Date Due

Jan 28 '42	May 16 '47	Oct 10 '64	
Feb 11 '42	May 27 '47	Feb 11 '66	
Feb 14 '42	Feb 7 '50	Mar 30 '67	
Jan 21	Feb 20 '50	Oct 15 '68	
Feb 16 '43	Feb 17 '51	May 26 '71	
Jan 26 '44	Jan 28 5 2	May 16 '77 P	
Feb 10 '44	Feb 13 5 2		
Feb 11 '44	Mar 29 5 2		
Feb 16 '44	Oct 13 5 2		
Feb 17 '45	Feb 14 '53		
April 11 '45	IN LIBRARY		
Jan 24 4			
Feb 18 4 6	Feb 11 '54		
Feb 23	Mar 7 '58		
Jan 1 8 '47	Mar 21 '58		
Feb 10 '47	Apr 8 '58		
Feb 15 '47	Jan 19 '60		
Feb 24 '47	May 14 '60		

WELLINGTON

By the same Author

THE DUKE OF WELLINGTON, 1815
From a painting by Sir T. Lawrence, R.A., at Apsley House.
By permission of the Duke of Wellington, K.G.

WELLINGTON

BY

PHILIP GUEDALLA

"I have been much exposed to authors"
—WELLINGTON to MRS. NORTON

NEW YORK AND LONDON
Harper & Brothers Publishers

WELLINGTON

Tenth Edition

TO

JOHN FORTESCUE

GRATEFULLY

PREFACE

HOW many English streets, squares, monuments, and licensed premises bear the name of Wellington? His title has become one of the commonplaces of urban, and even Imperial, topography. He has his thoroughfares and schools and clubs and institutions; obelisks and open spaces still take their names from him, though he has vanished from the bootmaker's. Yet his memory, in spite of all these verbal honorifics, seems a trifle faded. He cast so large a shadow once; all Europe was his province, and no public act was quite complete until the Duke approved. There was no other Duke; how could there be?

But he survives to later memory as little more than the instrument of a single victory and the gruff hero of a dozen anecdotes; and one is left reflecting on the contraction of that vast achievement to so meagre a residue. It was inevitable, perhaps, that his Indian career should be forgotten, since silence is posterity's one repartee to Anglo-Indian reminiscences. But seven years of patient and brilliantly successful warfare in the Peninsula, by which the British expeditionary force was brought from a beach in Portugal to the recovery of Spain and a victorious invasion of Napoleonic France, are less easily mislaid. Yet such a steady march to victory was, perhaps a shade inimical to his chances of lasting popularity in England. For a kindly nation seems to prefer its heroes slightly unsuccessful; its mind dwells more readily upon a last stand or a forlorn hope than upon the unchivalrous details of a crushing victory; and if it is to be allowed to choose, its favourite event will always be after the pattern of Rorke's Drift, its chosen hero in the manner of Sir John Moore. Judged by these sentimental tests, Wellington's career in Spain was far too successful to be really appealing. A second factor intervened to wither his Peninsular laurels, since British tradition is predominantly maritime and loves to murmur, with Admiral Mahan, that "those far-distant, storm-beaten ships, upon

vii

which the Grand Army never looked, stood between it and the dominion of the world." It is profoundly flattering to an island race to view sea-power as the deus ex machina *of war; and the Blue Water view of history is so picturesque. Besides, it substitutes for adoration the sprightlier figure of Nelson who, though victorious, at least atoned for his success by falling in the hour of victory. But it is hardly just to those British soldiers whose efforts actually won the war, which sea-power alone was* **impotent to win.**

And Waterloo? That, surely, cannot have been forgotten. Hardly; though a century of French assertion, combined with a steadily increasing Napoleonic cult, seems to have imposed the odd belief that Waterloo was lost by the Emperor rather than won by Wellington. His years of peace slide still more easily towards oblivion, since a generation with peace-treaties of its own is scarcely impressed by authors of earlier peace-treaties; though it might well spare a glance for a system which effectually silenced the guns of Europe for half a century and for a soldier who inspired such universal trust that the whole problem of Reparations was left by common consent in his hands.

His subsequent career in politics has done more, perhaps, than any other influence to efface his memory, since it provoked the Whigs. By a peculiar division of labour British history, quite considerable parts of which have been made by Tories, has been very largely written by Whigs; and Whig historians are a little apt to dispose summarily of Tory reputations. Viewed by such eyes, the Duke became a stiff-necked conqueror trailing an unwelcome scabbard into civilian assemblies. It was even feared that his faith in democracy was imperfect, that he did not trust the people. Why should he? Half his life had been devoted to a war against the French Revolution; and it was hardly likely that he would find revolution any more congenial because it happened to be English. Crowds had no sanctity for him—he had seen far too many—and the purely arithmetical basis of democracy failed to impress the Duke. Shocked by this revelation, the Nineteenth Century tended to belittle his entire achievement. Perhaps the Twentieth may feel inclined to number it among his merits.

At any rate, his portrait richly deserves to hang in the great gallery of English prose. But it is not there yet, though it is nearly eighty years since the Duke died. Stevenson, who was once to paint it for a series of Andrew Lang's, fingered the brushes for a little while. Many hands have sketched his long career (and I am indebted to almost all of them); but when Waterloo is passed, they nearly always falter, and the story dies away in a desultory stream of anecdote. I have tried to follow its whole course; and when novelists devote a quarter of a million words to the records of persons who did nothing in particular, I make no apology for requiring three-quarters of that quantity to describe the Duke of Wellington. Indeed, his career might even entitle him to the full ration customary for the portrayal of a thoughtful bank-clerk or an introspective commercial traveller. But in this case brevity has a real value, since his reputation seems to lie buried under the immense cairn of printed matter which posterity has raised in his honour. His correspondence has been printed in thirty-four volumes; and those 20,000 pages are the foundation of this book. I have done my best to supplement them by exploring the vast literature of his age and by using a mass of unpublished MS. material. The richest treasury of documents is, of course, at Apsley House; and the generosity of the Duke of Wellington in giving me full access to the papers has been of inestimable value. For the rest, the magnitude of the undertaking has laid me under so many obligations for unpublished material, illustrations, and other assistance that I am forced to tabulate my acknowledgments.

Duke of Wellington, K.G.	*Apsley House Papers and portraits*
Earl Beauchamp, K.G.	*Walmer MSS.*
Earl Camden	*Camden Papers*
Earl of Longford	*Wellington-Pakenham letter*
Viscountess Gough	*Pakenham information*
Lord Gerald Wellesley	*Mornington-Fortescue letters*
Miss Lowry Cole	*Lowry Cole Papers*
F. M. Guedalla, Esq.	*Wellington-Flint correspondence*
C. Hamilton, Esq.	*Hamwood Papers*

C. A. Oliver, Esq.	Wellesley-Gordon correspondence
Thomas U. Sadleir, Esq.	Irish researches and information
M. G. de la Villebiot	Angers information
Office of Arms	Mornington Declaration
Dublin Castle	

But though my thanks are tabulated, my gratitude is not.

One further source of information has been explored, since places are frequently as informing as documents. I have, therefore, so far as possible, studied the Duke's career on the spot. Whilst I make no pretence to supplement the military historians, numerous journeys to Spain and Portugal have familiarised me with the Peninsula; and I have made detailed studies of the ground at Salamanca, Talavera, Burgos, San Sebastian, and the lines of Torres Vedras. I have visited such points of minor interest as the Duke's school at Angers, and the scenes of his early life in Ireland. The kindness of the Duke of Wellington enabled me to conduct the greater part of my documentary researches in my subject's own library at Apsley House; and I am indebted to the Marchioness Douro for a sight of Stratfield Saye and to Earl Beauchamp for a thorough exploration of Walmer Castle. But I cannot conclude my thanks without particular acknowledgment of the sustained and various assistance which I have received from Lord Gerald Wellesley, who has made many of these expeditions possible, taken part in some of them, furnished unpublished documents, and given every aid to my undertaking.

The writing of this book, though it is founded upon much earlier reading and travel, was begun in 1928; and since that date it has extinguished all other interests (and almost all other occupations) for me. I feel bound to thank all who have borne with me during that time—and one dear person in particular.

P. G.

1931

CONTENTS

La gloire des grands hommes se doit
mesurer aux moyens qu'ils ont eus
pour l'acquérir.—La Rochefoucauld.

I

CASTES mark their children deeply; and as a caste, the English gentry resident in Ireland were pronounced. Every conquest leaves a caste behind it, since conquerors are always apt to perpetuate their victory in superior social pretensions. Had not the Romans been the noblemen of Europe? Even a Norman raid became an aristocracy in England; and in Ireland the Anglo-Norman conquest left a similar deposit. Such castes are frequently absorbed, assimilated by their subject populations. But where race combines with religious differences and recurrent insurrection to keep the two apart, the schism is absolute and the conquerors remain an alien caste. Such castes, where they survive, are aristocratic by necessity, since their *hauteur* is less a mannerism than the sole condition of their survival. For without a sinful pride the conqueror will vanish, merged in his subject population—the Norman turned Englishman, the Anglo-Irish a mere Irishman, and the Anglo-Indian "gone native." But while their pride remains, the little garrisons live on.

Generations of secluded life amongst an alien and subject population breeds aristocrats. For the perpetual proximity of inferiors is a rare school of high demeanour. Anglo-Irish magnates knew themselves observed by long, resentful rows of Irish eyes; and what conqueror could condescend before such an audience? The silent watchers made and kept them prouder than ever; and in the last half of the Eighteenth Century the Anglo-Irish magnate was indisputably *grand seigneur*. The visitor from England might stare at occasional crudities—at oxen roasted whole, at fourteen meat dishes for dinner, at a host who sat before his claret half the day and all night long, lord of "vast but unproductive" acres, dispensing in a mansion "spacious but dilapidated" hospitality that was "lavish but inelegant." The Irish *ton*, perhaps, was sometimes a shade barbaric. There was an awkward contrast between the Duke of Leinster's guests at Carton and the little houses of Maynooth huddled at its gates, while behind the big façade the house-party breakfasted to the sound of French horns off chocolate and honey and an immense table of "hot

3

bread—cold bread—brown bread—white bread—green bread, and all coloured breads and cakes." A chasm yawned between the classes, as it yawned between Versailles and France. But safe on the hither side the gentry lived their lordly lives, drank claret, toasted the "glorious, pious, and immortal memory," ran races, and matched fighting-cocks. Their very differences wore an aristocratic colour, since they adored the point of honour; and Dublin duellists met behind Lucas's Coffee-house near the Castle with more than contemporary gusto. Even their rivalries were lordly. As their rents rode ever higher on the mounting tide of Irish population, they scattered their argosies (and mortgaged their remotest prospects) in the lordliest game of all. For they built as recklessly as kings. The trim Palladian façades rose gracefully in every Irish county; tall windows looked down innumerable avenues of trees towards the ornamental water; obelisks defined the prospect; and Grecian temples ornamented the demesne with hints of the antique. Outbuilding neighbours afforded even richer sport than horse-racing; and a light-hearted gentry built with an increasing fervour, since rents could never fall while tenants swarmed in every cabin. Besides, borrowing was always easy; and the cheerful landlords sat before their wine in the new glories of their mansions, an aristocracy indeed.

They bore themselves, besides, with the immense patrician dignity that comes from superposition on a foundation of slavery. For the native Irish, even in the last years of the Eighteenth Century, were not far removed from slavery. The lash, the penal laws, the casual assault arouse misgivings in the onlooker. Misgivings turn to suspicion, when an English visitor notes that "a landlord in Ireland can scarcely invent an order which a servant, labourer, or cotter dares to refuse to execute. . . . Disrespect, or anything tending towards sauciness, he may punish with his cane or his horse-whip with the most perfect security. . . . Knocking down is spoken of in the country in a way that makes an Englishman stare." Suspicion deepens, as the same eye observes the strings of little Irish cars along the winding Irish roads "whipped into a ditch by a gentleman's footman, to make way for his carriage"; the "spalpeen broker," shipping his gangs of barefooted mountaineers to work in English fields, confirms it. It met the observant eye of Arthur Young a few years later—"Speaking a language that is despised, professing a religion that is abhorred, and being disarmed, the poor find themselves in many cases slaves even in the bosom of written liberty." And when a Lord-Lieutenant writes that "the poor people in Ireland are used worse than negroes by their lords and masters, and their deputies of deputies of deputies," the whole unpleasing truth appears.

For the nearest social parallel to rural Ireland was to be found three thousand miles away in the cotton-fields of Carolina. There, too, a little caste lived on its acres. The grace of Southern manners on the white-pillared porches of Colonial mansions matches the ease of Irish country-houses. There is the same profusion, the same improvidence against the same background of slavery. The same defects recur. Even the fighting-men and gamesters of the Irish countryside, who "kept miserable packs of half-starved hounds, wandered about from fair to fair and from race to race in laced coats, gambling, fighting, drinking, swearing, ravishing, and sporting, parading everywhere their contempt for honest labour," are reproduced in every unprepossessing detail on Mississippi levées. Ireland, it seems, had Southern wastrels as well as Southern charm. For who can fail to recognise the meaner types of Southern life in "the class of little country gentlemen, . . . bucks, your fellows with round hats edged with gold, who hunt in the day, get drunk in the evening, and fight the next morning"? Small wonder, then, that a mild critic finds the Irish upper classes "exposed to all the characteristic vices of slaveholders, for they formed a dominant caste, ruling over a population who were deprived of all civil rights and reduced to a condition of virtual slavery. They were separated from their tenants by privilege, by race, by religion, by the memory of inexpiable wrongs." The fires of religious persecution had burned low, since persecution connotes an enthusiastic faith; and enthusiasm was the last defect of an Irish Churchman in 1769. For a thoughtful Deist could hardly be expected to derive unlimited satisfaction from the spectacle of his brother-Deist at the stake. But though persecution had almost vanished, its legacy of social inequality remained. There were still serfs and, not less deeply caste-marked, "Protestant Bashaws." Slavery survived, and the vast dignity that marks slaveholders. For such a caste does not part lightly with the lordly faith that some are born to rule and some to serve. Elsewhere the same soil put out the stiff blossoms of Washington and Lee; and something, perhaps, of that unbending quality in war and statesmanship which grows in cotton-fields was latent in Ireland's Virginian gentry.

But though their aristocracy was real enough, the temptation (always strong) to view eighteenth-century life as a protracted costume play is nowhere stronger than in Ireland. Not that it was a genteel comedy of wigs and patches, devised by stage costumiers and laboriously played with carefully flirted handkerchiefs and dutifully taken snuff. The Dublin round—*ridotto*, dinner, dance, Italian opera, charity concert, Drawing-room—was natural enough. For one lived as other people lived in 1769, when all life in its more elegant forms had a faint air of *bal travesti*. But if the whole prevailing air was slightly unreal, still greater unreality hung on the air of Dublin, until it almost seemed a masquerade. Indeed, it was—a light-hearted masquerade where pleasant, slightly insignificant persons wore the impressive costumes of great officers of state. It was a little parody of England—Court, judges, bishops, Lords, and Commons—played out upon the stage of Dublin and watched with scared indifference by rows of Irish eyes. The stage was crowded; Lord Chancellors elbowed Masters of the Rolls; Privy Councillors nodded on every side to major-generals; bishops abounded; and there was a glorious profusion of Hereditary High Treasurers, Chief Barons, Remembrancers, and every known variety of public dignitary, with functions and without. The *rôles* were awe-inspiring; but the maskers often seem a shade inadequate under their dominoes. For lawyers, whose merits might reasonably have escaped detection in the Temple or Lincoln's Inn, appear in ermine on the Irish bench; and estimable clergymen, designed at best to fill a quiet canonry, inhabit vast episcopal palaces and preach to hushed cathedrals. It was the Irish masquerade, a delectable charade in which a little group of English families played at the government of Ireland upon a high and lighted stage in Dublin.

Dublin, in the spring weather of 1769, was never more Dublin. Some-where beyond the hard, blue waters of St. George's Channel the Irish packets found a city where the ordered elegance of pagan ornament proclaimed the Eighteenth Century. For it was eighteenth-century indeed. Grilles, cornices, and porticoes attested it. Flambeaux announced the fact with iron tracery; door after door insisted blandly with a delicious fan-light and a pair of elegant pilasters; it echoed from painted walls where the discreet festoons wandered from urn to urn; unnumbered chandeliers nodded assent with every gleaming prism; and where ceilings were an exquisite blend of stucco and mythology, marble deities reclined in bas-relief on innumerable mantelpieces. Murmuring (in heroic couplets) the last enchantment of the Eighteenth Century, Dublin sat decorously true to type beside its river. Other capitals might falter in their allegiance. In London the steady pulse of the century, shaken dangerously by the disordered tramp of Mr. Wilkes' supporters, wavered a little; it throbbed faintlier now in Paris under an ageing king; and, ingenious Mr. Townshend aiding with a tax on tea, tempers rose in Boston to a most inelegant pitch. Perhaps the Eighteenth Century might not last for ever. Boston rioters and Middlesex electors almost seemed to suggest a doubt. But could it ever end in Dublin? Dimly conceivable elsewhere, the notion there became wholly unthinkable. Every doorway seemed to deny it; each modish column barred the way; and carved divinities looked down in bland denial, refused the extravagant surmise with every attribute held in their marble hands or poured from their cornucopiæ and, the wild thought dismissed, resumed their allegories. So Flora's altar smoked again with stony clouds of incense, Ceres renewed her sheaves, and Endymion his slumbers. Behind the porticoes of Dublin it would always be the Eighteenth Century. For the stamp of its century was unmistakably on Dublin.

And on its people, too. It was not easy to be born in Dublin, where every wall exhaled it, and escape the Eighteenth Century. Had not Mr. Walpole informed Pitt's sister Anne a few years since that "all the spirit or wit or poetry on which we subsist comes from Dublin"? At the Castle on spring nights in 1769 loyal ladies dropped their curtseys to Lord Townshend by Viceregal candlelight, while their lords said hard things about him in the Irish House of Commons with a watchful eye upon the pension list. Perhaps the face of politics was slightly unprepossessing. Even Mr. Walpole had enquired a trifle acidly, "Pray, sir, how does virtue sell in Ireland now?" Placemen filled places, pensioners drew pensions, and in a dim perspective beyond Dublin landlords collected rent. Something, perhaps, was stirring on those shadowy hills where flitting figures burned outbuildings, houghed cattle, or cropped Protestant ears, as the Irish pipes wailed out *The Lad with the White*

Cockade. Rebellious Whiteboys were matched by Oakboys no less outrageous and even by Steelboys, while distracted soldiers shot impartially at either. But Dublin went on as usual. Ladies poured tea in Sackville Street; their lords fingered decanters; and Signora Cotilloni, fresh from her triumphs in "a neighbouring kingdom," begged leave of the *Dublin Mercury* to acquaint the nobility and gentry of her arrival and of her intention to open a Dancing Academy, and even to perfect her female pupils "in all the necessary manœuvres of coquetry, to manage the eyes to advantage, to smile a man into hopes or frown him into uncertainty, to deny favours without offending, and grant them with grace," the whole concluding with the loyal (and not untimely) sentiment, *Honi soit qui mal y pense.*

That week Lord Mornington, lately removed from Grafton Street, was with his countess at their new town house. They were in treaty with Lord Antrim for the lease; but the house seemed to be theirs already. Built in the latest mode, it stood in Merrion Street, and the two stately flambeaux were not unworthy to enlighten guests in search of Mornington House. Their ceilings were a graceful medley. Urns, shells, and garlands graced the new dining-room, where convivial Irish gentlemen might finger convivial Irish glass, while the ceiling in the drawing-room was a more womanish affair of birds and flower-baskets. But these new glories failed to engage Lady Mornington, since she lay upstairs in the big bedroom at the back. It looked across a little garden to the open space of Merrion Square. A harassed doctor called; the apothecary from Dawson Street brought round a soothing draught; and then a child—her sixth—was born on May Day, 1769. They called him Arthur, and the Dublin round was undisturbed. Fine gentlemen fought duels; coaches went up and down the street; ladies stepped out of chairs; wits rhymed; and the long tide crept slowly round the bay from Dalkey to the hill of Howth.

II

THE happy father was an earl. He was, besides, Professor of Music at Trinity College, Dublin. For he was an earl of parts. Earldom itself, indeed, was something of a novelty, since it was barely nine years old. Lord Mornington was a Wesley of Dangan, son of the first Lord Mornington who, born a Colley of Castle Carbury, had inherited both name and fortune from his cousin, Garrett Wesley, whose mother had been a Colley. The name of Wesley accompanied the money; and the same generous impulse had once suggested to the wealthier Wesleys a frustrated interest in Charles Wesley, then passing through Oxford on the long road to Methodism. The Colleys, emerging from the English Midlands in the later Middle Ages, had retained their English purity through three centuries of life in Ireland. No single Irish name adorns their pedigree; and when Richard Colley, as his cousin's heir, assumed in 1728 the no less English name of Wesley, they were still Anglo-Irish squires.

The Wesley fortune eased affairs. There was an ampler air; the family was moved to the big house at Dangan, and its new master entered the Irish House of Commons for the adjacent and well-disciplined borough of Trim. He planned improvements in the grounds, planted considerably, and dwelt upon the pleasing theme of ornamental water. There were to be canals that ships might ride on, lakes with islands in them, and a sufficiency of temples. It was an easy, cheerful home where everyone assembled in the hall for breakfast, shuttlecock, a little dancing, draughts, and family prayers, or strolled about the grounds and visited the temples. Apollo, Neptune, and Diana each received due honour in their shrines, and the company paraded gravely, bearing white staffs inscribed with their "Parnassus names" and complaining slightly that it made them look "like the sheriff's men at the assizes." For hospitality at Dangan extended even to the supply of classical allusions, and lady visitors were gratified by the *rôles* allotted them in Mr. Wesley's mythological charades. A delighted guest informed her correspondent that she was "nothing less than Madam Venus," whilst one belle united in her lovely person all three Graces, and their host was a trifle apt to nominate three rival goddesses and to reserve for the master of the house the arch *rôle* of Paris. He had an organ in the hall, and there was always a good deal of music. They often breakfasted to the harpsichord, to say nothing of a simultaneous game of shuttlecock. For bewildered guests found the Wesleys equal to the contrasted charms of drinking chocolate, the battledore, and counterpoint in the big hall at Dangan, all at once and without apparent interference with the enjoyment of either. Their picnics were invariably to music. Even on a little run from Dublin they hesitated to rely upon the unaided powers of "cold fowl, lamb, pigeon pye, Dutch beef, tongue, cockells, sallad, much variety of liquors, and the finest syllabub that ever was tasted." But the Muses were invoked, a lady placed at the harpsichord jangled a little, and afterwards Mr. Wesley's violin kept time to his daughters' dancing. For, as a courtly ear observed, he "played well (for a gentleman) on the violin." Sometimes, indeed, they essayed the grander pleasures of a water-concert on the canal at Dangan where, their flag hoisted on "a very pretty boat," they rowed harmoniously between the listening fields of Meath.

So, music and the classics aiding, the years passed pleasantly. An heir appeared; Mr. Wesley, presently ennobled as Lord Mornington, passed to the Irish House of Lords; the big house was burnt and sumptuously rebuilt. Mythology reigned in the grounds; the temples multiplied, and seats for exhausted worshippers graced every alley; obelisks abounded; and each sacred grove displayed the gracious gleam of statuary. Presently a visiting godmother found a small Garrett Wesley, whose one desire was to celebrate her arrival with an artillery salute. For he was governor of a tiny fort, as well as lord high admiral of a considerable fleet that rode on the canal, comprising the yawl *Fanny* and the barge *Pretty Betty*, the whole commanded by the flagship *Caroline*, a model of the King's yacht, carrying a battery of guns and a complement of two, destined originally for presentation to a royal duke and acquired by some happy accident for Dangan. But when the honour of a salvo was declined politely, his instinct for military courtesies was satisfied by hoisting all his flags at once.

The boy was musical. Indeed, one feels that unless he had been, life at Dangan with an organ in the hall and the harpsichord at breakfast would have been unbearable. But while the first Lord Mornington played well (for a gentleman), his heir stood in no need of such genteel allowances. For he approached proficiency of a more plebeian order. In fine, he was a prodigy. Almost from birth the infant marvel intimated his enjoyment of his father's performances by beating time; and as the air changed pace, awed onlookers saw the tiny hands alter their beat. Nor did his growth belie the promise of these talented gesticulations. The dawn of taste even preceded speech. For when a guest essayed to take the violin from his father, the infant interposed; and the transfer could only be effected while the small, indignant hands were held. But the visitor proving to be no less than the celebrated Dubourg, the fastidious infant, having once heard that virtuoso, was with difficulty persuaded to permit the noble amateur to resume his instrument. Indeed, when Dubourg was in the house, the child, with rare (if scarcely pious) discernment, would never let his father play. At nine he scraped a bow himself, rendering *Christ Church Bells* and *Sing one, two, three, come follow me*, and shortly afterwards played second violin in Corelli's Sonatas, an experience to which connoisseurs attributed that lifelong steadiness in time which never, it was said, deserted him. Then, pricked by the emulation which stirs musicians to their greatest efforts, he turned composer. For a local clergyman, having won considerable applause with a country dance of his own composition, Master Wesley responded with a minuet marred by a slight excess of fifths, and shortly afterwards achieved a duet for French horns and an *Andante*. His gifts survived the discouragements incidental to membership of a large and cheerful family, since his sisters drove him continually from the harpsichord in a sisterly opinion that he spoiled the instrument. But he played by stealth; and when an organ was installed in the chapel at Dangan, he startled the family by playing an impromtu fugue at the organ-maker's. His studies progressed; and though he lacked formal instruction, compositions flowed from his pen with such happy consequences that when he consulted Rosengrave and Geminiani, those masters modestly replied that they could not be of the least service to one who had already mastered the science.

The gentle youth grew up; and his godmother found him at thirteen "a most extraordinary boy," almost unnaturally good at lessons and playing the violin at sight. His varied accomplishments extended to shipbuilding and fortification as well as music; and their diversity was almost equal to her own somewhat injudiciously assorted passions for conchology, gossip, fossils, and every form of petrifaction. For she was no less than Mrs. Delany. At twenty-two he stepped sedately into the family borough, and uneventfully represented Trim in the Irish House of Commons. In the next year his father died, and he succeeded to the title. The exacting dowager found him a trifle lacking in "the punctilios of good breeding." Perhaps a nobleman required a thought more polish than the organ and Trinity College, Dublin, had power to impart; and when he chose a wife, her disapproval grew more pointed. His first choice was admirable. Lady Louisa Lenox was a duke's daughter; and all was smiles, until Mr. Conolly, of Castletown, offered his ampler means. The rival, as a loyal godmother confessed, had "double his fortune (and perhaps about half his merit)." But even dukes are human; and Lord Mornington was blandly informed that "the young lady had an insurmountable dislike to him." The wounded lover reeled; for the ducal alliance was not without its savour. But his wounds were promptly assuaged by Miss Hill, of Belvoir. Her father, though he had once kept a bank in Dublin, was younger brother to a viscount. Perhaps his manners were a shade excessive, since he was always apt to give a slightly unconvincing rendering of the fine gentleman. But, manners apart, he was agreeable, "with a *little pepper* in his composition," which might enliven the mild Wesley stock. The bride was turned sixteen, a fine young woman in Mrs. Delany's estimation, although "rather a little clumsy, but with fine complexion, teeth, and nails, with a great deal of modesty and good-humour." These charms prevailing, the young Lord Mornington paid his addresses. Mr. Hill was gallantly informed that the eager bridegroom asked no fortune, was even prepared to make a settlement himself; if the bride had any fortune, he chivalrously "desired it might be laid out in jewels for her." So all was smiles again. The clothes were bought; the settlements were drawing up; and Lord Mornington was seen at the play in Dublin, looking a little solemn.

They were a happy pair, though his exacting godmother still had her moments of uncertainty as to how far her qualities would remedy his defects. He was "a very good young man on the whole," if slightly lacking in punctilio; but Anne Mornington herself lacked finish, although she made shell flowers. (Yet even then she seemed wanting in distinction; for when she furnished Mrs. Delany with a shell or so for her endless decorations, they were nothing rare.) Unclouded by these mysterious defects, their life opened happily enough. They lived at Dangan or in Grafton Street. An heir was born in Dublin, and a grateful press recorded "the great joy of that noble family." King George II died; and the new reign brought Mornington a step in the Irish peerage. A pleasing fancy traces his earldom to the new sovereign's interest in music; but it had a likelier connection with the exigencies of Irish government, since the fountain of honour played steadily upon obliging Dublin legislators, and the next dozen years enriched the Irish nobility with thirty-three barons, sixteen viscounts, and twenty-four earls.

The new Earl of Mornington had his own interests. For the Muses followed him to Dublin, where he initiated a Musical Academy and supported burlesque productions in opposition to the Italian burletta of a rival theatre. It was an age of musical refinement, when Irishmen proudly recorded that "the god of music had taken a large stride from the Continent over England to this island . . . and it has been observed that Corelli is a name in more mouths than many of our Lord-Lieutenants." Respectful instrumentalists played Handel to listening cathedrals; and when Lord Mornington essayed a charity concert, an orchestra of noblemen and gentlemen obeyed his *bâton*. A Lord-Lieutenant's daughter sang; there was a peer among the flutes; a noble clergyman bowed diligently above his 'cello. The Italian taste prevailed; and one vocalist recalled to a disgusted ear Mingotti's "trills and squalls." But these ardours did not check Mornington's melodious pen, which ran mostly to Church music, with strong predilection for full harmony and the minor third, but had its lighter moments. For he could even stoop to glees, and grateful glee-singers rendering *Here in cool grot* and *Come, fairest nymph* acknowledged a noble author. *'Twas you, Sir*, was his work as well, to say nothing of *By greenwood tree* and *Gently hear me, charming maid*. Small wonder, then, that Trinity College conferred a Doctorate of Music and even advanced the earl to be professor. For music had quite vanquished his earlier leanings towards naval architecture and the principles of Vauban.

Meanwhile his family increased. They had named the heir Richard after the first Lord Mornington; and the happy infant bore the title of Viscount Wellesley, a prouder, mediæval form of Wesley. The second was called Arthur after her father; but he did not survive, and the first Arthur Wesley died in childhood. Then came a third son, named William, followed by a short-lived Francis, and a daughter, whom they christened Anne after Lady Mornington. The sixth child, born at the new house in Merrion Street, was a boy. They called him Arthur, too. So he got her father's name and perhaps (who knows?) something of her father's pepper.

III

LIFE opened for the child in Dublin; and as they brought him down the big staircase lit by its one tall, pillared window for his first outing in Merrion Street, the bland, unhurried days followed each other. Not that the times were bland. It was a wild decade, that opened (in Mr. Walpole's pained enumeration) with "no Government, no police, London and Middlesex distracted, the Colonies in rebellion, Ireland ready to be so, and France arrogant, and on the point of being hostile." Crowds had an ugly tendency to roar *God save great Wilkes our king*, and public men were in a flutter—"Lord Bute accused of all and dying in a panic; George Grenville wanting to make rage desperate; Lord Rockingham, the Duke of Portland, and the Cavendishes thinking we have no enemies but Lord Bute and Dyson, and that four mutes and an epigram can set everything to rights; the Duke of Grafton like an apprentice, thinking the world should be postponed to a whore and a horse-race; and the Bedfords not caring what disgraces we undergo, while each of them has £3,000 a year and three thousand bottles of claret and champagne." That summer— Arthur Wesley's first—London was alarmed by a terrific *revenant*. For at St. James's men heard the blind tapping of a familiar crutch across the palace floor, looked nervously behind them, and saw the tormented eyes under the peak of a great wig which were all that remained of Chatham. The old man had come to Court again, "himself" (as Mr. Walpole tittered "*in propriâ personâ*, and not in a strait-waistcoat"; and his sovereign's eyes protruded more than ever, as that imperial nose descended with tremendous deference to meet those ailing knees. Overseas the angry quaver of Mr. Samuel Adams's voice hung on the air of Boston; lion and unicorn still ramped cosily upon the State House; but who could say how long they would remain with an angry voice insisting that taxation was slavery, that Rome was never better than when it had no king, that thirty thousand men with bayonets and knapsacks would infallibly spring from the soil of Massachusetts. It was a flurried age, when Mr. Walpole feared the worst and England lived uneasily under the mosaic ministry of Burke's inimitable apologue, and in the wings Lord North was waiting for his turn.

But these discontents scarcely reached Mornington House. Burke wrote a pamphlet; and Lord Mornington composed a glee. The angry *Junius* strained the limits of invective; and that gentle nobleman made a mild addition to the English hymnal. Mobs roared; and he was seen, a little puffy now, bending a dark, shaven chin above deft fingers at the key-board. As America flamed into civil war, his peaceful *bâton* waved imperturbably above the busy violins of Dublin gentlemen at a charity concert. His calm was perfect—almost, it would seem, too perfect for his countess, since Mr. Walpole breathed to Lady Ossory a wicked "history of Lady Mornington," asking with finished malice "where should bawds and bishops pay court but to youthful hypocrisy! Could her Ladyship apprehend a cold reception where Lord Pembroke is a Lord of the Bedchamber?" Once, indeed, his calm was interrupted, when a Dublin footpad named Murphy stopped his sedan-chair, let off a pistol, and removed his lordship's gold watch with all his money. But the rogue was apprehended and left to dangle in a halter on the mound at the corner of St. Stephen's Green.

Sometimes they breathed the calmer air of Dangan; and from the big windows of his country home the small Arthur Wesley saw Meath rolling gently into the distance. They sent him to the little school at Trim, just down the road, where his brother Wellesley had displayed his early promise. That promise was, indeed, their pride. For Richard, their eldest, was exceptionally gifted; the other children lived in awe, and a loyal family prepared to applaud the rise of Richard Wellesley. He rose, whilst Arthur played at home with William and Anne, to Harrow. But Harrow failed to hold the aspiring youth for more than eighteen months, since a school riot, occasioned by the appointment of an Etonian headmaster, claimed him. Marked by these prejudices as a born Etonian, he was removed and sent to Eton. His faculties reviving in that nobler air, he became a prodigious Latinist and a considerable Grecian. They were all in England now; for the family (increased by the addition of a small Gerald, a still smaller Henry, and a tiny Mary Elizabeth) had let the Dublin house and moved to Knightsbridge. Lord Mornington was heard at the harpsichord one night at Lady Stamford's, where a distinguished amateur played first violin and a lady vocalist rendered *Dové sei* so sweetly that one grateful member of her audience "slept better than for many nights before."

Transplanted from his native island, the small Arthur Wesley studied the rudiments at Brown's seminary (later dignified as Oxford House Academy) in King's Road, Chelsea; and the splendid Richard passed on to Christ Church. That was the year that British armies laboured heavily through Carolina, while the mature intelligence of Lord George Germaine was busy organising defeat at the War Office. King George's guns thudded without conspicuous success in almost every hemisphere. The fires of victory burned low, and every tent was full of disappointed paladins. Gage was at home forgetting Bunker's Hill; Burgoyne was back in Hertford Street explaining Saratoga; and Howe was polishing his *Narrative*. Even the fleet, at war with France and Spain and heavily outnumbered, rode insecurely; and for a summer week of madness the mob ran wild for "No Popery" and Lord George Gordon, while the dull glare of burning houses glowed on the London sky. Small wonder that the harassed North begged to resign; but his inexorable sovereign pointed implacably to duty and the unique (though sadly underrated) perfection of the British constitution.

Like his afflicted country, Lord Mornington was not without his troubles. For the subsequent finances of infant prodigies are often far from cheering. His married life had opened with the rich prospect of eight or ten thousand pounds a year. But twenty years devoted to the Muses (at what cost the Muses only knew) had darkened the financial prospect. Few orchestras enrich their patrons; Musical Academies are rarely remunerative; and his man of affairs in Dublin surveyed a mournful landscape. For his later airs were pitched, like so many of his youthful compositions, in a minor key. Their migration to London, though hardly well-conceived as a measure of economy, had been in the nature of a retreat. They were rather stinted now, "not able to appear in any degree as we ought," though he still kept his coach. But lodgings in Knightsbridge were a sad decline for the noble *maestro*; and at the prospect of a continued effort to live on £1,800 a year Lord Mornington grew positively rebellious. There was so much to be provided—Richard's allowance, and the six younger children's education, to say nothing of the costly array of masters requisite if Anne's accomplishments were to be perfected with due elegance. One estate was already deeply mortgaged; but his dreams in Knightsbridge were haunted by an unpleasant sum of £16,000 that had to be raised somehow. Richard, of course, might join with him to raise it. But would he? After all, that eminent young man would shortly come of age; and he might not consent. Then, was it altogether wise to remove his property from his own power? For he had dismal recollections of too trusting parents sadly ill-treated by their unnatural offspring. It was a depressing problem, for which the hopeful earl found a solution in an ingenious scheme for raising £3,000 a year, rising in a yet more hopeful postscript to the cheering theme of lottery tickets—"If you will send me ten numbers I shall take two and give each of my Children and my Lady one, but don't let these numbers run all in order but different thousands if possible." Such expedients are not unfamiliar in the after-lives of patrons of the arts.

Nor was the brilliant Richard, trailing a nobleman's gold tassel from his cap at Christ Church, untouched by these melancholy concerns. His allowance was a family problem, since their touching faith persisted that he was "likely to make a figure in the world from his great abilities," and such prospects plainly called for at least four hundred pounds a year. But graver themes engaged him in the very moment of his triumph as Chancellor's prizeman for 1780 with a Latin ode on Captain Cook. His father was unwell, and a prudent counsellor in Dublin reviewed the unpleasing prospect. There was the mortgage, and the debts, and the eternal £16,000 that had to be raised somehow. If the earl recovered, he would really have to live at Dangan. If not, his heir must sell the Dublin house and travel. His adviser, having lived abroad himself and been twice to Italy, grew almost eloquent on travel. The sapient Richard was, he felt, unlikely to indulge in "any of the fashionable vices and follies wch ruin so many young Men," but touched with a nobler aspiration "to bring home a knowledge of the different Constitutions & Policy of the several States he visits," a sober programme, with the additional advantage of being vastly cheaper. For his adviser added with justice that "the flower of travelling may be gathered at a moderate expense, they ornament Character. The weeds are costly, they poison the mind & are a canker in the future." In fine, when he succeeded, the young gentleman would be well advised to economise abroad. His choice came all too soon. For Lord Mornington died in May, 1781, and the Madrigal Society lost their most zealous member. Music apart, he had always been a shade inadequate: Mrs. Delany had foreseen as much. And if she had foreseen his sons, what else could she expect? For fame reserves no niche for the father of the Gracchi.

So Richard became an earl at twenty, and Arthur at twelve had lost his father. They buried him with seemly state, and more than eighty pounds of Richard's inheritance vanished in the pious outlay—fourteen mutes with black gloves and truncheons; cloaks and crape hat-bands for the little party of eight mourners; and black gloves for the Knightsbridge landlady, to say nothing of a stupendous canopy (the undertaker's pride), nodding with sable plumes, and hired for the sad occasion. Two coaches followed him; and for once a Wesley outing lacked its music. Something of him, perhaps, lived on in Arthur's violin. For the small boy played; and if he remembered anything of his father, it was the pleasant, slightly ineffectual figure conjured up for him three-quarters of a century later by the Muse of *Jeames de la Pluche:*

> His father praps he sees,
>   Most muscle of Lords,
> A-playing madriggles and glees
>   Upon the Arpsicords.

IV

THE little family bore their bereavement. Now there were only eight of them—Lady Mornington, the fine young woman of Mrs. Delany's distant recollection, a dowager at thirty-nine; the incomparable Richard; William, just turned eighteen; and Arthur, a boy of twelve, with two small brothers and a pair of sisters. The young earl came down from Oxford and assumed his mournful post as head of the family. Mournful in more ways than one, since family finance in 1781 was uninviting. A thoughtful cousin had, it is true, reduced their burdens by leaving an estate in Queen's County to William (together with the name of Pole). But something must be done for his mother, to say nothing of five children all waiting for expensive educations and his own career. Besides, there were the debts. It was all highly disagreeable for a rising man. He came of age in June, and the next month he was in Dublin raising mortgages on the Meath lands. But the further programme of an in expensive Continental tour failed to attract him, since foreign spas afford few opportunities for statesmanship, and Richard was resolved to be a statesman. Taking his seat at the long table of the Irish House of Lords he quickly shewed that mild temper of rebelliousness which is the surest path to office. But the family were not sacrificed to this brilliant opening For that very year two of his brothers went to Eton.

The autumn mists of 1781 crept up from a Virginian river, and the British guns were flagging behind the crumbling works of Yorktown when Arthur Wesley went to boarding-school. The trap closed on Cornwallis three thousand miles away, as the two small brothers stared round at Eton. For there were two of them. He took Gerald with him; and this pair of Daniels (though one of them was only nine) kept one another in countenance among the lions of their new abode. Lions, indeed abounded. For Eton, in the spasmodic reign of Jonathan Davies, was a marked advance upon Brown's academy at Chelsea. Numbers alone were terrifying, since three hundred boys were quite enough to alarm two new comers from Knightsbridge. Had not the formidable Chatham confessed that "he scarce observed a boy who was not cowed for life at Eton; that a public school might suit a boy of turbulent forward disposition, but would not do where there was any gentleness"? But, turbulent or not, the two small Wesleys survived this stern initiation. Lower boys were scarcely disturbed by their vociferous headmaster. That slightly indecorous figure was almost as remote as royalty itself, which was always riding past the Long Walk with empty, staring eyes, or buttonholing stray promenaders on the terrace with his "Well, well, my boy, when were you last flogged, eh, eh?" or, more searchingly, "What's your name? who's your tutor? who's your dame?" concluding the invariable reassurance of, "*Very* good tutor, *very* good dame" from royal lips. The two small brothers were largely untroubled by these high matters. But the long ritual of lessons, "absence," chapels without number, and still more lessons, all to be performed under three hundred pairs of watching eyes, was quite sufficiently alarming.

They boarded at Naylor's, played in the muddy garden of the Manor House, and shared rooms with strangers. Decorum did not always reign, since Arthur fought a battle—his very first—with a schoolfellow named Smith, provoked by being stoned while bathing, for whom fate reserved the still more mournful destiny of being brother to a wit (even a thrashing from Arthur Wesley may well have been more palatable than a life-long course of Sydney's brightest sayings); and there were schoolboy jokes about the maids, who slept in a room just off the kitchen, termed, with exaggerated courtesy that stayed in Arthur's memory for forty years, the "Virgins' bower." Far more sedate was their scholastic progress. Not theirs the lofty destinies of Richard, whose declamations had drawn tears from royal eyes and compliments from Garrick; no statesmen, lured by their promise, drove down from London to enlist their gifts. For they were not, were very far from being their unnaturally gifted school-fellow George Canning; and no Mr. Fox stopped at their door. Early promise was the last thing about them. Breasting the slope together, they had advanced within the year to "Upper Greek," where they toyed with Ovid, Terence, and the Vulgate. By the next Easter they were both deep in the recesses of the Fourth Form, sustained upon a sober diet in which, though Ovid still predominated, there were nutritious extras in the way of Cæsar, Æsop, and Greek Testament. It was depressing to observe how close his younger brother trod to Arthur's heels; for if Wesley *ma.* sat fifty-third out of seventy-nine, Wesley *mi.* came fifty-fourth, the hounds of spring keeping assiduous company with winter's traces. The fact was not without its consequence for Wesley *ma.*, since he was shortly afterwards withdrawn from Eton. School bills were heavy, and Richard was moving up into the costlier arena of British politics. Besides, there was a third brother now in the abysses of the Lower Remove; and with Wesley *minimus* to pay for, the ant-like pace at which Wesley *ma.* scaled Parnassus scarcely rewarded outlay. So early in 1784 his brief rearguard action with the classics ended.

Its effects remain slightly mysterious. For the classical attainments, with which Eton equipped her sons for public life, were not for him. He once prescribed his rules of public speaking—"One is, I never speak about what I know nothing, and the other, I never quote Latin"—a wise abstention, since his quantities were always uncertain. Did not the nation's hero, in the full robes of Oxford Chancellor, once alarm the Sheldonian Theatre with a *Jacobus* whose second syllable was short, hastily atoned for by a *Carolus* whose second (and still more fatal) syllable was long? Yet, however impervious to Ovid, no Etonian could possibly escape a sense of the indisputable truths of revealed religion, since these were publicly rehearsed with impressive and even wearisome regularity. What else he learned is more obscure. Scarcely, it seems, a genius for friendship. Nor was he formed upon the playing-fields. Indeed, the playing-fields were hardly formed themselves. Cricket and fives were practised; but the remaining catalogue of Eton games varies between the infantile and the purely occult. It is not easy to believe that hoops and hop-scotch developed valuable qualities; few statesmen owe their eminence to early marbles; nor do the martial virtues thrive upon a simple diet of peg-top and battledore. The civic lessons of Bally Cally, Conquering lobs, and Hunt the dark lanthorn must remain enigmatic; but the heartening presence of Puss-in-the-corner may be felt to indicate that the stern reign of pure athletics was still far distant. Nor was Arthur's own recollection less unheroic. For revisiting the place in later years, he stared into Naylor's (then Ragueneau's) garden, and enquired affectionately for a broad black ditch he used to leap over, adding that in his own belief he owed his spirit of enterprise to the tricks he used to play there. The tribute may be found unsatisfying by athletic purists and a shade disappointing even to Etonians, since their playing-fields appear only in the attenuated form of a ditch in a dame's garden. But, such as it was, he paid it.

The next instalment of his education took him abroad. For, taste coinciding with finance, his mother chose to travel; and Arthur travelled with her. Not that they travelled far. For their brief journey ended in a town with which he was to have a fuller acquaintance, since they lay at Brussels. The cheerful, slightly equivocal little capital of the Austrian Netherlands lived uneventful days in 1784, only slightly complicated by the unlikely spectacle of a reforming Kaiser. For the solemn Joseph II, who ranked among the best-travelled men in Europe (since he had visited almost all his own dominions), suffered from the fatal illusion that he was a man of his times and—yet more fatal impulse—resolved to move with them. But the times, at any rate in Belgium, were sadly immobile; for the best intentions of Teutonic persons are often wasted upon Belgium, and his most progressive gestures were coldly received by a community that was still obstinately mediæval. To this accompaniment Lady Mornington and Arthur took up their residence in Brussels. It lasted for a year —the year that saw the last of Dr. Johnson and the first of Palmerston, that heard Mr. Pitt denouncing Mr. Fox above the lively uproar of the Westminster election, that saw the *Tragic Muse* begun and the *Decline and Fall* nearly ended. Arthur, perhaps, fell something short of her ideal. The retreat from Eton had not been altogether to his credit. And then he was fifteen. Few boys, whatever their moral excellence, are seen to the best advantage at fifteen: an excess of limb scarcely lends charm to an unaccustomed gruffness. Small wonder, then, that Lady Mornington vowed to God she did not know what she should do with her awkward son Arthur. Really, with Richard winning golden opinions in Parliament, William in the Irish House of Commons, Gerald destined for the Church, and Henry still too young to think about, Arthur's future began to be something of a problem. Meanwhile, it could do him no harm to learn a little French, if only with a Belgian accent.

French, it appears, was almost all he learned at Brussels. Their obliging landlord dispensed vague draughts of learning. But a fellow-pupil remembered Arthur Wesley mainly for his devotion to the violin. For the Muse was easier to woo in foreign lodgings than at Eton. So the world glided into 1785; and he played on, as the slow days went by in Brussels. Ste. Gudule struck the hours; the light slanted from the west across the uneventful fields by Hougoumont; and in a Brussels room an awkward boy was playing on the violin.

That year his education moved him on once more. Lady Mornington went home to England. But two years of Eton and twelve months of casual tutoring in Brussels being judged insufficient, he must go somewhere to be "finished"; and since his range included little in the way of manly accomplishments, he was consigned to Angers, where the fifth of a dynasty of riding-masters presided over a celebrated academy. It stood behind a noble grille of iron-work—such iron-work as Marie Antoinette, the Queen, passed through each time her coach rumbled discreetly off to Trianon and turned into the tiny drive before her tiny palace. But at Angers the shapely modern work was gracefully disposed under the very hulk of the Middle Ages, where King René's castle lay—striped, blackened, and truncated—like a grounded leviathan. The tall Academy behind the grille was modern too—trim angles of white stone, a rounded hall, and at the back a flight of stately little steps descending from the tall façade, where art had carved a sheaf of palettes, French horns, and books, contrasted decorously opposite a panoply of arms, such armour, baldricks, and cuirasses as classical hero never wore. Its educational resources consisted mainly of a riding-school. But the curriculum included dancing lessons, together with a course in fencing. This happy blend was customary in such establishments, when dancing was apt to start at dawn, followed by riding, fencing, and a little grammar with mathematics in the afternoon and a final dancing class to close the happy day. It was an age of elegance, when *haute école* and foils were felt to lack something if unaccompanied by Terpsichore. These studies, vaguely military in intention, were often followed by young gentlemen in search of a more general finish; and for about a year, his destiny being still uncertain, Arthur pursued them, walking the streets of Angers, seeing King Louis' soldiers in their white, or pounding round the riding-school in strict accordance with the rules of horsemanship. But the nicties of *haute école*, even when expounded with hereditary fervour by M. de Pignerolle, were scarcely more attractive than construing Ovid; and his attention often wandered. It was far pleasanter to pass the time playing with his dog or dining with the local gentry. He was often at the Duc de Brissac's, where the wine was poor and there was not much to eat, although their host had been an ornament of Versailles, under Louis XV. The old nobleman kept open house, though Pignerolle's cadets were a little apt to make themselves unpleasant to injudicious guests.

He saw a good deal of the French. There was one of them who had a brother in the Church named Talleyrand; and one day at the Duc de Praslin's table he met an Abbé Sieyès, full of vague politics designed for the new Assembly of Notables and preparing to astound the world with his conundrum, *Qu'est-ce que le Tiers État?* He even retained a dim (and, most likely, unfounded) recollection of meeting Chateaubriand, then a wild-eyed subaltern in the King's army. But his most congenial world was a small English set known, by the pleasing Continental practice of promiscuous ennoblement, as the *groupe des lords*. For more than one young gentleman of quality was sent to Angers, and among them a real lord or so. One pair, who lived in lodgings in the town and kept a famous cook, saw a good deal of Arthur. It was a cheerful world, where Pignerolle's cadets tried their very hardest to be manly, lose money at the tables, run into debt, and pick really grown-up quarrels (*bourgeois* French parents were mildly shocked by the establishment, because *"elle n'était remplie que de seigneurs Français ou Anglais, et . . . l'on ne connaissait pas de pays, où le libertinage, le jeu, le ton querelleur soient poussés plus loin que dans cette ville"*), although their manliest efforts were occasionally contradicted by the school confectioner's advertisements of sweets.

Arthur, staring up in the big round bastions of the castle or watching the gaitered infantry go stiffly by in their three-cornered hats, was seventeen. He had been two years abroad; and it was time for him to find a calling. They found one for him, since his mother had announced without enthusiasm that he was "food for powder and nothing more." Richard must use his influence and try to get him a commission. The rising man he was in the ministry now, one of Mr. Pitt's Junior Lords of the Treasury) approached the Lord-Lieutenant; and that potentate was presently informed of "a younger brother of mine, whom you were so kind as to take into your consideration for a commission in the army. He is here at this moment, and perfectly idle. It is a matter of indifference to me what commission he gets, provided he gets it soon." Dangan was mort-gaged, and there was not much to spare for the support of younger brothers. But Richard's nonchalance was less uncritical than might appear, since there was at least one variety of commission which he felt to be unsuitable for Arthur. For he declined the artillery, feeling perhaps that Arthur's birth (no less than Arthur's education) unfitted him for service in the learned arm. Such scruples were not universal. Watched by another family, another widow's son born the same summer and educated at another French academy was with his battery already. The pinched young subaltern, just seventeen and newly-joined, was deep in his gunnery. The guns attracted him; he even found a charm in mortars; and the frayed uniform grew dirtier than ever on the shadeless polygon of Valence. But then Lieutenant Bonaparte was not a Wesley, was not quite (as Arthur afterwards observed) a gentleman. Such ardours are not for Etonians. For Arthur's reading eschewed Rousseau; less ardent, he composed no novelettes of passion; and at no moment of his life was he capable of five perusals of *Werther*. More equable, he waited for the Lord-Lieutenant, through the good offices of Richard, to do something for him. And in due course he did. For on March 7, 1787, Arthur Wesley received the King's commission as Ensign in the Seventy-third. It was a Highland regiment; and, better still, it was in India, where there was not the slightest need for him to join it.

V

H E W A S gazetted Ensign just in time for his eighteenth birthday. It was the year of Mr. Pitt's *Entente Cordiale* and Hastings' impeachment. Mr. Burke was tuning up the deeper notes of his invective; Boswell was writing hard; and Mr. Gibbon, busy with his final volume, enjoyed the prospect of his lake. The century seemed at high noon, though the shadows fell a little longer as the sun, that decorously gilded sun, declined towards its last decade. Its melody was fuller than ever. *Don Giovanni* was heard that year, and Gluck's melodious shepherd mourned his Eurydice. Boucher was gone; but Fragonard still scattered rose-leaves. Countesses simpered for Gainsborough, and the cloaked Venetian maskers looked their most mysterious for Guardi. But they were all simpler (if a thought sweeter) now. For the sad tale of *Paul et Virginie* left no dry eyes that season, and the Queen of France was watching duchesses milk cows under the trees at Trianon, when Arthur Wesley first put on the red coat he was to wear, with impressive variations, halfway into the next century.

He had a calling now, though scarcely a profession, since he could hardly live upon an Ensign's pay; and their main anxiety was to find means of preventing him from following his unit to the East upon a pittance. Not that he shared their hesitations. The calling seemed to interest him and, as he said in later years, he "was not so young as not to know that since I had undertaken a profession I had better try to understand it." His curiosity, which Latin elegiacs had singularly failed to stir, began to move; and in a laudable pursuit of knowledge he had a Highland private weighed in full marching-order. But the family curtailed these barrack-yard experiments. For something better must be found for Arthur than bare regimental prospects; and hope gleamed, as usual, from Dublin Castle. That autumn there was a new Lord-Lieutenant, and Lady Mornington promptly asked him to do something for her boy. His reply was more than charming. For the obliging man made him an aide-de-camp the very instant that he had his own appointment.

27

Meanwhile, there was his leave to be arranged, his small belongings to be purchased, and (had he not been an Ensign for eight months?) something in the way of promotion. Advancement came to him through an ingenious series of exchanges rather than from any vulgar exercises in the barrack square. For the younger brother of a rising man found military life less arduous than a lonely gunner at Valence; and, after flickering uncertainly through the Ninth Foot, by Christmas he was a Lieutenant in the Seventy-sixth.

There was so much to be contrived for him, and his mother worked her very hardest. Now she was prouder of him. For Angers had done wonders for her awkward son. He had not learnt to dance for nothing, and the Duc de Praslin's table was a rare school of manners. Besides, the awkward age was over. He was eighteen; Eton was all forgiven now; and the grace acquired in French provincial *châteaux* quite effaced any shortcomings in his Latinity. So it was all written off to her two inseparable friends in Wales, and the "Dear Ladies" at Llangollen learned at becoming length from Lady Mornington how extremely obliging the Lord-Lieutenant had been, and how "there are so many little things to settle for *Arthur* who is just got into the army and is to go to Ireland in the capacity of Aid De Camp to Lord Buckingham, and must be set out a little for that, in short *I must* do *every thing* for him and when you see him you will think him worthy of it as he really is a very charming young man, never did I see such a change for the better in any body he is wonderfully lucky, in six months he has got two steps in the army and appointed Aid De Camp to Lord Buckingham which is ten shillings a day." Her pride in him was almost breathless; and there was still much to be arranged. For his new regiment had been raised for service in India; and if Dublin Castle was to see its latest aide-de-camp, he must exchange again. So she was busier than ever on his account (with the added torment of an intolerable bout of toothache)—"I have so much to get settled for Arthur, that I am sure it will not be done in the time. The King has given him leave to go to Ireland only upon condition of making an exchange into another regiment, as the one he is in is destined for the East Indies, and it cannot go without its full compliment of officers; this will cost some money and take some time to effect it; but at all events he will be a gainer." She seemed to grudge him nothing now; and it was all safely engineered at last. For in the first weeks of 1788 he got his transfer to the Forty-first; and, the laborious penury of foreign service thoughtfully eluded, the new aide-de-camp was packed off to Dublin. On the road he stopped to pay a call. For as they drove through Wales, he looked in upon the Ladies at Llangollen and earned the commendation of his mother's friends—"Lady Dungannon and Arthur Wesley arrived. A charming young man. Handsome, fashioned tall, and elegant. He stayed till two, then proceeded to Ireland."

So he was back in Ireland, his formal education ended. It had been a strange affair. Two years of Latin elegiacs, followed by two years of—what? Of French, of *haute école*, of ballroom deportment, of dinner at the Praslins'. Yet he had managed somehow to profit by it, though the virtues that won his mother's unexpected praise were rather social than military. His seat upon a horse was secure, if unattractive; his French was fluent, though he mastered it rather by vigorous assault than by more insidious methods (someone remarked in later years that he spoke French as he fought them—*bravement*); and in some mysterious way he had acquired a habit of private reading. But Dublin was unfriendly to studious habits, and Dublin resumed him—the cheerful, rather factious Dublin of 1788, where Lord Buckingham kept his Court and Mr. Grattan made his speeches. Chariots turned out of Dame Street, passed the Castle sentries, and set down before the Lord-Lieutenant's door; and lights shewed in windows, where gentlemen were losing money at the tables or Dublin hostesses received. The aide-de-camp was seen at parties—not always to his advantage. For somebody refused an invitation to a picnic until she was assured that "that mischievous boy" would not be there; and one heartless beauty, upon whom his company had palled, went home alone and left him stranded to get back as best he could with the musicians. The bright Vice-regal world enveloped him and, Dublin completing what Angers had begun, he learned to point a toe and turn a compliment. He played as well and naturally lost; and, these diversions straining a yearly stipend of £172 9s. 3d., he was occasionally left to stare disconsolately at the Liffey from his windows on Lower Ormond Quay. But his landlord, a sympathetic bootmaker, relieved the young gentleman's more pressing needs on loan, and was rewarded by full repayment and a place. Not all his rescuers were so fortunate. For a friend of his agent's brother, who advanced £100 to Lieutenant Wesley in 1789, was repaid by Major-General Sir Arthur Wellesley in 1806.

He had his duties too. For aides-de-camp were expected to ride out with the Lord-Lieutenant or to take their turn at Vice-regal ceremonies among the gilded pillars of St. Patrick's Hall; nor was it quite without significance that when Lieutenant Wesley first saw the world, he saw it from behind a throne. Besides, his brother Mornington, busy with his own career at Westminster, was always giving him estate business to do. So he had quite enough to think about in Dublin—his debts, his duties, and his violin; for he still played. He had a change of uniform as well, though without promotion. But it was a convenience for him to get a regiment that was stationed in Ireland. Since no acute professional interests attached him to the infantry, a fresh exchange transferred him to the cavalry; and he was now Lieutenant Wesley of the Twelfth Dragoons. Within the month a mob went roaring against the Bastille, and the first heads were bobbing through the Paris streets on the first pikes. Mr. Fox was in ecstasies; but Dublin (and the Eighteenth Century) went on. The ladies danced; their masters dined; the aides-de-camp rode out as usual, though Arthur's sister Anne enquired in some agitation of the Ladies of Llangollen, "A'n't you sorry for poor dear France, I shall never see Paris again"; and as the echoes died away, Lieutenant Wesley was putting on his new cavalry uniform.

A graver initiation waited, since he was nearly of age. Richard, the rising man in London, marshalled his forces. His brother William sat for their Irish borough. The post was not exacting; and, with Arthur growing up, William might very well be transferred to Westminster, while the young Castle aide-de-camp relieved him in the Irish House of Commons. So an English seat was found for William, and Arthur at twenty stood on the edge of Irish politics. Irish politics in 1790 were full of an uneasy stir. For there was positively an Irish question. Perhaps it had been answered at Bunker's Hill. Had not Mr. Flood announced that "a voice from America had shouted to liberty"? Napper Tandy might even be the voice of the people (which France was now so busy proclaiming to be divine); and conceivably the truth might be with that ecstatic commentator who had recently distilled an apocalyptic nationalism from the Book of Revelation and heartened the Lord-Lieutenant in well-doing by the coincidence between the harps, the sea of glass, the linen robes of Holy Writ and Ireland's coat of arms and leading manufactures. But borough-owners were largely untroubled by these lofty problems. For Castle politics in the age of Lord Chancellor Fitzgibbon were mercifully simple, consisting mainly in the humbler arts by which majorities are managed. Trim, represented by a Castle aide-de-camp, would be a unit in the Crown's majority; but before he could perform these simple evolutions, Arthur must qualify to represent it. First he became a Freemason, being initiated into Lodge 494, of Trim, co. Meath. Then he ran his first political errand. It was a matter of some delicacy that brought him into Trim one March day in 1790. For the Corporation, it seemed, was about to confer its freedom upon Mr. Grattan, a proceeding that could scarcely be congenial to the Castle. The family was bound to oppose it; and before an audience of eighty Lieutenant Wesley made his first recorded public speech. According to his own report, he "got up and said that the only reason given why Mr. Grattan should get the freedom of the corporation was his respectability, that really if we were to admit every man because one or two people said he was respectable, the whole community would belong to the corporation, that *he* could never be of any use to us and never would attend, and that I would certainly object, however great my respect for him." This was sensible enough. Then the orator grew more ingenious: "I said I should always vote for three sorts of people, those who were made to repel a party striving to turn the old family interest out of the borough," for a lawyer who might be serviceable upon election business, and for local residents. The meeting adjourned. But the young emissary was not inactive during the adjournment, since "I told my friends that it was a question of party, that they must stick by me"; and under this strenuous leadership the opposition carried the previous question in triumph. On the same eventful day he announced his candidature, and was promptly button-holed by an elderly voter, who declined to promise until he knew what Lord Mornington proposed to do about a bond for £70. This was extremely awkward; and the candidate, with rare discretion, "said I would have nothing to do with it, as in case of a General Election such a transaction would entirely vitiate my return." The simple appetites of eighteenth-century electors stirred on every hand; but the youthful politician, though considerably embarrassed, was not unskilful: "I was in the most difficult situation I ever experienced, and only got out of it by sticking up manfully to what I first said. I must say that, although I was plagued with requests of all kinds and totally unable and disinclined to make any promise . . . they behaved as handsomely as people could do. . . . They are all fine fellows."

Such was his first engagement. It ended in a modest triumph and a gratified despatch to Richard. But politics, it seemed, drew him as little as soldiering, since a postscript added that, "I am still of the same opinion with regard to your going abroad, and hope you will accept my offer to accompany you." Richard, however, stayed in England; and Arthur's duty called, however faintly, in Ireland. For, his regiment apart, the assault on Trim was promptly followed up; the Irish Parliament dissolved that spring; and Arthur was returned in 1790 for the family borough. There was some fear of a petition; for malice had been heard to whisper that the young gentleman was not quite of age when Trim elected him. These apprehensions kept him busy. He left his regiment in June, and posted to Dublin for grave consultations with the Lord Chancellor and the Attorney-General. But his constituency was not neglected, since that summer he subscribed five guineas to the local races. The House met in July, and the petition was set down for hearing. But the petitioners failed to proceed; and, all apprehensions set at rest, Lieutenant Wesley was beyond dispute Member of Parliament for Trim.

If contact with the Trim electors was an imperfect education in democracy, the Irish House of Commons was unlikely to impress its new recruit with the virtues of Parliamentary government. Two-thirds of that assembly owed their election to less than a hundred borough-owners; one-third were in receipt of salaries or pensions from the Crown; their collective appetites absorbed almost one-eighth of the Irish revenue; and it was not surprising that they rarely deviated from an inveterate conviction that the King's government must be carried on. Such was the first assembly in which Arthur Wesley learned to legislate.

Not that he legislated with any undue fervour. The rafters rang with the eloquence of Mr. Grattan; and he served modestly on a committee. Dublin repeated the latest sally of Sir Boyle Roche; and the Castle aide-de-camp was inconspicuously jobbing supporters into small places. His

zeal enriched the public service with a deputy barrack-master, whilst
another suppliant was safely lodged in the Lottery. But as the voices rose
and fell behind the portico on College Green, Arthur Wesley's never vied
with the solemn note of Sir Hercules Langrishe; and for two years after
his election he remained discreetly mute, a boyish-looking figure with a
high colour, a red coat, and a large pair of epaulettes, sitting among the
silent cohorts genially termed by Wolfe Tone "the common prostitutes
of the Treasury Bench." He was a Captain now, promoted in 1791 to
command a company in the Fifty-eighth Foot on the Irish establishment,
and regimental duty sometimes took him as far as Cork; though he
soon turned cavalryman again, exchanging into the Eighteenth Light
Dragoons in the next year. But he was mostly to be found in Dublin,
on duty at the Castle, or strolling to the House of Commons from his
rooms in Grafton Street, or else at Dangan deep in new tenancies, eject-
ments, renewals, and all the fierce joys of estate management. That
noble property was a sad trial to them now. There was the mortgage
interest to be found. And for what? The big iron gates were always
waiting, their tracery etched on the ragged skies of Meath; and the long
drive still led down the hill and over the bridge across the ornamental
water. But they never seemed to go there. No organ-music woke the
hall; the still canal heard no more water-concerts; and the garden gods
waited forlornly in their temples. Besides, the intrepid Richard needed
cash for his assault on Westminster. His ties with Ireland were always
of the slightest (did he not live to resent his own Irish marquessate as a
"double-gilt potato"?), and he had turned his back on Dublin. There
was the seat at Trim, of course; a vote on College Green was not without
its uses; and it would be as well for them to keep their hold on Castle
favours through the family borough. But Arthur could look after that.
There was no need for Dangan, though. Richard had never cared for it.
What did a rising man in London want with a mortgaged Irish mansion? Mr. Pitt could surely see his worth without that to set him off.
His discreetly orthodox opinions on the Regency question were even approved by Majesty itself, now happily restored to reason; and when
Windsor smiled, Dangan was surely far behind him. So before 1792 was
out, the place was for sale.

While Richard spread his wings in London for these impressive flights, obedient Arthur stayed behind in Ireland. His brother's deputy (and Irish patriots found hard things to say of "the petty pilfering, jobbing, corrupting tricks of every deputy of a deputy of an English minister"), he cultivated Meath electors, subscribed ten guineas to the Corporation plate, and earned Mornington's slightly condescending praises for his management of Trim, "where by his excellent judgment, amiable manners, admirable temper, and firmness he has entirely restored the interest of my family." Versed in these unobtrusive arts, he even made a maiden speech, rising to second the Address one January day in 1793. It was a fluttered world, in which the French—wild-eyed and shouting unfamiliar songs—threatened by turns to conquer Holland and behead their king, and an exuberant Minister of Marine promised his countrymen the added joys of a descent on England with the pleasing objects of depositing fifty thousand caps of liberty, planting its sacred tree, and holding out fraternal hands to the groaning subjects of King George. Small wonder, then, that Captain Wesley, seconding the Address on College Green, hazarded the blameless sentiment that "at a time when opinions were spreading throughout Europe inimical to kingly government it behoved us, in a particular manner, to lay before our gracious Sovereign our determination to support and maintain the constitution," with more (but not much more) to the same effect. Taking a wider survey he "reprobated, in very severe terms, the conduct of the French towards their king, and their invasion of the territories of foreign princes, and their irruption into the Austrian Netherlands." Then, returning homewards, he particularly approved a faintly liberal allusion to the Catholic question in the Speech from the Throne—"He had no doubt of the loyalty of the Catholics of this country, and he trusted that when the question would be brought forward, respecting that description of men, that we would lay aside all animosities, and act with moderation and dignity, and not with the fury and violence of partizans." It was a theme on which fuller reflection brought him worse counsel.

But Catholic Emancipation in 1793 was, by a queer inversion, the policy of sound reactionaries. Pitt was propitious; Burke could not forget that he was an Irishman; Popery itself grew daily more congenial to all who ranged themselves with Catholic allies against the godless excesses of Paris; and even the Castle gave a sulky acquiescence. Its drilled maiority, sometimes a little out of step, obediently passed a Catholic Relief Bill, which conferred the franchise and removed the major disabilities, excepting the exclusion of Catholics from Parliament. That must be maintained; for who would lay an impious finger on the palladium of Protestant ascendancy? Not Arthur Wesley, since he was positively chosen as the Castle spokesman to resist the bold amendment. It was his second speech in Parliament; and since his first the whole world was changed. For a king's head had fallen in Paris, and England was at war. The fact, though he might not suspect it, concerned him intimately. It concerned, indeed, his whole generation and Anglo-Irish younger sons more than most. For the bland decorum of the Eighteenth Century was sharply interrupted by a new age, which the fantastic calendar of Paris did well to date from the Year One. Elegance went out of fashion; and young gentlemen who trailed a graceful scabbard after the Lord-Lieutenant were a thought behind the mode. A stir was in the air, as Europe drifted into its long duel with the Revolution; and the war, of which a Castle aide-de-camp watched the opening from Dublin, came closer to him until, a little grey about the temples, he observed its final scene from the saddle above Hougomont.

But as the drums began to sound in February, 1793, he was speaking in the Irish House of Commons. This time he managed to abstain from general reflections. His tone, though unsympathetic to the full Catholic claims, was reasonable. For having voted for the Catholic franchise, he had no objection to giving the Roman Catholics the benefits of the constitution." But there were plainly limits; and a Parliament of Papists seemed to exceed them. When both sides were satisfied with a more gradual measure, the cautious young gentleman declined to "agitate a question which may disturb both." Not that he was a Protestant alarmist. His common-sense scouted the orthodox dismay at visions of enfranchised Papists voting solidly behind their priests—"Have not Roman Catholics, like Protestants, various interests and various passions by which they are swayed? The influence of their landlords—their good or bad opinion of the candidates—their own interests—and a thousand other motives? It appeared to him that they would not vote in a body, or as had been supposed, if the bill should pass in its present form; but if the motion of the honourable gentleman should be adopted, then indeed

they would undoubtedly unite in support of Roman Catholic candidates."
This was a fair sample of moderate opinion from a young gentleman on
the Castle list whose brother wished to stand well with Mr. Pitt. In
that judicious mood much might have been done for Ireland. But it
was the year 1793; and it is the fate of Irish hopes to be dashed by
European wars.

The world was stirring around him. But his interests seemed all to
lie in Ireland. His seat in Parliament, his place at Court kept him in
Dublin; affairs occasionally called him to Dangan; and regimental duty
took him no farther than an Irish barrack. There were other interests
as well. For Lord Longford had a sister; Kitty Pakenham had a pair
of bright eyes; and Captain Wesley often called at Rutland Square. Vows
were exchanged; but what are vows without a competence? Longford,
considering his sister's prospects on a Captain's pay, was stern. Plainly the
couple could not marry. But Arthur might find out a way—there was
no need for him always to be a Captain. Richard must manage something for him. So that spring he wrote to Richard; the purchase money
was advanced; and before April was out, he was a Major in the Thirty-
third. But it was not enough to be a Major. If Kitty was to be achieved,
he must rise in his profession. Cards had betrayed him more than once,
and card-playing was promptly forsworn. He had a deeper passion,
though, which seemed to stand between him and promotion. For music
(was he not his father's son?) absorbed his leisure; and a violin was
often in his hand. Music had brought his father almost to poverty, and
a little grimly he resolved to break the charm. Besides, it would never do
for a promising young officer to indulge in secret orgies of the violin.
To say the least, it was not martial. Brass, perhaps; or even wood-wind
(Frederick the Great had played the flute); but scarcely strings. His
head, if it was ever to wear laurels, must be filled with drill-ground
evolutions, not with the adorable intricacies of counterpoint or the sweet
wail of strings. So one day in that eventful summer of 1793 he burned
his fiddle. He never touched another, though the taste lived on in him.
For dinner-parties years away were carried off from Apsley House to
hear the Ancient Concerts; their host's preference was understood to
lie with Handel, and even with Corelli, though the severity of the
programme was somewhat mitigated by his invariable seat upon a special

sofa between two handsome women. He could still take pleasure in a lady's touch upon the harp, and was assiduous at the Opera, when Jenny Lind was singing; his wrist, although he only used it now for carrying the Sword of State upright in the House of Lords, remained supple as a violinist's; and once in later years, when Madame Lieven played some waltzes on the pianoforte, he supported her (an executant once more) upon the triangle. There was always a thin strain of music in him. But the charm was broken now. His father's fate had warned him; and when Major Wesley, in hopes of Kitty Pakenham, resolved to be a soldier, the flames licked a broken violin in Dublin. Perhaps an artist died. He never cared to have it spoken of.

VI

THAT summer, as the Queen of France sat waiting in her prison, the storm broke. It had climbed slowly up the sky; and as it climbed, the light died out of Europe. There was a hush, and the familiar sounds came plainly over the still air—the tap of heels, the rustle of polite society, the scratch of rhyming pens, the buzz of coffee-houses, and even the level voice of Mr. Pitt assuring the hopeful Commons that "unquestionably there never was a time in the history of this country when, from the situation of Europe, we might more reasonably expect fifteen years of peace than at the present moment." His hope died on the silence, and the dainty world began to lose its colours. For a cloud had swung across the sun, and a long shadow seemed to fall across the trim parterres. Even Mr. Pitt could see it now. "The war," he observed with a singular change of heart, "is not only unavoidable, but, under the circumstances of the case, absolutely necessary to the existence of Great Britain and Europe." The skies were leaden; and Burke raved in the gathering gloom, while Gibbon with grave elaboration begged leave to agree with him—"I admire his eloquence, I adore his chivalry, and I can almost excuse his reverence for church establishments." The century, the eternal Eighteenth Century, had turned to bay; and all its children —positive, polite, and sceptical—took up their places for the conflict. For the storm broke that summer; and the thunder which had muttered above Paris rolled halfway round the world. There was a sudden gleam of bayonets; and Europe marched, as the French rallied round the great voice of Danton. But before the stiff battalions of the Monarchies could reach their stations, France dashed to meet them, breaking like surf along the frontiers. Austrians pounded the northern fortresses; the Prussians barely held along the Rhine; Spain moved deliberately in the sunshine of the Pyrenees; and half the west was up in the King's name, while Britons resolved with loud huzzas to—

> stand by the Church, and the King, and the Laws;
> The old Lion still has his teeth and his claws;

Let Britain still rule in the midst of her waves,
And chastise all those foes who dare call her sons slaves.

Derrydown.

The surf rose higher now; a wilder melody hung on the air above its charges. But the seventh wave was still delayed. Perhaps it lurked among the shallows, where a lean captain of artillery trailed dustily along a road near Avignon in charge of sixteen gunners and two guns. It was his first command. For Captain Bonaparte was an apprentice, the long arm of Carnot sprawled in the dust of office floors across his maps to shift the candles with his armies, and the heads were falling fast in Paris, when Major Wesley took to soldiering.

But soldiering in such a season meant rather more than the punctual performance of regimental duties in Irish barrack squares. It was not quite enough for him to jingle spurs in Dublin corridors behind the Lord-Lieutenant; and that summer he was writing once again to Richard, desiring him "to ask Mr. Pitt to desire Lord Westmorland to send me as Major to one of the flank corps. If they are to go abroad, they will be obliged to take officers from the line, and they may as well take me as anybody else. . . . I think it both dangerous and improper to remove any part of the army from this country at present, but if any part of it is to be moved, I should like to go with it, and have no chance of being service except with the flank corps, as the regiment I have got into as Major is the last for service." He must see service, if he was to rise in his profession. But his application, if it was ever made, was disregarded fortunately, perhaps, since the flank companies despatched that year from Ireland went off to die of yellow fever in Martinique. So Arthur Wesley eluded the crowded cemetery at Fort Royal, to say nothing of the more dreadful fate that waits upon returned heroes of Colonial warfare. For their conversation, a just object of alarm, abounded in the tedium of concealed enemies and cocoa trees—"Here stood the enemy . . . and there, my love, are my fellows: there the cocoa trees. . . ." How the delicious Harriette learned to dread that opening in later years. But whatever else Miss Wilson had cause to fear from Arthur, it was never that. The Thirty-third still kept the peace in Ireland; and the assiduous Major drilled his men, as the world reeled through the stupendous calendar of '93. His century, with all that Arthur Wesley lived for—Dublin

Castle, Dangan, and the King's uniform—was assailed that year. *93 es*
la guerre de l'Europe contre la France et de la France contre Paris. . .
De là l'immensité de cette minute épouvantable, 93, plus grande que tou
le reste du siècle. He missed the rhapsody, perhaps, but caught a littl
of the uproar. For his countrymen were shouting Dibdin's chorus:

> Thus in famed Ninety-three
> Britons all shall agree,
> While with one heart and voice in loud chorus they sing,
> To improve *"Ça ira"* into "God Save the King!"

That summer, as the armies swayed along the frontier, Paris raved. Ther
was a fever of eloquence, a rash of tricolour cockades, a frenzy of citi
zenship. Voices rose shriller now on the still air above the stifling city
the big knife clanked down at briefer intervals in the great square be
yond the Tuileries; and France, beside herself, shewed the pale face o
the Terror like a Medusa's head to the oncoming battalions of the in
vasion. Marat died in those hot weeks and Charlotte Corday; and a youn
man stood muttering, as the cart went by, that it were beautiful to di
with her. But Arthur Wesley was still drilling redcoats in the soft Iris
sunshine. He went to England in the autumn. For Dangan had foun
a purchaser at last; and when Richard signed away the big square hous
Arthur witnessed his signature. They had no ornamental water now
the garden gods knew other owners; and the family, their castle gon
depended solely upon Richard and his soaring prospects. That day th
guns were opening above Toulon, watched by a "short, taciturn, oliv
complexioned young man, not unknown to us, by name Buonaparte
ranking now as Lieutenant-Colonel.

Arthur was soon promoted too; and as the gunfire echoed round th
hills behind Toulon, Lieutenant-Colonel Wesley went back to Irelan
to command the Thirty-third. (From Ensign to Lieutenant-Colonel in le
than seven years was creditable going—more creditable, perhaps, *
influence and army-brokers than to military science. But there was litt
need for a Lieutenant-Colonel to blush at twenty-four, when Kitt
Pakenham's brother was a Major at seventeen, and Cotton had a reg
ment at twenty-one and Lowry Cole at twenty-two.) As the leaves fe
the crisis deepened. Disordered tides of war raced round the coasts *
Europe; a Paris court-room heard the unpleasant voice of Fouquie

Tinville denounce a hunted woman, grey-haired at thirty-eight, as a Messalina, a Medicis, a Merovingian tyrant; the French infantry went roaring up the slope through the October mist at Wattignies; in Paris the knife fell and rose again and fell; and Arthur Wesley still sat on in Dublin, busy with regimental accounts. Late in the year, though, there was a vague hint of active service. For the strategy of British ministers is normally composed of a vast number of divergent gestures; and finding their commitments in Flanders, Provence, and the West Indies palpably insufficient for an army of 20,000 men, they gaily contemplated a descent on Normandy. A force was fitting out at Portsmouth for the French coast, and there was a notion that the Thirty-third would sail with it. Sudden departures are no less disturbing to gentlemen of honour than to their creditors, and Arthur made careful dispositions to discharge his Dublin debts, his income being assigned to an obliging tradesman who undertook to pay them off. But Moira's expedition started down-Channel on its aimless cruise without the Thirty-third; and as the year went out, Colonel Wesley was left standing in the wings, still waiting for his cue.

Dublin retained him, as a fresh year opened and the echoes of a world at war floated across St. George's Channel. They were still there in February. Spring came, the dreadful spring of '94, when Revolution, thirsting still and gorged with its enemies, turned unnaturally upon its own children. The Girondins had gone already, gone singing down the narrow street that ended in the waiting crowd, the planks, the angular machine. He was in Cork, still striking regimental balances the month a big, square-shouldered form came up against the evening sky in Paris and stared across a packed and silent square muttering, "Danton, no weakness." May found him there as well, still signing army forms. But the next month they got their orders; and Colonel Wesley prepared to take his first battalion on his first active service. It fell, by the symmetry of fate, in Belgium.

The skein of war was slightly tangled. Rarely without complexity for allies and always apt to yield its richest tangles to Austrian fingers, it bore extensive witness to the welter of cross-purposes which was the allied substitute for strategy. Soldiers of European standing did their solemn best to conduct a war as wars should be conducted. Having learnt

their profession fighting against or under Frederick the Great, the
took measures admirably calculated to outmanœuvre a Prussian army (
1760. But the delicate precision of their military minuet somehow faile
of its effect upon the coarser fibre of French *Demi brigades* in 179
Fashions, perhaps, were changing; and at Hondschoote the prim tacti
of the Eighteenth Century met the untutored onslaught of the Nineteent
with all the *gaucherie* of last year's fashions at a dress-parade. Beside
there was the Revolution. It appeared to affect them in the oddest ma▶
ner, so that troops, which by every rule were off the board, insisted upo
scrambling to the attack without a vestige of formation, shouting th
most unusual songs. It was all highly disconcerting. Military science wa
almost wasted on such adversaries. For armies threatened with con
plete (if theoretical) disaster by the loss of a strategical point failed fro
sheer ignorance to notice it, and pressed obstinately forward. The be
military minds had learnt to play at war as other men at chess; b▶
chess is rarely satisfactory with an opponent who declines to learn th
rules and is more than a little apt to spill the board. So the stiff *Kaise*
licks tramped dutifully in all directions, and nothing came of it. Whit
coated infantry faced with cerise, with mauve, with green, with ever
colour in the Imperial spectrum moved in strict obedience to order
gunners in grey tilted their big tricornes and served little guns; pr
posterously hatted units threw pontoon bridges across slow-flowin
Flemish rivers; while, furred and frogged, hussars of every shade—Kais
in blue, Barco in blue and green, Wurmser in green and scarlet—jingle
off, watched by respectful villagers, or dismounting stiffly from red sa
dle-cloths with the big Hapsburg cipher trailed their long scabbards ov
the Flemish cobblestones. It was a brave display; but nothing came of i
For the skein of war was tangled. Wound by the Emperor, the King (
Prussia, the *Reich*, King George, the Cabinet, the Duke of York, an
half the *Almanach de Gotha*, it abounded in sudden turns that led n
where, and was generously involved with every knot of European polic
(Few campaigns are less rewarding than those directed by Foreign Offi◀
strategy.) For in '94 the crusading march of outraged Europe upo
Paris had degenerated sadly. Checked at Mauberge the year before,
declined after Tourcoing to a precarious defensive strung awkward
along the Belgian frontier. France gathered strength in front of thei

and the invaders halted in a mood of dull bewilderment, resolved apparently to await its impact in the impressive posture of a sanitary cordon. But the dispositions convenient to frontier-guards in dealing with infected persons will not usually avail to check a nation in arms.

Somewhere towards the right of this depressed array a British contingent, shaken at Tourcoing and more than a little jaded by the endless series of aimless withdrawals and attacks that were not followed up, stood waiting in the Flanders plain. Waiting, indeed, appeared to be their leading occupation. For, apart from one major (and distinctly unsatisfying) engagement and a few dashing encounters, their derisive countrymen had summarised their operations with tolerable accuracy:

> The rare old Duke of York,
> He had ten thousand men;
> He marched 'em up to the top of the hill,
> And he marched 'em down again.

The Duke, indeed, was young; his command was in the neighbourhood of thirty thousand; and there were no hills in sight. But, these facts conceded, there was little fault to find with the disrespectful *précis* of their position and prospects. Vaguely alarmed, the Cabinet sent reinforcements. For Ostend was palpably in danger. It has been observed that Belgian ports hold a peculiar power of fascinating English statesmen; and their heads are sadly affected by names which, in the case of Queen Mary, were harmlessly engraved upon the heart. Ostend, like Antwerp, had the fatal charm. So the Thirty-third were moved at last: they sailed from Cork in the first week of June; and after nineteen days at sea Colonel Wesley landed his regiment at Ostend.

He was on active service now. Had not an elderly Colonel of the Guards warned him of its approaching trials—"You little know what you are going to meet with. You will often have no dinner at all. I mean," the horrified Guardsman had added, "literally no dinner, and not merely roughing it on a beefsteak or a bottle of port wine." The forecast was correct. For the Duke's army lacked almost everything. There was even a shortage of generals; and their exiguous supplies reached the dejected redcoats through the intermittent activities of the new Waggon Train, known (from their origins and tunic) as the 'Newgate Blues." Once more a British army swore terribly in Flanders.

For it was a continuation of Marlborough's wars conducted with muc
of Marlborough's equipment and lacking only Marlborough to comple
the resemblance. But Arthur Wesley and the rest of Moira's reinforc
ments were still among the sand-hills of Ostend. The Colonel foun
himself commanding a brigade of three battalions; and when Moir
marched away to join the main Allied army, Wesley's brigade was le
as rearguard "to settle matters at Ostend" (the French, including a youn
Colonel named Murat, were getting near) "and then to come on a
quick as I could." Ostend was promptly evacuated; and preferring
short sea voyage to a dangerous flank-march in face of an advancin
enemy, he re-embarked his men, put them on shore again at Antwer
and reached the Duke of York's position before the leading files o
Moira's force which had come overland. So his first minor operatio
comprised a deft retreat and a neat use of the ubiquity conferred by se
power on British expeditionary forces.

There was an agonised succession of Allied conferences, while the lir
still held uneasily in front of Brussels. They met at Braine-l'Alleuc
they met again, by a felicitous choice, at Waterloo. But with Austrian
to line it, that position was scarcely at its best. The French tide wa
running strongly across Belgium; and finally each Ally went his wa
For the last strand of Allied strategy had almost parted. The Austrian
trailed off towards the east, while the Duke of York, receding slowl
northwards, still undertook to keep the French out of Holland by th
united efforts of the Dutch, his own little army, and a few Germa
troops in British pay. Then the retreat began. There was a small affa
at Boxtel in Dutch Brabant one September day, when Arthur Wesle
took his battalion into action under the eye of Abercromby. The Thirt
third were competently handled, holding their fire in face of the or
coming French until their Colonel ordered a volley. The old Gener
(whose bushy eyebrows gave one, as someone said, "the idea of a ver
good-natured lion") called a few days later to convey "the Duke o
York's thanks and his to the Thirty-third for their good conduct on th
15th." But these laurels failed to dazzle him, since the same lette
which conveyed the news to Richard announced that he would be bac
in Ireland before the winter was out. There was the usual trouble wit
their Irish tenants; and as he lay in front of Nijmegen, Arthur's min

as full of small practical expedients of estate-management in Ireland. Not that his eye, as it turned homewards, was blurred by sentiment; or as he offered slightly contradictory counsels, he added tartly, "This Irish language, but not less true for that country of scoundrels."

The winter deepened round them, and the retreat went on through the dreary landscape and grotesque nomenclature of the Netherlands. They stood along the Waal; and Arthur, whose health was none too good, lived in a perpetual rearguard action. Now he commanded a brigade, and acted in virtual independence—"I was on the Waal, I think, from October to January, and during all that time I only saw once one general from the headquarters." But the young Brigadier, haunted by thoughts of leave, commanded without especial gusto. Hope gleamed a little, as the French hung on the edge of winter-quarters—"I think it impossible for any troops (even the French) to keep the field in this severe weather. As soon as their intentions are decided I intend to go to England." The French, alas! were ignorant of these refinements, and frankly disinclined to treat campaigning as a seasonal occupation. Besides, the season, however unpleasant, was particularly propitious for their offensive, since the frost eliminated water-lines which must otherwise have served as strong defences. So the war flickered along his outposts through the black nights of a Dutch winter—"We turn out twice, sometimes twice every night; the officers and men are harassed to death. . . . I have not had my clothes off my back for a long time, and generally spend the greater part of the night upon the bank of the river." By day the enemy were entertaining enough, "perpetually chattering with our officers and soldiers," and ready to oblige on request with lively performances of the *Carmagnole*. But as he watched the ice-cracks grinding in the Waal or wrote out his endless regimental accounts, he still thought of leave—"I intend to go to England in a few days, that is to say, if the French remain quiet, and if the regiment is relieved from the advanced post upon the river Waal, where it has been for above six weeks." The French, however, with republican discourtesy resumed the offensive; and in the last week of the year the Thirty-third cleared a Dutch village with the bayonet.

The year went out on his discomfort, on a winter land of freezing polders and ice-bound canals, on a ragged army straining precariously to

defend a country which had not the least wish to be defended. For th
Dutch found the French invasion more congenial than their Alli
champions. The countryside was frankly hostile, and there were ev
dark suspicions of the Dutch army. Arthur was once instructed to esco
a Dutch officer through his lines for a secret interview with Pichegr
Watched by the Colonel, two muffled figures met on the ice; and short
afterwards (it seemed a little sinister) the French were in Utrecht. Th
Dutch defences broke in all directions; there was a brief resistance
front of Arnhem, when the Thirty-third performed once more; th
the retreat went miserably on in the short winter days. With the Frenc
in the Dutch ports and solemn Dutchmen dancing round trees of li
erty in Amsterdam, there was no way to England for the retreating arm
except across the frozen heaths that lay between the Zuider Zee and th
North German ports; and their line of march slanted towards the ea
It lay across an endless plain of white under the dark winter sky. Tr
ing at first, the retreat soon deepened into tragedy. For the army w
practically unclothed; a few units had great-coats purchased by publ
subscription over a year before, and the remainder owed the sm
comfort of a flannel waistcoat to the private charity of officers.

An arduous winter on the long road from Antwerp to the north of H
land had left them in rags; and as the iron frost gripped these pitiab
scarecrows, they died along the frozen tracks. The last semblances of di
cipline almost vanished in its grip; for having no supplies they looted, an
having no enemy to fight they fought one another. All the torments
1812 were let loose upon them in one dreadful week of January, 179
The white plain lay behind them now; but it was marked with broke
waggons, with frozen pack-horses, with silent heaps that had been marc
ing yesterday, even with women. The worst was over then. They reache
the Ems at last; and a rueful General reported to the Duke of Yor
"Your army is destroyed; the officers, their carriages, and a large tra
are safe, but the men are destroyed. . . ." Life was easier now; discipli
returned, and Brigade Orders began to abound in prohibitions of pr
miscuous shooting of all edible forms of game. A Hanoverian unit (Jäge
in more than name) having found someone's deer quite irresistible, th
sporting instincts of the British were restrained by a threat of cou
martial for any soldier "detected in using his firelock except when

46

Duty." The winter turned to spring, and they dragged their way to the quaysides of Bremen. A period of endless embarkation returns set in. But Colonel Wesley, his duty in the field once done, eluded the confusion. They reached the port in March; and before the month was out, he was in London. His regiment was still abroad. Transports slid up the German river to fetch them home; and one Monday morning (it was April 3, 1795) the remnants of the Thirty-third were marched on board. The long campaign was ended.

Ended for Arthur Wesley also. Another chapter of his education closed, he was in England. It had been arduous—more arduous than the old Guardsman's forecast. But it had been instructive too. He said of it in later years that he had "learnt what one ought not to do, and that is always something." Few campaigns, indeed, were more admirably designed to perform the functions of the awful warning. The least attentive mind could hardly miss its lessons. It has been frequently observed that British armies are at their finest in retreat. But the higher command seemed almost over-anxious to display these qualities. Arthur himself was most unfavourably impressed by the limpness of headquarters, which left regimental officers in virtual independence—"We had letters from England, and I declare that those letters told us more of what was passing at headquarters than we learned from the headquarters themselves. . . . The real reason why I succeeded in my own campaigns is because I was always on the spot—I saw everything, and did everything myself." Not so the Duke of York and his headquarters. Besides, what they did was almost certain to be wrong—"There was a fellow called Hammerstein, who was considered the chief authority in the army for tactics, but was quite an impostor; in fact, no one knew anything of the management of an army, though many of the regiments were excellent." But, excellent or not, authority left them to freeze and frequently to starve; for it had yet to dawn upon the martial mind that orders on the day of battle are of far less importance than regular meals upon the intervening days. The lesson was not lost on Arthur. Nor, perhaps, the disastrous consequences of indiscipline upon retreating troops, or the effect of a judicious volley from British infantry in line upon the scrambling columns of the French. It was a dozen years before he saw their blue uniforms again, and the interval taught him the art of war. But he had learnt some of it in Holland through that dreary winter.

VII

RETURNED, but not conspicuously laurelled, the Colonel of th Thirty-third resumed the problem of his own career. The years we passing (he was twenty-six that spring), and so much remained to l achieved—promotion, Kitty Pakenham, even a competence. For the mo devoted younger brother could hardly be expected to live for ever upc Richard's prospects; and, these apart, Arthur had really not much more live on. Five hundred pounds a year, perhaps, comprised the total of Lieutenant-Colonel's pay with the allowances of a Castle aide-de-cam One could not cut a figure in the world on five hundred pounds a yea Indeed, it was distinctly doubtful if that income would suffice to meet th cost of past appearances. For Dublin and his creditors were waiting, ar the returning warrior faced the bleakest of financial prospects.

He faced it with resource; for Irish patronage was always a resour to those with friends at Dublin Castle. There was no need for him go to Dublin, though. The new Lord-Lieutenant was in London; ar Arthur promptly waited on Lord Camden with a modest intimatic that he should take some opportunity of stating the claims which l conceived himself to have upon the Government of Ireland. But Pit latest Lord-Lieutenant had more to think about than a remunerati place for Colonel Wesley. There was the rest of Ireland to be considere and Ireland in 1795 stood in need of full consideration. For whilst Arth Wesley had been countermarching on by-roads in Holland, Lord Fi william had been countermarching with no less vigour upon Catho Emancipation. Camden was to succeed that unhappy strategist; the who country was in a lively uproar; and with all his problems still unsolv the new Lord-Lieutenant went off a little grimly to take up his residen in Dublin. The faithful aide-de-camp, still close to the Viceregal e followed his chief and paced the Castle yard again. Dublin had dra backs for him, too. His tradesmen lived in Dublin; but a trifle of fo teen pounds to settle with a clothier was not to be thought of—was,

ct, suspended until the hero of Assaye, returning as a Major-General,
aid the account twelve years away.

The spring of 1795 grew bright above these cares. He lived in quarters
ow more advantageously than in his former lodgings. Catholics, United
ishmen, Defenders, Peep of Day Boys all pressed on Camden; but none
essed so hard as Arthur Wesley. The Thirty-third, returned from Ger-
any, were peacefully encamped in Essex. But their determined Colonel
aced his parallels and laid his mines, as he besieged the Lord-Lieutenant.
hat dignitary was evidently disinclined to be taken by storm; the March
connaissance in London had shown that. So Arthur settled down in
ublin to a siege *en règle*. All April he was in the trenches. He spoke
scretly to His Excellency "upon a certain object of mine in this
ountry"; he spoke of it again; he wrote a note enclosing—here he unasked his batteries—a letter from Lord Mornington in Richard's most
ajestic manner. That nobleman informed the Lord-Lieutenant, as one
rl to another, of his happiness at news of Camden's civility to Arthur—
ou may easily believe how happy this account has made me, and how
ongly I feel these proofs of your friendship for me." (A helping hand
Arthur was, it seemed, a mere form of courtesy to Richard.) But more
ight yet be done—"My Brother tells me, that the situation of Secretary
War . . . is likely to be opened soon"—and what more suitable to
thur, more gratifying to Richard, or more convenient to the public
vice? The note concluded with a scornful word or so on "His *çi-devant*
cellency," Fitzwilliam, and the sage reflection (familiar to belligerents
need of consolation) that the French "are very nearly exhausted even
their victories."

This bold attack encountered an insurmountable defence from the
sieged Lord-Lieutenant, which wrung from Arthur the slightly rueful
mission that "I see the manner in which the Military Offices are
ed, and I don't wish to ask for that which I know you can't give me."
ainly his next assault must take another road. But before the storming-
rty left his trenches, he prepared their way with slightly touching
genuity. He was still in Parliament; and if only he could be of service
the Castle, perhaps the Castle might be less impregnable. His chance
ived one night in May, when angry gentlemen denounced a former
rd-Lieutenant for the high misdemeanour of denuding Ireland of

troops. The voices rose; Lord Westmorland was sadly trounced; an
when Curran had dealt scornfully with "6,000 clowns, without shoe
and with ribbands in their hats," Grattan rose to a *crescendo*. Soarin
at once into his loftiest manner, he spoke boldly of impeachment, of
Lord-Lieutenant convicted of the very act for which King James ha
been deposed—"How can we otherwise dispose of him? here are th
laws which contain the covenant, and here are the army returns whic
contain the breach of it—can we connive with Lord Westmorland, an
combine and confederate with him against the law—against the Revolu
tion—against the Declaration of Rights—against . . . ." His lightning
played about the absent peer; and the official answer—that recruits ha
been raised to fill the gaps created by withdrawals—sped dancing lik
a dead leaf down the gale of his eloquence. "The new levies . . . . th
suggestion of an evasion, not of a defence, it is the suggestion of a tric
—of an impostorship—of a fraud; it is not a bad defence, but a scandalou
prevarication—a sort of clerk-like dexterity—but so clumsy, so miserabl
and so glaring—that it does not keep within the letter of the act, whos
object it professes to defraud, and of whose provisions it professes t
cheat the public." His closing sentence dropped a challenge—"It is
striking circumstance, that in a debate where the conduct of Lord Wes
morland towards the Irish army has been so publicly and so loudl
arraigned, no one veteran of the army, nor any old officer, has venture
to defend him." The challenge confidently made by Grattan was prompt
accepted. For Colonel Wesley rose to follow him. He had not spoken fo
two years; and even then he spoke without *éclat*. But the intrepid Colon
was prepared to follow Grattan in debate: men have earned medals fo
acts of lesser heroism. Not that he failed in the encounter. For as h
spoke, the chilling voice of common sense fell on the listening chambe
"What did the act require? 12,000 men for the national defence: Wer
they or were they not in the country? It was admitted that the publ
service demanded troops to send abroad, and an addition was therefor
made to the establishment by parliament. Was it the new levies ju
recruited that were to be sent abroad to meet an enemy, or the disciplin
soldiers? The question answered itself, and justified sending the ol
regiments out of the Kingdom, and retaining new corps." That cleare
Lord Westmorland; but he remained upon his legs a moment long

deal faithfully with a previous speaker who had described the new recruits as ragamuffins. "He congratulated that hon. baronet on his military sagacity, who would send ragamuffins upon foreign service; but he assured the hon. baronet that however he might treat the new levies with contempt, they were not objects of contempt to the enemies of their country." It was an adequate performance; and few acts in his military career were more courageous than the prompt reply to Grattan's challenge.

The House rose in the first week of June; and he went off to Trim to think about his own affairs. They owned no castle now, and Arthur had a bachelor's refuge—rectangular refuge of a bachelor growing slightly rectangular himself—among the trees at Fosterstown. The Lord-Lieutenant must be stormed again; and this time he launched a fresh assault against another face of the Viceregal fortress. His tone was not so lofty now:

"I assure you nothing but the circumstances under which I labour would induce me to trouble Your Excellency's Government at any time and the Offices to which Lord Mornington has desired me to look are those at the Revenue and Treasury Boards and considering the persons who are at present at these Boards, and those it is said are forthwith to be appointed to them, I hope I shall not be supposed to place myself too high in desiring to be taken into consideration upon the first vacancy at either of them. If Your Excellency and Mr. Pelham are of opinion that the Offices at those Boards are too high for me, of course you will say so; and as I am convinced that no man is so bad a judge of the justice of a claim as he who makes it. . . .

"You will perhaps be surprised at my desiring a civil instead of a military Office. It certainly is a departure from the line which I prefer; but I see the manner in which the military Offices are filled, and I don't wish to ask you for that which I know you can't give me. Although the necessities under which I labour from different circumstances have nothing to do with the question whether I have a claim to the Offices I have mentioned, I again repeat that nothing but them should induce me to trouble Your Excellency's Gov't at any time."

always his wretched circumstances. They haunted him that year. It was one now; and as he sat waiting for the Lord-Lieutenant's answer in his little house at Trim, he faced a cheerless outlook. After all, a place in

the Irish Revenue would mean security; and he might even sell the
King's commission for the price of a home with Kitty Pakenham. For
there had been little in his Dutch campaign to kindle military ardour.
Strange that the summer, which saw Arthur Wesley contemplate civilian
life, witnessed the stranger spectacle in Paris of General Bonaparte ap-
plying for transfer to the Turkish army.

But Arthur's manœuvre failed completely; and as the summer turned
to autumn, he launched his last attack supported by his invariably heavy
gun, Lord Mornington. The Lord-Lieutenant was informed discreetly
that the incumbent of an Irish post would shortly be resigning; that
there was "the best reason in the world why he should"; that someone in
England would have a grievance if he did not; that, in fine, a vacancy
might be expected in the eligible place of Surveyor-General of the Ordnance for Ireland; and that Arthur "should prefer to have that office
to any of those which I mentioned in my letter to you." He would not
for the world have pressure put on the incumbent to resign. For one thing
he was an uncle of Kitty Pakenham. Besides, place-hunting has its etiquette: one does not forcibly create the vacancy that one desires to fill.
But Camden, still obdurate, resisted every assault. Foiled by the long
defence, Arthur drew off his forces and, resigned at last to military life,
raised the long siege of Dublin Castle: sieges would never be his *forte*.

That autumn he was with the Thirty-third once more. They were in
England still, waiting for the tangential strategy of Mr. Pitt to dispose of
them. The regiment lay near Southampton under orders for the West
Indies; and their Colonel wrote to inform the Lord-Lieutenant that he
proposed to go with them. The Earl, relieved from his besieging aide-
de-camp, was distinctly gratified. He was, as courtesy required, "very
sorry we are likely to lose you next winter," but could not but "approve
of your determination to accompany your reg't to the West Indies, as
I am convinced that a profession once embraced should not be given up.
I shall be very glad if I can make some arrangement satisfactory to you
against you come back, but if a vacancy should happen in the Revenue
Board I fear the Speaker's son must have the first." That written, he
turned again to a distracted Ireland, and Arthur went about his regimental duties. He was not well that autumn, seemed slightly feverish,
and consulted a physician. His Dutch winter might well have left

mark. Besides, a touch of fever was the right preparation for a soldier's grave in St. Domingo. So he lived once again in the shadow of Miss Harriette Wilson's dreaded cocoa trees. They were ordered to Barbados first, and then to capture the Dutch islands; for the Cabinet, having singularly failed to rescue Holland, had resolved upon the more prudent course of rescuing the Dutch colonies. Meanwhile they waited near Southampton, as autumn turned to winter and the Channel grew daily less inviting. They sailed at last; and as the fleet of transports with the tall ships of their convoy swept with all sails set past Weymouth one November day, men crowded to the shore to watch. But the November day was followed by a November night. A gale went screaming over Portland; and in the morning seven wrecks were grimly aligned along the wind-whipped Chesil Beach. The rest put back to Portsmouth, sailed once more in the first week of December, and more venture-some than ever tempted the Channel in the teeth of a midwinter gale.

It blew for seven weeks, blew one of them clean past Gibraltar to the Spanish coast, scattered a hundred into the unknown until they dropped weeks later, one by one, into West Indian harbours, and blew thirty—Arthur's amongst their number—back to the sheltering Solent after seven vivid weeks of crowded maritime adventure. So the Thirty-third saw England once again; and their Colonel completed an unpleasant spell of duty, which had comprised one storm at sea and seven weeks of gale. But few gales have ever done more useful service. For it spared him a campaign in the West Indies and (most likely) the West Indian grave that generally followed. "It's very hard," as the redoubtable *Major Monsoon* informed *Charles O'Malley*, "to leave the West Indies if once you've been quartered there," since "what with the seductions of the coffee plantations, the sugar-canes, the monsoons, the brown skins, the rainy season, and the yellow fever, most of us settled there."

The voice of duty called, though not quite so raucously, in the first weeks of 1796. Restored to their unwilling country, the storm-tossed regiment reposed at Poole. They passed the winter there in the deep calm of Essex. Meanwhile, their destinies were altered; for Whitehall, which had proposed them for the Western hemisphere, consigned them to the Eastern. Now they were under orders for India and sailed in April. But

their Colonel was not well enough to go with them. He was still convalescent in Dublin. There was so much to be arranged before he could
leave Ireland—a paper to be written for his successor on the management
of Trim electors, his post as aide-de-camp to be resigned, his brother's
interests, estate affairs, to say nothing of his own. These dismal occupations filled the spring days in Dublin, as a ragged army swept through
the passes into Italy and the names of Bonaparte's first victories—Lodi,
Montenotte, Mondovi—were sounded upon silver trumpets. But Colonel
Wesley, getting back his health, went patiently about his business. He
was full Colonel now. The Castle was still vaguely benevolent, assured
him of its continued sympathy, and murmured something indistinct about
a future prospect of the Revenue Board, adding to Richard that it felt
"so much the propriety and spirit of Col. Wesley's conduct in going to
the E. Indies that I should be very happy to relieve his mind from the
embarrassment it feels on account of some pecuniary arrangements which
he was obliged to leave unsettled when he left England. He mentioned
these circumstances to me"—and His Excellency, it seems, had vanished
in a haze of insubstantial promises of profitable places. So Ireland slipped
behind him, rattling miserably down towards the melancholy rapids of
'98 in a froth of violence, night drilling, and informers, with the fatal
miasma of rebellion "creeping" (in Grattan's words) "like a mist at the
heels of the countryman."

In June he was in London, lodging at 3 Savile Row, and wafted on
his way by the good wishes of an agent, who could not quite suppress
an anxious hope that he would leave express instructions to Lord Mornington to pay, should the worst happen, £955, 4s. 8d. of outstanding
bills. He did his final shopping at a bookseller's in Bond Street; and before the month was out, he was at Portsmouth waiting for a wind. The
Thirty-third had sailed in April; but a fast cruiser should overhaul them
before they passed the Cape. And so, his trunks packed, his lot decided
now, he waited on the Hard. Among his baggage a large corded trunk
contained the last additions to his library. Now, men will frequently
buy books with the simple object of display, but rarely when the books
are to be their sole companions in distant countries. Such libraries are
more revealing. Arthur's was newly bought from Mr. Faulder, the
bookseller in Bond Street, whose corner shop became that very year the

background of Gillray's agreeable record of Lord Sandwich's encounter with a more than usually bouncing barrow-wench. The bookseller's account survives with its particulars of solemn quartos, of barely sprightlier octavos, of Oriental phrase-books and forbidding pamphlets, down to the corded trunk itself:—

HONBLE. COL. WESTLEY

June 6, 1796. B^{ot} of R. Faulder.

	£	s.	d.
Crawfurd's Sketches of the Hindoos		6	6
Dow's History of Hindostan. 3 vol. 8vo	1	1	
Verelst's Bengal. 4°		7	6
Vansittart's Narrative. 3 vol.		18	
Bolt's India Affairs. 3 vol.	1	11	6
Scrafton's Reflections on Bengal		3	
Holwell's Historical Events with other Tracts		6	
Cambridge's War in India		6	
Dirom's Campaigns. 4°	1	1	
Monro's Narrative	1	1	
Mackenzie's Campaigns. 2 v.	2	2	
Fullarton's Account of India. 8°		6	
Scott's History of the Dekkan. 2 vol.	2	2	
Analysis of British India. 3 v.		18	
Plans for the Government of India. 4°	1	1	
Hastings' Memoirs of Bengal		3	6
History of Hyder Ali Khan. 2 v.		5	
Rennel's Map and Memoir	2	2	
D'Herbelot, Biblotheque Orientale	1	18	
Richardson's Persian Dict*y*. 2 vol.	12	12	
Hadley's Persian Grammar		7	6
Moises Persian Interpreter. 4°		16	
Halhead's Bengal Gram.	1	1	
Account of the Siege of Mangalore		6	
Jones' Hist. de Nadir Shah		18	
Fraser's History of Kati Jehan		3	6
Volney's Egypt. 2 vol.		16	
Savary's Egypt and Greece. 3 vol.	1	1	
Cæsar's Commentaries		4	6
Plutarch's Lives. 6 vol.	2	2	
Locke's Works. 9 vol.	4	4	
Paley's Works. 5 vol. gilt	5	5	6
Blackstone's Commentaries. 4 vol.	1	16	
Smith's Wealth of Nations. 3 vol.	5	5	
Ainsworth's Dictionary. 8°		10	6
Tableau de l'Histoire Moderne. 3 tom.		10	6

	£	s.	d.
Bolingbroke's Works. 4 vol.		3	3
Swift's Works. 24 vol.		2	10
Voyage de Bernier. 2 tom.		5	
Russell's Laws of the India Company	2	2	
" Hist. of the India Company		5	
Trunk, Cord, &c.	1	11	6
	£58	2	6

His programme of reading was severe, but salutary. For nearly half his acquisitions were palpably designed to equip him for the East with a substantial grasp of its history, language, and administration. His purchases were strong upon the late wars with Tippoo; excepting Cæsar, all his new military works were purely Indian; nor was current Indian controversy disdained. It was plain from these elaborate researches that Colonel Wesley destined himself for a long stay in India, since officers in quest of quick promotion and the first passage home scarcely require such full documentation. Dublin was fading from his vision now. And Richard wrote of him in the next year, "If Arthur has good luck, he will be called to act on a greater stage than dear Dublin." His stage, it seemed, was India; and the bookseller's bill shewed that he meant to learn his part. It was his chance in life—the very first that had come his way. For Dublin Castle had been little more for its anxious aide-de-camp than an expensive pastime; and military reputations were scarcely to be made in Holland. But India was different. Richard, a student of Indian affairs, could see that "the Station is so highly advantageous to him, that I could not advise him to decline it." For India might make something of him—and he of India. At any rate, he meant to try. So much was plain from the forbidding volumes in his trunk.

The rest were no less arduous—Cæsar to be attempted with a Latin dictionary and vague memories of Eton afternoons; Plutarch (in English); the foundations of belief to be explored with Locke and Paley, the mysteries of commerce with Adam Smith, of law with Blackstone, and of Toryism with Bolingbroke. One item only amongst his new purchases was for recreation—a set of Swift. Arthur, it seemed, was just a shade sardonic in his tastes. Besides, what amateur of Irish politics could fail to savour Swift? There was a link between them, too; for

Laracor, the little church near Dangan, had been a living of the Dean's as well as Wesley property. So Swift, in twenty-four small volumes, was packed in Arthur Wesley's trunk for India.

He had other books, of course. His London purchases did not compose the whole of Colonel Wesley's library, though they formed almost half of it; since a later list survives in his own writing, which includes his recent acquisitions together with books that manifestly came from his rooms in Dublin:—

LIST OF BOOKS

No. 1

Vols.		Vols.	
2	Richardson's Persian Dictionary	1	Howell's Events
2	Herbelot's Bibliotheque Orientale	24	Swift's works
3	Reports Secret & Select Committees	13	Hume's History of England
1	Harleian Miscellany	8	Smollett's Continuation
5	Œuvres du Roi de Prusse	9	Woman of Pleasure
2	Volney's travels	10	Faublas

No. 2

Vols.		Vols.	
4	Blackstone's Commentaries	7	Raynal's Histoire des Indes
1	Verelst India Affairs	1	Hastings' Trial
3	Bolt's India Affairs	1	Account of the Siege of Mangalore
3	Orme's Indostan	1	War in Asia
2	Edward's West Indies	1	Walpole's Answer to Bolingbroke
1	Petit Neptune François	3	British India Analysed
9	Locke's works	1	Moore's Narrative of Little's Detachment
5	Paley's works		
1	Graves' regulations	1	Sketches of the Hindoos
3	Smith's Wealth of Nations		

No. 3

Vols.		Vols.	
1	Manufactures and Commerce of Bengal	1	Proceedings of Com^ee of Officers at home
1	Dirom's Narrative last campaign		
1	Plans for British India	1	Munro's Letters on ye last war
1	Russell's India	3	Dow's Indostan
1	Statutes relative to E. In. Company	3	Voltaire Fables
2	Scott's Deckan	1	Hastings' memoirs
1	Persian Grammar	4	German dictionary
1	Account of 1st June	1	Jones' Persian Grammar
1	Memoir and Map of Indostan	1	Arabick Grammar
2	McKenzie's War in Mysore	1	Universal politician

Vols.

1 Hadley's Grammar
1 Papers on Maroon War
1 Hadley's Persian Grammar
2 Savary's letters
1 Savary Greece
1 Nadir Shah
1 Memoires Marshall Saxe
1 Abregé Chronologique Histoire de France

Vols.

1 Chapman Venereal disease
1 Transactions in India
1 McIntosh Vindiciæ Gallicæ
1 Cambridge's War in India
1 Cæsaris Commentaria
3 Vansittart's Narrative
1 Reynell's Marches of the B. Armie
1 Clarendon's Irish Affairs

No. 4

Vols.

1 Johnson's dictionary
1 Ainsworth's dictionary
2 Memoirs Baron de Tott
1 German Grammar
3 Gazetteer of France
3 Loyd's War in Germany
1 Dundas Quarto
   Proceedings of Officers
   Map of France
   Bengal Army List
   Roads of Bengal
1 Fullarton's India
1 Scrafton's reflections
1 Robertson's Historical Disquisition

Vols.

1 Dundas Cavalry Tackticks
1 Dumourier's campaign in Flanders
   Pamphlets
3 Dumourier's life
2 Histoire d'Hyder Ali
2 Bernier
1 Crebillon 2nd Vol.
1 Leonora
9 Royal register
   Pamphlets
   Allan's views of Hill Forts, &c.
7 Nouvelle Heloise
8 Robertson's works

This library was evidently formed before he left for India, thou
more than half of it consists of volumes that do not appear in Fauld
bill. The Colonel's list was made (for packing purposes, no dou
on the occasion of his move from Calcutta to Madras in August, 1'
But one can hardly doubt that almost all the books had come w
him from Europe. More than a hundred of the volumes had b
bought in Bond Street just before he sailed; and the rest were p
pable survivors from his Dublin library, since it was barely thinka
that Clarendon's *Sketch of the Revenue and Finances of Ireland* (
relic of his vain designs upon the Irish Revenue Board) was bought
reading in Calcutta, and two items—*Papers on the Maroon War*
Edwards' *History, Civil and Ecclesiastical, of the British Colonies in*
West Indies—had manifestly been acquired when the Thirty-third w
destined for that theatre of war. Besides, he had a habit of reading
was unlikely to discard his entire library in favour of the new bo

from Faulder's shop: a man, whose interests impel him (at a moment of financial stringency) to spend fifty pounds on books, inevitably has more books at home. So the list represents his choice of books at a decisive moment; and men reveal themselves in their selection of reading for a sea voyage of six months and a long residence abroad.

What does his library disclose? A military man of rather solemn tastes, whose books were almost all for use. There were no flourishes. His latest purchases reveal his concentration on India; for India filled his horizon. But there was more than India among his books. He was inclined to history and (the East apart) took out no less than thirty volumes, distributed between the venerated, if slightly alarming, names of Hume, Robertson, and Smollett. Nor were his thoughts confined to Britain, since French history was included. Even the Revolution engaged him, and from an unexpected angle. For he possessed a copy of Mackintosh's *Vindiciæ Gallicæ*, that judicious answer to Mr. Burke's fevered denunciations of French excesses. The Revolution was by far the most conspicuous fact in Europe; but one would expect a British Colonel to examine it (if he examined it at all) through the congenial medium of a hostile publication—unless, of course, he were genuinely concerned to ascertain what could be said in favour of it. But in that case he would be a most unusual Colonel. Perhaps he was. His literary tastes, indeed, might seem to show as much. For his light reading, apart from a new set of Swift, comprised two foreign authors who were, to say the least, unusual in military circles. King George's officers were seldom to be found with Rousseau in their hands. Yet seven volumes of his *Nouvelle Héloïse* accompanied the Colonel; and Arthur's sensibility could thrill with the melting *Julie* and enjoy the exquisite delineation of an English nobleman in *Mylord Édouard Bomston*. Voltaire, his second choice, displayed a more astringent quality that might well commend itself to a reader of Swift. But the combination of Voltaire with Rousseau on Arthur Wesley's shelves is undeniably intriguing. That he was not unacquainted with French literature in its naughtier moods is evident from his inclusion of an odd volume of *Crébillon*—with the appended note, touching to bibliophiles, "2nd vol." Apart from these, his literary tastes, though French, were almost commonplace. For he endured, it would appear, nine volumes of the *Woman of Pleasure*, to say nothing of ten more containing Louvet's interminable *Aventures du Chevalier de Faublas*, and a translation of the latest German romance, *Leonora*. An odd volume of the *Harleian Miscellany* kept eccentric company with these sparks and nymphs, serving the Colonel, it would seem, for intellectual recreation between the lilies and languors of Louvet and the roses and raptures of Rousseau.

His military reading was of a graver cast. Upon the present war in Europe he was content with the writings of the refugee Dumouriez. Dundas supplied a meagre textbook of drill and tactics. But Arthur's choice of masters in the art of war was more significant. Frederick the Great in fifteen small volumes, Marshal Saxe in quarto, and Lloyd's *History of the late War in Germany between the King of Prussia and the Empress of Germany and her Allies* formed his equipment. Frederick was plainly to be studied at full length in his own *Histoire de Mon Temps* and *Histoire de la Guerre de Sept Ans*. (It may be justly doubted how far the studious Colonel penetrated the last ten volumes of that monarch's works, where the dust gathers on his odes, his rhymed epistles, and his endless correspondence with the *coryphées* of French philosophy.) But Frederick, however instructive in military practice, rarely theorised upon the art of war. More theory, as well as sound correctives of undue subservience to Prussian views, was to be found in Major-General Lloyd's volume of *Reflections on the General Principles of War*, with which his narrative concluded. Slightly obsessed by the eighteenth-century delusion that wars could be won without battles by the simple (and magic) occupation of decisive points, and that "if you possess these points, you may reduce military operations to geometrical precision, and may for ever make war without ever being obliged to fight," the General was fairly sound on strategy. His tactics, in spite of an eccentric predilection for the pike, were more suggestive, since he departed from the Frederician line, and proposed to meet cavalry attacks with infantry formed into squares:

"I will join the four companies, and form a complete square; can they break this? No; they will not say they can: for, exclusively of the musket, lances, and pikes, I will venture to say that no body of horse, with any degree of velocity, is able to break through a body of infantry of sixteen ranks, because the quantity of action produced by a horseman on full gallop (for one only shocks at a time) is not equal to the resistance of sixteen men placed behind each other, so near as to support in a mass the shock of the horseman.

"I conclude that, armed as I propose, a battalion of infantry will beat in the open field twice the number or indeed any number of horsemen formed and armed as they are at present."

This was strange reading in 1796; but after Waterloo, perhaps it did not read so strangely.

The thoughtful Lloyd was equally inclined for change in his extended use of *tirailleurs*. Light infantry was to operate on a wide front before the troops in line.

"The fire of our two light companies will alone produce a greater effect than that of the enemy, for this obvious reason, that our light infantry acts where and how they please, aims at their leisure, crosses their fire along the enemy's whole front, goes upon their flanks, &c.; in short, it acts with all the advantage of real and expert chasseurs."

For these new purposes he recommends that their numbers should be expanded to one-fifth of each battalion:

"The number of the latter may appear too great; and in fact it is so, if they are confined to that kind of service only in which they are now employed. . . . But according to our plan, they will perform all the duties commonly done by light troops; and likewise in a day of action, they shall be employed in such a manner, as will enable them to render more real service than the heavy infantry."

Here, in his little library of 1796, was the germ that may have led an officer in 1809 to attach a rifle company to each brigade of his command in the Peninsula, to form Portuguese infantry brigades with one battalion to every five—Lloyd's exact proportion—trained and equipped as *Caçadores*, and to put out a line of skirmishers whose fire could invariably hold the French *voltigeurs*. So perhaps his country's debt was greater than it ever knew to Major-General Lloyd, late of the Austrian army, and variously denominated by a choleric historian of Frederick "Epimetheus Lloyd," "surly sagacious Lloyd," and "a man of great natural sagacity and insight; decidedly luminous and original, though of somewhat crabbed temper now and then; a man well worth hearing on this and on whatever else he handles."

Arthur's last military instructor was no less suggestive. For Marshal Saxe survived in his *Reveries* as a singularly active mind, busy with every topic from the desirability of body-armour to the endowment of motherhood. Inclined by nature to an excessive ingenuity in details of equipment that faintly recalls the preparations of the White Knight for active service, that accomplished soldier was severely practical upon the theory of war. The soldier's health engaged him; he was strong for vinegar as the secret of Roman vigour, and insists in detail upon care of the feet. He was admirable upon the leg—*"Le Principal de l'Exercice sont les jambes & non pas les bras: c'est dans les jambes qu'est tout le secret des manœuvres, des combats, et c'est aux jambes qu'il faut s'appliquer."* (One almost catches, in this firm abstention from heroics, the ring of a later voice.) Not that he failed to explore the higher regions of the military art. He was sagacious on the merits of reserving fire till the last moment—*Le quel emportera l'avantage, de celui qui s'est amusé à tirer ou celui qui n'aura pas tiré? Les gens habiles me diront que c'est celui qui aura conservé son feu, et ils auront raison*—a salutary lesson which the French, omitting to absorb it from Saxe, had ample opportunities of learning on Peninsular battlefields. The villainy of army contractors roused his invective; he was emphatic on the value of light infantry; and his whole survey of warfare was conducted with the cold gaze of a realist.

Such, if he read them, were Colonel Wesley's first masters in the art of war. Saxe, Frederick, Dundas, Dumouriez, and Lloyd hung like fairies, good or bad, above his professional cradle to bestow their gifts. Not that war bulked largely in his library. For, India apart, it accounted for barely twenty of his two hundred volumes. India was his main interest; almost a quarter of his books related to the East. Yet he was disinclined to think of India as a mere battlefield. For India had civil problems, which were included in his studies. He could even refer them to first principles, finding his politics in Bolingbroke, his law in Blackstone, and his economics in the *Wealth of Nations*. It was a statesman's library in miniature—but all designed for use, and none to awe visitors.

His purchases revealed him, as another library, bought two years later for another soldier, revealed its owner. For General Bonaparte, just leaving for the East and scrawling a list of purchases for Bourrienne in '9 entered the same confessional. The list was more impressive. It was analytical and erudite. It had an air.

BIBLIOTHÈQUE DU CAMP

1° *Sciences et arts.*
2° *Géographie et voyages.*
3° *Histoire.*
4° *Poésie.*
5° *Romans.*
6° *Politique et morale.*

Sciences et Arts

	Vol.
Mondes de Fontenelle	1
Lettres à une princesse d'Allemagne	2
Le Cours de l'École-Normale	6
Aide nécessaire pour l'artillerie	1
Traité des Fortifications	3
Traité des Feux d'artifice	1

Géographie et Voyages

	Vol.
Géographie de Barclay	12
Voyages de Cook	3
Voyages français de La Harpe	24

Histoire

	Vol.
Plutarque	12
Turenne	2
Condé	4
Villars	4
Luxembourg	2
Duguesclin	2
Saxe	3
Mémoires des Maréchaux de France	20
Président Heinault	4
Chronologie	2
Marlborough	4
Prince Eugène	6
Histoire philosophique de Indes	12
D'Allemagne	2
Charles XII	1
Essai sur les mœurs des nations	6
Pierre le Grand	1
Polybe	6

	Vol.
Justin	2
Arrien	3
Tacite	2
Tite-Live	
Thucydide	2
Vertot	4
Donina	8
Frédéric II	8

Poésie

Ossian	1
Tasse	6
Arioste	6
Homère	6
Virgile	4
Henriade	1
Télémaque	2
Les Jardins	1
Les chefs-d'œuvre du Théâtre-Français	20
Poésies légères (choisies)	10
La Fontaine	

Romans

Voltaire	4
Héloïse	4
Werther	1
Marmontel	4
Romans anglais	40
Le Sage	10
Prévost	10

Politique

Le Vieux Testament.	
Le Nouveau.	
Le Coran.	
Le Vedam.	
Mythologie.	
Montesquieu.	
L'Esprit des Lois.	

There were pretensions here. Besides, the General had ten thousand francs to spend, compared with Arthur's fifty pounds. So he bought three times as many volumes. Yet how few of all their purchases appeared in both selections. Both owned a set of Frederick the Great; each bought the *Reveries* of Saxe; they both agreed in reading Voltaire and the *Nouvelle Héloïse*; and both sailed with Plutarch in their baggage. That was the mode, of course; and the coincidence of choice scarcely argues a taste in common. Born the same year and living in the last decade of the Eighteenth Century, they could scarcely hope to escape Plutarch. But it is pleasant to discover a classical allusion shared between these two admirable subjects for a Plutarchian diptych.

What else do the two trunks reveal? Arthur's was full of his resolve to master India, to learn Indian warfare and administration. But there was little about Egypt in Bonaparte's. He preferred to soar with *Orlando Furioso,* to explore the deeps of melancholy with *Werther,* or to draw a gentler sigh over the destinies of *Manon.* Even his military works ranged every age and nation; his classics were impressive; and his collection of travels qualified him rather for the conquest of the world than for an exact knowledge of the Syrian Desert. In fine, it was a gentleman's library in perfect miniature—perhaps a shade too perfect to be quite a gentleman's. "You find me," he could exclaim to callers, "among my books." Arthur's were far less universal. But then the Colonel of the Thirty-third would not have to sustain exhausting conversations with French *savants* on the voyage out. Neither was he inclined to class the Bible as *Politique et morale*; but then, perhaps, he did not need to buy one for the journey. Heroic poems had no charms for him; life would, it seemed, be tolerable for Arthur without the Iliad; he took no tragedies in verse. Indeed, had fate exchanged their trunks, one doubts how much of Bonaparte's he could have endured. Voltaire undoubtedly, and Rousseau, and the military history. But the sardonic amateur of Swift must have jettisoned almost all the other's lighter reading. For his choice was more austere. But then austerity is frequently the note of books selected by intending travellers. How many of them get a reading, how few survive the journey, are dark questions rarely answered. In Arthur's case, however, the later list remains to show how many of his purchases of '96 were still by him in '98. Swift survived; but Bolingbroke alas! had vanished. He had Locke and Paley with him still; his *Wealth of Nations* kept its charm, his Blackstone too. But though Cæsar was retained, the classics lost their hold on him. For the six volumes of Plutarch no longer darkened his bright Indian horizons. But as he waited for his passage out, his trunk was full of them, and he of high resolve to read them.

64

He was at Portsmouth still in the last week of June, 1796, waiting for a wind for India to take himself, his sword, and the light baggage of his education ten thousand miles from England. For he was twenty-seven, his education ended now. It had been a singular affair from start to finish. His family, perhaps, had taught him least of all. They saw so little of him. Besides, their interest was always centred on Richard's bright ascent—Richard's success would surely atone for all his backward brothers. But if he learnt little from his family, had Eton taught him more? Angers, perhaps, imparted polish and a notable distinction of manners. And Dublin? Dublin and Trim had been his university, where he learned all the arts of management, the shifts of personal finance, Viceregal deportment, and the under-side of Parliamentary affairs. That had been his civilian education. As to his profession, had he not studied it in the sombre academy of his Dutch winter? Formed by a varied past, he waited for the wind at Portsmouth. A wind sprang up; the frigate sailed and Europe faded into the summer haze behind him.

Sepoy General

Contra la mar salada conpezo de
    guerrear
A oriente exe el sol e tornos a esa part.
                        Poema del Cid.

A TEDIUM inseparable from the professional recollections of retired administrators broods impenetrably above the brightest pages of Anglo-Indian history. Besides, there are so many of them, and almost uniformly bright. That glorious circumstance, perhaps, contains the secret of their tedium; since bright surfaces repel protracted contemplation. Viewed by posterity, there is a lack of vicissitudes about them that is almost distressing. That lofty destiny, those prescient forerunners, and the long roll of their inevitable victories sweep past like a political speech to its foregone conclusion. We see the goal; we note the all too steady progress; and our starved dramatic sense cries out for a hitch somewhere. But it cries in vain; and our ingratitude almost forgets that no victory is inevitable until it has been won. Familiar in its outline, the story seems to pall by reason of its very grandeur. For a continent subdued is vastly less exciting than a city saved or an election barely won. It has all the unimpressive vastness of astronomical dimensions, and fails as dismally of its effect upon our fainting comprehension. Eastern history is often disappointing to the Western mind. Did not Macaulay, in a famous Minute, expose to impolite derision "history abounding with kings thirty feet high and reigns 30,000 years long, and geography made up of seas of treacle and seas of butter"? Something, perhaps, of those staggering proportions survived to haunt the latest phase of Indian history, to infect the conquerors themselves, and touch the annals of the British conquest with Oriental tedium.

Yet India in the first stages of the British conquest was far from tedious. Familiar objects of the Anglo-Indian horizon were not yet conspicuous or existed only in the most rudimentary forms. Not yet the grave Civilian; not yet his lady. The stupendous flood of Indian reminiscence was a modest rill, still near its source. No voice rehearsed the endless anecdote of how, "when we were at Dumdum in '36, we ate some colt. Don't you remember Jubber's colt—Jubber of the Horse Artillery, General?" For India was still a land of promise, gleaming with faint allurement over the edge of the world. But Eldorado draws livelier company; and India, though less improving, was distinctly brighter. For it was Hastings', Francis', Impey's, Hickey's India, where a cheerful world, pleasantly redolent of factors, writers, and supercargoes, defied the climate upon claret or withdrew sedately to more dignified repose beneath a Latin tag in a Calcutta graveyard. The scene was bright with powdered heads, with gentlemen in white, with smiling ladies who could smile the brightlier for a comforting knowledge that "the men are out of all proportion to the female world." They rode; they danced, sometimes they danced themselves into a decline. They strolled at sunset on the Fort or aired themselves in more adventurous mood upon the water. Oars dipped, as families reclined in pinnaces and bands of music floated by. For the Eighteenth Century, disinclined to pine in exile, viewed the waters of Babylon rather as an invitation to a water-concert than as a signal to hang up its harp. It was a masculine society, where life was planned delectably for male diversions; and the lively exiles ate the bread of affliction with a certain gusto. They ran wild for masquerade and supped heroically off oysters, while gentlemen amateurs unendingly rehearsed the parts that they could never get by heart. Life was inalterably eighteenth-century, as though Bengal had been a sultrier Bath and the Great Tank reflected the Piazza at Covent Garden. Did not the pen of *Asiaticus* deplore in a Calcutta journal the sad decease of a young lady "celebrated for her poetry and misfortunes," who—cruel to relate—had "died of pure sensibility"? How clear it rings, the authentic voice of the Eighteenth Century, speaking quite unmistakably with bland, familiar accents in its unusual surroundings. Europe might have its moments of uncertainty, as the harsh voices of the Revolution fell on its ear. Europe, perhaps, was changing now; something was stirring in the air of Europe that might mean a change of season, and the Eighteenth Century was putting on its wraps. But, whatever hour the clocks might chime in Paris, it was still the Eighteenth Century in India. A traveller would find it there and, once landed at Calcutta, need never leave his comfortable century. Indeed, the journey would prolong it, as summer prolonged for travellers who follow summer round the world.

One traveller found it indubitably so, obtaining by his timely exile a prolongation of the Eighteenth Century, a reprieve for that delicious prisoner of Time, who lay in Europe under sentence. Born at its height behind a Dublin fanlight, he had passed his youth in it; for what was more *dix-huitième* than a Viceregal world and Dublin Castle? But as the glow began to fade from Europe, he passed on to India, where he world still walked by its unwavering light. Splintered at home, the mirror of the Eighteenth Century was still intact in India. The judicious traveller could point a toe in its smooth surface and survey himself still framed by its gracious gilding. For the century enclosed him still; there was no need for him to leave it yet. Had he not followed ts summer round the world to India? He had always lived in its easy weather; and in India, it seemed, he would live in it still. Indeed, e would find it far from pleasant to encounter other seasons: they vere unthinkable for him. Perhaps he would resist them, when they ame.

I

The ship sailed on. Portsmouth was far behind them now, and the im headlands of the Spanish coast. The road to India led southward own the broad sea-lanes of the Western Ocean, and Teneriffe stood p out of the summer sea to watch them pass. The summer turned to utumn, as they made the long haul past St. Helena to the Cape. Those were the days when travellers paused at the Cape to taste its vine and eat its grapes and stretch their legs with a ride to Constantia nd a scramble up Table Mountain. But now the Cape was more conenial than ever, since British enterprise had lately rescued it from the nworthy Dutch. For though the French might overrun the Netherlands nd indulge the antics of their preposterous Batavian Republic, they nould never have the Cape: the sheltering arm of Britain would secure from the dread contagion. Indeed, it had just done so, finding the escue of Dutch colonies less arduous (and more rewarding) than that Holland. So Colonel Wesley found himself ashore in the very latest ritish garrison. He found the Thirty-third as well, and resumed his egimental duties in the intervals of paying his respects in Cape Town two young ladies, fresh from school in Bloomsbury and on their way India. Miss Jemima Smith was gay, satirical, and enterprising; but liss Henrietta, aged seventeen, conquered the Colonel with her more tiring manners, to say nothing of a "pretty little figure and lovely

neck." And a caller at the house found him "all life and spirits" and
the very image of John Philip Kemble. His blue eye was clear; his
nose was large; his speech was rapid, "with, I think, a very, very slight
lisp"; and a beard of obstinate growth placed him under the distressing
necessity of shaving twice a day. Before they sailed, he wrote in the
interests of his career to the Governor of Madras. Then they sailed on
to India, enduring "a most tedious passage" in the *Princess Charlotte*
East Indiaman. Even the composition of a second letter to Lord Hobart
failed to relieve the tedium. He had his regiment; he had his box of
books; he had his thoughts. But the bright spaces of the Indian Ocean
stretched endlessly away, and India still lurked somewhere behind the
haze. A line of coast appeared at last. The sea became the Roads; the
Roads dwindled to the Hooghly; the Hooghly turned to Garden Reach;
and halfway through February, 1797, the Colonel landed at Calcutta.

Once safe ashore, he had his duties. For there was the Governor
General to be called upon. There was not a notion yet that Richard
might be summoned to fill that lofty throne. When Arthur sailed, Lord
Mornington was deep in politics at home with every expectation of
staying there; and Sir John Shore sat modestly in Warren Hastings'
seat. That potentate recalled (after a fitting interval) his first prophetic
estimate of Arthur. For the discerning Governor-General observed that
if Colonel Wesley should ever have the opportunity of distinguishing
himself, he would do it. He even found in the young man "a union of
strong sense and boyish playfulness." Both would find scope in India.
Indeed, his playfulness seemed likely to be called upon before his sense.
For one muggy night in March Mr. Hickey found him presiding at
the Calcutta dinner for St. Patrick's Day and doing the duties of the
Chair with peculiar credit to himself—and in matters of conviviality
Mr. Hickey's standards were exacting. Now he was in the cheerful
world that went for morning rides, paid calls, and made its bow at the
Governor-General's levée. It was Dublin Castle over again, but Dublin
Castle with a difference. For the Calcutta *ton* was often quite inseparable
from its hookah, drew fragrant puffs between the hands of cards, or
smoked discreetly in the back of theatre boxes. A mob of pipebearers
sometimes came in with the dessert, and furtive devotees had been
occasionally known to snatch a sly cheroot in guestrooms. Even the fair

could not escape the strange infection. (Here was a novelty for Arthur, a variation upon Dublin Castle.) For long years before the Nineteenth Century could draw its first emancipated whiff, pale ladies in Calcutta tasted smoke. But when they stooped to smoke, they smoked with grace; since eager beaux approaching with the pipe put a fresh mouthpiece on, uncoiled the snake, and offered it respectfully to the fair novice. Once that spring he went up the river to Chinsurah and stayed with Mr. Hickey and a men's party. The house was new, the company select; after mornings pleasantly divided between horse exercise and billiards they sat down twelve to table; and having dined, a cheerful company "pushed the claret about very freely," while somebody obliged with a song. He was there again in June. They rode races every morning, and the King's birthday was celebrated with loyal ceremony. For the convivial Hickey had procured a turtle and some venison, to say nothing of the very best champagne, hock, claret, Madeira, and "an eminent French cook" imported from Calcutta for the occasion. Small wonder that they fell to glees and catches, and a General rendered *The British Grenadiers* with the utmost spirit. But these diversions failed to distract the Colonel. His mind still ran on Indian campaigns; and when the General invited his opinion upon the introduction of light artillery, he could respond with a wealth of technicality, though not "regularly bred to artillery," in a paper citing the late wars in Mysore, the defects of recent operations, and the scarcity of horses in India. For he had read to some purpose his forbidding library of Indian history.

That summer a hope of active service dawned. For Spain, having rashly entered the war on the French side, the British formed a sage resolve to appropriate the Spanish colonies in the Pacific. The Philippines were most inviting; so were the Dutch establishments in Java; and a combined attack from India was freely talked of. While the expedition was deliberately fitting out, there was a chance that Arthur might be given command of the Bengal contingent. He was alert at once, drew plans for submission to the Governor-General, and displayed a terrifying intimacy with monsoons, the defences of Batavia ("surrounded by a light brick wall, which has no defence. It has on the eastern side of it a citadel, which stands close to the bay, but which, however, is not within shot of the artillery-ground. . . . In the rear of the town, at some distance, are two redoubts; in which, however, as I am informed, there are no guns"), and the comparative merits of Malay harbours. The Colonel was unusually thorough; and he wrote hopefully to Richard of his prospects of the command.

> "I desired the person who communicated his wishes to me to decline it in my name, and to propose Doyle. If any thing should prevent Doyle ... I intend to accept of it; taking the chance that the large force they intend to send, the known pusillanimity of the Enemy, and my exertion will compensate in some degree for my want of experience. I hope to be at least as successful as the people were to be to whom Hobart wishes to give the command. ... Of course the Chief Command of this expedition would make my fortune; going upon it at all will enable me to free myself from debt."

The prospect was alluring; but the offer, alas! was not renewed. His initial gesture of abnegation had been successful—more successful, possibly, than he intended—and he sailed with no higher rank than that of Colonel commanding the Thirty-third. But before the expedition left he had a touch of fever. India, perhaps, seemed less attractive now—"have not yet met with a Hindoo who had one good quality, and the Mussulmans are worse than they are. Their meekness and mildness do not exist." Cruelty, deceit, and perjury formed a depressing background, and he began to feel a little lonely, having "no news from England since I left it, which is extraordinary, considering that that was in June '96." Now it was July '97; and almost wistfully he asked his brother to "let my mother, &c., know that I am well."

But within a fortnight a mail arrived with the sublime intelligence that Richard was to come out to India as the next Governor-General. So that bright promise was to be fulfilled at last, and Richard awaited with serenity its rich fulfilment. Imperial attitudes had always suited him, and his new appointment would enable him to strike the most imperial of all. For what spoke plainlier of Rome, what more reminiscent of the legions and the eagles, than a proconsul? Not that the prior associations of the office were conspicuously proconsular. His countrymen had strikingly declined to award the civic crown to Warren Hastings; few warriors were less adapted to the pallium than Lord Cornwallis; and he judicious qualities of Sir John Shore—"a good man, but cold as a greyhound's nose"—were scarcely of the order that cries out for bronze to be their record. But these predecessors could not conceal its rich possibilities from the discerning Richard. It was, he could see that it was "the most distinguished situation in the British Empire after that of Prime Minister of England"; and he was modestly prepared to discharge its functions. Meanwhile (since Roman dignities were often followed by a Roman triumph) it would be just as well to think about a marquessate, if one should come his way. For Mornington was quite resolved to be Marquess Wellesley; and Ulster King of Arms, in his secluded room at Dublin Castle, was kept busy with Richard's eager inquiries upon heraldic points—had he the right to quarter Cusack, Keneville, and De Lacey with Wellesley? who married Walter Cowley of Castle Carbury in the reign of Henry VIII? and what was known about a shadowy ancestor traditionally thought to have been standard-bearer to Henry II and feudal holder of some lands near Wellington in Somerset? These lofty themes engaged him, as the new Governor-General prepared to enter on his splendid province. But he had living relatives as well, whose prospects might be gilded as Richard's luminary rose in the skies of patronage to become, in Burke's splendid image, "lord of the ascendant."

Richard, it seemed, had other views, though his brother Henry went with him as secretary. For his Roman qualities appeared to include the austerer forms of Roman virtue; and one hopeful applicant received the chilling answer that a young gentleman, for whom his favour was desired, would receive—

"every encouragement and assistance; and if he deserves it (not otherwise) I will take care that he shall rise as quickly as the Regulations of the Company's Service, and the attention due to the merits of others will permit; more I will not do for my own Brother; nor would I accept this high station, unless I were assured of my possessing firmness enough to govern the British Empire in India without favor or affection to a human being either in Europe or Asia. The integrity of my own character in such a government is the best provision which I can make for any branch of my family; and if this were not good policy, as well as morality, I have

vanity enough to be resolved to sacrifice every consideration (but th
public interest) to the preservation of a just and well-founded fame."

This was austerity indeed; for it was the golden age of patronage, an
India was almost sacred to nepotism. But Arthur was not unprepare
for Richard's Roman virtues, since his reception of the news of th
great appointment concluded with an almost formal offer of "servic
to you in your Government" and the rueful supplement that "such ar
the rules respecting the disposal of all patronage in this country, tha
I can't expect to derive any advantage from it which I should not obtai
if any other person were Governor-General." It gratified him, though
Had he not pressed his brother to entertain the appointment within
month of his own arrival in India? He even offered reasoned consola
tions for Richard's approaching separation from his domestic hearth
though "I acknowledge that I am a bad judge of the pain a man feel
upon parting from his family." For the twelve months' absence of
line from home still seemed to rankle.

Meanwhile, with Richard brushing up his quarterings at home
Arthur went soberly about his duties, untroubled by heraldic problem
or the lands once held by spectral ancestors near Wellington. What wa
Wellington to him? They would be sailing for Manilla soon; and th
Colonel plagued Government for mess allowances and a prompt amend
ment of the system by which ships' surgeons were to be made responsibl
for his soldiers' health at sea—"It takes out of my hands entirely th
superintendence and control over the management of the sick. . . .
shall be deprived of that part of the superintendence over my corp
which is most gratifying to me when they are embarked, and by exerci
ing which I can render most service to the soldiers." For he was stror
upon their health (had he not watched an army die in Holland?); an
his regimental orders for the voyage were a judicious code of hygien
that included frequent fumigation of the decks, daily exercise wit
dumb-bells, and the sterner prescription that "the men should be mad
to wash their feet and legs every morning and evening, and occasional
water should be thrown over every man; every day if possible." Th
new practitioner did not disdain such unheroic aids to war.

Not long before they sailed, he had a word with Mr. Hickey on a lofti
theme. The Thirty-third, it seemed, were unprovided with a chaplain

a friend of Mr. Hickey's had a nephew; and the Colonel "in the handsomest manner" promptly appointed him. The appointment, it must be confessed, disclosed a somewhat languid interest in their spiritual health, since the new chaplain was "a young clergyman of very eccentric and peculiarly odd manners," whom he had met at Hickey's house. They sailed in August; but the ships were barely three days out from land before the new regimental chaplain disgraced himself completely. For this unaccountable young man became intolerably drunk and gave a public exhibition of extreme impropriety. Then, seized with contrition, he refused all nourishment and stayed secluded in his cabin. The captain's consolation failing, Colonel Wesley came on board and plied the penitent with kindly arguments—"that what had passed was not of the least consequence, as no one would think the worse of him for the little irregularities committed in a moment of forgetfulness: that the most correct and cautious men were liable to be led astray by convivial society, and no blame ought to attach to a cursory debauch." But all in vain. The unhappy clergyman continued to repent, drooped for a week or so, and died. Meanwhile, the little fleet pursued its way through the still summer days, until they reached "the shallow sea that foams and murmurs on the shores of the thousand islands, big and little, which make up the Malay Archipelago." For the first stage was ended in the long journey to Manilla; and Arthur Wesley walked ashore among the palms that overlook Penang.

That region of romance, of Malays and Chinamen, "of shallow waters and forest-clad islands, that lies far east, and still mysterious between the deep waters of two oceans," was more mysterious still in 1797. But the Colonel seemed impervious to mystery and, Malays and palm-trees notwithstanding, wrote sturdily to Dublin ordering some Irish linen for his back. His tone was reassuring—"I don't think that people get quite so rich in India as it is imagined in England that they do, but I must say that I am richer now than I ever was & I hope in the course of 4 or 5 months to have it in my power to send you home at least a sufficiency to pay 2 years Interest on my debts." Here was good news for an anxious agent, and the cheerful Colonel breathed the soft Malayan air more lightly for its despatch. But before their first attack was launched across the Straits upon the unsuspecting Dutch in Java, an impulsive

Government recalled the little force. The French, it seems, commande
by the atrocious Bonaparte, had lately made the most disquieting progre
in Italy. Besides, the peace of India itself was vaguely threatened; and fe
these somewhat occult reasons it was thought well to concentrate th
British forces in the East. So the expedition to Manilla sailed home aga
from Penang, and Arthur never walked the shadowy stage of romanc
where silent rivers creep mysteriously past Malay Stockades and drun
throb in vast, unlistening forests.

Indeed, he resolutely declined to see its mystery and instead compos
a memorandum on the material advantages of holding Penang. I
defences, garrison, and revenue were minutely estimated; and the tre;
ment of commercial problems seemed to shew that his Adam Smith w
not unopened. This freight of views returned with him to India, whe
he was seen again at dinner with his mess or dining with a broth
officer at Alipore. Hickey was with them more than once and fou
"eight as strongheaded fellows as could be found in Hindostan." Aft
the cloth was off, they despatched twenty-two toasts "in glasses of cc
siderable magnitude"; then discipline relaxed, the Chair considerat
ruling that gentlemen might drink as little as they choose; but a che
ful company persisted bravely with the task until they staggered (
to find their carriages and palanquins a little after two, leaving N
Hickey to enjoy an excruciating headache, which lasted forty-eig
hours and extorted the impressive tribute that "a more severe debau
I never was engaged in in any part of the world." This was high pra
indeed. Such relaxations aiding, Arthur resumed his regimental li
Not that his interests were exclusively military, since he still had
books and composed a lengthy memorandum in refutation of son
one's heretical *Remarks upon the Present State of the Husbandry a
Commerce of Bengal*. This malcontent had assailed the British c
nection through the East India Company, and the resourceful Colo
offered a detailed defence. His economics were self-taught; he ventu
boldly on the sugar question and devised an ingenious naval argument
support of Great Britain's preferential tariffs in favour of West Ind
produce by insisting upon the necessity of the Atlantic trade as a sch
of seamanship. The Colonel was growing positively encyclopædic; a
he improved his Indian knowledge with a visit to Lord Hobart at F

t. George, where he found the little world of "hum-drum Madrassers" nd the more pressing problems of a Presidency which dwelt in un-omfortable proximity to the unrestful Tippoo. But he was back in alcutta on the May day in 1798 that Richard—dapper, aquiline, and ately—made his auspicious landing. The frigate which had brought im out was so "encumbered" (to the irreverent eye of the *Morning hronicle*) "with stores, carriages, and baggage, that should the ren-ntre of an enemy make it necessary to prepare for action, Lord Morn-gton will inevitably suffer from clearage in the course of six minutes loss of at least £2,000." Such were Richard's imperial paraphernalia.

Lord Mornington was still an Irish earl; but, halfway to his goal ready, he was Lord Wellesley in the English peerage now. They called s brother Henry by the new name of Wellesley, too. Richard had ways seemed to prefer the fuller version, writing their surname, with a int contempt for its abbreviated form, "Wellesley, otherwise by cor-ption Wesley." It had an ampler air; and since the family must do their yal best to live up to Richard, Arthur felt bound to make the change well. For it would never do for Colonel Wesley to persist, when the remost name in India was Wellesley. So Arthur made the change; d within two days of Richard's landing he signed his first letter in e more impressive style of "Arthur Wellesley."

II

H E W A S a person of importance now, with Richard safely installe
in Warren Hastings' seat and Henry, his younger brother, at th
new Governor-General's elbow as private secretary. What could be o
better augury for Arthur than these highly-placed relations? Not tha
their influence would waft him straight into preferment. For Calcutt
was not Dublin Castle; and the cruder forms of patronage were checke
effectively by the Company's regulations, to say nothing of Richard'
stern resolve to play the Roman parent. But Richard, however lofty, wa
still Richard. Had he not always been the architect of Arthur's caree
brought him into Parliament for Trim, advanced the purchase price o
his promotion, even supported him in the vain pursuit of Irish places
His principles might indispose him to endow his brother as an India
placeman; but Lord Mornington was not reluctant to use him for th
public service.

The new proconsul was inclined by nature to become a thunderbo
of war. But the technique of war presents an obstacle that even the mo
high-spirited of civilians find awkward; and Arthur was welcome to h
brother in the capacity of technical adviser. The post was strictly u
official. But since the Company omitted to supply their Governor-Gener
with a military cabinet, that enterprising potentate proceeded to repa
the omission by employing Arthur Wellesley as an informal chief
staff. Unofficial or not, the post was real enough; and Colonel Wellesl
was kept busy writing memoranda for the Governor-General upon
forward policy in Mysore, troop movements in the Carnatic, supply, for
fications, professional grievances in the Company's army, and the d
fences of the north-west frontier. His detail (he was always strong o
detail) was abundant; he projected forts without omitting to estima
their armament, and "said nothing about Dindigul, as I have not se
it, and don't understand anything relating to it." Supply engaged hi
quite as deeply as strategy; and, always disinclined to soar, he kept h
feet firmly on the ground of practicable operations—"It is impossible

arry on a war in India without bullocks. . . . Order that the collectors f the different districts under the Company's Government should en- eavour to ascertain the number of bullocks they have in their districts, id what number they could collect without doing much injury to the ultivation of the country." This was the prose of war; and few officers ere better fitted to dispense it than Lord Mornington's unofficial ief of staff.

But Arthur Wellesley still remained a regimental officer. He was Colonel still. Not quite an ordinary Colonel, though. He had his ooks; and in a list of them he made that summer there was abundant idence of reading that was far from habitual with Colonels in 1798. e had discarded little of the library that had come out with him o years before. His irony still fed on Swift; Paley and Locke still uded him towards the eternal verities, Blackstone and Adam Smith wards a just apprehension of earthly problems; and India still formed e staple of his library. Cæsar, Saxe, Lloyd, and Frederick were still s counsellors upon the art of war. Indeed, he found his Cæsar curiously levant to Indian military problems; for he confessed in later years w much he learned from him, "fortifying my camp every night as did," and borrowing Cæsar's methods of crossing rivers by basket- ats. But Bolingbroke had gone. Was it not Mr. Burke who had ered the scandalised enquiry, "Who now reads Bolingbroke?" Not thur Wellesley, it would seem; and the attempt on Plutarch was ndoned—or, his six volumes read, a triumphant reader had dis- ded them. He even weeded his light reading; and a judicious pen s drawn through *Faublas* and the *Woman of Pleasure*, as he made his of books for packing. For he was ordered south that summer, and . Hickey was deprived of the society of the Thirty-third. They sailed August for Madras, and reached port after an arduous four weeks navigation, that comprised collision with a reef outside Calcutta, a k, a spell of pumping, and a supply of drinking water that spread entery on board. Arthur was not immune himself, lost fifteen men, l was left reviling the commissariat for its shortcomings—"I conceive o be very inconsistent with the principles of the Christian religion give people bad water when he had notice of the probability that it uld be so. . . . A Gentile could not have done worse than give us a

bottle of good rum by way of muster, and fill the casks with the wor
I ever saw." The convalescent was still fuming a month later—"
is unpardonable, as I warned him of it, and I am afraid that I mu
make a public complaint of him."

Now he was in Madras, where officers took evening rides on th
Mount Road acknowledging profound salaams from the old Nabob
Arcot, as he rode, turbaned and long-bearded, in a venerable Engli
chaise behind his black postillions. But, his regiment apart, Colon
Wellesley was in Madras on special duty. His enterprising brother
Calcutta was inclined for war with Mysore. Somewhat unduly shocked
an egregious gesture of the French, Lord Mornington fingered h
thunderbolts. For a flurried Frenchman at Mauritius had produced
sonorous proclamation calling for volunteers and reciting that Tipp
was only waiting for French aid to drive the British out of Ind
Such ill-considered eloquence is habitual with revolutionaries. B
Mornington jumped almost fiercely to conclusions; and exasperati
visions of "Citizen Tippoo" planting trees of liberty, while gratef
Mysoreans performed the Carmagnole, danced angrily before his ey
The French were everywhere; they were in Egypt now; a dragg
shipload of them had even reached Mysore; and with India in dang
would not a prescient Governor-General be wise to strike before wo
happened? Besides, prompt action would enable him to settle the anci
reckoning with Tippoo. Arthur, consulted on his policy, was less
flammable and wrote a chilling memorandum. The French alliance w
Mysore appeared to leave him singularly calm. While Richard's fa
kindled with the dreadful prospect of Tippoo allied with the Repub
One and Indivisible, Arthur was coldly counting heads—"the con
quence of that alliance has been an addition to the forces of Tip
of 150 men at most." And even if the French should send a force fr
Europe, he estimated that it could not exceed 3,000 men, who m
first elude the British squadrons at the Cape and in Indian wa
before they could appear in Mysore. Once there, a chain of ca
lovingly enumerated would reduce their efficacy by three-quarters. In f
the Colonel was not alarmed by the alliance and concluded that "i
be possible to adopt a line of conduct which would not lead immedia
to war, provided it can be done with honour, which I think indispensa

n this Government, it ought to be adopted in preference to that pro-
osed in the conversations. . . . Let the proclamation be sent to Tippoo
vith a demand that he should explain it and the landing of the troops.
Don't give him reason to suppose that we imagine he has concluded an
lliance with the objects stated in the proclamation; and finding he has
erived so little benefit from the alliance, there is every probability that
e will deny the whole, and be glad of an opportunity of getting out
f the scrape. In the meantime we shall believe as much as we please,
nd shall be prepared against all events." This was the wisdom of the
erpent. His chief of staff declined to soar with Richard; for soldiers are
ometimes less given to military moods than spirited civilians. The
olonel's view received abundant confirmation and, to his brother's deep
egret, prevailed. The *rôle* of Mars postponed, Lord Mornington pre-
ared his plans, organised allies, and waited for his moment.

Colonel Wellesley's mission in Madras was closely connected with
iese preparations. He brought instructions to the Commander-in-Chief,
xpounded Richard's strategy, wrote freely in cipher to Calcutta com-
nenting on his seniors, and exercised unwearied pressure to secure a
egree of military readiness. His major task, more delicate, was to ensure
-operation by the Governor of Madras. Lord Clive was difficult and dull,
st in the mould that Nature favours to obstruct the bold designs of
ever men. His speech was slow, but easily kept pace with his thought;
id the resulting compound formed an unlikely partner for the leaping
ichard, who angrily enquired of a colleague, "How the Devil did he
t there?" Arthur, a shrewder judge, was doubtful "whether he is so
ill as he appears, or as people here imagine he is." So the judicious
olonel took the slow-spoken peer in hand. Scarcely articulate them-
lves, such types are frequently impervious to the spoken word. But
rthur's diplomacy prevailed; indeed, he was so far successful that there
is even a danger of his being almost permanently attached to this un-
spiring duty, "merely because there is a chance that endeavours may be
ade to set Lord Clive against the measures which the Supreme Gov-
ament have thought necessary." Meanwhile, his backward pupil made
atifying progress, and was presently discovered by Mornington to be
very sensible man . . . on the most intimate and cordial footing."
was Arthur's first diplomatic triumph.

But his diplomacy found more strenuous exercise in importuning languid authorities to move the siege-train nearer to the frontier of Mysore, to have a plan of operations, to locate supplies "upon the line which it may be intended to follow," and to substitute effective commissaries for "the vague calculations of a parcel of blockheads, who know nothing, and have no data." His efforts, though extremely trying to the temper, were successful. But the success left him unsatisfied. He was still unconvinced that Richard's dashing policy was sound, and urged that Tippoo should not be pressed too far—"Nothing should be demanded which is not an object of immediate consequence. . . . I would confine the demand to his receiving an ambassador from us." Besides, his personal position as Richard's legate *in partibus infidelium* was particularly awkward; and his embarrassments were confided to his brother Henry with strict injunctions to say nothing of them to Mornington. They had a more material side as well. For his situation in Madras denied him all chances of obtaining a command elsewhere; and though his tone was highly disinterested—"whether I return £500 richer in consequence of having been in a command, or poorer in consequence of having been in Fort St. George, is a matter of indifference to me"—it was not surprising that his eye wandered in the direction of an impending vacancy in Ceylon, "if there be no war." But even if there were, his mood was curiously cool. It would, he felt, be long and doubtful; and he appeared to view with calm his own recall to Europe whenever seniority should make him a Major-General. Even when Mornington obligingly proposed him for the Staff in India, he acquiesced without marked enthusiasm, preferring European service, but conceding gloomily that "as I am obliged to serve in some part of the world, however disagreeable the country is, I don't know whether I may not as well remain here as go to any other place. I have been perfectly well in India, and I don't much care about being in a disagreeable place."

The drums of war, it seemed, scarcely made music in his ears. Meanwhile he struggled dutifully on, pestering supine officials and mitigating his exile with a shipment of delicacies from the Governor-General's *maître d'hôtel* and the more graceful *rôle* of witness at Belle Johnston's wedding. The tone of Richard's correspondence with Mysore began to deepen ominously. Tippoo was still profuse in his desire for "gladdening

tters notifying your welfare"; but Mornington, past compliments, re-
ponded grimly (and with a creditable mastery of Oriental idiom) that
dangerous consequences result from the delay of arduous affairs." His
orrespondent countered with an exasperating rigmarole rich in allusions
 Jamshyd, the major constellations, and his continuing anxiety for
urther intelligence of Richard's health, concluding with the unhelpful
formation that "being frequently disposed to make excursions and hunt,
am accordingly proceeding on a hunting expedition," adding however
.at a British envoy "slightly attended (or unattended)" would not
 unwelcome. Lord Mornington, his moment come, permitted himself
e luxury of impatience; and Tippoo was informed that further ne-
otiations would be conducted by the Commander-in-Chief of the British
my in the field. Richard, it seemed, was going hunting too. Indeed,
 wrote almost savagely to England that "I have had the satisfaction to
cceed completely in drawing the Beast of the jungle into the toils . . .
ur own army is the finest which ever took the field in India; and by
nt of scolding and flattering I have equipped it within a period of
ne perfectly astonishing to the old school." Much of the scolding
.d been Arthur's.

The Colonel's preparations for the field included a soup-tureen and
shes for a mess of twelve. He was still deep in questions of supply and
rned the unusual tribute from the Commander-in-Chief that "the
dicious and masterly arrangements in respect to supplies . . . were no
s creditable to Colonel Wellesley than advantageous to the public
vice, and deservedly entitle him to my thanks and approbation."
all wonder that this adept viewed with profound disgust "two Com-
ny's officers; one of them . . . so stupid that I can make no use of
n, and the other such a rascal that half of my occupation consists in
tching him. . . . Besides this, they neither of them understand one
lable of the language; have never even been in a camp, much less
 service." His own experience was scarcely extensive; but the young
lonel (he was close on thirty now) began to know his mind. Before
 y took the field, however, a trying incident engaged him. Consulted
 an angry Colonel who was deep in an aimless wrangle with sub-
linates over a minor point of regimental accounting, Arthur advised
n to abstain from issuing an irritating order. But since good advice is

rarely welcome, his incensed colleague insisted, and Arthur (alway
eminently practical and excusably a trifle ruffled) enquired, "Then why
if you had made up your mind to do so, consult me on the subject?
The injudicious order issued, the inevitable duels followed between th
Colonel and his juniors; and the unhappy man, after a death-bed inte
view with his "dear Arthur," expired, another melancholy instance (
the degree to which a trying climate can exalt the sense of honour, a
well as of the prevailing taste—high-spirited, but how uncalled for—
British officers for avoidable casualties.

The war was ready to begin. Arthur, who had been in tempora
charge of the whole army, commanded a division of native allies wi
a slight stiffening of English troops, consisting (in his own enumeratior
of "the 33rd, six excellent battalions of the Company's sepoys, fo
rapscallion battalions of the Nizam's, which, however, behaved well, a
really about 10,000 (which they called 25,000) cavalry of all nation
some good and some bad, and twenty-six pieces of cannon"—a respectab
command, its nucleus being formed by the Nizam's contingent, who
presence in the field was largely due to Mornington's acceptance
Arthur's earlier advice to eliminate French influence at Hyderabad by
prompt *coup de main*. The Colonel had been reading his Dumouriez
"You have read Dumourier's account of his organizing the Poles; I a
employed in a business of much the same kind. My Poles fight too, a
that not badly, I assure you." The "ponderous machine" moved slov
up towards the highlands of Mysore, and Arthur viewed without elati
the prospects of the war. His misgivings were sharply accentuated by
enquiry from Madras whether Richard should take the field hims
Arthur's negative was prompt and unqualified—"All I can say up
the subject is, that if I were in General Harris's situation, and you joir
the army, I should quit it." Such frankness was, perhaps, a trifle m
than brotherly; but Richard, to his credit, took it extremely well, add
his satisfaction at the general praise of Arthur's management—"I w
to God the whole were under your direction; but even as it is, I th
our success is certain." Arthur did not. His mood was notably s
dued. Henry was warned that "our war cannot be successful in
campaign"; and he was at extreme pains to water Richard's wine m
liberally than any stranger would have dared—"I am glad that you

repared for a failure. . . . My despondency goes thus far, and no
rther. . . . I think I have done better to make it known to you, than
tell you that it was impossible that we should not succeed. It is better
see and to communicate the difficulties and dangers of the enterprise,
d to endeavour to overcome them, than to be blind to everything but
ccess till the moment of difficulty comes, and then to despond."

His spirits rose a little as they penetrated deeper into Mysore—"There
not *now* a doubt but that we shall bring that monstrous equipment
Seringapatam, and, in that case, we shall certainly take the place."
hey had a brush with the Mysoreans in the last week of March, and
e Thirty-third charged with the bayonet. His tone was higher now—
We are here with a strong, a healthy, and a brave army, with plenty
stores, guns, &c., &c., and we shall be masters of his place before
uch more time passes over our heads." But Arthur's health was
ghtly affected. His trying spell of duty in Madras left him a little
w; and the heat of Mysore, in April combined with bad water
bring on dysentery, "which did not confine me" (so Richard was
formed), "but teased me much. I have nearly got the better of it, and
hope to be quite well in a few days." Before it left him, though, he
as tried harder than is entirely good for any man with dysentery. For
the very night he wrote about his health to Richard, the Colonel was
charge of a small column engaged in clearing the approaches to
ringapatam. The night was "dark as pitch *forward*, and in the *rear*
wards our camp the fires and lights burnt brilliantly, which increased
e darkness in front." The column stumbled through the night into a
tle wood, which nobody had reconnoitred. Entangled in the darkness,
ey were heavily fired on and lost formation; the gloom filled sud-
nly with shots and shouting; a spent ball struck him on the knee;
mewhere in front the leading files were captured in the night; and as
nfusion deepened, the Colonel—a trifle unaccountably—left them to
port his failure. Shaken and unwell, he reeled back to camp. It was
t far from midnight; and the exhausted man, his nerves all frayed,
ng himself face down across the mess-table to sleep. Attacking in the
orning, he retrieved himself and carried the position; but the night-
are of the little wood had left him with the bitter flavour of defeat—
ad," as an officer recorded, "with this ill success"—explaining ruefully

to Richard his "determination, when in my power, never to suffer a attack to be made by night upon an enemy who is prepared and strongl posted, and whose posts have not been reconnoitred by daylight." An forty years away he could still draw a sketch-map in explanation of th affair at Sultanpettah Tope. For the unpleasing night lived in hi memory. Such lapses are occasionally final. Arthur's, happily, was no That icy rigour of control, it seems, which led his countrymen to a unkind suspicion that nerves had been omitted from his compositio came to him only by degrees. He was not born, but made himself, th unmoving soldier of later years; and learning his lessons as they cam he learned some of them (since night attacks are a rough school war) that night at Sultanpettah.

The siege was duly opened with the becoming ritual of parallels an breaches; and Arthur found himself one evening in charge of a su cessful operation against an outlying work. But on the day of the assau he was in reserve, commanding in the trenches, while General Baird e joyed the unusual treat of storming a fortress in which he had once bee a prisoner. Baird's part was played to perfection; his sword was draw his big voice roared, "Then forward, my lads"; a flag fluttered in t breach; and panting Englishmen scrambled into Seringapatam. But wh they found Tippoo's body, Colonel Wellesley was at the eager Genera side, and Arthur's careful hand assured them that no life remained. T captured fortress was a problem, since it contained vast quantities treasure and a scared native population. The situation plainly called f skilful handling by the command; and the heroic Baird was scarc likely to display the requisite touch. Had not his mother, hearing ye before that he was chained to a fellow-captive at the tail of one of Tippo guns, gaily exclaimed, "I pity the mon wha's tied to ma Davie." A Arthur's portrait of him, drawn in later years, was no less distinct— gallant hard-headed, lion-hearted officer; but he had no talent, no *tact*; h strong prejudices against the natives; and he was peculiarly disqualifi from his manner, habits, &c., and it was supposed his temper, for t management of them. He had been Tippoo's prisoner for years. He h a strong feeling of the bad usage which he had received during captivity." This was unpromising for the prospects of good governm in Seringapatam; and Baird received a morning call from Colo

Wellesley. He disliked the Colonel, since he had always resented Arthur's command of the Hyderabad contingent, overlooking the fact that Arthur was almost wholly responsible for its existence and that the Nizam's son had asked expressly for the Governor-General's brother to be appointed. Seated at breakfast with his staff in the palace, he heard the Colonel say, "General Baird, I am appointed to the command of Seringapatam, and here is the order of General Harris." The angry General rose, turned to his staff, and said, "Come, gentlemen, we have no longer any business here." But Arthur, upon whom rhetoric was invariably wasted, politely added, "Oh, pray finish your breakfast."

Such was Arthur Wellesley's entry on his first responsible command. His fiery senior departed in a blaze of protests, wrote angrily to the Commander-in-Chief, and received no vestige of satisfaction. For General Harris was not disposed to vary his selection, though he let Richard know that the appointment had occasioned comment. But Richard could reply with perfect justice that he had "never recommended my brother to you, and, of course, never suggested how or where he should be employed." He added, though, that Arthur was "the most proper for that service"; and Arthur's own reflections after thirty years confirmed his verdict—"I must say that I was the *fit person* to be selected. I had commanded the Nizam's army during the campaign, and had give universal satisfaction. I was liked by the natives." The choice, at any rate, was not his brother's. Arthur had earned the prize from the Commander-in-Chief; and if, as he declared in later years, "it is certainly true that this command afforded me the opportunities for distinction, and then opened the road to fame," he owed it to himself.

III

THE new Governor of Seringapatam succeeded at an awkward moment, with half his subjects actuated by a strong desire to plunder the other half. Indeed, for a brief interval the army enjoyed a spell of looting, in which gold ingots changed hands for a bottle of brandy and one judicious Scot acquired the Sultan's jewelled armlets at a modest price from an impulsive private. Meanwhile the Colonel sent grimly for the provost-marshal, and "by the greatest exertion, by hanging flogging, &c., &c., in the course of that day I restored order among the troops." Four of the criminals were hanged and confidence returned to the scared population, though the new commandant's embarrassments were not diminished by the hungry presence of the late Sultan's collection of live tigers. Colonel Wellesley held himself responsible for Tippoo's subjects, and urged with emphasis that "General Harris ought to get away as soon as he can, as the plunderers of his army and that of the Nizam still occasion great confusion and terror among the inhabitants and tend to obstruct our settlement of the country." He seemed to pride himself that he had "gained the confidence of the people." For his mind was busy with civilian problems; and Richard was advised at length upon the future of Mysore. He still kept his independence though, insisting with his former clarity that Richard should not act the *rôle* of conqueror in person—"Many persons in camp . . . are exceedingly anxious that you should come here to settle everything. I am (as I was upon a former occasion) of a different opinion." The conquered state was duly partitioned, surviving under British influence in a diminished form, while the Company shared its remaining territories with Richard's native allies. Freely consulted on the settlement, Arthur advised with all his shrewdness—"I recommend it to you not to put the Company upon the Mahratta frontier. It is impossible to expect to alter the nature of the Mahrattas; they will plunder their neighbours, be they ever so powerful. . . . It will be better to put one of the powers in dependence upon the Com-

any on the frontier, who, if plundered, are accustomed to it, know how
to bear it and to retaliate, which we do not."

Richard, the war successfully concluded, prepared to bind his sheaves.
The Cabinet was promptly informed that a marquessate, or else the
Garter, would be acceptable. But the fountain of honour was distant, and
mails were slow. Meanwhile the conquering army offered him the insignia of St. Patrick tastefully composed of Tippoo's jewels. Richard
first declined the gift; but the Company overbore his coy refusal,
adding an offer of £100,000. Once more the Governor-General had
scruples, whereupon his Board with sound commercial instincts substi-
tuted an annuity of about half the value. The news of victory reached
England and elicited the thanks of Parliament; the fountain of honour
began to play, and Richard's sovereign was pleased to advance him in the
peerage as Marquess Wellesley. It was his marquessate at last; but the
marquessate, alas! was Irish. His disgust was eloquent. A letter home
was signed "Mornington (not having yet received my double-gilt potato)"; and the angry nobleman declared that "as I was confident there
had been nothing Irish or pinchbeck in my conduct or in its results, I
felt an equal confidence that I should find nothing Irish or pinchbeck
in its reward." What now remained but for them to "dispatch the overland express; and for God's sake bring me home, home, home; home first,
home last, home midst"?

Remote from these impassioned outcries, Arthur sedately governed
Seringapatam. He had his troubles too, though the prize-money seemed
to afford a brighter prospect. Richard was promptly advised that "my
share . . . will enable me to pay the money which you advanced to purchase my lieutenant-colonelcy, and that which was borrowed from Captain Stapleton on our joint bond." But Mornington refused the offer
with the utmost chivalry. Arthur was still embarrassed, though. Campaigning with a staff (and without increased allowances) had proved a
heavy burden; his present post was quite as costly; and he concluded
gloomily that "I am ruined." Yet he was disinclined to leave it. For
when Richard proposed that he should go home with the trophies of
Seringapatam, he made an unconvincing gesture of consent, "if it is
thought that I can be of any use." But his pen was busy with reasons
for remaining in Mysore. Had he not "the most respectable and the best

situation for me that I could have in India"? Besides, the thought of hi
successors filled him with alarm—Baird was impossible, and Generals wer
"generally so confoundedly inefficient." So, if the choice were left t
Arthur, he should prefer to stay; he might "render service to the public"
and as the year wore on, he was confirmed in command of the Com
pany's forces in Mysore.

He was a satrap now, immersed in local administration and nativ
grievances. How seriously he took the last appears from his anxiety t
be dissociated from a somewhat ill-considered order of the Commande
in-Chief, which outraged local feelings by a search of Tippoo's zenan
for hidden treasure—"I had nothing to do with it excepting that I obeye
the General's order, and . . . I took every precaution to render the searc
as decent and as little injurious to the feelings of the ladies as possible
Indeed, before the year was out, he gave still stronger proof of his respe
for native customs. For when the redoubtable Abbé Dubois, labourin
in the Indian mission-field for a revival of native Christianity, demande
the return of two hundred Christian women from the late Sultan
zenana, Arthur reluctantly declined, "although the refusal is unju
because, the Company having taken this family under its protection,
is not proper that anything should be done which can disgrace it in t
eyes of the Indian world, or which can in the most remote degree ca
a shade upon the dead, or violate the feelings of those who are aliv
The limit of his concessions was to demand a census of the Christi
women, which would enable the eager missionary to re-marry any me
bers of his flock whose wives had died behind Tippoo's purdah; t
Sultan's heirs must be assured that "it is not intended to ask for a sin
woman," though warned that refusal to comply would involve a r
erence to Government, which might be followed by unpleasant con
quences, since "I am by no means certain that if the matter came bef
Government they would not be obliged to give up every woman
them. Justice and all our prejudices and passions are on the side of
Christians. . . . If the Princes and the family here carry *their* prejudi
so far as to refuse compliance . . . the result will then be most proba
that Government will give orders not only that every Christian wom
but every woman detained in the Zenana against her consent, may
allowed to depart." How many colonels in 1799 would have decline

berate the Christian captives of a defeated Moslem? This was modera-
on with a vengeance. Not that his temper was un-Christian, since he
ibmitted an official request for a chaplain, so that the garrison of Ser-
igapatam might "have the advantage of regular divine service, and
:her duties which a clergyman could perform." But he administered
a awkward province with a due sense of native rights; and when he
ithorised a lengthy code of regulations for the re-establishment of nave justice, he sanctioned separate tribunals for Hindu and Moslem law
ogether with short forms of pleading and a compulsory reference to
bitration before trial) in terms that reflected equal credit on his Black-
one and his Indian library.

The Colonel laboured to restore his province. The battered city was
built under a watchful eye—"This morning I was there at half-past
i, and the people who mix up the chunam were then coming to work,
number about 12, and there were no other persons near the work"—
d calm gradually returned to Seringapatam. But the country districts
ere disturbed, and the remaining months of 1799 passed in the strenu-
is pursuit of an elusive enemy. The *terrain* was uninviting, since
erilla warfare in the jungle is hardly favourable to the higher flights
strategy; and Arthur found few openings for Frederician manœuvre,
ough the ingenuities of Saxe were not without their lesson. Such opera-
ns (rendered acceptable to tender European consciences by the term
acification"), which are the aftermath of every conquest, normally
ound in opportunities for minor misadventure. But Arthur pacified
th skill, distributing his force in flying columns with defined objec-
es and orders that were invariably distinct and detailed. He took the
ld himself and toured his frontier posts, enjoining a respect for native
lings on troops engaged in punitive operations, and stigmatising ex-
ions from the villagers as a departure from "the first principle of a
dier, which is fidelity to the trust reposed in him." He was still deep
the absorbing task of pacification when Richard offered him a new
nmand. The unworthy Dutch were now to be relieved of Batavia;
: operations would be light, the credit ample, and the prize-money
re than rewarding. This lucrative excursion was proposed to Arthur,
ovided you can safely be spared from Mysore." But Mysore, alas!
l claims upon him. Madras was loud with outcries at the prospect

of his departure; Lord Clive grew almost eloquent upon the impossibili
of replacing the energetic Colonel; and he regretfully put by the chanc
—"I do not deny that I should like much to go; but . . . my troops a
in the field"—assured consolingly by Richard that "you could not qu
Mysore at present. Your conduct there has secured your character ar
advancement for the remainder of your life, and you may trust n
for making the best use of your merits in your future promotion."

Promotion tarried in the most provoking way; and Richard, wl
detected an affront to his own dignity in any check to Arthur, fum
over the fate of "Colonel Wellesley not only unnoticed but his prom
tion protracted so studiously, that every Intriguer here believes it
be delayed for the express purpose of thwarting me." A Colonel sti
he took the field again in 1800 to remove the last reproach of insurrecti
from his province. One *insoumis* still stained the bright horizon
Mysore, where Dhoondiah Waugh hung on the northern border, wea
ing the slightly excessive title of "King of the Two Worlds." Arth
more modestly concerned with only one, resolved on "the destruction
this man," and moved against him in force. His correspondence—a p
tracted litany of bullocks and road-making—shewed how completely
had mastered the lesson that transport is the key of war; and he w
disinclined to linger on the awkward problem of Dhoondiah's prec
status—"he either belongs to the Mahrattas, or he does not: if he belo
to the Mahrattas, they ought to remove him to a greater distance, as
state has a right to assemble on the frontier of another such a fo
as he has on ours; if he does not belong to the Mahrattas, and he
there contrary to their inclination, they ought to allow us to drive h
away, and to join with us in so doing." In May he started from S
ingapatam; in June he was one hundred and fifty miles to the north
an exasperating region where rivers rose and fell at precisely the wr
moments; in July he was storming forts in the Mahratta country a
these obstacles removed, prepared for the agreeable *finale* of round
up his adversary. But as the operation entered on its closing phase,
elusive Dhoondiah was far from passive in the hands of fate, and
dian rivers almost uniformly failed to co-operate with Wellesley's ti
table. In August the hunt turned eastward towards Hyderabad;
pursuing columns converged; and as the net was drawn round h

Dhoondiah dashed at its meshes, encountering Colonel Wellesley and his cavalry. They met on a September day in 1800, and Arthur enjoyed the exhilarating luxury of leading a cavalry charge. Four regiments in line behind him drove at the enemy who broke, leaving the monarch of the two Worlds (expelled with violence from one) to explore his other kingdom. The campaign had lasted fifteen weeks—the summer weeks of 1800, in which Bonaparte, First Consul now, dazzled the Austrians by the consummate swordsmanship of Marengo. Arthur was rounding up a robber-chief; and if his later exploits were a somewhat doubtful progeny of Eton playing-fields, the pursuit of Dhoondiah derived more obviously from hide-and-seek in Naylor's garden. For the Colonel had achieved a business-like triumph over a shadowy foe and the unmanageable facts of Indian climate and geography, leaving his brother to announce with sober exultation that "we have now proved (a perfect novelty in India) that we can hunt down the lightest footed and most rapid armies as well as we can destroy heavy troops and storm strong fortifications." The novelty and the proof were alike Arthur's.

The disturber of its peace removed, he was engaged once more in the settlement of Mysore. Land tenure, flying columns, and the incalculable proceedings of native potentates absorbed him. One night a dismissed favourite from Hyderabad poured endless grievances into his ear during the cheerful uproar of a nautch; and as duty kept him on the advancing frontier of Richard's empire, he surveyed the new problem of the Mahratta confederacy, where Scindia threatened to achieve "that which we learn that all our policy ought to be directed to prevent, viz. one man holding and exercising nearly all, if not all, the power of the Mahratta empire." Not that he favoured the heroic surgery of preventive war—"one country has no right to commence a war upon another because at some time or other that other may form an alliance with its enemy. . . . The question of peace or war is not, and cannot be, only the probability of success, but must depend upon other circumstances, and in this country must depend upon the prospect of being attacked by the power with which it is proposed to go to war." Late in the year these speculations were sharply interrupted by an order transferring him from Mysore, and a fresh prospect opened. For Richard's war-like eye, sweeping the western skies, observed the French to be more menacing than ever. Were they not still in Egypt? Besides, Marengo had been fought that summer. A British force was concentrating in Ceylon with the spirited design of making trouble for the French; and Colonel Wellesley was to lead it, though Richard was perfectly aware that "great trouble will arise among the general officers in consequence of my employing you; but I employ you because I rely on your good sense, discretion, activity, and spirit; and I cannot find all those qualities united in any other officer in India who could take such a command." So he departed from his province, leaving behind a military testament of impressive detail, which enlightened his successor on the topography of Mysore, together with exhaustive notes upon supplies, civil government, and lines of operation; and for a time Seringapatam knew him no more.

IV

BEFORE the year was out, the Colonel was at Trincomalee (with six cases of claret, six of Madeira, and six of port), deep in demands for vinegar, tea, sugar, beef, Staff officers, and rum. Their destination was a trifle vague. It seemed to oscillate between Mauritius and a voyage through the Red Sea to take in rear the French whom Bonaparte had left marooned in Egypt. Mauritius was their first objective; and Richard offered the agreeable prospect that "if you should succeed in taking the Isles of France and Bourbon, I mean to appoint you to the government of them, with the chief military command annexed." Arthur was then to choose between this novel eminence and a return to his command in Mysore. Meanwhile he cross-examined likely informants on the approaches to Mauritius, the French defences, tides, landing-places, and the unfamiliar problems of amphibious war. His little army waited in Ceylon. But, the customary dislocation prevailing between the services, the fleet was nowhere to be found; and its delays ended all hope of a surprise attack upon the islands. Early in 1801 the Colonel warned his brother of the altered prospect; the Admiral, a distant voice in the Straits of Malacca, declined (from Penang) to attack Mauritius without an order from the King; his muffled protest was decisive, and the expedition was diverted.

Richard's next notion, since Batavia was always tempting, was to send them to attack the Dutch in Java. But before the plan matured, orders from England changed their direction once again. Egypt was now their goal; the waiting forces in Ceylon were destined for a protracted spring across the Indian Ocean, past Aden and the bald Arabian littoral of the Red Sea, and on to the Egyptian coast. Once there, they might reach Suez, or a desert march from Kosseir would take them into Upper Egypt. But Arthur's part in this amended programme was sadly diminished. For the angry Generals had prevailed, and Colonel Wellesley was to sail (as Colonels should) as second in command—and second in command, by an unhappy dispensation, to the most trying of his seniors,

Major-General Baird. Before this intimation reached him, he had gathered up his force, put it on board the transports, and shipped it to
Bombay *en route* for Egypt. The blow fell while he was still at sea.
Letters from the embarrassed Richard broke the news as best he might:
that potentate, in a rare mood that bordered on apology, explaining
almost timidly to Arthur that the postponed attack upon Mauritius
should be reserved as a tit-bit for him, that he could not have had the
command in Egypt without a breach of every service regulation, that
Baird should prove to be a charming colleague who was quite sure to
listen to his views, that Richard would not feel offended if Arthur chose
to return to Mysore, though he should much prefer him to remain with
Baird. But Richard's preferences were Arthur's last concern. He was
exceedingly annoyed. For this supersession seemed to his angry eye to
ruin his professional prospects; and the indignant Colonel rained resentful letters on his brother Henry, who sent consoling answers but
discreetly kept the correspondence from the Marquess. Here he was—
"at the top of the tree in this country" and trusted equally by two Presi-
dencies—degraded suddenly, without stated cause, from an attractive
command. The General might be his senior; but Richard had no right
to raise his hopes, to make use of him for the preliminary drudgery
and—least of all—to give no public explanation of the sudden change.
"I have not been guilty of robbery or murder, and he has certainly
changed his mind; but the world, which is always good-natured toward
those whose affairs do not exactly prosper, will not, or rather does not
fail to suspect that both, or worse, have been the occasion of my being
banished, like General Kray, to my estate in Hungary." This was a
novel tone for Arthur, since he grew almost shrill at the thought of the
affront, of all his wasted efforts in Ceylon, of his subordinates misled
into an unpleasant trip with Baird, of his own career in danger.

That was a novel thought. Arthur—the patient, rather listless Arthur
—had a career. He had not seemed to think so in the bleak discomfort
of his Dutch campaign six years before, when his mind ran mainly upon
prospects of leave. Had he not done his best on his return to Dublin to
become something in the Irish Revenue? And even in India he seemed
almost indifferent as he balanced the prospects of a return to Europe
against an Indian career—"I don't know whether I may not as well

main here as go to any other place." His tone had mounted slightly, when he announced his preference for staying at Seringapatam; and now the angry Colonel, raging round Bombay in an unenviable mood, was anything but indifferent to his prospects.

His first impulse was to stay in India, to sulk anywhere in preference to serving under Baird. Before the month was out, however, his mood changed. News came in March that Abercromby was already striking at Egypt from the north; and if the Red Sea expedition was to serve any purpose, it must move at once. Baird had not yet arrived, and Arthur resolved to sail immediately and make a start in Upper Egypt—"my former letters will have shown you how much this will annoy me; but I have never had much value for the public spirit of any man who does not sacrifice his private views and convenience, when it is necessary." This was more soldierly. Not that Arthur was unconscious of his own virtue, since he wrote later of his "laudable and highly disagreeable intention." But the gesture was frustrated; for he was promptly taken ill. His illness was anything but diplomatic, since he was assailed after a touch of fever by an unpleasing malady termed the Malabar itch. The drastic therapeutics of Bombay plunged the sufferer into nitrous baths, which positively burned his towels; and as his cure progressed, the expedition sailed with Baird. The Colonel, partly reconciled by an unusual display of manners on the part of his chief, collaborated loyally with a voluminous memorandum on Egyptian warfare; he had been studying local politics, the desert, and the Nile and gave Baird the benefit of his researches. But Egypt in 1801 was not his destiny. Richard restored him to the command in Mysore, and he returned with evident relief to Seringapatam. The incident almost parted the brothers. For Arthur's "My dear Mornington" cooled instantly to "My Lord," reverted momentarily to "My dear Mornington," and was succeeded by an awful silence. The brothers ceased to correspond; and, this breach apart, the *imbroglio* of the Egyptian command revealed the interesting fact that Arthur had ambitions.

V

THAT summer he returned with sober elation to his province. The voyage south was uneventful; but once ashore the convalescent travelled at breakneck speed, lending interest to the long ride up-country by leaving his little escort far behind, and remarking cheerfully to young captain, "If we are taken prisoners, I shall be hanged as being brother to the Governor-General, and you will be hanged for being found in bad company." A day was spent *en route* in courtesies to native ruler, of which Arthur's Persian stood the strain admirably, even rising to corrections of the Company's interpreter. Then he resumed the dash to Seringapatam. On the road they heard of a promotion Colonels to be Major-General; he brightened at the news and called for an Army List; but when he found that he was not included, he wistfully exclaimed, "My highest ambition is to be a Major-General in Her Majesty's service."

A Colonel still, he entered on his little kingdom once again, assured by a consoling friend that honour and wealth awaited him at Seringapatam and by Henry that he was "still at the top of the tree as character. . . . I have never heard any man so highly spoken of, nor do I know any person so generally looked up to. Your campaign against Dhoondiah. . . ." His lot was enviable enough, though his grievance still haunted him and he hinted darkly to Henry that "I have some thoughts of going home in the next winter if I don't see some prospect of being actively employed in India." But this was little more than brotherly *boutade,* since he lived in a happy whirl of local administration and cheerful company. They sat down eight or ten to dinner in the old palace, the Colonel opposite his saddle of mutton. He ate well though his recipe for health in India was "to live moderately, to drink little or no wine, to use exercise, to keep the mind employed, and, if possible, to keep in good humour with the world. The last is the most difficult, for, as you have often observed, there is scarcely a good-tempered man in India." Arthur was one of them, however; for roast mutton was his chief indulgence. He rarely took more than four or five glasses beyond his pint of claret; and such abstinence seemed almost total in an age when military manners prescribed officially a monthly ration of fteen bottles of Madeira as the bare limit of necessity, with such extras as beer and spirits and water by way of luxuries. Not that the abstemious Colonel was a gloomy host. For he was always gay at his own table, talking in his quick way of his past successes in the field (a meagre theme for Wellesley in 1801), of intrusive seniors—"we want no Major-Generals in Mysore"—and of commissariat iniquities, which moved him to inform the mess one day that if he ever commanded an army of his own, he should not hesitate to hang a commissary. So the lively Colonel talked the afternoons away over his mutton and claret at Seringapatam. He was just thirty-two, a little grey already about the temples; but that was a mere legacy of fever, since his brown hair (he wore it cropped and disapproved of powder on hygienic grounds) still crowned a young man's face. Sometimes he got a game of billiards; and occasionally they went after antelope with Tippoo's hunting leopards, the Colonel following the hunt in his own howdah. They had feminine society as well. For wives were not excluded; and Arthur shewed a distinct partiality for wives. A brother-officer recalled him as the wearer of "a very susceptible heart, particularly towards, I am sorry to say, married ladies." A prudish aide-de-camp was shocked; an interfering lady interfered; but if eyes were bright and husbands negligent, who could blame the Colonel? He might, perhaps, have thought of Kitty Pakenham. But Kitty Pakenham was ten thousand miles away.

With these agreeable mitigations he laboured at his oar, writing innumerable letters about public works and army stores and the illimitable theme of transport bullocks, or taking the garrison's salute after an early morning parade in a cocked-hat, long coat, white pantaloons that ended in Hessians and spurs, and an impressive sabre with a big silver hilt. His official life from ten to four was mainly filled with a supremely distasteful enquiry into the malversation of large quantities of stores. It ended, after dragging him through "scenes of villainy which would disgrace the Newgate Calendar" in stern sentences upon the guilty officers. But though the Colonel's duty was performed down to its most un-

pleasant particular, he was still capable of pity, writing to the Governor
of Madras:

> "I take the liberty of addressing your Lordship in favour of an old
> man, (the late) Lieutenant-Colonel ——, whom I have lately been the
> means of convicting of very serious crimes before a general court-martial
> and I do so, not from any doubt that I entertain of the reality of his guilt
> but from a conviction of his former good conduct as an officer, and of
> the extreme poverty and distress to which he has been reduced in con-
> sequence of the sentence of the general court-martial. I understand that
> when he will have paid the Company the sums which are due to them
> in consequence of that sentence, he will be left entirely destitute; and
> without attempting to justify any part of his conduct, I may safely say
> that he becomes an object of charity.
>
> "Allow me, therefore, to entreat your Lordship to give him some small
> pension to enable him to support himself, or that you will recommend
> him for some provision to the Court of Directors on account of his long
> services and his present reduced situation."

Few causes have been better pleaded. For Arthur, incapable of false
sentiment, was genuinely moved to pity.

His other interests survived. He resumed the never-ending struggle
to secure respect for native rights and customs, though he had few illusions as to native virtues, writing acidly that "every native who gets a
paper signed by the name of a person having any power makes a bad
use of it and generally contrives by its means to extort something
which he has no right." But he shielded villagers from requisitions,
insisted on behalf of Tippoo's zenana that "the greatest attention must
be paid to their prejudices and customs. . . . Keep everybody at a distance from them, and prevent all intrusion upon them, which can be
occasioned only by a desire to gratify a vain curiosity"; and even promul-
gated a sentence on an army surgeon for maltreating natives with the
stern comment that the prisoner "ought to have known that he is a
part of a body of troops placed in this country to protect the inhabitants, and not to oppress them." He had little taste for the strong hand.
"I long for the return of the civil government. Although a soldier myself,
I am not an advocate for placing extensive civil powers in the hands
of soldiers merely because they are of the military profession, and I have

always opposed the idea excepting in cases of necessity." His correspondence, though, was not uniformly official. A colleague was assured
that "I shall send to Mrs. Stevenson in two days some cabbage and
celery plants, and in about a week her rose-trees." He was a gardener
himself, sent cuttings to his friends, and quite early in his residence at
Seringapatam made judicious use of creepers on unsightly walls. Sometimes he enclosed drawings of native monuments with notes on Jain
theology; and once the Governor of Bombay received from Arthur a letter
that was positively arch. A young lady, it seems, had sent him a portrait
of himself; this tribute elicited the grim comment that "the two or three
glances which you mention made very little impression upon the fair
artist, as the picture is as like anybody else as it is to the person for
whom it is intended." This was ungrateful. But the Colonel's chivalry
was equal to the occasion, since he proposed to write to her himself,
to tell her that I am glad to find that those few glances made an impression upon her memory so exceedingly favourable; and I have employed a gentleman here to draw the picture of a damsel in the character
of a shepherdess, which I shall also present as the effect of the impression
made upon my memory by the fair artist." Here was the Colonel in a
graceful mood.

He had other moods as well. An awful silence still prevailed between
him and Richard, and he seemed to view with equanimity his brother's
possible recall to England in 1802. His tone with Baird was friendly;
the rough General seemed to have won him in Bombay, and Arthur
wrote him all the news of India to brighten his campaign in Egypt. He
took the field himself quite soon in order to dispose of an insurgent
rajah in the west. This time, early in 1802, he undertook the complexities
of forest warfare; and the campaign in Bullum was a neat and punctual
operation by three converging columns. The leading rebel was run to
earth and hanged in pursuance of Arthur's grim determination on
"he suspension of the Rajah"; and the whole salutary process was concluded in three weeks. The expedition appeared to leave him with few
illusions on the subject of British authority in India, since he wrote that
year on the necessity of military power "for a government which exists
only by the sword." But he rarely generalised; the news from Europe
excited little beyond gruff disapproval of Addington's limp pacificism—

"There is too much moderation and candour for these bad times. . .
I see that they have submitted to abuse from the opposition, and instead
of retorting it according to the good old custom, they have deprecated
it"—and he was soon back at Seringapatam, lost in the familiar jungle
of timber contracts, errant subordinates on whom he sometimes turned
a slightly indulgent eye—"He has a wife and family (who in my eyes
cover a multitude of sins, &c.)"—and mess disputes that drew from him
the sage opinion that "a drunken quarrel is very bad, and is always
to be lamented, but probably the less it is inquired into the better." A
small godson engaged him, receiving kisses in the postscript of official
letters; and Arthur, with a sense of duty rare among god-parents, was
at pains to have his namesake submitted to the mysteries of vaccination
for the cowpox. He had lighter interests too. For that year the Colonel's
mess was swept, if one may judge from Arthur's bills, by a passion for
theatricals; and his purchases of plays appear among dozens of Madeira
casks of ale, lamp-glasses, and potatoes. Some remain enigmatic; for
his acquisition of "1 Book plays" and "8 plays" reveal little of the station's taste in drama. But Schiller's *Robbers* shewed them in a tragic
mood; though a sprightlier taste appeared in his purchase of Sheridan
(though no particular play was specified), no less than of Davies' *Play*
written for a Private Theatre. The last, published in 1786, had just attained the degree of staleness appropriate to amateur performance, though
no record survives to shew whether Arthur played *General Blunder*,
M.P., in *News the Malady*. The same account records his literary diversions, which consisted of a complete set of *The Novelist's Magazine*
and a French novel. Duty was tempered by these mild alleviations. Promotion came at last; gazetted in April, 1802, the news reached him in
December; and the world heard at length of Major-General Wellesley
commanding the troops in Mysore, Malabar, and Canara.

Whilst Arthur loyally hewed regimental wood and drew provincial
water, Richard—a Marquess now—surveyed imperial horizons. The little
autocrat was more august than ever. Seated majestically in the state
replica of Kedleston that rose at his command (to exasperate his parsi-
monious Directors with its "style of Asiatic pomp and display" and to
direct the juvenile attention of a successor to India, implanting "the
ambition, from an early age, to pass from a Kedleston in Derbyshire to

edleston in Bengal"), Lord Wellesley held the gorgeous East in fee with peculiar enjoyment of the fact that it was gorgeous. "The drums and banners, the turbans and the flowing robes, the spears, the silver maces, the elephants with their canopies of State" entered his splendid repertory, as he "elevated" (in a successor's envious phrase) "the spectacular to the level of an exact science." His taste for grandeur found appropriate expression in an expanding Body Guard which, fifty strong at his accession, rose to two hundred in a year or so, mounted in two years more to three hundred men and two guns, and twelve months later reached the impressive total of four hundred men, two guns, and a band. Small wonder that Cornwallis was a little staggered on his arrival to succeed this Cæsar; the old soldier lost himself in endless corridors, was startled by Richard's innumerable sentries—"If I show my head outside a door, a fellow with a musket and fixed bayonet presents himself before me"—and the embarrassed veteran ended by ordering his galaxy of martial state back to the guard-room. Not that Richard's splendour was all for show. It was easy to ridicule "the sultanised Englishman"; but even Mr. Hickey, always a trifle fretful, could not withhold a tribute to "the pompous though undoubtedly able little Knight of St. Patrick." For he transformed "a little patchwork of crimson spots on the map of the Indian Continent" into an Indian empire. This process was observed with growing horror by an ungrateful Company. Leadenhall Street breathed its concern into the ear of Westminster; the Board of Control transmitted softened versions to the Governor-General; and that dignitary, resolved that India should be "ruled from a palace, not from a countinghouse; with the ideas of a Prince, not with those of a retail-dealer in muslins and indigo," and mounting

"the high horse he loved so well to ride,"

became increasingly impatient of restraints. His resignations grew in frequency, since he was by nature ill-adapted to a system of government based rather on the principles of ventriloquism than upon those of Montesquieu; and even Arthur, scarcely a sympathetic witness now, was moved to resentment of "the corrupt and vulgar interference of Leadenhall Street in the operations of his government." He felt for Arthur too, when an ill-timed economy curtailed his allowances for the Mysore command; for official disregard of Arthur's claims seemed to the angr Richard to "have offered me the most direct, marked and disquietin personal indignity." Their paths converged again, since he had worl for Arthur now.

The last stage in Lord Wellesley's strenuous conversion of "a Britis Empire *in* India" into "the Empire *of* India" was the extension of Britis influence to the vast territories of the Mahratta confederacy. As usua action was preceded by a preliminary phase of diplomacy. Arthur wa not consulted upon this stage, since the brothers' intimacy was still ir terrupted by their Egyptian misunderstanding. But Richard's finge vigorously thrust into the rich compound of Mahratta jealousies, dre out the unquestionable plum of a treaty with the Peshwah, that dignitar engaging to submit to British influence in exchange for restoration his throne. Arthur was promptly notified that his force in Mysore woul be required to take the necessary action. The order was not unexpecte since he had composed a paper in the previous year on the subject operations against the Mahrattas; and he plunged with gusto into h customary preparations. Bullocks and rice became the burden of h official correspondence, because "if I had rice and bullocks I had me and if I had men I knew I could beat the enemy." His strategy w simple:

"It is obvious that the intentions of the British government regardi the affairs of the Mahratta empire cannot be carried into execution unle Holkar's army is either defeated or dissipated. The object of the campai must therefore be to bring him to a general action at as early a period possible. . . . If it be our intent to bring Holkar to a general action, it his to avoid it; and it may be depended upon that he will avoid it long as possible.

"His army is light, and chiefly composed of cavalry. The whole compo tion of our armies is heavy . . . Holkar, therefore, will have not only t inclination but the means of avoiding the result which, I take it f granted, can alone bring the war to a conclusion. . . . Therefore I co clude that, after a certain period for which our stock of provisions w have been provided, we shall be obliged to return to our own country a fresh supply.

"There are but two modes of carrying on this war by which we m

avoid this disagreeable result: one is to place the seat of it in a country
. . . near our own resources . . . ; the other is to keep up our communication with our own country, whatever may be the distance from it
of the seat of war. In regard to the first, viz., to command the seat of war,
I have to observe that we shall no more be able to do that than we shall be
able to command its operations. . . .

"The second mode then is that alone by which we can succeed. By this
mode we shall always supply ourselves; the enemy may protract his defeat, but sooner or later it must happen."

This was clear-eyed. It was to be a commissariat war; and, omitting
. heroics, General Wellesley waded ankle-deep in questions of supply.
e called for beef; he called for sheep; he called for forage; he was
eticulous upon the packing of his provisions, specifying gunny bags
r his rice, kegs for his salt beef, and casks "with iron hoops of four
llons each" for his arrack. Depots were stocked in northern Mysore
jacent to the Mahratta border; and though operating from the south,
conceived the unusual project of an advanced base somewhere along
e western coast, to which he could transfer his communications on
ching the region of Poona—"by this arrangement we should carry on
e war at Poonah . . . with the resources of Bombay; and we should
orten our line of communication many hundred miles." (The same
nœuvre was to shift a later army's base from Lisbon to the north coast
Spain, as they worked northwards into the Pyrenees.) For months he
ed in an ecstasy of preparation; and though the breach with Richard
s not yet bridged by a single letter, Arthur's feelings were a shade
der now, since he urged him indirectly to come south to Madras
the ground that "nothing but Lord Wellesley's presence can keep
government of Madras in the direct line." The army moved in
oruary, 1803; in March they crossed the border; and at the moment
nvading Mahratta territory Arthur broke the long silence with a letter
the Governor-General (though he was still "My Lord"), expressing
ie uncertainty as to his own future in Mysore. Richard responded with
hole-hearted testimonial to "his approved talents, firmness, temper, and
egrity," concluding with a vigorous insistence on his retention in the
sore command. These powers at peace once more, the war proceeded
oothly. The long march was almost uneventful, and in April General

Wellesley rode into Poona after a final dash of sixty miles with fou
hundred cavalry. His dealings with the Mahrattas were almost uniforml
satisfactory, and in the view of one highly competent observer this eas
progress had been largely due "to the admiration which the Mahratt
chiefs entertain of that officer's military character, and the firm relianc
which the inhabitants place on his justice and protection."

With the Peshwah safely restored to his throne at Poona, the fir
stage of the war was over. Richard was promptly notified of the succe
in terms which made it plain that Arthur approved his policy and woul
deal faithfully with the "croaking" of his brother's critics; the fami
alliance was almost reconstituted now, the General resenting with e
emplary warmth the latest slight upon the Governor-General—"the lett
from the Court of Directors to the Governor of Fort St. George is shoc
ing. I hope that you do not propose to stay in India longer than the end
this year. Such masters do not deserve your services." At first it seem
unlikely that there would be any further need of military operatior
Mahratta bands were still at large in the northern provinces, and f
these his strategy was shrewd and practical:

> "Press him with one or more corps capable of moving with tolera
> celerity. . . . The effect produced by this mode of operation is to obli
> him to move constantly and with great celerity. . . . He cannot ventu
> to stop to plunder the country, and he does comparatively but little m
> chief, at all events; the subsistence of his army becomes difficult a
> precarious; the horsemen become dissatisfied; they perceive that th
> situation is hopeless, and they desert in numbers daily; and the freeboo
> ends by having with him only a few adherents, and he is reduced to su
> a state as to be liable to be taken by any small body of country horse."

But he wrote cheerfully of his "great hopes . . . that the combination
the northern Chiefs will end in nothing. . . . I think that, althou
there will be much bad temper and many threats, there will be no hos
ity." He made his preparations, though, his mind running on pontoon:
a means of obtaining superior mobility by crossing rivers that remair
impassable for native armies. His correspondence soon abounded in fi
inch cables, anchors, graplins, and measurements of boats; and as
work advanced, he discovered an increasing disrespect for native al
who "think that when once they have put the seal to a treaty with

ey have nothing to do but to amuse themselves and sleep." (In a long xperience of allies Arthur was generally disappointed.) The summer onths of 1803 passed slowly by; and he was still detained in Poona by a endless web of Mahratta diplomacy. He was not altogether easy, since e seemed to have his doubts of Richard's eternal forward policy—"One d consequence of these subsidiary treaties is, that they entirely annihilate e military power of the governments with which we contract them. . In my opinion we ought to withdraw from Poonah, and leave some ance that the principal chiefs may have the power of the state in their nds; . . . I would preserve the existence of the state; and guide its :ions by the weight of British influence." The General was disinclined war, if war could be avoided. He could still write in June, as intermin- le *pourparlers* proceeded with the Mahratta chiefs, that "my object is e preservation of peace"; in July he was a shade more sceptical—"If re be any truth in a Mahratta durbar, we shall have peace." Taking a nd himself in the negotiations (Richard presently conferred full pow- on him in the most complimentary terms), he bluntly challenged onsla and Scindia to withdraw their forces, still clinging gallantly to conviction that peace was "very probable." But he wisely fixed no e for the expiry of his ultimatum from a practical desire "to keep in own breast the period at which hostilities will be commenced; by ich advantage it becomes more probable that I shall strike the first w, if I should find hostile operations to be necessary." Then, as the skein of procrastination wound slowly off the reel, he grimly in- ned his incorrigible correspondents in the first week of August that had offered "peace on terms of equality, and honorable to all parties: have chosen war, and are responsible for all consequences."

His first movement was a swift attack on Ahmednuggur. The place stormed with a precision which elicited the rueful compliment that se English are a strange people and their General a wonderful man. :y came here in the morning, looked at the pettah-wall, walked over :illed all the garrison, and returned to breakfast." This capture deftly ered Poona from the Mahrattas. Then he moved north to find them, sing the Godavery in full flood by means of his precious basket s. His plan was simple—"I do not expect that we shall be able to g the enemy to an action, but we must try to keep him in movement,

and tire him out." He was at peace with Richard now, writing tha
month to "My dear Mornington" once more; and his main preoccupa
tions consisted of dealings with the natives, in which he lived up to a
exacting standard ("If we lose our character for truth and good faith
we shall have but little to stand upon in this country"), and the eterna
problem of military hygiene—"I consider nothing in this country s
valuable as the life and health of the British soldier." After an interlud
of countermarching to the east and back again, he moved north an
stumbled on his enemy, a day earlier and in considerably greater for
than he anticipated, at Assaye.

The *rencontre* on September 23 was unexpected, since his intelligen
was far from perfect. Nearly half his force had been detached to follo
by another route, and the men with him had marched twenty miles th
morning. The odds were serious, since the enemy had 40,000 men
line to his own 7,000; and the situation was uninviting, as they we
strongly posted in the angle formed by two rivers. Plainly he must
tack at once, since his little force was manifestly unequal to sustaini
the weight of an attack by an enemy of six times their numbers. Succe
depended on a double gamble. If the enemy would have the court
to keep reasonably still, he might cross their front and reach their flan
once there, if only they would oblige by still continuing to face in
same direction, he might roll them up. His flank march across their fr
was uninterrupted, and the first perilous throw succeeded. Guessing a
ford, he got his force across one river, and drew it up with 40,000 n
in front and two rivers behind. This seemed a trifle reckless, altho
the gamble might succeed, if an unwieldy enemy continued to expose
unprotected flank to his impending blow. But the enemy, less unwie
than Wellesley had hoped, changed front with admirable precision
faced his little force in its perilous peninsula. Then his attack
launched, and the result was "one of the most furious battles that
ever been fought in this country." With little scope for tactics, he han
the attacking units well, led infantry charges against guns, and had
horses killed under him. The Mahrattas were well drilled and am
provided with artillery; they broke at last, however, leaving Welle
in possession of the ground and ninety-eight of their guns. But he
almost spent; and that night Wellesley sat motionless among the cas

es, his head between his knees. His gay strategy—"Dash at the first
fellows that make their appearance, and the campaign will be ours"—
was justified, but at a singularly heavy price.

Richard received the news with stately raptures. He had observed their
march "with much solicitude for the success of our operations on public
grounds, and with every additional anxiety, which affection could inspire"; and now the watcher had been gratified in "all my affection and
all the pride of my blood." He had foreseen it all—"It was not more
than was expected from you"—and a majestic hand waved Arthur forward to his niche in a blaze of Ciceronian commendation. Arthur was
melted visibly; and, until lately satisfied with a bare "Believe me, &c.,"
he now became ever Richard's most affectionately. Meanwhile, the army
bound its wounds, assisted by a dozen of the General's own Madeira for
every tent of casualties, and moved off in pursuit. Two months of marching, to an accompaniment of dilatory negotiations (and a touch of fever
for the General), ended in a second encounter with the Mahrattas at
Argaum on November 29. Unlike Assaye, this was premeditated; and
the affair proceeded with perfect regularity, though Arthur personally
checked a panic of his native infantry. He wheeled his cavalry into position, riding sedately at their head, and presided calmly over an inexpensive victory. The last stage of the war was the storm of Bhonsla's
fortress of Gawilghur. Arthur directed the attack against both faces of
the place, riding a daily circuit of fifty miles. It duly fell; and the year
ended with a pair of peace-treaties which satisfied even Richard's exacting
notions of conquest, and left him in ecstasies over "a brilliant point in
the history of this country, and a noble termination of your military
glory."

By comparison, the next year was almost restful. Indeed, after three
years in tents the General began to need a rest; for early in 1804 he
found himself "much annoyed by the lumbago." But his repose was
interrupted by a minor operation, in which he moved five regiments sixty
miles in thirty hours and wrote exultantly that "we now begin to beat
the Mahrattas by the celerity of our movements." Had he not once in-
stinced to a colleague that "time is everything in military operations"?
Then he returned to Poona and received a presentation from his officers.
The triumph continued at Bombay, where he rode through crowded

III

streets, received addresses, made sedate replies, dined at the theatr
(confronted by "an elegant transparency" of his own coat of arms), an
"had much conversation with mercantile gentlemen there." Even h
correspondence took a gentler turn; a Colonel's lady in Bombay wa
asked to procure

> "some pickled oysters, and I wish you to prepare some and send the
> here. You must lose no time, as I understand that the oysters at Bomb
> become best when the rains commence.
>
> "Don't send them by Coleman, as he will eat more than his share befo
> he reaches camp; nor by any of your great eaters, or I shall get none
> them. . . .
>
> "Tell Colonel Gordon that I see that all the offices of subordinate Colle
> tor in Malabar are filled up, and that his brother-in-law has no chance. B
> as a recommendation from a *great Man* is always a good thing I write th
> day to Lord Wm. Bentinck to recommend Captain Watson to him."

Arthur, it seems—unlike the stately Richard—could positively jest abo
his greatness. His next letter was no less familiar, since it announc
with relish that

> "the oysters were excellent; everybody likes them. . . .
>
> "As for your susceptible youths, I consider three days full enough
> them at Bombay, particularly when I want them elsewhere. But whenev
> you have a mind to detain one of my champions as you call them, y
> have my permission to do so, and I shall not be the 'Deaf Adder' of t
> reasons which you will give for detaining them, provided that you do
> allow them to marry. After that they would not answer my purpose."

This was no grim disciplinarian. The sprightly General even press
his correspondent to visit them in camp:

> "We get on well, but we want you to enliven us. Allow me to prev
> upon you. If you'll come I'll go and meet you with my Servts. at the
> of the Ghaut, so that you will only have 24 miles to travel in palanque
>
> "There is excellent galloping ground in the neighbourhood of car
> and the floor of my tent is in a fine state for dancing and the fiddlers
> the Dragoons and the 78th and Bagpipes of the 74th play delightfully."

Here was a charming mood. His proximity to Bombay enabled him
replenish his library as well; and purchases of books appear amc

vord-belts, expensive saddlery, pale ale, York hams, and Gloucester
neeses. His taste for drama still prevailed; for Bell's Shakespeare (in
nineteen volumes) and the *British Theatre* (in thirty-four) entered his
brary that year. Dow's *History of Hindostan* (to replace, perhaps, a
issing copy, since he had brought out a set from England), together
ith a work on Egypt followed the line of his earlier reading, though
e purchase of Gentz's survey of *The State of Europe before and after
e French Revolution* showed plainly that his thoughts were turning
meward. A sheaf of pamphlets—*Brief Answer . . , Cursory Re-
rks . . , Substance of a Speech . . , Report of the Cause . .* —kept
m abreast of current affairs. He bought some military books—two
lumes of French tactics, Smirke's *Review of a Battalion of Infantry,*
d Porter's *Military Instructions,* to say nothing of a *Summary Account
d Military Character of the several European Armies that have been
gaged during the late War.* For Arthur was beginning to envisage
er theatres of war than Mysore and other enemies than contumacious
ahs. This work (which chilled its latest reader with the depressing
ervation that "an English general, who returns from India, is like an
miral, who has been navigating the Lake of Geneva") surveyed the
ropean armies. French methods were well summarised; the Austrians
re sternly judged; and no reader could retain illusions as to the mili-
y efficiency of Spain after reading its choleric verdict—"a Spanish regi-
nt . . . looks like an assemblage of beggars. . . . During a siege, they
e been known to destroy the trenches . . . in order to steal the earth
s, and sell them for a few pence." A terrifying appendix warned
lers of the *Parallel of the Policy, Power, and Means of the Ancient
nans and Modern French; shewing the real Designs of the latter
inst the Independence of Europe; particularly of Great Britain and
nd.*

ot that Arthur's reading was exclusively professional. For at the
e time he bought the *Sporting Magazine* for 1802–3, together with
e odd numbers of the *Universal Magazine.* His latest acquisitions—
natic, military, and miscellaneous—were added to the General's little
ry; and one work, a shade more unexpected than the rest, appeared
is bookseller's account. He positively bought a copy of Dr. Priestley's
ates and Jesus Compared,* and Arthur Wellesley faced that slightly

condescending examination of the enlightened pagan. But his purchas
were not invariably literary in design or male in destination. For
Brilliant hoop Ring and 2 pearl guards to ditto, 150 Rs." reveal a gentl
mood. He was not easy, though, contemplating an early return to E
rope and pressing Richard to resign before an ungrateful Company d
missed him. But Lord Wellesley, fairly launched on his career of conque
was disinclined to stop. Fresh provinces beckoned him on to furth
wars; and Arthur wrote ruefully that "the system of moderation a
conciliation by which, whether it be right or wrong, I made the treat
of peace . . . is now given up." His own principles were plain:

> "I would sacrifice Gwalior, or every frontier of India, ten times ov
> in order to preserve our credit for scrupulous good faith, and the advanta
> and honor we gained by the late war and the peace; and we must
> fritter them away in arguments, drawn from over-strained principles
> the laws of nations, which are not understood in this country. W
> brought me through many difficulties in the war, and the negociati
> for peace? The British good faith, and nothing else."

Small wonder that the questionable ingenuities of Richard's later dip
matic manner left him "dispirited and disgusted . . . beyond measur
War was resumed, with Arthur as a gloomy commentator. He watch
the operations from a distance; but this time there were few victor
and the epitaph of the campaign was written in his grim comment t
he did not "think that the Commander-in-Chief and I have carried on
so well by our deputies as we did ourselves." For Lake and Welles
had made 1803 glorious by Laswaree and Assaye; but Monson's retr
and Lake's failure at Bhurtpore clouded 1804.

Arthur was growing restless now. Had he not "served as long
India as any man ought, who can serve any where else"? There was
prospect of service in Europe, in which I should be more likely to
forward." (This seemed a trifle selfish; but his distaste for Richa
policy hardly increased the hold of India upon him.) Besides, his rh
matism would not be improved by another rainy season under can
The course of operations in 1804 rendered him almost superfluous;
after setting his administrative house in order, he withdrew to Calcu
where he sat to Home for a head-and-shoulders at the modest pric

)o rupees, and assisted the Governor-General with a steady stream of
memoranda, including a lengthy vindication of the earlier phases of his
Mahratta policy. Calcutta had its softer side as well, attested by the pur-
hase of a pearl necklace with some bracelets and a "silk worked shawl."
ut Monson's "retreat, defeats, disgraces, and disasters" (Arthur was not
indulgent to these "woful examples of the risk to be incurred by advanc-
g too far without competent supplies") recalled him to the south again,
ore convinced than ever that "against the Mahrattas in particular, but
against all enemies, we should take care to be sure of plenty of provi-
ons." Before the year was out, he was back at Seringapatam. The at-
osphere was peaceful now; and the Colonel's lady from Bombay was
formed of his "great dinners daily" and a sufficiency of dances, together
ith the General's gallant wishes for her return to Bombay "in high
ealth and beauty to be again its ornament."

He was quite clear about his destination now—"I certainly do not
propose to spend my life in the Deccan; and I should not think it neces-
ry, in any event, to stay there one moment longer than the Governor-
eneral should stay in India." The clouds were gathering round Richard
some foreshadowing resignation, others shaped perilously like dismissal;
d Arthur foresaw "a variety of subjects in discussion, relating to this
untry, upon which some verbal explanation is absolutely necessary. I
nceive, therefore, that in determining not to go into the Deccan, and
sail by the first opportunity for England, I consult the public interests
t less than I do my own private convenience and wishes." India, he
t, had been a hard mistress, from whose penurious Directors he "had
ver received any thing but injury. . . . I am not very ambitious; and
cknowledge that I have never been very sanguine in my expectations
t military services in India would be considered in the scale in which
considered similar services in other parts of the world. But I might
ve expected to be placed on the Staff in India. . . ." This was a stand-
; grievance with him. Besides, British India was not in danger—had
een, he "should not hesitate a moment about staying, even for years"
nd he concluded almost angrily that "these men or the public have
right to ask me to stay in India, merely because my presence in a
ticular quarter may be attended with convenience." His plans were

definite in the first days of 1805; he should resign, if quiet continued on
the northern borders of Mysore. Richard consented; and the General
promptly notified the authorities. A Madras official was advised of his
desire to secure a passage home—"I am not very particular about accom-
modation, and I would take any rather than lose the opportunity . . . and
I don't care a great deal about the price. I should prefer, however, either
half a round house or the starboard side of a quiet cabin; and I don't
much care who the captain is, or what the ship." This was almost precipitate. But his departure was delayed by endless complications—official
business to be wound up, his staff to be provided for, portraits distributed
to friends, and the safe bestowal of two elephants presented to the departing traveller by a devoted rajah at the last moment. Before he started
he found time for an unusual act of kindness. Years before, when he
defeated Dhoondiah, the dead man's son was captured; Arthur had
taken the boy under his own protection; and on leaving India he settled
a sum of money on him, taking steps at the same time to assure his
future. Whilst he was waiting at Madras (and very far from well), he
received a pleasant piece of news which he passed on to Richard:

> "A fleet arrived from England this morning; it sailed on the 4th
> Sept[r.] I enclose a paper of the 3d. containing an extract of the Gazette
> of the 1st Sept[r.] by which it appears that General Lake is made Lord
> Lake of Delhi and Laswaree, and I a Knight of the Bath. I have
> heard no other news, excepting that Captain Fitzgerald of the 34th in-
> formed me that the fleet had spoken a Ship which left England the 2
> Sept[r.], the Captain of which ship informed them that there was ever
> probability of war between France and the Northern Powers. He did r
> recollect the name of the ship, or of the Captain, or where he saw the shi

So the world heard for the first time of Sir Arthur Wellesley, thou
the recipient's sense of his new honour appeared to be almost effaced
his contempt for Captain Fitzgerald's inexactitude of mind. A passeng
who went on board ten days later to find his own luggage inform
Sir Arthur that there was a box "kicking about the *Lord Keith*," wh
contained his insignia. Then he prepared to start for home. His fi
purchases comprised a selection of reading-matter for the voyage; a
it is pleasant to observe a marked deterioration in the severity of

Arthur's tastes. Nine years before the Colonel had acquired a library which would not have disgraced a public institution. But Major-Generals need relaxation, and his choice of books in 1805 would have given entire satisfaction to a girls' school. *Love at First Sight* (in five volumes) was matched by *Lessons for Lovers* (in two); his fancy wandered from *Illicit Love* to *Filial Indiscretion or the Female Chevalier*. His book-seller supplied him with a dazzling array of the most brilliant popular successes in recent fiction, which appeared (if their titles could be trusted), to concentrate upon family complications. For the eager traveller was regaled with four volumes of *The Rival Mothers* and three of *The Supposed Daughter,* to say nothing of *The Disappointed Heir* and the wider horizons suggested by *Fashionable Involvements* and *The Fairy of Misfortunes*. In all, he bought twenty-six novels by authors ranging from Madame de Genlis to Mrs. Gunning. Almost the sole exception to his prevailing thirst for fiction was *Beauties of the Modern Dramatists*, a purchase which appeared to shew that his theatrical interests survived exile from the dramatic circle in Seringapatam. Nor was an earlier allegiance overlooked in his acquisition or Crébillon's *Letters of Madame de Pompadour*. The spirit of Crébillon almost seemed to haunt another entry in the same account, which debited Sir Arthur, homeward-bound, with ten pairs of ladies' shoes—small gifts of Oriental elegance for Western wearers.

The last farewells (including a convivial evening with the field officers and captains of the station, which "passed off with great harmony" and ended in a young gentleman's inexcusable refusal to sing and the arrest in error of a completely innocent captain by an inebriated Town Major) were safely said and due answers returned to the grateful addresses of Madras, Seringapatam, and his own Thirty-third. They sailed in March, Sir Arthur with a comfortable conviction that "in India at present there is not, or will not in a short time, be anything for a military man to do." But he had Richard's business to transact at home—"Send me all your commands to England; I shall have nothing to do excepting to attend to them, and I will exert myself to forward your views." Richard was still his chief; though Arthur, who was nearly thirty-six, had learnt his trade and, in his own later judgment, "understood as much of military

matters as I have ever done since." Once more the breeze sprang up
a frigate sailed; and India faded behind him.

At midsummer an island stood up out of the sea; and Arthur Wellesley went ashore at St. Helena. His health, in spite of *mal de mer*, wa
better now; and he found "the interior of the island . . . beautiful, an
the climate apparently the most healthy that I have ever lived in." (Ricl
ard confirmed his view a few months later, deriving satisfaction from "i
singular beauty and delightful climate," as well as from a congenial a
mosphere of deference, and testifying to its beneficial effects upon a del
cate young man, whose "health is restored by this climate.") Sir Arthu
stayed there for three weeks, rode into Jamestown for a christening, an
derived peculiar enjoyment from a Governor of antique cut—"a goo
man, but a quiz, of a description that must have been extinct for near
two centuries. I never saw anything like his wig or his coat." Tl
General lodged at The Briars; the house (it had another lodger late
lay pleasantly among the trees in a deep valley close by the road
Longwood. The names were unfamiliar to Sir Arthur—and still mo
so to an eager man, who waited in those summer weeks of 1805 f
news of a fleet that he had flung halfway round the world to set a tr
for Nelson, whilst his bugles rang upon the hills above Boulogne. B
for three weeks in 1805 a malicious fate enjoyed the brief paradox
Napoleon at large and Wellington at St. Helena. Then, in July,
Arthur Wellesley sailed on to Europe: the island waited.

One of Ireland's many tricks is to fade away to a little speck down on the horizon of our lives, and then to return suddenly in tremendous bulk, frightening us.—Ave.

I

THE ship sailed home across the summer seas of 1805. Their course was northward now; and as the bright Atlantic waves danced before *Trident*, Sir Arthur Wellesley sat writing in his cabin. His pen was busy with a paper upon Indian famines, in which he wrote learnedly of irrigation and native agriculture; and he replied at length to a proposal of Lord Castlereagh's for the employment of Indian troops in the West Indies and the substitution in India of West Indian negroes. Though strong upon the sepoy's virtues—"I have tried them on many serious occasions, and they have never failed me"—he was sceptical of the experiment, and suggested that Malays might answer better, whilst he was more than doubtful about garrisoning India with negro slaves.

There was a pause in Europe; and as *Trident* brought Sir Arthur home, the world was waiting. London, a little anxious, waited for news of Nelson, last heard of halfway to America in pursuit of phantom Frenchmen; the big hills above Boulogne waited to pour two hundred thousand men across the Channel into Kent; Sir Robert Calder waited doggedly off Finisterre to bar the road to England; and in a little room behind Boulogne the Emperor was waiting for a fleet that never came. *Trident,* in company "with about forty sail of Indiamen and Chinamen," sailed decorously homeward up the broad avenues of the Atlantic. Far to the west Nelson, eager and miserable in his feverish pursuit of Villeneuve, hunted the French towards their ports; and in those summer weeks of 1805 Nelson and Wellesley both rocked to the Atlantic swell. The General was nearing Europe now. Portugal heaved slowly out of the sea as they sailed by, and the Spanish mountains stood ranged behind the mists. But nothing stirred in the Peninsular sunshine. They passed the coast of France; but all the hutted alleys of Boulogne were emptying. For the Emperor had changed front abruptly, turned a scornful back on the derisive cliffs of Dover, and flung himself angrily against Vienna. Eastwards across the world obedient Russians in the last of Mr. Pitt's despairing Coalitions moved stiffly forward to the tap of their **monotonous**

121

drums, and Austrians fumbled with their arms, as the Emperor's *berlin* rolled into Germany. Gold-braided Marshals in stupendous collars tilte hats of pantomime proportions; the French cavalry jogged eastward through the blinding summer dust in the full coquetry of sabretache an dolman under a nodding avenue of busbies, shakoes, and immens brass helmets with plumes, with crests, with horse-hair tails, with strip of leopard-skin, with great imperial ciphers, as the long lines of bayone wound across France behind their clanging bands to write Austerli upon their eagles.

Sir Arthur read his novels, walked the deck, and wrote notes to fellov passengers. They reached England in September, and the General set c for London to lay siege to ministers in Richard's interests. One day had a strange encounter in "the little waiting-room on the right hand" the old Colonial Office in Downing Street. Another visitor was waitin there already—a sad-eyed little man, "whom from his likeness to his p tures and the loss of an arm" Sir Arthur promptly recognized as Nelsc home from the sea and happy in a few weeks of Emma Hamilton an "dear, dear Merton." The Admiral began to talk and, as Wellesley rec lected drily, "entered at once into conversation with me, if I can call conversation, for it was almost all on his side and all about himself, a in, really, a style so vain and so silly as to surprise and almost disgust m (Sir Arthur was unlikely to be captivated by the manner which, wh expressed in an excess of stars and ribbons, had elicited from John Moc the pained comment that their wearer seemed "more like the Prince of Opera than the Conqueror of the Nile.") Then, suspecting somethir the sailor left the room, learnt the identity of the spare military man, a came back transformed. All that the General "had thought a charlat style had vanished, and he talked of the state of this country and of t aspect and probabilities of affairs on the Continent with a good sense, a a knowledge of subjects both at home and abroad, that surprised equally and more agreeably than the first part of our interview had dor in fact, he talked like an officer and a statesman." So the French march to Austerlitz, and the first broadsides of Trafalgar came faintly up wind, as Nelson and Wellesley sat talking one September day in a ro off Whitehall. Lord Castlereagh was busy; and they talked above half hour. The talk stayed in Sir Arthur's memory; and after thirty years udged that "I don't know that I ever had a conversation that interested me more," adding the shrewd reflection that "if the Secretary of State had been punctual, and admitted Lord Nelson in the first quarter of an hour, I should have had the same impression of a light and trivial character that other people have had, but luckily I saw enough to be satisfied that he was really a very superior man; but certainly a more sudden and complete metamorphosis I never saw." They never met again.

All that autumn he besieged ministers with rare assiduity. His first assault was on Lord Castlereagh. Born the same year, they had seen something of each other in Dublin as young members of the Irish House of Commons. The other's legislative triumphs as Chief Secretary and pilot of the Act of Union through the muddy shallows had fallen in Sir Arthur's absence. But as Pitt's understudy Castlereagh now assisted another pilot to weather a severer storm, and the Secretary for War and President of the Board of Control took for his province the whole world (including India). Wellesley was soon correcting his Indian opinions, submitting memoranda, reading draft despatches, and setting Richard's proceedings in the most favourable light. He saw Lord Camden too, and told him bluntly that the Prime Minister's support of Richard left much to be desired. Pitt promptly sent for Sir Arthur; and, deep in Indian ㅤㅤs, they rode slowly into town together—two noses of rare quality jogging comfortably side by side down the long road from Wimbledon. Then he was off to Cheltenham for a rest. Not that his visits were confined to ministers; for on the way he stopped at Stowe to prospect the opposition. The Whigs were full of promises, pressed Richard to return to his old political friends, and to remember above all that the Prince of Wales was younger than the King. The shrewd General surveyed an unfamiliar problem, took counsel with his brothers, and reached the sage conclusion that Richard would be well advised "to remain neutral for some time and observe the course of events." This was judicious strategy. His own prospects were slightly obscure. The Duke of York was gracious, and ministers shewed a mild tendency to make use of his advice on military questions. He met them all that autumn, when he was staying at Lord Camden's house at Chislehurst. They rode twenty miles a day; and Mr. Pitt's invalid refreshment of steak and bottled porter was sent on ahead; then they rode home again to Camden Place, changed their splashed clothes, and held a Cabinet on how to foil the French. (A strange irony sent the last Emperor of the French to die in the same house three-quarters of a century later.) Once or twice Sir Arthur was consulted upon proposals for Continental expeditions. At one moment it was hoped that Prussia could be induced to take the Emperor in rear; and the notion commended itself to Mr. Pitt, whose strategy consisted less in striking blows than in making agitated passes above the map of Europe. But this slightly feverish prestidigitation scarcely commended itself to Wellesley, who predicted grimly that the Prussians could not be "raised, equipped, and on the Danube in less than three months"; and the event proved him correct. These consultations left Sir Arthur with a less favourable impression of Mr. Pitt than Mr. Pitt's of him. For while the soldier gauged the civilian defects of the Prime Minister—"the fault of his character was being too sanguine . . . he conceived a project and then imagined it was done, and did not enter enough into the details"—the admiring statesman found that Sir Arthur "states every difficulty before he undertakes any service, but none after he has undertaken it." This was a blessing, after the querulous paladins with whom Pitt was normally condemned to work.

The autumn passed away. The sagacious Mack marched twenty thousand Austrians into the iron trap of Ulm; Nelson lay murmuring in the half-darkness of the cockpit; and one November night Sir Arthur at table in Guildhall heard the Prime Minister returning thanks in two immortal sentences "for the honour you have done me; but Europe is not to be saved by any single man. England has saved herself by her exertions and will, as I trust, save Europe by her example." One of the cheering voices was Sir Arthur Wellesley's. He soon had an opportunity to display the quality of uncomplaining service which had impressed Mr. Pitt. For in December, 1805, he was appointed to command a brigade in a Continental expedition affording the most ample grounds for complaint. A Hanoverian officer, who bore the slightly unpromising name of van der Decken, had proposed to plant a British army in Hanover with the laudable design of worrying the French; the Cabinet complied; and through the winter months of 1805 an aimless stream of reinforcements was maintained. An infantry brigade of three battalions was commanded by Sir Arthur Wellesley. He was a week at sea, passed an unpleasant Christmas Day in a gale among the sands of Heligoland, and landed below Bremen seeing once more the unpleasing levels of the winter landscape which Colonel Wesley of the Thirty-third had left behind in '95. They saw the rain; they saw the unpleasing news of Austerlitz; they never saw the French. As the stricken Pitt dragged home from Bath to die, orders were sent to bring them home again; and Sir Arthur's second taste of European warfare—six uneventful weeks in the neighbourhood of Bremen—had been scarcely more inspiring than his first.

Returned to England in February, 1806, he subsided equally into the modest dignity of a brigade at Hastings, "in command of a few troops stationed in this part of the coast, the old landing place of William the Conqueror." The post, since all danger of invasion had perished with the French navy at Trafalgar, was not conspicuously exacting. But when someone asked how he endured it after his greater days in India, his answer was impressive—"I am *nimmukwallah*, as we say in the East; that is, I have ate of the King's salt, and, therefore, I conceive it to be my duty to serve with unhesitating zeal and cheerfulness, when and wherever the King or his government may think proper to employ me." Besides, the Whigs were in and Castlereagh was out; as Sir Arthur wrote to a friend in India, "*we* are not actually in opposition, but we have no power"; and it was hardly likely that professional plums would fall into his lap. Not that his situation was unfavourable; he was gazetted to the Staff as well as to the lucrative dignity of the colonelcy of his old regiment, and he wrote comfortably that these appointments "have made me rich."

Perhaps he needed to be rich in 1806. At any rate, he assumed at least one fresh liability that year. For in the spring he married. It was in some ways the most obscure of all his actions. There are no maps of such affairs; the heroine herself confessed that there were no love-letters; and the surviving facts barely suffice to indicate the meagre anatomy of his unpromising romance. He had loved at twenty-four, when the bright vision of Kitty Pakenham first danced before his eyes. Because he loved, his violin lay smouldering in a Dublin grate, and he resolved to be a soldier. That was in '93. A taste of soldiering in Holland almost cured him of military views. But love survived; and at twenty-six, a lover still, he set his modest hopes in '95 upon a civilian situation under the Irish revenue and a home in Dublin. What felicity for Kitty Pakenham, designed by Providence to be his little Dublin wife. But Providence un-

kindly omitted to provide her with a Dublin husband. For in '96 the
quays, the Castle, and the Custom House receded; and for nine years he
walked an ampler stage under a deeper sky. At thirty-six the East restored
him. Was he her lover still? If so, he had been unusually passive. For
they never wrote. This singular departure from romantic ritual was confessed upon the highest authority. Kitty attested it herself in answer to
the Queen; for when she went to Court, the royal couple beamed approval. Her Majesty was pleased to be inquisitive—

"I am happy to see you at my court, so bright an example of constancy
If anybody in this world deserves to be happy, you do. But did you really
never write *one* letter to Sir Arthur Wellesley during his long absence?"

"No, never, madam," answered Kitty.

"And did you never think of him?"

"Yes, madam, very often."

But fortunately his enquiring sovereign never asked Sir Arthur how
often he had thought of Kitty. Hardly, it would seem, with embarrassing
frequency. Never when writing letters; nor at the jeweller's. Yet during
their nine years of separation he both wrote to ladies and bought jeweller
—but not, it would appear, for Kitty, since she never wrote to thank him
for it.

Was he her lover, then? If he was, he scarcely seemed to know it. But
her world appeared to think so. Perhaps it was not, at first sight, the
sort of world that might be expected to carry weight with Sir Arthur
For it was the slightly high-pitched world of Dublin beaux and Longfor
belles, where young ladies romped and languished in provincial mansion
or flushed and paled in Merrion Square over matrimonial prospect
Their skies were filled by her Excellency the Lord-Lieutenant's wife
the Castle season, and the latest breath of London fashion; and whe
little Miss Edgeworth of Edgeworthstown distilled her raptures ov
"sweet Kitty Pakenham," she drew an air that was nothing if not provi
cial. But it was not unfamiliar to Sir Arthur. (How long was it sin
Captain Wesley, a stiff Castle aide-de-camp, made his first awkward bo
in Dublin?) So he was not surprised to hear a Dublin voice one day
Cheltenham, as General Sparrow's lady greeted him. She was a daught
of Lord Gosford's; besides, he had seen something in the East of

brother-in-law Lord William Bentinck, the Governor of Madras. But the Sparrow twittered; and Sir Arthur heard with more surprise her sudden assurance that Kitty Pakenham's sentiments towards him were still unchanged. What, the startled gentleman enquired, did she still remember him? And did the Sparrow think he should renew his offer? If so, he was prepared to. The chivalrous reply did credit to his self-command; and chivalry combined with Lady Olivia Sparrow to seal his fate. For Arthur Wellesley found himself Prince Charming unawares, hero (or victim) of a one-sided romance.

The next step was easy; for if Dublin drawing-rooms expected him to marry, what other course was open to a Castle aide-de-camp? His dignity (to say nothing of the lady's feelings) seemed to demand it. Besides, her attitude was distinctly flattering; and, his family apart, Sir Arthur was a little lonely. His friends were all in India, and the Longfords were a respectable connection. So he laid siege to Kitty in due form. Sieges were ever his strong point; but it was the most successful of his sieges, though perhaps the fortress fell just a thought too easily. For Kitty Pakenham, at thirty-three, surrendered at discretion; Sir Arthur won his prize; and in the spring of 1806 he went to Ireland to bring home his bride. Pretty? Perhaps. Young? Well, not quite so young as she had been in Dublin. Devoted? Ah, devotion was her *forte*.

They married at St. George's, Hill Street; and every *amateur* of romance in Dublin thrilled with delight at the lovers parted for long years, the maiden's vigil, her knight in peril overseas, the hero's homecoming, and then a leap into his arms, rapture, and wedding-bells. Miss Edgeworth plied a gleeful pen over "one of those tales of real life in which the romance is far superior to the generality of fictions," hoped ecstatically that "the imagination of this hero and heroine have not been too much exalted, and that they may not find the enjoyment of a happiness so long wished for inferior to what they expected," and asked with fervour what Sir Arthur looked like. An unreliable observer at the Castle informed her that he was "handsome, very brown, quite bald, and a hooked nose." But though he retained an admirable head of hair, he fell lamentably short of his romantic *rôle*. For his Irish wedding-trip was accomplished inside a week; and when he sailed for England, he travelled by himself.

True, he had overstayed his leave to be with her. That was a saving touch of romance. But was it kind to leave the bride to travel after him "under the care of his brother, the clergyman"? It almost seemed to lend substance to the dreadful whisper that when the couple drove home from the honeymoon, a startled world beheld the bride inside the carriage, the bridegroom on the box. And yet, perhaps, she found it a relief: she was always scared of him.

So Prince Charming, contrary to precedent, came home alone; and the bride followed later in charge of a relation. This was a shade discouraging; but when his hands were full, Sir Arthur was not easily discouraged, and at the moment he had other things to think of. There was his brigade at Hastings, which occupied him with agreeable problems of coast-defence; he read stimulating papers on the Rye inundations and the military virtues of Winchelsea Castle. Besides, that summer he went into Parliament. His motive for the step was not ambition or any appetite for politics, but the defence of Richard. For, loyalty apart, the family viewed Richard's fame as their main asset. Resigned at last, the splendid Marquess was back in England, draped in the dignity peculiar to returned proconsuls. But his attitude, though always regal, was not wholly free from uneasiness. A pertinacious Anglo-Indian named Paull had dogged him spitefully for years. This mischief-maker had succeeded in entering the House of Commons, and was now engaged in a series of manœuvres unpleasantly suggestive of impeachment. Impeachment was the mode that year. Lord Melville was already well on the road to Westminster Hall; and if Paull had his way, Lord Wellesley seemed likely to follow him. (Such persecution seemed, if he might judge from the dismal precedent of Warren Hastings, the customary reward of Indian service.) If Pitt had been alive, the Marquess might perhaps afford to disregard his persecutor. But Pitt was gone; the obnoxious Paull had Whig connections; and it was doubtful how far Whig ministers would undertake Richard's defence. Slightly alarmed, he mobilised his little cohort. Henry was busy on official doorsteps; William was in the House already; and in April Arthur was returned for Rye.

The campaign was not exacting, since the Rye electors listened more closely to their proprietor than to any candidate. Their simple appetites appear in his election accounts:

	£	s.	d.
Wine &c. &c. at the Meeting at the Court Hall	3	8	0
Supper for Corporation at Nomination	37	10	0
Cold Collation day of Election	15	8	0
Election Dinner Tea Supper &c.	123	0	6
do. do. for Freemen Wives & Families	88	12	6
Town Clerk's Fees &c. &c.	26	5	0
Serjeant's Fees	13	2	6
Ringers	5	5	0
Waiters at the Inn	5	5	0
Donation to the Poor in lieu of Garlands &c. &c.	50	0	0
	£367	17	0

The freemen dined; the corporation supped; the ringers rang; the waiters waited; the poor of Rye were richer by fifty pounds in lieu of wearing Wellesley's colours; and on these reasonable terms the obliging borough sent Sir Arthur to the House of Commons.

II

H<small>E TOOK</small> his seat in April, 1806, when politics were complicated
by the strange ministerial interlude of "All the Talents," and the
gunpowder muzzle of Charles Fox hung like a benevolent thundercloud
over the Treasury Bench. Before the month was out, he was at grips with
Paull, challenging his brother's assailant to state his charges; and Mr.
Secretary Fox, who spoke in the debate, discovered a diminished taste for
India impeachments in distressing contrast with his robust appetite when
in Opposition. A few days later Mr. Paull launched his First Charge,
rather inaudibly, and only found a seconder after a most embarrassing
pause. Sir Arthur followed with a fervent hope that the House would
"consider the feelings of his noble relative, and come to such decision as
would lead to a speedy and full discussion of the whole case"; and William testified with deep emotion to his respect for Richard. Unmoved by
this affecting spectacle, the persevering Paull retorted in the subsequent
debate that "the hon. but indiscreet Knight of the Bath was an accessory
to many of the facts," eliciting from Sir Arthur the curt answer that "as
to the observation that he himself was implicated in some of the proceedings, his short reply was, that what he did in India was in obedience to
the orders he had received; and for the manner of that obedience, and
its immediate result, he was ready to answer, either to that House, or to
any other tribunal in the realm."

It was adroit of Arthur to appear as Richard's leading advocate. The
laurels of Assaye formed a becoming ornament of the defence; and as
through the summer, his days divided between rooms in Clifford Street,
the House of Commons, and an uneasy feeling that he ought really to
be back with his brigade at Hastings, he laboured at his forensic oar.
He harried Mr. Paull with a zest once savoured in the pursuit of Mahratta chieftains, pressing him for specific charges, moving for papers, and
scrambling over discovery of documents with a professional gusto worthy
of the Temple. In July he made a Parliamentary appearance on a larger
scale, though India was still his theme; for he exercised himself at length

upon the Indian Budget, chosen hunting-ground of all sun-dried legislators, with a wealth of figures and a grasp of public finance highly creditable in a soldier. He spoke once on army matters in favour of increased
rates of pay for junior officers. Then the House rose, and he escaped from
Westminster.

Not that he found his *rôle* particularly congenial. The company was
stupid; and two sporting members, deep in discussion of their books,
were vastly entertained when the General, who sat between them, asked
gravely to what books they alluded. He informed a friend in India that
"I am in Parliament, and a most difficult and unpleasant game I have to
play in the present extraordinary state of parties." For it was not easy,
even for a skilled tactician, to align all parties in support of Richard,
though the egregious Paull ably seconded his efforts. Besides, there was
his own profession and the brigade at Hastings. After midsummer the
General resumed his military avocations in the plain little town, still
innocent of attractions and parades, where a green haze of tamarisks
hung about every street. But even there his pen was busy with a long
vindication of Richard's policy; and they still corresponded upon Parliamentary business. Sir Arthur was managing the St. Ives election for him,
securing the return of two members at the slightly exorbitant rate of
£3,500, payable within fourteen days after the meeting of Parliament.
But Westminster was plainly not his own destination. Sir Arthur was
growing restless, and his brother was informed that "it is such an object
to me to serve with some of the European Armies that I have written
to Lord Grenville upon the subject; & I hope that he will speak to the
Duke of York." His eyes had strayed from Mr. Paull to more interesting
horizons. For the war in 1806 was more widespread than ever, with the
French slowly bearing down on Prussia, a British army in the toe of
Italy, and unlikely Russians on the Adriatic. A military friend in Calabria
sent him a full account of the victory at Maida, which confirmed his own
impression that the French column could be beaten by British infantry
in line. There was even a vague notion of sending a small force to Portugal. Surely employment could be found somewhere in the world for
a Hastings brigadier.

Since his experience of active service was confined to Europe and Asia,
ministers consulted him exclusively upon operations in America. The war

with Spain had opened vast colonial perspectives; and delirious ente
prises swam constantly before their eyes. Nine hundred bayonets, fo
guns, and six dragoons were hopefully consigned into the vast spaces
the Argentine to capture Buenos Ayres; five battalions were entrust
with the flattering mission of rounding Cape Horn, occupying Chile, a
crossing the Andes; and the same lofty disregard of time and space d
tated a third project, which verged on the sublime. Two forces starti
in two separate hemispheres were to converge on Mexico. One, based up
Jamaica, had the relatively simple task of striking at the Atlantic s
board; but the other, destined for a simultaneous attack on the Paci
coast, was to travel by a route devised in Bedlam. Embarking at Madr
it was expected to proceed to Mexico by way of Singapore, the Phil
pines, and Botany Bay. The tedium of its voyage would be relieved
capturing Manilla on the way; and having sailed halfway round
world, it should arrive punctually in Mexico to co-operate with the c
tingent from Jamaica. This promising command was offered to
Arthur, "if Lord Grenville can arrange it for me, & if upon the exa
ination of the papers in the Secretary of State's office, & upon a conv
sation with the persons who have been in that Country I should thi
the plan likely to succeed, & Gov^t. should still be of opinion that i
desirable to obtain possession of Mexico." (The papers, it appeared, w
being studied at the moment by a Colonel Robert Craufurd, destined
Government for another *rôle* in their South American extravaganza, w
whom Sir Arthur was to be better acquainted.) The General confer
with the Prime Minister on the egregious project, and even wrot
paper in which it was examined with perfect gravity, arguing w
painstaking lucidity that the time-table was wholly impracticable, t
a garrison of one thousand men could not maintain themselves with
comfort on an island with a population of two millions, and tha
Mexico was to be attacked at all, the attack had better start fr
Jamaica without Pacific complications.

Small wonder that he turned almost with relief to Richard's poli
urging him to bow to the spirit of the age and seek journalistic alli
"It appears that the Newspapers have at last made such progress in g
ing what is called publick opinion in this Country, that no Man

oks to publick station can attain his objects, without a connection with
assistance from some of the Editors." Even editors and politicians might
ell seem preferable to Cabinet strategy; and in the autumn he expressed
s own readiness to come into Parliament again and even to contribute
his brother's party fund. (That week the Emperor struck once again
Jena, and Prussia crumbled into dust.) The enterprising Richard hoped
mobilise a group of eight members with a total outlay of £7,000, which
: Arthur judged to be "certainly cheap." He was prepared to sit with
em himself, and to give £1,500; for his finances were distinctly brighter,
d old Dublin debts began to melt before the rising sun of unaccustomed
luence. Not that he was reconciled in any way to a career as a back-
ncher. His battalions were being steadily withdrawn for active service,
d he was anxious to go with them—"and I don't care in what situation.
m only afraid that Lord Grenville does not understand that I don't
nt a Chief Command if it cannot be given to me; and that I should
very sorry to stay at home when others go abroad, only because I
not command in Chief." This was a very different tone from the
ignant outcries with which he had once refused to go to Egypt as
ond in command to Baird. But now all the world was in the field—
n Moore and Lowry Cole in Sicily, Beresford on the River Plate, and
n Craufurd off to some eccentric destination—and it would never do
Wellesley to remain in command of a few martello towers at Hastings.
he Cabinet detained him still with South American enquiries. He
te copiously upon the coast of Mexico, and was condemned to the
sperating company of political exiles, spies, and noblemen with bright
s. His views were shrewd, and on one vital point his grasp of
xican realities was quite surprising:

"The French gentlemen who have turned their thoughts to this subject
ave recommended that one of the French princes should be established
king in New Spain, and the English and Spanish writers have recom-
ended an independent government, without specifying of what nature it
ould be. None, however, have pointed out in what manner the govern-
ent recommended to be established in that country should be kept in
istence, carried on, and supported after the revolution should have been
ected, particularly against the attempts which might be made upon it
the United States."

133

Such foresight, exercised two generations later, might have saved Max
milian and Bazaine; and uttered by Sir Arthur Wellesley in 1806,
came near to prophecy. But though vague on the political prospects, h
was prepared to conquer Mexico with eleven thousand men and liste
the requisite supplies with admirable precision. A sounder instinct tha
the French displayed in 1861 dictated that "the object . . . upon the a
rival and disembarkation of the troops in Mexico must be to remov
them from the low countries on the coast to the higher and more healtl
parts inland. I have asked for horses, mules, and pioneers, with a vie
to this object principally." But the mirage of Mexico dissolved; and l
was left at Deal, writing stray paragraphs for Richard against the ou
rageous Paull.

That winter he returned to Parliament, elected in the first weeks
1807 for a Cornish borough which lurked obscurely under the *aliases*
St. Michael and Michael Midshall, otherwise Mitchell. He had a hou
in Harley Street; and in February, as the French felt their way acr
the snow to Eylau, a child was born there. He still favoured ministe
with his opinions on Central America, commenting shrewdly that th
high-minded action in abolishing the slave trade would scarcely enl
the enthusiastic support of the slave-owners of Venezuela. The defen
of Richard was resumed in Parliament; and once at least Sir Arthur l
his heir's cradle in Harley Street to get some hunting at Hatfield. E
before March was out, these agreeable exercises were sharply interrupt
by a change of Government. A threat of toleration for his Catholic su
jects aroused the sleeping dragons of King George's conscience, a
Whig ministers were abruptly consigned to outer darkness. Pitt's he
returned in force; Lord Castlereagh resumed the War Department, wh
Mr. Canning took the Foreign Office, and the Duke of Portland inspi
general confidence as Prime Minister in time of war by the twin circu
stances of being seventy years of age and in failing health. Sir Artl
Wellesley was invited to accept the post of Chief Secretary for Irela
The offer marked him as a Tory. But the Tories had befriended Richa
and he accepted. His reasons, which were transmitted with unusual d
cacy to the late Prime Minister, were almost wholly governed by
exigencies of his brother's position. As this manifestly demanded a T
connection—

"the only doubt I had . . . was whether I should accept a civil office the duties of which might take me away from my profession. I have consulted the Duke of York upon this point, & he has told me, that he approves of my acceptance of the office, & that he does not conceive that it ought to operate to my prejudice; & the Ministers have told me that they consider me at liberty to give up the office in Ireland whenever an opportunity of employing me professionally will offer, & that my acceptance of this office, instead of being a prejudice to me in my profession, will be considered as giving me an additional claim to such employment."

A minister on this unusual tenure, he left his infantry brigade; and in March, 1807, his career as a back-bencher ended, Sir Arthur Wellesley as Chief Secretary for Ireland.

DUBLIN resumed him in the third week of April, 1807. It was t
years since he had lived there; and both of them were change
His haunt was still the Castle. But the Castle aide-de-camp living a sha
precariously on credit was now a Major-General, K.B., and Chief Sec
tary at the eccentric salary of £6,566. He was the great Sir Arthur no
And Dublin? Dublin had waned a little. For the slow poison of t
Act of Union was working. There was no Parliament to meet on C
lege Green; coaches were rarer now in Dame Street; and fewer gent
men kept up their houses in Merrion Square. The city's pulse was slow
But Ireland was more feverish than ever. For deprived by Union of
traditional leadership of its resident gentry, an impatient country turi
from its natural leaders to more exciting substitutes. The new Chief S
retary lost his illusions rapidly. Within a month he was assuring mi
ters that "no political measure which you could adopt would alter
temper of the people of this country. They are disaffected to the Brii
Government; they don't feel the benefits of their situation; attempts
render it better either do not reach their minds, or they are represen
to them as additional injuries; and in fact we have no strength here
our army." Relief for Catholics scarcely promised a solution, since
retained in later years a strong conviction that "Ireland has been I
connected with Great Britain by the distinction between Protestants
Catholics since the Act of Settlement. The Protestants were the Eng
garrison. Abolish the distinction and all will be Irishmen alike, v
similar Irish feelings. Shew me an Irishman and I'll shew you a
whose anxious wish it is to see his country independent of Great Brii
. . . I was astonished when I was in office to find the degree in which
opinion had grown that Ireland could stand alone as an indepen
country among gentlemen of property, persons in office, and conne
with government. The connection with Great Britain has decrease
popularity since the Union, the abolition of jobs, the curtailment o
patronage of the Crown. . . ." Small wonder that as he paced a

uare in Portugal, he once proclaimed his belief that "independence is
hat the Irish really aim at, and he is therefore for giving no more, but
oceeding upon King William's plan to keep them down by main force,
r he thinks that they have too much power already, and will only use
ore to obtain more, and at length separation."

So Dublin Castle taught him to be a Tory. There are few better schools;
d Sir Arthur was a likely pupil. For the accident of his career had kept
n in the East for nine decisive years between 1796 and 1805. In those
urs the movement of ideas at home sent many thoughtful men to study
familiar topics, and the principles that underlay the Revolution were
wed by calmer eyes than Burke's. Soldiers were not exempt from
h reflections; John Moore was something of a Whig; and Wellesley
nself had owned a copy of *Vindiciae Gallicae*. But whilst the leaven
the Revolution was working in English minds, he was governing
sore. He stepped ashore again in 1805, quite untouched by any ques-
nings. The accident of Richard's grievances aligned him with the
ries; the Tories sent him to Dublin Castle; and the Castle made a
ry of him.

anded in Dublin after a most unpleasant crossing, he plunged into
duties; and before the month was out, he was knee-deep in patronage,
ensing promises with easy grace and draping refusals with profound
ets. The dissolution of Parliament doubled his work, since the Chief
retary acted as head organiser for Government in all the Irish seats,
he was soon desiring the Whips' office in London "to make me ac-
inted with the price of the day." Some borough-owners were reported
ell to the highest bidder; others were more amenable, responding to
nely hint of Church preferment for a brother. But in some lively in-
ces his martial instinct was rewarded by the tumultuous delights of
ntested election; and he reported gleefully upon the prospects of
ting out," and even "kicking out," an opposition candidate. An Irish
est had a rare flavour, affording ample scope for military attainments
, in *Charles O'Malley's* cheerful recollection—

ne adverse parties took the field, far less dependent for success upon
evious pledge or promise made them, than upon the actual strategem of
e day. Each went forth, like a general to battle, surrounded by a num-
us and well-chosen staff; one party of friends, acting as commissariat, at-

tended to the victualling of the voters, that they obtained a due, or rath
undue, allowance of liquor, and came properly drunk to the poll; othe
again broke into skirmishing parties, and, scattered over the country, c
off the enemy's supplies, breaking down their post-chaises, upsetting the
jaunting cars, stealing their poll-books, and kidnapping their agents. Th
there were secret service people, bribing the enemy and enticing them
desert; and lastly, there was a species of sapper-and-miner force, who i
vented false documents, denied the identity of the opposite party's peop
and, when hard pushed, provided persons who took bribes from the enen
and gave evidence afterwards on a petition."

Duels abounded; the military were present in force "which, when no
ing pressing was doing, was regularly assailed by both parties"; and "t
man who registered a vote without a cracked pate was regarded as a ki
of natural phenomenon." Sir Arthur's bulletins recorded that Tippera
mobs, "parading through the country with green flags and feathers," h
broken up conveyances taking electors to the poll; that the dragoo
were out; and that a Wexford candidate had killed his opponent i
duel, adding a little grimly that "as this is reckoned fair in Ireland
created no sensation in the country." He pressed reluctant voters,
proached placemen whose support of Government left something to
desired, suggested skilful arguments "on the ground of the Protest
interest and on Talbot's revolutionary speech on the first day of
election," and generally proved himself a worthy manipulator of
electoral machine. The experience was scarcely calculated to increase
respect for representative institutions. But the Irish elections of 1807 w
perhaps, the most remarkable (and not the least successful) of Welli
ton's campaigns.

His own electoral career was less adventurous. Relinquishing his C
ish seat on grounds which may be surmised from its earlier history
Michael had cost Clive so much that he was driven back to India
glory on the field of Plassey), Sir Arthur stipulated that its successor n
be inexpensive, rejected Ipswich, and with admirable simplicity "dire
Justice Day to return me for Tralee." That luminary complied; tho
Sir Arthur was simultaneously returned for Newport, Isle of Wight,
which he subsequently elected to sit. His fellow-member was a fr
faced young gentleman just down from Cambridge, who had succee

ecently as Viscount Palmerston. Till the House met, work kept him at
is desk in Dublin. He was housed comfortably at the Chief Secretary's
odge in Phœnix Park, left his bow-fronted home each morning, and
ode across the Park with the Lord-Lieutenant's daughters. They parted
: the gate (as yet unshadowed by any Wellington Testimonial); and
e rode **slowly down** the quays towards the Castle. His work was wait-
g on the table in the Chief Secretary's room; and through the summer
ays he sat writing courteous letters to his official correspondents. His
orrespondents all had wishes; and with rare unanimity their wishes
emed to run in one direction. For they invariably coincided in a disin-
rested anxiety to see deserving friends accommodated at the public
xpense. A bland Chief Secretary was "concerned that he cannot adopt
is opportunity of gratifying your wishes," politely indicated obstacles
which may, and indeed must, retard the accomplishment of your wishes,"
d confessed how happy he should have been "in being instrumental
forwarding your wishes." The gentle sibilant ran, like a mild refrain,
rough all his correspondence. But he could still be firm, refuse a pen-
on to a peeress, and write firmly to his sister that there was no vacancy
the Dublin packets, and that if there were "it may be expected that
e Duke of Richmond or I, who have been all over the world, have
val friends of merit, but not rich, to whom we may be desirous of
ving such a provision." Matters of larger policy occasionally interrupted
e absorbing business of distributing loaves and fishes. He wrote wisely
the defence of Ireland, dismissed martello towers in favour of mobile
val defence, and assumed judiciously that "Ireland, in a view to mili-
y operations, must be considered as an enemy's country." But he was
pable of moderation, and could refuse leave for a Yeomanry celebration
the events of '98 upon the admirable ground that "it appears impos-
le to celebrate the victory at Vinegar Hill without recalling . . . the
rsons over whom that victory was gained, and all the unfortunate cir-
mstances of the times which concurred to bring about that state of
airs which rendered that battle and victory necessary. His Grace can-
t believe that those who wish to commemorate their military achieve-
nt are desirous to hurt the feelings of others, however blameable and
lty they may have been; and he does not suppose that they can wish
perpetuate the memory of the unfortunate circumstances which led

to the contest in question." For long memories, the standing curse of Ir
land, were best discouraged; and a wise Chief Secretary checked th
throb of Orange drums.

Indeed, his ears were tuned that summer to the sound of other drum
For a rumour reached him of an expedition to the Baltic, and he w
soon pressing Castlereagh to release him from his desk—"It will l
understood and said that I had avoided or had not sought for an oppo
tunity of serving abroad in order to hold a large civil office. As I a
determined not to give up the military profession, and as I know that
can be of no service in it unless I have the confidence and esteem of t
officers and soldiers of the army, I must shape my course in such a ma
ner as to avoid this imputation. If, therefore, you send the expedition
wish you would urge Lord Hawkesbury to fix upon a successor for n
as I positively cannot stay here whether I am to be employed with it
not." But, for the moment, duty called at Westminster, and Sir Arthu
eye surveyed civilian ranks. For the House met in June; an Irish relat
was gaily informed that "we must get our troops over by the 22nd
this month . . . and I think your presence here in the next week
hurry the fellows away might have good consequences"; and before
month was out, he sailed for England. As they left Dublin, his observ
eye was caught by a defective pier, and he learned something on
passage about the grievances of packet captains. Kitty was left behind
Phœnix Park. For she was his little Dublin wife; and, instinctively p
haps, she stayed behind in Dublin. But Sir Arthur was back at Har
Street, deep in correspondence upon Church patronage or speaking
the House of Commons on an Irish sinecure. He was still pressing
egregious Paull to state his charges against Richard; and the Chief S
retary found himself introducing a Coercion Bill inherited from his
decessor. In the best Castle style he proposed a duration of seven ye
and experienced the unpleasant sensation of being thrown over in
debate by the Chancellor of the Exchequer. He was heard once aga
this time on Indian finance—wrote countless letters about military loa
and ecclesiastical fishes, pressed a young sailor's claims upon the F
Lord of the Admiralty with the dry commendation that they v
"founded upon his being the favourite son of his mother, who wa
favourite of yours about thirty years ago," and did his best to gov

eland from his room in Harley Street, opining tartly that "it would be st to take no further notice of the trees of liberty at Tipperary" because Lord Landaff will be tired of furnishing trees as often as those planted ll wither." One day in June, as the slow waters of a northern river irrored a barge on which two Emperors shared out the world, Sir rthur Wellesley was busy writing dutiful injunctions about a Castle former.

Small wonder that he turned with evident relief to his own profesnal prospects. For the vague expedition to the Baltic had now a less certain outline. A descent on Denmark was suddenly projected; and the last week of July ministers acceded to Sir Arthur's application to ve with the expedition—"I don't know, and I have not asked, ether I am to return to my office when this coup-de-main will have n struck or will have failed." Indeed, he scarcely seemed to mind. For r was his profession; and "no political office could compensate to me loss of the situation which I hold in the army, and nothing shall ince me to give it up." They gave him a division; and, Chief Secretary l, the strange pluralist posted from Harley Street to Sheerness and ed in the *Prometheus* fire-ship for Copenhagen.

IV

IN THE Danish expedition of 1807 Great Britain's policy again[st]
Napoleon became, for the first and last time, Napoleonic. A friend[ly]
neutral was curtly summoned to give up its fleet. True, there was reaso[n]
to suppose that France was on the point of seizing it herself. Beside[s]
Great Britain undertook to hold the ceded warships as a "sacred pledg[e"]
until the war was over. But Albion, rarely perfidious, seemed sudden[ly]
resolved to earn her title. An unaccustomed ruthlessness transformed tho[se]
amiable features; scruples were hastily discarded by the vivacious Ca[n]-
ning; King George appeared in the aggressor's *rôle*; and this departu[re]
was rendered still more shocking by its complete success.

The expedition to the Baltic was hastily diverted from its random [ex]-
ploration of seaside resorts and strongly reinforced. Sir Arthur took co[m]-
mand of the reserve, though he did not owe the appointment "to a[ny]
favour or confidence from the Horse Guards. . . . In the first place, th[ey]
thought very little of any one who had served in India. An Indian victo[ry]
was not only no ground of confidence, but it was actually a cause [of]
suspicion. Then because I was in Parliament, and connected with peo[ple]
in office, I was a politician, and a politician never can be a soldier. Mo[re]-
over, they looked upon me with a kind of jealousy, because I was a lor[d's]
son, '*a sprig of nobility*,' who came into the army more for ornament th[an]
use . . . they thought I could not be trusted alone with a division. . [. .]
When the Horse Guards are obliged to employ one of those fellows l[ike]
me in whom they have no confidence, they give him what is calle[d a]
second in command—one in whom they have confidence—a kind of [a]
nurse." Sir Arthur's nurse, a thoughtful brigadier named Stewart, w[as]
admirably chosen; and half his command came from the infantry tra[in]-
ing-camp at Shorncliffe, where John Moore forged the Light Briga[de.]
They sailed in summer weather, and he went ashore in the first week [of]
August beneath the battlements of Elsinore. His professional custod[ian]
was discreetly helpful at every turn—"during the embarkation, the v[oy]-
age out, and the disembarkation General Stewart did everything. I s[aw]

kind of objection to anything he suggested, and all went *à merveille.*" is command landed with "one simultaneous and tremendous cheer" the summer dawn to the north of Copenhagen. The city was invested; d when a Danish force that had been left at large shewed a disturbing ndency to interrupt, Sir Arthur was detached to deal with it. His plan as simple: whilst he attacked the enemy in front, a second force was sweep round and take them in rear. But chance, a broken bridge, and mebody's mishap denied him the complete success; and though he und the Danes at Kioge on August 29, attacked with spirit, and de- oyed them, he was left lamenting that "not a man would have made s retreat if [General Linsingen] had carried into execution his part of e plan; but, as it is, they have been sufficiently beat to prevent their sembling again." It was a neat performance, and the credit was all his vn. For when the helpful Stewart began to make suggestions, "I pped him short with 'Come, come, 'tis my turn now.' I immediately ade my own dispositions, assigned him the command of one of the ngs, gave him his orders, attacked the enemy, and beat them. Stewart, e a man of sense, saw in a moment that I understood my business, and sided with (as far as I saw) good humour into his proper place." The British forces could dispose of Copenhagen at their leisure now. was to be bombarded, though Sir Arthur felt a strong distaste for this m of coercion and would have preferred to starve the city. But the ns played on it, whilst he ranged the open country and exchanged valrous correspondence with defeated Danes. He met a gentleman med Rosencrantz, and resisted, as he afterwards confessed, a strong ptation to ask him after Guildenstern; a General conveyed his grati- e in imperfect English "for your human and generous conduct . . . s a great pitty that political views should counteract the private feelings he individuals"; one grateful Dane thanked him "sincerely and of my rt for the protection you have given me in these days your troops have in my neighbourhood"; and an indignant Princess, whose property been tampered with, was so far mollified by his courtly apologies its prompt restoration as to offer a shy gift of fruit—*"pleignant seule- nt qui'ils ne soyent pas meilleures"*—and to invite Sir Arthur, *"comme hevalier est amateur de chasse,"* to shoot her coverts. These amenities d into the autumn. The city fell; and in recognition of his services

at Kioge Sir Arthur was detailed to negotiate the terms of its capitulati
Then he recalled that he was still Chief Secretary for Ireland, and t
the days were drawing in—"the *long nights* are approaching fast, and
I am to have any concern in the government of that country, it is de
able that I should be there." So he was given leave at once and sai
home, shortly followed by the surrendered Danish fleet. His sole memel
of the expedition was a likely colt named "Copenhagen."

 H E world was more than usually out of joint that autumn; and
 England seemed to run before the gale under bare poles. How
udly she had sailed with Mr. Pitt for pilot and all the sails of Coali-
 set. But now the last shreds of her allies had vanished, as gust
 gust swept across Europe from the west. Austerlitz had carried
stria away; Jena took off the Prussians; and the inconstant Czar,
ken at Eylau, went dancing down the wind of Friedland. There were
allies left for England excepting a mad King of Sweden, who was too
d even to change sides. Small wonder that the Emperor, parading
rope with a troupe of kings and dealing continents like cards, shared
 the world with Alexander on the barge at Tilsit. For the world
yed him now. His writ ran from Naples to the Baltic; and the Pope
 a mere bishop—one of his bishops. He could make dukes like
 flowers (he made twenty-six that year), give laws to the whole
ntinent, leave England starving on its island, its goods shut out by
douaniers from every port. For every port seemed to be his. True,
tugal still kept a narrow doorway on the Atlantic. If so, then Portugal
st take his orders; and when the Emperor commanded, who could
y him?

ir Arthur Wellesley sailed sedately home from Copenhagen, landed
armouth, and was stopped at a country house in Suffolk to confer
 Castlereagh. There was a notion of sending him back to Denmark
continue the negotiations, but Lord Hawkesbury demurred. The
eller reached London "in high spirits." For the brush at Kioge stood
is credit, and ministers appeared to value him. Had not Lord Castle-
h written that "we shall want him for Flushing"? But fate spared
 Walcheren; and he returned to Dublin, the Castle, and his Lodge
hœnix Park. Not that he meant to stay there, since he assured a
d in India that he was even ready to return to the East, though
on't think it probable that I shall be called upon . . . men in power
ingland think very little of that country, and those who do think

of it feel very little inclination that I should go there. Besides that,
have got pretty high upon the tree since I came home, and those
power think I cannot well be spared from objects nearer home." S
Canning was informed that "I shall be happy to aid the government
any manner they please, and am ready to set out for any part of t
world at a moment's notice." Meanwhile he governed Ireland.

His problems varied. There was still, there was always the multitu
waiting to be fed; and the Chief Secretary performed his daily mira
from a diminishing supply of loaves and fishes. Tithes engaged h
deeply; and that adaptable intelligence produced a system of refo
which even included "a law to compel the residence of the clergy
their benefices." (Junot's men were winding through the passes i
Spain.) His busy mind ran on Irish education; and though Sir Arth
valued the curriculum less highly than public order—"I believe it v
turn out that there are more schools in Ireland, and more people tau§
to read and write, than in England. We want discipline, not learnin
—he was still capable of writing with sudden enlightenment that
my opinion the great object of our policy in Ireland should be to
deavour to obliterate, as far as the law will allow us, the distinct
between Protestants and Catholics, and that we ought to avoid anyth
which can induce either sect to recollect or believe that its interests
separate and distinct from those of the other. I would apply this p
ciple to the education which you intend to propose to the Board." (
marching columns of the French had left Spain behind them no
Sir Arthur wrote respectfully to the Lord Primate of Ireland enclos
a return of private schools to be filled up by his clergy; and that
Junot's ragged infantry limped into Lisbon.

With the French in Portugal, official minds began to fear a raid
Ireland, though Sir Arthur predicted wisely that the invader "n
make up his mind to the loss of his communication with France
every purpose excepting that of intelligence." His plan for its defe
was drawn upon the sage assumption that "no position will be
excepting where the troops will be"; and quite unruffled, he returne
tithes and education. One hopeful clergyman sent him a play to r
which he undertook to "send and recommend to the manager of
playhouse, but you must be aware that no recommendation of that

ᵢ ensure it success"; and as the year went out, he was opining that
ᵣeland is not a country on which the experiment of sudden and rapid
ₒrms of abuses can be tried. However enormous the latter may be,
ₑy are too inveterate and of too long standing to bear the sudden
plication of the former; but I know that neither the abuses which
st, nor the reforms which can be applied to them, have been lost
ht of since I have been in this country." How many tenants of the
ief Secretary's Lodge have stared across the Park and murmured the
ne good intentions towards the Wicklow mountains?

As 1808 came in, the Emperor pervaded Europe, and Sir Arthur
ellesley was signing departmental letters in a room at Dublin Castle.
would be forty soon; and Alexander had conquered the world at
rty-one. But as the *rôle* of Alexander seemed adequately filled at
sent, Sir Arthur was confined to writing lucidly upon the government
Ireland. His task was modest, since it scarcely amounted to more
n the preservation of an English bridgehead on a hostile island. For
land, once a little parody of England, was barely more in war-time
n a mere parody of Ireland. French agents flitted up and down;
ormers in back streets composed incredible reports or crept mysteriously
he Castle; the Tipperary mails were robbed; there was an argument
ut Maynooth; innumerable busybodies asked for official favours; and
Chief Secretary presided imperturbably over the simple operations
unrepresentative government upon a countryside whose leading crop
a luxuriant nobility. It was a singular employment for Sir Arthur,
o gave no signs of impatience. His second son was born in January;
before the month was out, he left for England to attend the House
Commons. (He was unwell, and asked the Lord-Lieutenant to keep
news from Kitty "as it is only making a piece of work out nothing.")
iness was unexciting. One afternoon he sat demurely in his place to
en to the Speaker's thanks for the Copenhagen expedition and man-
d a becoming answer. He was still capable of an injured speech upon
eternal charges against Richard; and when the virtuous Whitbread
cked the conduct of the troops in Denmark or grudged Lake a pen-
, he replied. Perhaps the predestined futility of all war-time Opposi-
s helped to make a thorough Tory of him. But he could navigate
vexed waters of a debate upon religious education with the rational

complaint that the Catholics instructed Irish children out of textbool
calculated "to breed them up in a fixed and rooted hatred to Protestants
to say nothing of the dreaded writings of Tom Paine.

But he had other interests. For Castlereagh employed him to advi
once more on operations in America. The vague design of raising insu
rection in the Spanish colonies persisted; and he conferred at length wi
General Miranda, whose company was not congenial. The revolutiona
shocked him—"I always had a horror of revolutionising any country f
a political object. I always said, if they rise of themselves, well and goo
but do not stir them up; it is a fearful responsibility." Besides, he cou
not bear Miranda's symmetrical constitutions "of a Republican for
and too regularly constructed ever to answer any practical good effe
. . . All the old institutions in the country ought in the first insta
to be maintained, and to be changed and amended only as time a
experience would point out what would suit both people and coun
better." For Sir Arthur was still Chief Secretary; and it would never d
concede in South America the very principles which he was combat
in Kerry. But he wrote careful memoranda on the prospects of a desc
on Venezuela and made detailed estimates of army stores.

As 1808 wore on, Sir Arthur seemed to be the military maid-of-all-w
of a bewildered Cabinet—"considered here very much in the ligh
the *willing horse,* upon whose back every man thinks he has a righ
put the saddle." His views were asked for on a Swedish expedition
trusted to John Moore; and when France and Russia appeared
contemplate a combined attack on India by way of Persia, he supp
ministers with the lines of a defensive campaign. But his official s
were filled with Ireland. There was still a full budget of outrages; he
deep in a scheme for providing Dublin with a police force; and fav
were asked for daily, though he was learning to be stern with applic
regretting his inability to oblige even the Duke of Kent. One nigh
confessed to the House of Commons in defence of an unduly secta
appointment that "his own opinion was, that without distinctio
religion, every man ought to be called upon to do service to the
where he was particularly qualified to do that service"; and he
even capable of drafting regulations positively countenancing th
tendance of Catholic soldiers at mass. But that week a longer shadov

cross his office table. For "the Government have lately been talking to
e about taking the command of the corps destined for Spain, which is
 be assembled at Cork"; and 1808 moved to a livelier measure.

 The air, as airs are apt to be in New Castile, was minor, the per-
rmers odd. King Charles of Spain—high-nosed for Bourbon and
rongly, too strongly chinned for Hapsburg—performed an uncertain
ss, Ferdinand his heir a piercing treble. Two voices rendered the
elody—the Queen with amorous *roulades*, and Manuel Godoy, Prince
 the Peace, with romantic *brio*. For Queen and Prince were lovers,
n and father enemies. A deeper note intruded on this discord at Aran-
ez as,

> Cannon his name,
> Cannon his voic ,

poleon sounded the dominant fifth. The voices were unfairly matched;
d the part-song became a solo. For it was barely human to put the
hless purity of that Canova profile against the collective imbecility
 a Bourbon family group by Goya. The sharp voice at Fontainebleau
ered a principality in Portugal to Godoy, a French princess to Ferdi-
d, and in a swift aside called Joseph, King of Naples, to Bayonne.
s troops were moving now. The marching columns wound through
 pale winter sunshine of 1808 down the long road towards Madrid;
ot was safe in Lisbon; and Murat, furred and frogged, jingled
ough Burgos. The air quickened suddenly in March, as King Charles
nounced his abdication and, watched by incredulous French troopers,
dinand succeeded. The uneasy vocalists were summoned to Bayonne;
 the sharp voice resolved their discords. One night in April King
dinand, who shambled in before the rest, received a message after
ner that the House of Bourbon had better cease to reign. (Sir Arthur
llesley was busy with his papers, and wrote a few days later to the
d-Lieutenant that "there is nothing new.") Before the month was
 the caste assembled at Bayonne for the strange harlequinade—the
King as Pantaloon, Godoy a sadly dishevelled Harlequin, and his
oted Queen an indomitable Columbine. The Emperor surveyed his
pe; and the charade began. (In the House of Commons Sir Arthur
llesley was harmlessly augmenting the stipends of Irish curates.)

Charles abdicated first, then Ferdinand—and Spain was his to dispo
of. King Joseph waited for his cue. But Spain was not so passive. F
beyond the mountains Murat's cavalry was sabring the *Madrileños*, ar
the dull volleys of his firing-parties rolled across Madrid: it was the fir
gun-fire of the Peninsular War. (That day Sir Arthur wrote about a pi
in Meath.) Then, their *rôles* concluded, Clown, Harlequin, and Pant
loon shuffled off the stage; the Emperor turned happily to other matte
—to Italy, to Poland, to the little son just born to Hortense (they h
better name him Charles-Louis-Napoléon), to the defences of Ancor
to the fleet, to canals in Lombardy, to Marmont's defalcations in D
matia and the prospects of a French mission to Morocco; while Sir Artl
Wellesley thought of Church affairs and entertained the House of Co:
mons with the innocent theme of first-fruits.

VI

THAT summer England heard the news from Spain. A little force
was fitting out at Cork for a raid on Venezuela; and Sir Arthur
Wellesley, just promoted Lieutenant-General and deep in preparations
for his expedition, was quick to see the chance. Some months before
he had sent out a spy to Spain "to pick up what he can find out." But
when the news came in May, he wrote ministers a paper. For if Spain
was really in revolt, "this would appear to be a crisis in which a great
effort might be made with advantage; and it is certain that any measures
which can distress the French in Spain must oblige them to delay for a
season the execution of their plans upon Turkey, or to withdraw their
armies from the north." He proposed to divert the Venezuela expedition to Gibraltar and to employ it in raising Spain against the French
by organising a general exodus of Spaniards to South America upon the
model of the loyal Portuguese, who had left Lisbon for Brazil. The
notion was experimental—"one month would probably be sufficient to
ascertain the chances of advantage to be derived from the temper of
the people in Spain"—and if none appeared, the expedition could proceed to South America according to its former plan. But the chance of
distracting the Emperor by a diversion in Spain appealed to him—"the
manner in which his armies are now spread in all parts of Europe,
each portion of them having great objects and ample employment, which
cannot be given up without injury to his affairs, afford (*sic*) an opportunity which ought not to be passed by." This simple conception, born
in May, 1808, somewhere between the Irish Office and his house in
Harley Street, brought seven years of war to the Peninsula, and raised
on the smooth surface of the Empire the "Spanish ulcer" (in Napoleon's
displeasing image) which ultimately drained its strength.

Ministers were more than usually receptive; and on June 1 Sir Arthur
wrote in greater detail of "the plan of operations at present in contemplation," enumerating with precision the quantities of stores required
for its two objectives. By June 4 ministers were talking of Wellesley for

the command; and two days later the plan had been officially espouse
by Castlereagh. Two lions waited in his path—Kitty's wifely tears an
the disappointed hopes of General Miranda. Both were alarming; an
Sir Arthur handled both with rare discretion, postponing Kitty with
warning to the Lord-Lieutenant—"Don't mention this subject, as I don
write it to Lady W. till it be positively determined"—and, by a wise pr
caution, breaking the unpleasant news to the Venezuelan patriot in
London street "to prevent his bursting out. But even there he was
loud and angry, that I told him I would walk on first a little that v
might not attract the notice of everybody passing. When I joined hi
again he was cooler." But until he cooled, Sir Arthur was follow
down the street by Spanish curses. "You will be lost," the disappoint
patriot informed that trim, retreating back, "nothing can save you; th
however, is your affair; but what grieves me is that there never was su
an opportunity thrown away." Yet Venezuela's loss was Spain's, P
tugal's, and ultimately Europe's gain.

It was decided, then. They were to try their chance in Spain *en ro*
for Venezuela; and if they made anything of Spain (the first mor
or so would show), Sir Arthur Wellesley must win his laurels e
where than on the Orinoco. At any rate, there would be laurels to v
since he had got a command. For on June 14 Majesty traced its las
uncertain signature in the top, left-hand corner of a commission appo
ing him to command a force "employed on a particular service." T
evening Mr. Croker dined with them in Harley Street; Kitty, who l
come to town, was there as well. Their guest was to take charge
Irish business in the House of Commons while the Chief Secretary
abroad; and there was some conversation after dinner upon the rous
theme of the Dublin Pipe Water Bill. Mr. Croker was inclined to arg
and suggested that his host should write him on the subject. "No, no,"
Arthur said in his quick way, "I shall be no wiser to-morrow than I
to-day. I have given you my reasons: you must decide for yours
Then his attention seemed to wander. He fell silent; and for a
nothing was said in the dining-room at Harley Street, until his g
enquired what he was thinking of. "Why, to say the truth," Sir Ar
told him, "I am thinking of the French that I am going to fight. I l
not seen them since the campaign in Flanders, when they were ca

ldiers, and a dozen years of victory under Buonaparts must have made
em better still. They have besides, it seems, a new system of strategy
hich has out-manœuvred and overwhelmed all the armies of Europe.
is enough to make one thoughtful; but no matter: my die is cast,
ey may overwhelm me, but I don't think they will outmanœuvre me.
rst, because I am not afraid of them, as everybody else seems to be;
d secondly, because if what I hear of their system of manœuvres be
ue, I think it a false one as against steady troops. I suspect all the
ntinental armies were more than half beaten before the battle was
gun. I, at least, will not be frightened beforehand." Thoughtful but
afraid, he soliloquised to Mr. Croker, and sat thinking in his chair
Harley Street of British infantry in line waiting for the French columns
attack.

At any rate, he would get back to his profession now. He had piloted
: Dublin Police Bill through Committee, and politics were palling on
n. For the Opposition intoned an endless and repetitive litany of fault-
ding, and even ministers seemed to fail lamentably in unanimity—the
t duty of ministers, as viewed by Sir Arthur. Not that his tenure of
new command was quite secure. For the veiled deities of the Horse
ards were adverse. In those discriminating eyes he was still a novice
d (what was worse) a politician. Venezuela, perhaps, might be en-
sted to such hands with safety; but the command in Spain appeared
essive for the youngest Lieutenant-General in the Army List. Ministers,
course, might feel a natural partiality for the Chief Secretary. But
le they did their best, the Duke of York had other views, and Majesty
lf was understood to frown. The Horse Guards, by the customary
ice, gave him a second in command; Sir Arthur dutifully visited
ldsor; but the outraged gods were still unappeased.

the third week of June he went off to Ireland to prepare the em-
cation of his new command. He was seen driving down Whitehall
a post-chaise and four, spent the evening at Coombe Wood with
d Liverpool, and slept at his married sister's. On the road to Holy-
d he stopped to see some old friends of his mother's at Llangollen;
the inseparable Ladies made a peculiar addition to his equipment.
they supplied a Spanish prayer-book, from which Sir Arthur "learnt,"
grateful inscription testified, "what he knows of the Spanish lan-

guage." Armed with this unusual *vade mecum*, he prepared to start f
the Peninsula. His actual destination was uncertain, since Spain w
in an uproar. The cold voice of history, wiser than usual after tl
event, may diagnose "the Spanish revolution, like a leafy shrub in
violent gale of wind, greatly agitated but disclosing only slight u
connected stems." But to contemporary eyes Spain in the early summ
of 1808 was a more heartening scene, where province after provin
assembled an indignant *Junta*, declared its independence and rose. T
French, thrown suddenly on the defensive, fumbled a little; fortresses
old as time, armed with museum pieces, failed to surrender at th
summons; and bewildered Generals faced the incalculable prospect
an endless war against an unforgiving population. The infection
revolt spread to the Portuguese, and Junot was forced back on Lisb
Great Britain, until recently so friendless, had her allies now. A ple
ing delegation from the north of Spain appeared in London; even
Whigs, unmoved by monarchs in distress, were melted by the angu
of a nation struggling to be free; and ministers enjoyed the rare a
pleasurable experience of hearing their noble sentiments echoed
Opposition speakers, when they announced a crusade in the Peninsula.
precise destination, though, was still obscure. Sir Arthur was not und
sanguine—"I think the whole question depends upon whether the Ju
of Andalusia had been assembled. If they had, and had submitted
the French Government, the game appears to be over." It had not en
yet. Indeed, it had not quite begun, with the French staring helple
into Saragossa and Dupont groping among the hills of northern Ar
lusia. Sir Arthur's orders were to drive Junot out of Portugal. He
to concentrate on that objective, though he might look in at Vigc
Corunna on his passage out; and in a cheerful whirl he made his prep
tions for departure. Old habits revived; he gave directions for the tr
at Cork to be landed frequently from their transports, as "it will t
much to the health of the men, and will make them feel less unpleasa
the heat and confinement"; he wrote with eloquence on the supe
convenience of "small tin kettles"; and in utterances that recalled
the bullocks of Mysore he made desperate endeavours to secure
ficient transport. The troops were ready now; and he lay waiting f
wind at Cork. Lord Castlereagh desired him to go straight to Portu

etaching someone to report on conditions in the north of Spain. But
ir Arthur thought better of it, and preferred to see the Spaniards for
mself, since "it appeared to me that the intelligence which I should
ceive here might decide on the expedition, and that I could trust
o person excepting myself with such a decision." He was not trustful.
or it was his way to see for himself: his strength lay in the fact—and,
rhaps, something of his weakness also. So he should sail ahead in a
st frigate, touch at Corunna, and rejoin the expedition before they
me in sight of Portugal.

Through the first days of July, 1808, he lay waiting for the wind to
from Ireland towards Spain. He was to fight the Frenchmen whom he
d not seen since Flanders; and what else had life formed him for, if
t for fighting Frenchmen? For their unholy challenge threatened his
ole tradition. His eyes had opened to the tap of heels on Dublin floors
der the marble eyes of drawing-room divinities; his first games were
yed among the garden gods at Dangan; and he learned manners at
silken knees of the Eighteenth Century. Its sad, tinkling melody had
ed his ears at home, at Dublin Castle, on College Green, at West-
ster, in the Chief Secretary's lodge. The age enfolded him; and, in-
rably eighteenth-century, he walked its minuet. But France turned
lently from the Eighteenth Century and with an impious hand waved
rope on towards the witches' cauldron of the Nineteenth. The harsh
llenge of the Revolution broke in upon the ordered dance. Hoarse
es called outside; there was a glare of torches, a sudden hammering
the doors. They splintered; and as the intruders flooded in with
d eyes and snatches of discordant song, the mounting numbers of the
rseillaise rose on the air. For the scared violins had fallen silent. The
ce had stopped. They were not dancing now. But frightened ladies
dled into corners, and their angry partners confronted a new age
drawn swords. What other course but fighting Frenchmen was
to a gentleman?

esides, it was his trade. He was by choice a soldier; and he found
ore than usually congenial to fight in such a cause. For it engaged
as deeply as a duel engaged other men, since the issue of the war
in its way, a duel. His home, his origins, his life, his century
all been challenged by the French; and now he was to meet them

on the four-square ground of the Peninsula. The trim duellist of th *ancien régime* stepped smartly forward, measured the distance with steady eye, tested his sword against the turf, and waited. A wind spra up on July 12; he put to sea at last; and by the divine inconsequence British institutions the Chief Secretary for Ireland sailed in a cruis named *Crocodile* to deal a death-blow to the French Empire.

Devers Espaigne vei venir tel bruur,
Tanz blancs osbercs, tanz elmes
    flambïus!
Icist ferunt nos Franceis grant irur.
                    Chanson de Roland.

E WAS at sea once more; and as the big Biscayan rollers staggered beneath a creaking ship, Sir Arthur crossed the Bay. It was past midsummer, 1808, and the Peninsula was waiting. That was where he was to fight the Frenchmen; and it was a noble theatre of war. For here would be room to fight in the Peninsula. Portugal, perhaps, was tightly cramped between the mountains and the sea. But Spain lay beyond; and he would find room enough in Spain. Those wide horizons would give him back the freedom of manœuvre that he had once known in India. For Spain, where interminable uplands stretched endlessly away in tall sierras, was the most spacious country in Europe—perhaps the only one (Russia alone excepted) where there was really room to fight. Vast, inhospitable distances lay between dead cities strung at intervals on crumbling roads; grey olives marched interminably across red, rounded, and unlikely hills; and discouraged rivers wandered aimlessly with shrunken waters past fantastic cliffs or died away in the wide spaces of immense, unwelcoming plains. It was all singularly baffling to Marshals trained on trim South German pastures or in the neatly chequered fields of Italy. For as they entered Spain, they passed beyond the certainties of Europe; Africa received them now; and they were left to play disconsolately across an unfamiliar stage, where cues were missed, and the scenery was ill-adapted to the triumphant tableaux of Napoleonic warfare. But to eyes accustomed to the East, the Spanish scene was less bizarre; Indian experience might serve his turn in the Peninsula; and there would be room enough to fight.

There was one drawback, though. For it was an empty land; and to fight (he knew it well) one must indubitably feed. But armies left at large to wander down the broad corridors of Spain were lamentably apt to starve. They could not hope to live in the French style upon the country, since the country barely lived itself. Great armies could support themselves in Central Europe by wayside requisition; but in Spain they must transport their food. A war of transport and supply waged across starving provinces was novel to the French; but to a soldier of the East India Company it was the most familiar mode. He was accus-

tomed to intone an endless litany of commissariat bullocks, and ha
mastered the eternal truth of Indian warfare that "if I had rice and bul
locks I had men, and if I had men I knew I could beat the enemy.
So if it was to be the bullocks of Mysore over again, it was as wel
perhaps, to be a Sepoy General.

I

He was a week at sea. *Crocodile* was a fast sailer; Ireland faded in
the haze behind them; and in the third week of July, 1808, the stern
outline of Corunna stood up out of the summer sea. The Spaniards i
the north, supported on a heady diet of non-existent victories, were mo
encouraging; and Sir Arthur, whose credulity was still undimmed by i
timacy (or any great command of Spanish), reported happily that "t
accounts of these successes, although credited, are only private; but
credit them." Then he wrote a note to the Lord-Lieutenant about t
Clare election and sailed to meet his transports off Cape Finisterre. I
left the fleet again and landed at Oporto. The Portuguese were slight
lacking in enthusiasm; but a startled bishop undertook to send five hu
dred mules to meet his force when it was landed. Sir Arthur sail
again, rejoined his transports, and coasted southwards. They were
land at the mouth of the Mondego and move on Lisbon. Meanwhi
he found a moment for a line to the Home Secretary about some C
toms patronage at Cork. Then he turned happily to more immedi:
problems.

There was strange news from Spain. Far to the south Dupont a
eighteen thousand Frenchmen stumbling through the Andalusian gla
where mud roads wander circuitously towards white villages, had walk
into a trap. Leaving Andujar in the plain, its brown towers aligned
tween the broad Guadalquivir and the green sierra, and groping unc
tainly towards the hills, he found across his road to safety a Spanish ar:
under a Swiss commander with the unlikely name of Reding. The Sw
the Spaniards, and the French fought through a blazing summer d
The Frenchman failed to clear Reding from his road; Castaños w
more Spaniards lay in his rear; and Dupont was trapped at Baylen. 7
trap closed in due form with a capitulation; and when Dupont s

:ndered, it dawned upon a pleased and startled world that the tricolour, ι spite of eagles, Emperor, and *Marseillaise*, was not invincible—grati-ing intelligence for a General hanging off the coast of Portugal with ders to drive it from the Peninsula.

His news from home was less exhilarating. For the veiled divinities the Horse Guards had prevailed, and he was to be superseded in com-and of the expedition. Ministers had done their best for a colleague; ιt, as the austere Moore recorded, "he was so young a Lieutenant-Gen-al that the Duke had objected to it." Age would be served; the Cabinet ccumbed; and as "the King and the Duke of York objected to him," mething more venerable than Wellesley must be found to drive the ench out of Portugal. For it would never do to win a battle with a nior Lieutenant-General. Greybeards abounded in the Army List; d a greybeard in command would at least save them from John Moore. ·r that Galahad was home from Sweden. His troops were added to the pedition; he had a perfect right to follow his command to the Peninsula; d if he went, he would command as Wellesley's senior. This prospect ιs distasteful to the Cabinet, exasperated by his Scottish rectitude, a ;htly Whiggish flavour, and an unhappy aptitude for being very ιrly always right. (Few qualities are less rewarding, since Cabinets, apt to err themselves, prefer a saving touch of human frailty in their truments.) It was resolved to irritate John Moore into resignation by amiliar artifice. For he was curtly informed that if he went to the ιinsula, he went as junior to Sir Hew Dalrymple and Sir Harry rrard. These paladins, both Guardsmen, were of unquestionable senior- ; one had served against Washington with Howe; and both now oyed the dignified repose reserved for governors of fortresses, Sir w residing in the flowered shades of the Convent at Gibraltar, and Harry exercising a less arduous tutelage of Calshot Castle. The ιinet, rendered aware of their existence by research (mitigated in the : of Sir Hew by some activity in his relations with the Spanish insur- ion), decreed that they should take command in Portugal. This was udied insult to John Moore, who was expected to throw up his *rôle* go off to mutter in the wings. But though the fuse was lit, no ex-ιion followed; for the tiresome man possessed, in addition to his other lities, the virtue of long-suffering. Besides, he was determined not to

miss a chance of active service. So he drove off to Portsmouth after
snappish interview with Castlereagh; and one more General was adde
to the lengthening list of Wellesley's seniors in the field.

The unpleasing news reached him as they lay off the Mondego. Th
blow was tempered by a note from Castlereagh assuring him that th
Secretary of State had "made every effort to keep in your hands th
greatest number of men, and for the longest time that circumstanc
would permit." For the Cabinet still favoured him; and Wellesley w
commended to his new commander as "an officer of whom it is desirab
for you, on all accounts, to make the most prominent use which the ru
of the service will permit." This was promising. But with Sir Hew, S
Harry, and Sir John each on his way to Portugal, Sir Arthur's days
command were numbered. He had a second in command as well; b
"I came to an immediate explanation with him; I told him I did r
know what the words 'Second in command' meant, any more th
third, fourth, or fifth in command; that I alone commanded the arm
that the other general officers commanded their divisions; that if anythi
happened to me, the senior survivor would take the command; that
contemplation of such a possibility I would treat them, but him
particular, as next in succession, with the most entire confidence, a
would leave none of my views or intentions unexplained; but tha
would have no *second in command* in the sense of his having anythi
like a joint command or superintending control; and that, finally a
above all, I would not only take but insist upon the whole and undivi
responsibility of all that should happen while the army was under
command." This was plain: until Sir Harry or Sir Hew appeared,
Arthur would command.

As time was short, he prepared to land his force; and Portugal v
told that her allies were fighting "for all that is dear to man—the
tection of your wives and children; the restoration of your lawful Prir
the independence, nay, the very existence of your kingdom; and for
preservation of your holy religion." This was strange language fror
Chief Secretary. But he was always tender of native customs (had
not kept a missionary out of Tippoo's zenana?); and in a General O
that would have scandalised Dublin Castle he prescribed a code
manners for the use of Protestant soldiery in a Catholic country:

"It is almost essential to the success of the army that the religious prejudices and opinions of the people of the country should be respected, and with this view the Lieutenant-General desires the following rules may be observed:

"1st. No officer or soldier belonging to the army is to go to any place of religious worship, during the performance of Divine service in such places, excepting with the permission of the officer commanding his regiment, and the General officer commanding the brigade to which he belongs.

"2nd. When an officer or soldier shall visit a church, or any other place of religious worship, from motives of curiosity, at periods when Divine service is not performed, he is to remain uncovered while in the church.

"3rd. When the Host passes in the streets, officers and soldiers, not on duty, are to halt and front it; the officers to pull off their hats, and the soldiers to put their hands to their caps. When it shall pass a guard, the guard will turn out and present arms; when a sentry, the sentry must present arms."

This was the statesmanship by which Mysore had once been governed. Indeed, it shewed a little more than judicious tenderness for local prejudices; for his little code concealed an ingenious measure of toleration for the Catholics in his command. As he wrote twelve months later,

"The soldiers of the army have permission to go to mass, so far as this: they are forbidden to go into the churches during the performance of divine service, unless they go to assist in the performance of the service. I could not do more, for in point of fact soldiers cannot by law attend the celebration of mass excepting in Ireland. The thing now stands exactly as it ought; any man may go to mass who chooses, and nobody makes any inquiry about it. The consequence is, that nobody goes to mass, and although we have whole regiments of Irishmen, and of course Roman Catholics, I have not seen one soldier perform any one act of religious worship in these Catholic countries, excepting making the sign of the cross to induce the people of the country to give them wine."

But his preparations were not entirely spiritual, since another order specified with his old precision the loads of pack-mules and bullock-waggons. For he was eternally the Sepoy General.

The surf that thunders along Portuguese beaches was roaring in their ears, as they landed in the first week of August. That was the ground-bass, audible ten miles out to sea and uncomfortably evident inshore in the form of drowned men and broken boats. They landed fifteen thousand strong; Sir Arthur came ashore; and presently the leading *motif* of his Peninsular symphony fell on their ears. For the dusty air filled with the shriek of solid wheels revolving slowly under bullock-carts. That shrill *falsetto* creaked its unchanging melody above all other noises; newcomers to the country always caught it first; the squealing axles were even audible to dashing Light Dragoons; and to the more delicate sensibilities of a German commissary "the scratching of a knife on a pewter plate is like the sweet sound of a flute beside them." With this music in their ears they toiled southward through the dust to find the French. They found them first across the road to Lisbon near Obidos on August 15. A scuffle ensued; and the French fell back upon an admirable position at Roliça, against which Sir Arthur two days later launched a serious attack. The ground was difficult, and he preferred to impose retreat upon his enemy by the persuasive method of outflanking rather than by the brutal (and costly) insistence of a frontal attack. But an impulsive Colonel compromised his plan, and it cost Sir Arthur close on five hundred casualties to dislodge the French from Roliça.

His southward thrust brought the French swarming out of Lisbon like angry wasps. Junot gathered thirteen thousand men and moved north to meet him. Sir Arthur's numbers were increasing now, as two more brigades from England had anchored off the coast; and he took post on the hills above Vimeiro to cover their landing. Unhappily they were accompanied by one of Wellesley's seniors. For Sir Harry Burrard was in the *Brazen* sloop; and his arrival automatically relieved Wellesley of the command. That afternoon (it was August 20), just as Sir Harry's boat was ordered to land him, Sir Arthur came on board. He was inclined to advance; but his senior, more cautious, favoured a waiting game, and Sir Arthur dutifully cancelled his orders for a fresh offensive, writing disconsolately to Castlereagh that "this determination is not in conformity with my opinion, and I only wish Sir Harry had landed and seen things with his own eyes before he had made it." Sir Harry did not land; like every traveller, he had letters to write; another night on board his sloop seemed preferable to the dubious hospitality of a Portuguese beach; and Wellesley remained in charge for a few hours longer. Perhaps it was as well. For the French moved that night; and two days later he could write gleefully to the Lord-Lieutenant that "as I am the most fortunate of men, Junot attacked us yesterday morning with his whole force, and we completely defeated him." Sir Harry landed in the morning, rode hurriedly inland to the sound of guns, and found the action in progress at Vimeiro. Sir Arthur "in few words explained to me the position occupied by the Army, and the steps taking to beat the enemy. . . . I had reason to be perfectly satisfied with his disposition, and the means he proposed to repulse them, and I directed him to go on with an operation he had so happily and so well begun." So, thanks to Sir Harry, Wellesley had his chance.

It was a simple affair. The French in their white summer uniforms came on in columns of attack, and the British waited on the ridge in scarlet lines. The columns panted uphill in the hot August sunshine, and the long lines received them with a volley and then the bayonet. As he recalled with a grim smile in later years, they came on "with more confidence, and seemed to *feel their way* less than I always found them to do *afterwards*. I received them in line, which they were not accustomed to." The columns broke; and this simple process having been repeated several times at various points, the shattered French drew off. Sir Arthur turned to his exiguous cavalry with a lift of his cocked hat and "Now, Twentieth, now is the time." He turned to Burrard too, who sat beside him on an indifferent mount, and watched proceedings through his glass, observing, "Sir Harry, now is your time to advance. The enemy are completely beaten, and we shall be in Lisbon in three days." But the rules of war lay heavy on Sir Harry. He was a pardonably cautious man; for his professional experience was almost limited to unsuccessful expeditions. So he resolved to wait once more; and once again delay was fatal to his own chances of distinction. For in the morning Sir Arthur, early on the beach, observed a fresh arrival and reported to Sir Harry, not without glee, that he was superseded in his turn by the appearance of Sir Hew Dalrymple. That thunderbolt of war was even less inclined to sudden action, since his last (and sole) experience of active service had been in Flanders fourteen years before with the Duke of York. He, too, preferred to wait on events. What could Sir Arthur do? His seniors chose to waste his victory, and he was irritably helpless.

Not that his victory was altogether wasted. For the French, with a somewhat juster appreciation of the consequences of Vimeiro, surrendered. Their action caused a flutter, since an impulsive Portuguese vedette had diagnosed the approach of a dismal little group, consisting of two squadrons of dragoons with a white flag and a French General with a slight grasp of English, as a French offensive. But when its nature was disclosed, Sir Hew received the emissary. A long afternoon of negotiation ensued—"from about halfpast two till near nine at night, with the exception of the short time we sat at dinner"—in the hot little room at Vimeiro. Sir Harry and Sir Arthur were both present, though the latter was uneasy with his new commander and disliked the terms of the armistice. As he wrote to Castlereagh on the next day, "I beg that you will not believe that I negotiated it, that I approve of it, or that I had any hand in wording it. It was negotiated by the General himself in my presence and that of Sir Harry Burrard; and after it had been drawn out by Kellermann himself, Sir Hew Dalrymple desired me to sign it." Wellesley dutifully complied, with the comment that it was an extraordinary paper, promptly silenced by his superior's retort that it did not contain anything that had not been settled.

He was extremely uncomfortable—"my situation in this army is very delicate one. I never saw Sir Hew Dalrymple till yesterday; and it is not a very easy task to advise any man on the first day one meets him. He must at least be prepared to receive advice." Sir Hew was no Advice from Wellesley was the last need he felt; and the veteran was no rendered more receptive by Castlereagh's expressed desire that he should make of Sir Arthur the most prominent use permitted by the rules of the service. For, as he testified, "those rules, and my own feelings what was due to myself, and to the distinguished Officers senior Sir Arthur Wellesley . . . would not allow of my making any extensive use of the talents of that General after my whole force was assembled Small wonder that Sir Arthur's letters grew almost plaintive—"I should prefer going home to staying here. However, if you wish me to stay, will: I only beg that you will not blame me if things do not go on you and my friends in London wish they should." Things undeniably d not. The imperfect armistice became a still more imperfect Convention; the French were to evacuate Portugal; but as the precious weeks before the autumn rains went by, the British hung uncertainly about the outskirts of Lisbon. Wellesley was more uncomfortable than ever. Slighted by Dalrymple, he found consolation in defiant presentations and addresses from his military colleagues and in angry letters home—"I am sick of all that is going here, and I heartily wish I had never come away from Ireland, and that I was back again with you." That might be compassed; but before he went, he made a singular approach to Moore. Drawn to him by a generous letter of congratulation after Vimeiro, Sir Arthur was still more attracted by Moore's chivalrous attitude: "I have told both Sir Hew and Sir Arthur that I wished not to interfere; that if the hostilities commenced, Sir Arthur had already done so much, that I thought it but fair he should have the command of whatever was brilliant in the finishing. I waived all pretensions as senior. I considered this as his expedition. . . . I should aid as far as I could for the good of the service, and, without interference with Sir Arthur, I should take any part that was allotted to me." These feelings were reciprocated on Sir Arthur's side by a positively mutinous determination to secure the substitution of Moore for Dalrymple in command of the expedition. He wrote to him at length, offering to press the Cabinet in this direction; they talked the matter over; but John Moore, always impeccable, replied a shade severely that he "could enter into no intrigue upon the subject." He was frankly disinclined to save ministerial faces by making "a submission, or anything that tended to it, which I thought unbecoming," though he admitted stiffly that he should be obliged to Wellesley or to any other friend who might remove the unfavourable impression that he had made upon the Cabinet.

There was no more for him to do in Portugal. He had declined a fatuous proposal of Sir Hew that he should go to Madrid upon a diplomatic mission; and he was equally unenthusiastic about a scheme of Castlereagh's for sending him to report upon the north of Spain—"I am not a drafsman, and but a bad hand at description. . . . I have told Sir Hew Dalrymple that I was not able to perform the duty in which you had desired I should be employed; that I was not a topographical engineer, and could not pretend to describe in writing such a country as the Asturias." He grasped the problem, though. Where soldiers like Moore irritably denounced Cabinet strategy as "a sort of gibberish which men in office use and fancy themselves military men," Sir Arthur helped ministers towards a plan. Before he sailed from Portugal, he wrote a luminous survey of Spanish prospects. His estimate showed few illusions as to his country's allies:

"I doubt not that, if an accurate report could be made upon their state, they want arms, ammunition, money, clothing, and military equipments of every description; and although such a body are very formidable and efficient in their own country, and probably equal to its defence, they must not be reckoned upon out of it; and in any case it is impossible to estimate the effect of their efforts. In some cases equal numbers will oppose with success the French troops; in others, 1,000 Frenchmen, with cavalry and artillery, will disperse thousands of them, and no reliance can be placed on them in their present state."

He was prepared to contemplate the conduct of combined operations with these allies by a British force of 15,000, which "should advance from Portugal, to which Kingdom it would be in the mean time a defence. But he drew a great distinction between the risks that could properly be taken with this relatively small British contingent and the bulk of the expeditionary force:

"The next consideration is the employment of the remainder of the army now in Portugal, amounting by estimate to about 10,000 men, with an additional corps of 10,000 men assembled and ready in England, and some cavalry. I acknowledge that I do not think the affairs in Spain are in so prosperous a state as that you can trust, in operations within the kingdom, the whole disposable force which England possesses, without adopting measures of precaution, which will render its retreat to the sea coast nearly certain. Besides this, I will not conceal from you that our people are so new in the field, that I do not know of persons capable of supplying or, if supplied, of distributing the supplies, to an army of 40,000 men (British troops) acting together in a body. Even if plenty could be expected to exist, we should starve in the midst of it, for want of due arrangement. But the first objection is conclusive. We may depend upon it that whenever we shall assemble an army, the French will consider its defeat and destruction their first object, particularly if Buonaparte should be at head of the French troops himself; and if the operations of our army should be near the French frontier, he will have the means of multiplying and will multiply the numbers upon our army in such a degree as must get the better of them. For the British army, therefore, we must have a retreat open, and that retreat must be the sea. . . .

"The only efficient plan of operations in which the British troops can be employed, consistently with this view, is upon the flank and rear of the enemy's advance towards Madrid, by an issue from the Asturias. If it be true, as is stated by the Asturian deputies in London, that their country is remarkably strong, and that it is secure from French invasion —if it be true that the ports of Santander and Gijon, the former particularly, are secure harbours in the winter—and if the walls can give to both, or either, the means of making an embarkation, even if the enemy should be able to retreat through the mountains—the Asturias is the country we should secure immediately, in which we should assemble our disposable forces as soon as possible, and issue forth into the plains, either by Leon or the pass of Reynosa. The army could then have a short, although probably a difficult communication with the sea, which must be carried on by mules, of which there are plenty in the country. . . ."

Meanwhile the British striking force of 15,000 might join the Spaniards further to the south. Their lot, he granted, would be more precarious; but he was prepared to face the risk.

"First, I conceive that there is a great deal of difference between the risk of the loss of such a corps as this, and that of the loss of the whole of the disposable force of Great Britain. Secondly, it does not follow that, because the whole British army could not make its retreat into Portugal, a corps of 15,000 could not. . . . I conclude, then, that although this corps might be risked, and its retreat to the sea should be considered in some degree *en l'air*, that of the whole disposable force of Great Britain ought to be, and must be, saved."

These bold designs differed completely from the prevailing character of British operations. For sea-power, which kept an easy line of retreat permanently open behind every British expedition, had largely atrophied strategical conceptions; and most contemporary soldiers were satisfied with "our old style of expedition,—a landing, a short march, and a good night, and then a lounge home again." Even John Moore had once made

use of the disastrous term, "a littoral warfare." But this innocuous form
of military "tip-and-run" was unlikely to modify the European situation
For in 1808 the French Empire was broadbased upon its undefeated
armies. The last word of sea-power had been spoken at Trafalgar; and
if the world was ever to be freed, the victory must be won on land
Baylen had shewn the way; Vimeiro followed; and Sir Arthur saw the
long road that lay before his country.

Meanwhile, there was no prospect of immediate operations. The French
were gone; the rains were imminent; a high official at Dublin Castle
had just died; and he applied for leave. He scarcely seemed to mind
what prospect offered, so long as Dalrymple did not darken it, since
he wrote to Castlereagh that "it is quite impossible for me to continue
any longer with this army; and I wish, therefore, that you would allow
me to return home and resume the duties of my office, if I should still
be in office, and it is convenient to the Government that I should still
retain it; or if not, that I should remain upon the Staff in England; or
if that should not be practicable, that I should remain without employment." For Dublin Castle, the Horse Guards, or half-pay were preferable
to an endless farce with a cast consisting almost wholly of preposterous
veterans—of an old gentleman who habitually alluded to the Thames
when he meant the Tagus, and the less endearing figures of Sir Harry
and Sir Hew, who lived on in his exasperated memory as "the Gentlemen." So he turned an indignant back on Portugal, and went down to
the water-front at Lisbon. A ship received him; the brown forts of
Cascaes slid by; the tall hills above Cintra receded in the autumn mist
and he was homeward bound once more.

II

His homecoming was not triumphal—quite the reverse. For the people of England, always a trifle irresponsible on military matters, had decided to resent the Convention under which the French evacuated Portugal. Opinion settled down with gusto to a noisy hunt for scapegoats, and from the accident that Dalrymple's despatch enclosing the Convention was dated from Cintra,

> "Britannia sickens, Cintra! at thy name."

This temper was excusable, since the treaty was a bitter disappointment. A defeat would have been easier to bear; for defeats were usual. But to be starved of victory for fifteen years, to thrill with the glad tidings of Vimeiro, to wait on tip-toe for a crowning triumph, and then to learn that the defeated enemy were to be shipped comfortably home was beyond bearing. The mild eyes of Mr. Wordsworth flashed fury at the outrageous thought of "turning the British Lion into a beast of burthen, to carry a vanquished enemy, with his load of iniquities, when and whither had pleased him." Small wonder that, in *Childe Harold's* memory,

> "Pens, tongues, feet, hands combined in wild uproar;
> Mayors, Aldermen laid down the uplifted fork;
> The Bench of Bishops half forgot to snore;
> Stern Cobbett, who for one whole week forbore
> To question aught, once more with transport leapt,
> And bit his devilish quill agen, and swore
> With foes such treaty never should be kept,
> While roared the blatant Beast, and roared, and raged and—slept!"

The explosion was universal and ranged the whole gamut of abuse from shrill invective in newspapers with funeral borders and angry caricatures of the three Generals wearing white feathers or dangling from gallows to Canning's bland announcement that he should in future spell "humiliation" with a "Hew."

These clouds were mounting in the sky, as Wellesley sailed for England. He reached Plymouth on October 4 and gathered his forces to resist the onslaught. His strategy was deft, since he promptly wrote a friendly letter to a leading member of the Whig Opposition. As he had written to John Moore, "I am no party man"; and at such moments there was something to be said for a slight cultivation of the mammon of un righteousness. Not that he was afraid. For his sturdy temper appeared in the note he sent to Richard upon reaching Harley Street once more

> "I arrived here this day, and I don't know whether I am to be hanged drawn & quartered; or roasted alive. However I shall not allow the Mob of London to deprive me of my temper or my spirits; or of the satis faction which I feel in the consciousness that I acted right."

The Wellesley clan was mobilised in his defence—William at the Admir alty, Henry at the Treasury, and Richard in the solemn shades wher returned proconsuls await the summons (often long delayed) to high office—whilst angry Whigs confessed themselves "not sorry to see th Wellesley pride a little lowered," and Cobbett railed against "the arro gance of that damned infernal family." The family, indeed, was veerin slightly. For their hopes, so long pinned upon Richard, were positive turning to Arthur. Their mother, with a slight lapse of tact, congratulate him on his younger brother's victory—"upon the glorious success of or Beloved Hero! God bless him . . ."—and Richard was left broodir darkly on the fate reserved for the brothers of great men. But he was st head of the family; and Kitty, sometimes a little apt to gush, poured o her troubles to him after Vimeiro.

> "Even the Hopes with which the Newspapers are filled are too agitati not to give great uneasiness. But I am a Soldier's Wife and the husband whom it is the pride of my life to think shall find that he has no reas to be ashamed of me. All promises well, the Cause is a glorious one, a Please God we shall see our friends return safe and successful. My Bo are well and lovely."

Arthur's first errand was to Castlereagh, where he did his best Moore and reported to Sir John that "I am placed under your comma than which nothing can be more satisfactory to me. I will go to Cort immediately, where I hope to find you." They never met, though; for postscript added that he must first appear in the enquiry to be held i the Portuguese *imbroglio*. Tempers were rising; and when he ask

Castlereagh to drive him to the Levée, the cautious statesman "hemmed and hawed, and said that there was so much ill-humour in the public mind that it might produce inconvenience, and, in short, he advised me not to go to the levée."

Sir Arthur had an answer ready. "When I first mentioned it," he said, "I only thought it a matter of respect and duty to the King; I now look upon it as a matter of self-respect and duty to my own character, and I therefore insist on knowing whether this advice proceeds in any degree from His Majesty, and I wish you distinctly to understand that I will go to the levée to-morrow, or I never will go to a levée in my life." Sir Arthur went.

His sovereign, who had faced mobs himself, was uncommonly civil; and whilst he was at Court, the General enjoyed the spectacle of the Corporation of London petitioning for an enquiry into the Convention and being royally snubbed. But no Government could resist the public pressure indefinitely, and a military tribunal was appointed to inquire into the late Armistice and Convention concluded in Portugal, and into "all the circumstances connected therewith." Meanwhile Sir Arthur went to Ireland, saw Kitty once again, and steadily refused to take part in the public controversy. Friends were informed that "I will publish nothing, or will authorise the publication of anything by others"; strangers who volunteered assistance in the press were faced with a polite refusal to furnish material or correct their text; and the obliging Croker, who had laid his pen at the Chief Secretary's feet, learned that Sir Arthur had "not had even one, much less all, the calumnies which have been circulated against me during my absence in Portugal." Not that he was inactive. For he corresponded with his Whig connections, read interminable arguments in his defence composed by William, and returned to London in November, when the Board was ready to sit.

It was a strange tribunal. Solemnly convened at Chelsea Hospital by royal warrant, the Board of General Officers met under the tall windows of the Great Hall. There were seven of them—three peers, a baronet, two commoners, and a knight. But the knight presided, since Sir David Dundas was blest with seniority compared with which Sir Hew Dalrymple was a schoolboy. Had he not served on one of Chatham's expeditions in the Seven Years' War? The War of Independence found him

deep in military erudition; he wrote profusely upon tactics; at sixty he
commanded a brigade in Colonel Wesley's first campaign; and now at
seventy-three, known with affectionate derision as "Old Pivot," he pre
sided in the court by which Sir Arthur and his seniors were to be tried
The other members, a galaxy of minor talent with reminiscences of Bun
ker's Hill and Pitt's less successful expeditions, presented an array o
martial eminence less formidable in the field than in White's window
Sir Hew, Sir Harry, and Sir Arthur were summoned to their bar in th
Great Hall at Chelsea, where they sat before mellow panelling not ye
ennobled by the names of Sir Arthur's victories. These instruments c
justice moved with becoming deliberation. They called for bales of co
respondence; disdaining hasty study, they listened patiently whilst a cler
recited it *vivâ voce*; they summoned witnesses and, with all eternity b
fore them, invited written narratives. Sir Hew disclosed his spite again
Sir Arthur at the first opportunity, complaining of newspaper attacks "fo
the purpose of rescuing a more favoured Officer from the unlooked fo
unpopularity of a measure he most certainly approved." Wellesley r
torted with a comprehensive denial of complicity in any press campaig
and blandly admitted his concurrence in "the principle of the measur
viz. that the French should be allowed to evacuate Portugal," addir
that he "did not think it proper to refuse to sign the paper on account
my disagreement on the details." (That day the Emperor beneath tl
spires of Burgos watched his marching columns flooding southwar
across Old Castile; for the *Grande Armée* was bearing King Joseph ba
to his capital.) Sir Arthur's narrative was put in evidence, and he m
a written cross-examination with bare, but convincing, references to t
correspondence. He was at pains to spare Sir Harry "not only out
regard to him, but because I think it fatal to the public service to exp
officers to the treatment which I have received, and to punishment f
acting upon their own military opinions." His whole difference was w
Dalrymple, and his defence was plainly stated:

"It is perfectly true that I advised the principle of the arrangeme
that I assisted the Commander-in-Chief in discussing the different poi
with General Kellermann; and that I gave him my opinion when he as
it, and when I thought it desirable to give it him. But I was not
negociator, and could not be, and was not so considered, the Comman

of the Forces being present in the room, deciding upon all points, and taking part in all discussions. If indeed, the Commander of the forces had given me instructions to negociate this instrument, and I had then negociated it, I might have been responsible for its contents; or at all events, for the manner in which it was drawn up; but as it is, my signature is a mere form."

This was plain enough; and as the case went on, he called his witnesses. The French were still in flood; Polish lancers cantered against entrenchments in the throat of a Spanish pass; and the Emperor breasted the mountains that look down on Madrid.) Sir Arthur was still answering questions beneath the picture of King Charles II, who caracoled across a wall in Chelsea resisting the discreet allurements of a whole bevy of feminine mythology. His closing speech was lucid and assured. The Board took three meetings to consider its Report, one more to draft it, and a final assembly for signature. It was December now. The French were marching north again. For John Moore, emerging warily from Portugal, had thrust into Leon "bridle in hand; for if the bubble bursts, we shall have a run for it." The run was just beginning; for the Emperor had divined the threat to the long road that wound behind him towards France and turned sharply north to meet the challenge. The hunt was up; John Moore edged northwards; and his pursuer crossed the Guadarrama in the teeth of a midwinter storm, tramping angrily among the freezing, cursing files with the snow driving in his face.

That day the Board at Chelsea Hospital signed their Report. It was a cautious document, less actuated by an overwhelming sense of justice than by a professional desire to spare everybody's feelings. It found the facts, praised Wellesley for Vimeiro, arrived at no decision on the sole point to be decided, and concluded in a mood of hazy benevolence that "no further military proceeding is necessary on the subject." The Duke of York perused it and unkindly pointed out the evasion, writing with reasonable sharpness on Christmas Day that the Convention of Cintra "has been altogether omitted." Faced with the unpleasant necessity of taking a decision, the Board (while Moore's rearguard were breaking bridges on the long road to the sea) had one meeting more and approved the armistice by six votes to one and the Convention by a narrower majority of four to three.

This terminated the proceedings, though the public mind continued
to be exercised. Mr. Wordsworth, writing at some disadvantage from his
retreat at Grasmere, explored the larger issues in the *Courier*. He quoted
Milton and the Georgics and ransacked the outer regions of Petrarch and
Dante for damaging quotations. But though he tramped up the bare
shoulder of Dunmail Raise to meet the post, polemics at long range were
far from easy; and when his noble lucubrations were expanded into "the
last great example of a Miltonic tract" and (De Quincey aiding with the
proofs) put out in a pamphlet, few of the five hundred copies were sold,
though Walter Scott agreed with his sentiments. But while disapproving
of the treaty, Scott was very far from disapproving of Sir Arthur—"I
would to God Wellesley were now at the head of the English in Spain.
His late examination shows his acute and decisive talents for command;
and although I believe in my conscience that when he found himself
superseded, he suffered the pigs to run through the business, when he
might in some measure have prevented them—

> 'Yet give the haughty devil his due,
> Though bold his quarterings, they are true.' "

But the haughty devil was relegated for the moment to the lowlier duties
of Chief Secretary for Ireland and, as 1809 came in, sat modestly behind
his writing-table at Dublin Castle. Moore's men, vowed unforgettably to
"glory, disgrace, victory, and misfortune," were reeling through the snow
to Lugo, as Sir Arthur fingered official tape once more. Ireland was quite
unchanged. The same gentlemen still asked for the same favours, and
the same Yeomanry pursued the same offenders. But Wellesley was not
disposed to govern it indefinitely. "I shall go to England for the meeting
of Parliament, and mean to join the army as soon afterwards as I shall
be allowed to go." His martial inclinations were encouraged by loyal
tributes from Londonderry and Limerick; and Castlereagh was duly
advised of his intention to "join the army if it should remain on service
in Spain within a limited time." Meanwhile Sir Arthur wrote to the
Lord Mayor of Dublin upon street improvements, and Moore turned at
bay on the jagged hills above Corunna.

The House met in January, 1809; and he was in his place to receive
the thanks of Parliament for Vimeiro. Kitty gave a parting ball in Dublin

and followed him to England. When his own pluralism was challenged
by the Opposition, he undertook to resign his civil office upon being appointed
to another command; and to accelerate, perhaps, this welcome
event he spoke in defence of the Duke of York, now labouring in sad
disgrace by reason of unkind suggestions, the sprightly Mrs. Clarke, and
the list of promotions pinned to the royal bed-curtains. There was a
long debate on the Convention; and when Tarleton spoke against it, Sir
Arthur assured that dashing relic of the War of Independence that he
would much rather follow his example in the field than his advice."
On the next day he testified before the Clarke committee to the excellence
of the Duke of York's work for the army; and before March was
out, the House of Commons heard him on the blessings that canals
could confer on Irish agriculture. It was his swan-song. For on April 7
he resigned his seat.

There was more work for him abroad; and he escaped from Westminster
with obvious relief. All Spain was now submerged by the
French tide; and as the rising waters flooded into Portugal, Cradock,
who had succeeded John Moore, waited uneasily near Lisbon. The Cabinet
(as Cabinets will in times of military doubt) looked in two directions.
For Canning fixed a fascinated stare upon Cadiz and thought hard
of campaigns in Andalusia, while Castlereagh's mind ran on Portugal.
The latter still relied on Wellesley for military advice. Sir Arthur had
not lost his confidence; his brother Charles still wrote to Castlereagh
in the Peninsula, "Would to God we had the hero of Vimeiro at our
head now"; and in March Wellesley wrote a paper for the Secretary of
State on the Defence of Portugal. His views were simple:

"I have always been of opinion that Portugal might be defended whatever
might be the result of the contest in Spain; and that, in the mean
time, the measures adopted for the defence of Portugal would be highly
useful to the Spanish in their contest with the French. My notion was that
the Portuguese military establishments, upon the footing of 40,000 militia
and 30,000 regular troops, ought to be revived, and that, in addition to
these troops, his Majesty ought to employ an army in Portugal, amounting
to about 20,000 British troops, including about 4,000 cavalry. My opinion
was that, even if Spain should have been conquered, the French would
not have been able to overcome Portugal with a smaller force than 100,000

men; and that, so long as the contest should continue in Spain, this force, if it could be put in a state of activity, would be highly useful to the Spaniards, and might have eventually decided the contest. . . .

"The first measures to be adopted are to complete the army in Portugal with its cavalry and artillery, and to horse the ordnance as it ought to be. As soon as this shall be done, the General Staff officers should go out. . . ."

They took him at his word. For when Canning's Andalusian design went thoroughly astray, Castlereagh prevailed and the Cabinet submitted Wellesley's name for the Portuguese command. Their tone, in writing to the King, was diffident. For "your Majesty's servants have not been unmindful of the inconvenience that might arise, in case of any considerable increase of this force, from Sir Arthur Wellesley's being so young a Lieutenant-General. But, as any material increase of the army in Portugal cannot be at present looked to as probable . . . they humbly conceive that your Majesty's service (without prejudice to the claims of the distinguished officers in your Majesty's army who are his seniors) may have the benefit of Sir Arthur Wellesley's being employed where he has had the good fortune of being successful, and that it will remain open for your Majesty's future consideration to make a different arrangement of the command, if, under all the circumstances, it shall appear to your Majesty proper to confide it to a general officer of higher rank." This oddly apologetic tone served his turn; Majesty concurred, and Wellesley was appointed.

It was the end of March, 1809; and he was free to go. Ireland receded now (though there was still time for a note to the Irish Office upon Mr. Croker's attitude towards the Dublin Paving Bill) and, his seat and office gleefully resigned, he made his preparations. As the Lodge in Phœnix Park was given up, Kitty would want a place in England. The Lord Lieutenant offered obligingly to let them a small house near Goodwood; but Sir Arthur thought she would be going to Malvern when the weather got warm enough. Then he went down to Portsmouth and waited for a wind. Before sailing he called for a complete print of "the Spanish Portuguese papers, including Mr. Frere's correspondence with Sir John Moore," together with a volume of evidence on Indian patronage as lighter reading in Portugal. He felt some scruples about superseding Cradock and, with a lively recollection of his own embarrassments at

imeiro, declined to do so "if he had been in any manner successful";
or Sir Arthur was disinclined to play the *rôle* of Sir Hew. For days he
ared across the Solent, waiting for a wind; and when it blew, it blew a
ale. *Surveillante* sailed; and as they pitched down-Channel in the roaring
arkness, the despairing captain thought of running them ashore on the
le of Wight. It was just bedtime, when an excited aide-de-camp in-
rmed Sir Arthur that it would soon be all over with them. "In that
se," his studiously undramatic chief replied, "I shall not take off my
ots."

III

IT WAS the month of April, 1809, when he sailed once again for t]
Peninsula. Each time the curtain rose on a new scene to the sar
overture. For each chapter of his life appeared to open with the sar
interlude at sea. The boatswain piped, blocks creaked, the waves we
dancing by, and the sea-wind sang in the halyards. Sometimes it w
the Dublin packet taking a small boy to England, sometimes a transp
ferrying an anxious Colonel to his first campaign; tall East Indiam
carried him round the Cape and up the Hooghly to Calcutta or, mo
respectful of their passenger, sailed up-Channel homeward bound w
a tanned General. It was not long since *Crocodile* had stood across
Bay, taking an eager man to Portugal; and now he sailed in the sa
track for the last time. For five busy years he knew the sea no mo
since the Peninsula was waiting, its mountains ranged behind the mi
and his road wound endlessly across the bare hillsides, past empty tov
and dim cathedrals, until the folded mountains lay all behind him ;
he could look back to Spain. France lay before him then, mile a
mile, spread out below the Pyrenees. When he next stepped on bo
ship (it was at Calais), a Duke came up the gangway and a discar
Emperor sat idly in the sunshine of 1814, watching the summer w;
that broke on Elba. But now it was mid-April, 1809; and the l
road still lay before him, winding all the way from Lisbon to
Pyrenees.

He would be forty in a week or so; and Alexander, he could
reflect, had conquered the world at thirty-one. But then, had Alexa
governed Mysore or sat in the Chief Secretary's room at Dublin Ca
These odd preliminaries of conquest had filled Sir Arthur's life. (Per
they taught him lessons Alexander never knew.) Besides, Sir Ar
took his time. Rarely impulsive, he proceeded with a measured tr
and now his sober pace took him once more to Portugal. If figl
Frenchmen was his business in life, there were Frenchmen in abund
to be fought in the Peninsula. Life, indeed, seemed to hold little els

m. For he was not leaving much behind. There was always Kitty,
be sure. Poor, fluttered Kitty did her best to be "a Soldier's Wife." He
as her pride—the slightly alarming object of her veneration. But what
as she to him? When England dropped below the horizon, Kitty, one
els, dropped with it. His fancy was unvisited by images of Kitty; or
they came to him, they wore a slightly exasperating aspect—of Kitty
th her frightened manner running into debt, or sitting in the big
rouche with her face hidden in a book. He hated debts; he had seen
bts enough when he was young; but Kitty could never manage money
d was too shy to tell him until she had fallen into arrears. And then
e always read a book when she drove out, because she was dreadfully
ort-sighted. For Kitty could never recognise the bowing figures in the
opic haze along the pavement and sought refuge in her book—un-
rthy artifice for the wife of a coming man. Small wonder that, as he
e steadily, she lagged a little. For she was born to be his Dublin
e; and as Dublin receded, Kitty—short-sighted, muddled about ac-
unts, and a little scared—receded with it. She was uneasy, too; for
the news of his next victory, her brother expressed without undue
fidence a hope that "it may ultimately produce as much comfort to
family as honour to his Country." It evidently had not brought
ch comfort yet.

o Kitty waited for the news in Harley Street, and the ship sailed
taking Sir Arthur back to the Peninsula. He was not leaving much
ind. Perhaps the thought made him a little hard when other men
lied for leave. Perhaps the dusty distances of Spain dried up some
ng with him. At any rate, the void at home left him free to con-
rate upon his problems. His plan was formulated on paper within
days of his arrival at Lisbon:

"I intend to move towards Soult, and attack him, if I should be able
make any arrangement in the neighborhood of Abrantes, which can give
e any security for the safety of this place during my absence to the
rthward.

"I am not quite certain, however, that I should not do more good to the
neral cause by combining with General Cuesta in an operation against
ictor; and I believe I should prefer this last, if Soult were not in pos-
ssion of a part of this country which is very fertile in resources and of

the town of Oporto, and if to concert the operations with General Cuest
would not take time which might be profitably employed in operation
against Soult.

"I think it probable, however, that Soult will not remain in Portug
when I shall pass the Mondego: if he does, I shall attack him. If he shou
retire, I am convinced that it would be most advantageous for the commo
cause, that we should remain on the defensive in the north of Portugal, an
act vigorously in co-operation with Cuesta against Victor. . . .

"I am convinced that the French will be in serious danger in Spa
only when a great force shall be assembled which will oblige them to co
lect their troops; and this combined operation of the force in this countr
with that under General Cuesta, may be the groundwork of further measur
of the same and a more extended description."

The design was simple—a thrust at Soult in northern Portugal, fo
lowed by a joint Anglo-Spanish attack upon the French in centr
Spain. He made his customary preparations, assembled bullock car
called loudly for horse transport, and reviewed in detail the supply
rangements of his Portuguese allies. His flank was shielded from t
French in Spain by the simple-minded expedient of collecting all t
boats in which they might have crossed the flooded Tagus. Then
moved northwards against Soult. One novelty was introduced into
command. For he attached a company of riflemen to his infantry briga
—a memory, perhaps, of early reading in Lloyd's *History of the t
War in Germany* (purchased by Colonel Wesley in 1796 before his v
age to India), assisted by his observation of the French columns of
tack at Vimeiro. A strange interlude engaged him, when a French C
tain of Dragoons appeared mysteriously in the British lines. His story
obscure. Soult, it appeared, assuming royal airs at Oporto, encoura
crowds of Portuguese to shout for "King Nicholas." After all, if M
was King of Naples and Joseph Bonaparte of Spain, there could be
impropriety in Soult's becoming King of Northern Lusitania. Cro
were in fashion; but some of his brother-officers, either from env
revolutionary austerity, resented the new mode and were prepare
kidnap the aspirant, if Wellesley would oblige with a timely offen
Furtive interviews with mysterious strangers were not Sir Arthur's f
nature had not designed him for a conspirator. But he saw Argenton

icked up some useful information upon Soult's dispositions, though
e retained his determination that he "should not wait for a revolt,
ut shall try my own means of subduing Soult." His visitor returned
ne night. They met over a camp-fire beside the road; and Argenton re-
eated his incitements, obligingly presenting Wellesley with a paper upon
oult's line of retreat. But Sir Arthur persisted in his endeavour to eject
oult from Portugal by fair means, leaving Argenton to a feverish
areer of hairbreadth escapes that was ended, before the year was out,
y a French firing-party at Grenelle.

His march towards the French continued through days bright with
owers showering from grateful windows and nights thrilling with false
arms and the never-ending song of frogs. Soult was still waiting for
m at Oporto, sweeping the seaward sky for a first glimpse of his sails.
ut Sir Arthur was ashore and marching north. True, the broad Douro,
wing beneath its cliffs, glinted between his marching columns and the
wn; but had not fording Indian rivers formerly been one of his
complishments? Some barges were discovered; the bank was quite
guarded; and one morning he launched a surprise attack with the
obtrusive recklessness of his gruff "Well, let the men cross." The
ounding throw succeeded; and the French, surprised in broad day-
ht, were hustled out of Oporto on May 12 at a cost of one hundred and
enty British casualties. Soult, headed off from every practicable road,
nged miserably off in driving rain into the hills towards the north.
s guns, his bullion, and his stores were sacrificed; and after a week
arduous retreat by winding tracks that hung precariously above terri-
ng gorges a starving, tattered mob, that had once been the Army of
rtugal, staggered to safety in the first Spanish town. Sir Arthur's
ning move was a complete success, though he wrote home resentfully
t "if the Portuguese troops had been worth their salt," his adver-
y "would have been hard pressed and probably could not have
ped." A fortnight had sufficed him to manœuvre Soult out of Orporto,
l in less than four weeks from his landing he had cleared Portugal.
hen he turned south again to carry out the second part of his design
deal with the French in central Spain, writing briskly to a colleague
"as you have seen Soult out, you might as well see what we can
ith Victor." Much might be done with Victor. For the operations of

the French were unco-ordinated beyond Sir Arthur's wildest dream
King Joseph hunted his rebellious subjects with a divergent pack o
Marshals, who bayed in all directions—Junot and Mortier in Arrago
Ney in Galicia, St. Cyr in Catalonia, and Sebastiani among the dust an
windmills of La Mancha. At intervals King Joseph sounded an ineffectu
horn; and at longer intervals the post brought Imperial rescripts full o
detailed instructions in the familiar *staccato* manner, months out o
date and hopelessly inapplicable to Spanish conditions. The Emperc
deep in another war, was off again in Central Europe; and the sha
voice came faintlier now from bivouacs along the Danube—from Ec
mühl, from Ratisbon, and at length from the echoing corridors o
Schönbrunn. Left almost to themselves, the Marshals plunged about Spa
a little wildly, and Sir Arthur had an unequalled opportunity to inte
rupt their gambols. Far to the north Soult irritated Ney; Ney revil
Soult; their officers fought duels freely; and a Marshal's sword w
positively drawn upon a brother-Marshal. Small wonder that their ope
tions lacked unity of purpose, and that the King of Spain was left
learn the news of Soult's eviction from Oporto by the circuitous route
a despatch from Paris. Victor, in this strategic whirlpool, had essay
an isolated thrust almost up to the Portuguese frontier; and if the ripo
were swift, much might be done with Victor.

But Sir Arthur had allies, and the delights of combined operations w
a Spanish army were new to him. He was already equal to the shag
geniality of up-country *guerrilleros*, all side-arms and moustaches;
grave-eyed generals by Goya, whose elaborate courtesy almost invaria
ran to full uniform and decorations but rarely kept appointments, w
a more serious affair. His present collaborator was Don Gregorio de
Cuesta, Captain-General of Estremadura. This paladin, now ris
seventy, was less menacing as an adversary than as an ally; for he loo
back upon an uninterrupted record of sanguinary (and frequently av
able) defeat. Composed in equal parts of pride and failing health, he
the embodiment of Spain at its very worst—old, proud, incompetent,
ailing—and Sir Arthur could hardly hope to have a more instruc
object-lesson in the joys of allied operations. With his illusions str
upon him he moved southward, while Cuesta proffered imbecile s
gestions for a combined attack on Victor, which rested on the

ypothesis that Victor would oblige by keeping absolutely still while
ney annihilated him at leisure. But Victor, who had not been trained in
uesta's school, fell back. Sir Arthur was not altogether easy, though for
ne moment the causes of his uneasiness were domestic. For his army
ave him grave reason for dissatisfaction. Discipline left much to be
esired. As he wrote, "we are not naturally a military people; the whole
usiness of an army upon service is foreign to our habits . . . particularly
a poor country like this." He hated looting and wrote angrily that "I
ave long been of opinion that a British army could bear neither success
or failure, and I have had manifest proof of the truth of this opinion
the recent conduct of the soldiers of this army. They have plundered
e country most terribly. . . ." The Government was pouring its best
oops into the thirsty levels of Walcheren; and perhaps Sir Arthur got
ore than his share of Irish units. At any rate his complaints ended in a
im announcement: "the army behave terribly ill. They are a rabble who
nnot bear success any more than Sir John Moore's army could bear
lure. I am endeavouring to tame them. . . ." Besides, supplies were
ort (these were the days when he assured a ruffled commissary that
a General had really threatened to hang him, he would keep his
rd); and Mr. Huskisson at the Treasury was slow in meeting his de-
nds for currency.

ut he moved slowly forward, writing cheerfully that "the ball is
w at my foot, and I hope I shall have strength enough to give it a
d kick." In the last week of June they left Abrantes; on July 3 they
sed the frontier into Spain; and for ten days they lay at Plasencia.
en he reviewed the Spanish army and knew the worst. He reviewed
owing to a slight lapse of Spanish staff-work, at night; but even by
ch-light the aspect of his allies was far from reassuring, and their com-
nder's scarcely more so. For Cuesta, whose cavalry escaping hastily
n his last defeat had ridden over him, was in the habit of command-
from a coach, though he had been hoisted for the occasion on to a
se, where he was precariously maintained by pride and two assistants.
had already impressed Sir Arthur in correspondence with being "as
inate as any gentleman at the head of any army need be," and he was
easier in conference, where his refusals to comply with his ally's sug-
ions were filtered through an English-speaking Chief of Staff named

(with a friendly reminiscence of Dublin) O'Donoju. Victor was waiting
for them near Talavera by the slow waters of the Alberche. When the
came up with him, Cuesta was lifted from his coach, deposited upon it
cushions, and invited by Sir Arthur to co-operate in an attack; but th
chance was missed. The French fell back once more; and his enemy hav
ing withdrawn, Cuesta became unnaturally enterprising. Faint but pu
suing in his coach, he pressed after them across the endless plain tha
rolled dustily towards Madrid, leaving Wellesley at Talavera darkl
resolved to go no farther. Cuesta grew "more and more impracticab
every day. It is impossible to do business with him, and very uncertai
that any operation will succeed in which he has any concern." Besides, h
could not move without supplies; the Spaniards fed themselves and le
their allies to starve. So he resolved to halt and, if necessary, withdra
from Spain. Meanwhile, the impulsive Spaniards in full cry towar
Toledo and Madrid, stumbled into forty thousand Frenchmen wi
Marshal Jourdan and King Joseph at their head and hastily fell ba
towards Sir Arthur. He watched them streaming in and begged his c
league to retreat a little farther. The Spaniards, he conceived, would n
be at their best, if they engaged the French with a river immediately
their own rear. So he sought Cuesta; but his ally was invisible. It was
July afternoon, and the old General was (not unpardonably) sleeping
his retreat. Sir Arthur interrupted his prolonged siesta and found h
more than usually obstinate. For if it was bitter to have lost the brig
vision of Madrid, whose gleaming towers had danced before his ea
eyes during the brief advance, would it not be galling beyond words
watch his ragged, scared battalions trailing back under the cold eyes o
contemptuous ally? Sir Arthur pleaded, argued, coaxed, and positiv
knelt to the exacting mummy to whom fate had bound him as an a
Then the old *hidalgo's* pride was satisfied; and he consented to fall ba
a little farther. The British were to stand on the green hills that shoul
their way towards the plain of Talavera. The mules of Cuesta's co
jingled incongruously by; and as the old gentleman sat in the shadow
cross on the roadside, his staff scandalised a German commissary by sta
ing round with cigarettes. There was a scuffle, as the French passed
Alberche; Sir Arthur galloped to the front and was almost caught am
their skirmishers. Then he rode off to rally the agitated Spaniards in

dusty plain between Talavera and the green hills that climbed towards the
all sierra. Their officers appeared to have abdicated; and the Sepoy General, who was not unaccustomed to fluttered auxiliaries, took charge
himself.

That night (it was July 27-28) his command was roughly aligned to the
north of Talavera facing eastwards, and the brook Portiña crawled
along their front. The position—half hillside, half dusty levels—had nothing very much to commend it. But at least his troops were all assembled
here, and the French, it seemed, would be good enough to attack. They
were; indeed, they did so in the night. They attacked again at dawn; and
through the heat of a long summer day they flung themselves against the
scrubby sides of the Portiña gorge or streamed across the plain. Sometimes there was an interval, when panting men crept to the little stream
between the armies and gulped its uninviting pools. But Wellesley cantered up the line or sat watching on the green hill that looks across
Talavera and its brown towers to the carved cliffs beyond the Tagus.
Once a spent bullet bruised his chest. But the day faded, and the French
attacks died down. King Joseph saw his armies fail; and in the night
they marched away. Judged by the strictest tests, it was a muddle. For Sir
Arthur insisted upon doing everything himself; and as he could not be
everywhere at once, there were imperfections. But a muddle ending in the
retreat of forty thousand French before twenty thousand British was a
victory.

He was more hopeful now, "after two days of the hardest fighting I
have ever been a party to." For in the morning Robert Craufurd brought
up the Light Brigade (which later years swelled to the Light Division),
having marched to the sound of the guns and covered forty-three miles in
twenty-two hours at Moore's celebrated quickstep of three paces at a
walk alternating with three paces at a run. Small wonder that Sir
Arthur wrote that day, "We shall certainly move towards Madrid, if not
interrupted by some accident on our flank." But his instinct was sound
enough. The accident occurred, since the next day brought news that the
French had come down from the north behind him and were threatening
the homeward road to Portugal. The pack of Marshals were all baying in
the same direction now, Jourdan and Victor in front of him, and Ney and
Soult behind. So there was nothing for it but retreat. That, indeed, would

probably have been imperative even without the French. For if he stayed much longer in the parched valley of the Tagus, he was faced with a prospect of starvation. In the first week of August he wrote grimly that it was "almost impossible" for him to stay in Spain—"a starving army is actually worse than none. The soldiers lose their discipline and their spirit. They plunder even in the presence of their officers . . . and with the army which a fortnight ago beat double their numbers, I should now hesitate to meet a French corps of half their strength." This was unpleasing, and their situation was not improved by their allies, who were apparently content to let them starve. Sir Arthur's pen poured acid in all directions. Lisbon was informed that "we are starving, and are ill-treated by the Spaniards in every way. . . . There is not a man in the army who does not wish to return to Portugal"; Lord Castlereagh learnt that "we want everything and can get nothing; and we are treated in no respect as we ought to be; and I might almost say not even as friends"; and Spanish statesmen were naturally aghast at his resolve to leave the country.

"I am fully aware of the consequences which may follow my departure from Spain. . . . But I am not responsible for these consequences, whatever they may be. Those are responsible for them who, having been made acquainted with the wants of the British army more than a month ago, have taken no efficient measures to relieve them; who have allowed a brave army, that was rendering gratuitous services to Spain, that was able and willing to pay for every thing it received, to starve in the centre of the country, and to be reduced by want almost to a state of inefficiency; who refused or omitted to find carriages to remove the officers and soldiers who had been wounded in their service, and obliged me to give up the equipment of the army for the performance of this necessary duty of humanity."

Now he had no illusions left about his allies and wrote bitterly to Castlereagh that "the information which I have acquired in the last two months has opened my eyes respecting the state of the war in the Peninsula." The sole accomplishment of Spanish troops appeared to be rapid dispersal followed by "reassembly in a state of nature"; and his angry litany was echoed in the shrinking ears of the Junta by a majestic voice. For Richard had consented to appear in Seville as Ambassador Extraordinary.

It was a strange reversal. For he was Arthur's armour-bearer now.
There were odd visitors to the Peninsula that summer. Lord Byron walked
he quays of Lisbon, admiring "Cintra's glorious Eden" and noting how

> "Fandango twirls his jocund castanet,"

neditated freely upon history, legend, and current politics, and passed on
o meditate at appropriate points along the Mediterranean and to carve
is name upon selected fragments of the antique. But Lord Wellesley was
stranger visitor, running civilian errands in Seville, whilst Arthur won
is battles. His family, which had no tact, was always congratulating him
n Arthur's latest triumphs; and here he was, a mere second on the field
: honour, writing dutiful reports to Canning in place of Mr. Frere. That
lept at light verse had vanished; and, the sublime succeeding the ridicu-
us, Lord Wellesley occupied his post. But the requisite diplomacy was
uite to Richard's taste, since his leading duty was to make the Spanish
overnment feel small. This feat was well within Lord Wellesley's range.
deed, it was his *forte*. He echoed Arthur's strongest invectives to the em-
rrassed Spaniards and derived unlimited satisfaction from informing
e of them with stately vehemence that he "would not trust the protec-
n of a favourite dog to the whole Spanish Army."
But strong language could not mend Sir Arthur's case or feed his
ops; and he retreated sulkily, slanting south-west towards the Portu-
ese frontier on the Guadiana. His mind was quite made up—"I have
ned in many troubled waters, but Spanish troubled waters I will never
n in again." There were to be no more combined operations, and he lay
tably at Badajoz. But there were compensations. For Cuesta, worn out
last—or shocked by his unaccustomed participation in a victory—had a
oke. Besides, Talavera brought recognition to Sir Arthur. The Spani-
ls gave him presentation chargers and the rank of Captain-General
which he declined the pay, refusing "to become a burden upon the
unces of Spain during this contest for her independence"); the House
Commons voted him £2,000 a year for three years; and his sovereign
s moved to elevate him to the peerage. He was to be a Viscount; and
problem of his title raised questions of rare delicacy which William
dled for him, while Kitty and her boys were by the sea at Broadstairs.
could not well include Talavera in Arthur's style without Spanish

consent; and if he made any reference to Wellesley, what would Richard
say? Some feudal ancestor, it seemed, had held lands near Wellington. So
much was safe; and William risked the rest. The General should become
Baron Douro of Wellesley and Viscount Wellington of Talavera; and in
the autumn of 1809 Sir Arthur vanished in the new glory of Lord
Wellington.

IV

THE leaves of 1809 were falling, as the last addition to the Peerage waited in Estremadura with his back to Portugal. He signed his new name for the first time on September 16 to the usual letter about biscuit and cash balances (for Lord Wellington was very like Sir Arthur), adding a modest application to the Portuguese for leave to shoot a royal covert across the frontier. (His prayer was granted, and subsequent advices record his prowess with ball cartridge among the Braganza deer.) But though Sir Arthur was unchanged, the scene was changing round him. For the French wound homewards from Vienna with the name of Wagram on their eagles. Now there was time for them to think of Spain once more. Berthier was to be Chief of Staff there; a hundred thousand men were on the march for the Pyrenees; and as his cavalry jogged southward once again and booted Marshals in their blue and gold tilted enormous hats and muttered about Spain, the Emperor spoke of going with them. But he stayed behind that autumn, detained in Paris by an ageing, pretty woman who trailed about the Tuileries holding her head low so that they might not see how red her eyes were; and as Josephine dragged miserably towards divorce, his armies surged into Spain once more. The English, waiting for their impact, were a shade distracted by the news from home. True, the new Viscount received the comforting intelligence that his brother Henry was to be Minister at Lisbon, prompting Lord Byron to the ribald enquiry

> "How many Wellesleys did embark for Spain,"
> As if therein they meant to colonise.

But the family *bloc*—Arthur at Badajoz, Richard at Seville, and Henry at Lisbon—was soon dislocated. For the Government collapsed with the consonance peculiar to governments in war-time. The Duke of Portland, who was still Prime Minister (if only people could remember it), was then ill. That did not matter much. But his surviving colleagues failed to agree on a successor. The Foreign Secretary refused to serve under the

Chancellor of the Exchequer; the Chancellor returned the compliment
the Secretary of State for War resigned and (better still) fought a due
with the Foreign Secretary; the Prime Minister, who had been quite for
gotten in the scuffle, resigned as well; and with these agreeable prelimin
aries his startled country passed to the rule of Mr. Spencer Perceval, K. (
This modest figure (one contemporary termed him with friendly di
paragement an "honest little fellow") assumed the disconcerting task (
forming a Cabinet in circumstances strongly reminiscent of Casabianca'
Canning and Castlereagh, the duellists of Putney Heath, had gone; b
since the pressing needs of war and foreign policy had not gone wit
them, Perceval adopted the expedient of bringing Richard Wellesle
home from Seville to the Foreign Office and giving the War Departme
to Lord Liverpool and the rosy-cheeked young Palmerston (who thoug
it "suited to a beginner"). This was grave for Wellington, since Castl
reagh had always been his sponsor at the War Office, and he wrote
him in grateful terms:

> "It would appear that your friendship for me, of what I believe in t
> instance referred to I ought more properly to call your sense of what w
> just to me and others, was the original cause of the dissatisfaction of yo
> colleague. . . .
> "I have experienced many acts of friendship and kindness from y
> If I had been your brother you could not have been more careful of
> interests than you have been in late instances, and on every occasion it
> always appeared to me that you sought for opportunities to oblige me a
> to mark your friendship for me; of all which I assure you that I
> not forgetful."

The scene was changing fast. He had new masters now; that was a no
(and not particularly reassuring) circumstance in Wellington's rear.
who could tell how far Lord Liverpool would share Castlereagh's
lightened taste for Peninsular adventures? True, Richard could answ
for his brother in Cabinet. But since Walcheren had failed, overseas
peditions were a trifle out of favour. In front of him the change
almost as disconcerting, since the French flood was gathering. The tra
of marching feet came nearer; the Young Guard were filing through
passes of the Pyrenees; and he could almost catch the sharp orders of
Emperor. There was one consolation, though: the Spaniards remai

almost wholly unaltered. For they passed the autumn in their customary pastime of superfluous defeats, engaged, as he wrote bitterly, in "doing Bonaparte's business for him as fast as possible"; and after Tamames and Ocaña Wellington occupied the position of an allied General with the unusual advantage that his allies had been annihilated.

But there was still Portugal; and while Portugal remained, he had his plan. So early as the month of August, in the hot weeks that followed Talavera, he faced the problem:

"The next point in this subject is, supposing the Portuguese army to be rendered efficient, what can be done with it and Portugal, if the French should obtain possession of the remainder of the Peninsula? My opinion is, that we ought to be able to hold Portugal, if the Portuguese army and militia are complete.

"The difficulty upon this sole question lies in the embarkation of the British army. There are so many entrances into Portugal, the whole country being frontier, that it would be very difficult to prevent the enemy from penetrating; and it is probable that we should be obliged to confine ourselves to the preservation of that which is most important—the capital.

"It is difficult, if not impossible, to bring the contest for the capital to extremities, and afterwards to embark the British army. . . . However, I have not entirely made up my mind upon this interesting point. I have a great deal of information upon it, but I should wish to have more before I can decide upon it."

sound instinct told him that when the French arrived in force, "their first and great object will be to get the English out"; and as the autumn passed, his mind was busy with his plan for a defensive. As usual he must see the ground for himself; and in October he slipped away to Lisbon. Twelve months before, in the exasperating days that followed Vimeiro, he had tried to break into Lisbon, while Junot lay among the big hills in front of Torres Vedras. He would see Torres Vedras once again; for Torres Vedras might serve his purpose now. So he spent half October riding in and out among the great green hills that climb along the sky; the bare ruin of a Moorish keep above the little town watched him go by; and before he left, he had composed a Memorandum of twenty-one pre-cise instructions for his Engineers. He saw more besides; for that watchful detected a mule-cart which a Major of Light Dragoons had appro-

priated for his own baggage, and a visit to a Lisbon theatre inspired the
acid comment that "officers who are absent from their duty on account of
sickness might as well not go to the playhouse, or at all events upon the
stage, and behind the scenes."

The plan was clearer now. He should not stand upon the frontier—
"the line of frontier of Portugal is so long in proportion to the extent and
means of the country, and the Tagus and the mountains separate the
parts of it so effectually from each other, and it is so open in many
parts, that it would be impossible for an army acting upon the defensive
to carry on its operations upon the frontier without being cut off from the
capital." He should stand nearer to the sea, because (as he wrote later)
"when we do go, I feel a little anxiety to go, like gentlemen, out of the
hall door, particularly after the preparations which I have made to enable
us to do so, and not out of the back door, or by the area." So he prepared
the hall, devising for his adversary an impenetrable blend of field fortification and mountain warfare; and bewildered Portuguese were se
digging on the tumbled sky-line above Torres Vedras.

Then he was back at Badajoz, posted to Seville, saw Richard off t
England from Cadiz, and returned to his command once more. A bus
winter lay before him. For if he had resolved on making Portugal
fortess, someone must organise the Portuguese. Their army and militi
vigorously drilled by British officers and re-equipped in a fair semblan
of British uniform, were slowly coming into shape under Beresford. F
Wellington had little faith in patriotic emotion as an unaided instrume
of national defence and passed a shrewd judgment on the French:

> "As to the enthusiasm, about which so much noise has been made ev
> in our own country, I am convinced the world has entirely mistaken
> effects. I believe it only creates confusion where order ought to prevail .
> and I fancy that, upon reflection, it will be discovered that what was deem
> enthusiasm among the French, which enabled them successfully to resist
> Europe at the commencement of the revolution, was force acting through t
> medium of popular societies and assuming the name of enthusiasm, a
> that force, in a different shape, has completed the conquest of Europe a
> keeps the continent in subjection."

At any rate, the Portuguese (unlike the Spaniards) were to wear
strait-jacket of British discipline; and, to do them justice, they wore

with some credit. A sterner test awaited them, since his reading included "*Mémoire de la Campagne en Portugal, l'an 1762,*" and "Correspondence relative to the War in 1762," and he had resolved to use their ancient weapon of the *Ordenanza.* As an historian of the Spanish war of 1762 had written, the King of Portugal commanded "his subjects to fall upon the invaders, and the national hatred always excites them to execute the Ordinance.' As the Spanish army pushes on, the villages are depopulated, and the inhabitants fall back on the capital." That was the plan—an exodus before the French, leaving an empty countryside in front of them. For starvation was to be the glacis of his fortress.

His mood was almost cheerful now, since the plan stood clearly in his head. That autumn he got "pretty good sport" after the red deer near Badajoz; and the new Cabinet agreed with his conviction "not only that we cannot in good policy give up the Peninsula, but that we may be able to continue the contest in Portugal with success, and that we shall finally bring off our army." That was the comforting reflection which lay behind his forecasts of the next campaign: their retreat was safe. For the new lines at Torres Vedras would, in the last resort, ensure a sheltered embarkation; and if they had to go, he meant to take the Portuguese, though "shall not have a single ton for a Spaniard." The campaign, of course, would have to be defensive; there would be a dearth of brilliant deeds; and he should "be most confoundedly abused, and in the end I may lose the little character I have gained." But that would not greatly matter, though he paid a shade more attention than usual to Opposition attacks upon him, welcoming Mr. Croker's heroic poem upon Talavera and forwarding a narrative of the campaign of 1809 to a correspondent with an accustomed warning: "If it is desired to publish anything upon the subject founded upon the enclosed, pray let it be so disguised that it cannot be supposed to come from me. I think, however, that a publication might be of some use." He was inclined to view the English critics with philosophy—"You see the dash which the Common Council of the city of London have made at me! I act with a sword hanging over me, which will fall upon me whatever may be the result; but they may do what they please. I shall not give up the game here as long as it can be played." He saw clearly now, as the last weeks of 1809 went by, how he meant play it. The ground was chosen. For they turned their backs on Spain before the year was out; and as 1810 came in, they were waiting for the French among the piled and tumbled rocks of Beira. Best of all, he wrote with gleeful underlinings that he had *"an unanimous army."* They were not perfect (he complained to Liverpool that "if I succeed in executing the arduous task which has devolved upon me, I may fairly say that I had not the best instruments, in either officers or men, which the service could have afforded"); but at least they did not argue with him. Indeed they trusted him—not yet, perhaps, with the blind confidence of later years. But Lowry Cole, who had come out to take command of a Division bore striking testimony:

"I never served under any Chief I like so much, Sir J. Moore alway excepted, as Lord W. He has treated me with much more confidence tha I had a right or could be expected from anyone. Few, I believe, possess firmer mind or has, as far as I have heard, more the confidence of the Army.

Cole's good opinion was, it would appear, reciprocated; for his com mander wrote to him that week, "I have got two dozen of excellent po for you, which I do not know how to send you." (There were some con pensations for making war in Portugal, though Lord Wellington anxieties sometimes included the delivery of his tea.)

The weeks went by; and he was waiting "in a situation in which r mischief can be done to the army, or to any part of it; I am prepared fe all events; and if I am in a scrape, as appears to be the general belief England, although certainly not my own, I'll get out of it." He slippe off to Lisbon in the winter for a final look at his new works; and fro the orders that he left behind, in case the French attacked in his absenc it was plain that he had already chosen ground near Busaco for an actio Then he returned to his position just inside the Portuguese frontie waiting, like any duellist, for some invisible second to give the signal. Th time his duel was to be fought with Masséna. He was ascending in t scale of Marshals; and it was fitting that—with Junot, Soult, and Jourd already to his credit—he should be matched with Masséna. The Prince Essling was, at fifty-two, a shade past his prime, with a weakness f feminine society in its more portable forms; but he was extremely able in his adversary's judgment, "the ablest after Napoleon." He was a lit tired, perhaps. But he brought nearly 80,000 Frenchmen into play agai

Wellington's 25,000 British (with the dubious addition of the Portuguese); and the long columns wound towards Portugal under the wide horizons of western Spain. Somewhere behind the blue distances Lord Wellington was waiting with his sober "doubt whether they can bring that force to bear upon Portugal without abandoning other objects, and exposing their whole fabric in Spain to great risk. If they should be able to invade it, and should not succeed in obliging us to evacuate the country, they will be in a very dangerous situation; and the longer we can oppose them, and delay their success, the more likely are they to suffer materially in Spain." That was his purpose now; that was the meaning of the Lines. There might be a battle, "if the enemy should invade this country with a force less than that which I should think so superior to ours as to create the necessity for embarking." But his taste for battles was very far from insatiable—"I am not so desirous as they imagine of fighting desperate battles; if I was, I might fight one any day I please. But I have kept the army for six months in two positions." Small wonder that impatient men grew more impatient, that the Staff gossiped and preferred "writing news and keeping coffee houses" to their own business, and positively croaked at their gloomy predictions, while their irritable chief expressed his displeasure with the doubters by continuing to entertain the meanest opinion of his instruments, professing to be "apprehensive of the consequence of giving them in any nice operation before the enemy, for they really forget every thing when plunder or wine is within their reach," and informing William (who was now Chief Secretary for Ireland) that "the army was, and indeed is still, the worst army that was ever sent from England." Nerves were a little strained by the long wait for Masséna. Sometimes, indeed, his outcries verged upon somewhat boisterous comedy:

"I have received your letter announcing the appointment of Sir William Erskine, General Lumley, and General Hay to this army. The first I have generally understood to be a madman. . . . Really when I reflect upon the characters and attainments of some of the General officers of this army, and consider that these are the persons on whom I am to rely to lead columns against the French Generals, and who are to carry my instructions into execution, I tremble; and, as Lord Chesterfield said of the Generals of his day, 'I only hope that when the enemy reads the list of their names he trembles as I do.' Sir William Erskine and General Lumley will be a very nice addition to this list! However, I pray God and the Horse Guards t deliver me from General Lighthume and Colonel Sanders."

But he did not despair. For he retained a sound conviction that he kne best—better than his subordinates, and far better than Masséna. Beside the new Government appeared to trust him; and Majesty itself positive vouchsafed a favourable opinion of him before a final lapse into insa ity. Kitty was well; his little boys were over their whooping-cough; an he waited briskly for the French.

They came slowly on, as summer mounted in the sky. He fell bac before them, curbing Robert Craufurd's inconvenient aptitude for expe sive rearguard actions. For that eager warrior was ill-attuned to Fabi exercises; and, as he disregarded orders, his blue chin projected farth than ever above the high peak of his saddle. But he found Wellingt indulgent; for "if I am to be hanged for it, I cannot accuse a man wh believe has meant well . . . although my errors, and those of others al are visited heavily upon me, that is not the way in which any, much les British army, can be commanded." Craufurd meant well enough; but alacrity marred the smooth perfection of their withdrawal from the C Then ill-luck took a hand; and a stray French shell sent up the powd magazine of Almeida in thunder—"a great and unexpected misfortu I had hoped that the place would have detained the Enemy for some tir and that I might have relieved it if circumstances had favoured m But its guns were silent now, and they fell back upon the deep windi of the upper Mondego. The French came slowly after them throug jumble of fir-clad hills across the heather towards Busaco. The grou was almost perfect for defence, and he stood to fight them on the ridge. It was September 27; 60,000 Frenchmen faced 50,000 Allies, hal whom were Portuguese; but through an autumn day Masséna launc forty-five battalions against his twenty-four and failed to dislodge th The British fought according to their custom, and the Portuguese wi new vigour. Their stout defence surprised Masséna; but that autu Masséna was not spared surprises. For a fortnight later, as he follo Wellington's receding columns towards Lisbon and the sea, the big of Torres Vedras climbed slowly up the sky, and he was faced by inspired introduction of the broad facts of geography into the art of

A nervous Staff excused itself for its omission to report upon the Lines by explaining apologetically that Lord Wellington had made them. *"Que diable,"* the Marshal snapped, *"Wellington n'a pas construit ces montagnes."*

They loomed stolidly in front of him, from the great bulk of Sao Vicente to the rectangular green slopes that curve away towards the gleaming reaches of the lower Tagus, where the Dutch sails of wherries seem to drift through the water-meadows. The whole foreground was full of mountains; and the mountains were all full of guns and Englishmen and Portuguese. It was most disconcerting. And that, though Masséna did not know it yet, was not the worst; for behind the Lines that filled his grey horizon a second line of field-works stood waiting for him on the big, bare hills beyond Mafra, and even a third traced in the dusty plain between the river and the Cintra hills. That was the triple step of Wellington's enormous fortress, the citadel of Portugal.

It was October now; and the clouds hung low above the Lines. The autumn rain drove down, and the French were raking a dun wilderness of scrub for food. To Wellington's intense annoyance, they found a little. For the Portuguese, though improved out of all knowledge, had failed to rise completely to his Fabian conception of an evacuated desert (perhaps it is impracticable to play Roman *rôles* without a Roman Senate); and the Regency had left gaps in the projected glacis of starvation, which impelled their exasperated ally to fish at intervals in the muddy waters of Portuguese politics and even to the impassioned outcry that "if Principal Souza is to remain either a member of the Government, or to continue at Lisbon . . . he must quit the country or I shall." But the French lay angrily before the Lines, hesitating to attack with a lively recollection of Busaco, and hoping with increasing fervour that Wellington would sally out. That wary fighter, finding himself "in sight of a very numerous but starving Army, which has been in our front now for ten days, and does not appear to like to attack us," looked down one day from a redoubt and thoughtfully remarked, "I could lick those fellows any day, but it would cost me 10,000 men, and, as this is the last army England has, we must take care of it." So he took care of it in the Lines. As he had written to Arbuthnot of the Treasury, "they won't draw me from my cautious system. I'll fight them only where I am pretty sure of success." Besides, what need was there to fight a battle, when Masséna chose to starve himself? The "sure game" was best, and Wellington preferred to play it. He watched them starving in the plain, as autumn turned to winter. But one November night, as the fog lay in banks along the Lines, the French slipped off. Their hungry columns groped northwards through the mist towards Santarem, and he followed warily—"Feeling, as I do, all the consequences which would ensue from the loss of a battle, and the risk which I must incur, in the existing situation of affairs, if I should fight one, I have determined to persevere in my cautious system, to operate upon the flanks and rear of the enemy with my small and light detachments, and thus force them out of Portugal by the distresses they will suffer, and do them all the mischief I can upon their retreat. Masséna is an old fox and is as cautious as I am; he risks nothing." With an uneasy feeling that he "could not attack them without incurring the risk of placing the fate of the Peninsula on the result of a general action, in which the advantage of ground would be much in favor of the enemy," Wellington remained almost stationary when Masséna halted for the winter. The old fox had gone to ground, and a wary huntsman was content to wait.

As 1810 went out, the French were still in Portugal. But so was Wellington. That was the miracle. The Emperor had put reinforcements into the Peninsula to the surprising tune of 100,000 men; but by some strange perversity the British still maintained their 25,000 there, and their commander wrote proudly home that "I am at the head of the only army remaining in the Peninsula—or, I believe, in Europe—that is capable and willing to contend with the French." Small wonder the delighted Lowry Cole wrote that "the ability displayed by Lord Wellington is universally acknowledged and I hope the good folks in England will do him equal justice. He certainly is in the literal sense of the word a fine fellow with the best nerves of anyone I ever met with." Busaco and the Lines had added Masséna to his bag of Marshals. Better still, a British army had faced the Empire at its widest, when a man could walk from Genoa to the Baltic on French soil, and had stared it out of countenance. The slow tide was turning; and though the Peninsular War was not yet won, at Torres Vedras it could not well be lost.

V

THE military problem of the Peninsula was almost maddeningly simple. The French objective, from which the Marshals were inter-mittently distracted by the allied lures of loot and sideshows, was to find and destroy the British expeditionary force. It was two years since the Emperor had announced, with a slightly hysterical blend of heraldry and natural history, that "the Leopard" would shortly be driven into the sea. That was the essence of French strategy. And the British problem was just as simple. For it presented two objectives—to avoid expulsion and then, resuming the offensive, to expel the French. The first goal was reached when Masséna, with the whole weight of the Empire behind him, turned back from Torres Vedras. It was plain from that moment that Wellington could not be driven out of the Peninsula. But could he drive out the French? That was his second problem, and in 1811 it was still unsolved. Its elements were simple, too. For the French occupation of Spain hung by one precarious chain—the great road from Bayonne to Madrid. If that were snapped, their armies must recoil from every province, since they could not maintain themselves with a British force across the road to France. If it were threatened, they must all come swarming north to safety. (Had not John Moore touched them on that nerve-centre in 1808 and seen the Emperor whip round towards him like an animal upon whose tail an unexpected foot had trodden?) If Wellington could get across their road to Paris, the game was won. That was the short way with the French. So he must thrust eastwards out of Portugal across Old Castile and break the road to France somewhere between Madrid and the Ebro. There was one point at which an angle of the road brought it nearer to him; the angle was at Burgos. That must be his goal, as it had once been John Moore's. But this time there would be no sudden dash for Burgos. For it was no part of his programme to make a gallant raid into Spain and scramble on board his transports at Corunna. The judicious Wellington was indisposed to risk himself beyond the shel-ter of his mountains, unless the gates of Portugal were safely held behind

him. He must be free to move decorously out of Portugal and to re-ente
it at will; and this privilege would not be his unless he held the gates. S
Badajoz and Ciudad Rodrigo must be his first objective; and, these onc
secured, he might make his decisive thrust towards the road to Par

I

As 1811 opened, the deadlock on the Tagus held. Masséna's m
starved at Santarem with a will that impressed their adversary as "
extraordinary instance of what a French army can do. It is positive
a fact that they brought no provisions with them, and they have r
even received a letter since they entered Portugal. With all our mone
and having in our favour the good inclinations of the country, I assu
you that I could not maintain one division in the district in which th
have maintained not less than 60,000 men and 20,000 animals for mo
than two months." That was written in December; by the first we
of March their transport was a shadow, their shoes a memory, a
their supply the stray outcome of marauding forays across a ch
waste of empty villages. Then, with Junot wounded and Ney fran
mutinous, Masséna turned to go. Withdrawing deftly, he slipped
towards the north with Wellington shepherding him on his way
trifle gingerly. For he was disinclined to risk unnecessary battles, w
it was far simpler to preside over the inevitable disintegration of
French from a safe distance. Had he not in his charge the last army
England? Defeated, it would let the tide of war surge into Britain—"t
would His Majesty's subjects discover what are the miseries of
of which, by the blessing of God, they have hitherto had no knowled
and the cultivation, the beauty, and prosperity of the country, and
virtue and happiness of its inhabitants would be destroyed, what
might be the result of the military operations. God forbid that I she
be a witness, much less an actor in the scene. . . ." But victoriou
might be the instrument to end the interminable European war—"I
equally certain that if Buonaparte cannot root us out of this country
must alter his system in Europe, and must give us such a peace as
ought to accept." He saw the goal; and in his marching redcoats he
the means to reach it. For he had more work for them to do than

ing rearguard actions against Masséna. His mind was ranging eastward ow towards the Spanish frontier; the gates of Portugal began to gleam n his horizon; and he preferred "to keep my own army entire, rather nan to weaken myself by fighting them, and probably be so crippled as ot to have the ascendant over the fresh troops on the frontiers. Almeida nd Badajoz are to be retaken."

They were to be his next objective. Meanwhile, he followed warily as Masséna struggled back to Spain. They scuffled on the road at Pombal nd again at Redinha, while Ney displayed the sombre aptitude for arguard actions that was soon to light a larger army down a longer, arker road. (That month the guns in Paris flashed and boomed for a heir born to the Emperor: all that remained was to retain an Empire r him.) Masséna's ragged columns wound slowly through the moun- ns after a running fight at Foz d'Aronce; their road was littered th discarded transport, and they left a growing legacy of weary, refoot men to be gathered in by their pursuers. The spring rains were ling now; Ney had gone raging off under virtual arrest, when the ny of Portugal, enlivened by the *feux de joie* for the small King Rome, fought a confused engagement in the fog at Sabugal, which ly served to strengthen Wellington's conviction that "these combina- ns for engagements do not answer unless one is on the spot to ect every trifling movement." (Had he not been his own "general of alry and of the advanced guard, and leader of two or three columns, netimes on the same day," throughout the long pursuit?) Then sséna crept out of Portugal, leaving behind 8,000 prisoners and 17,000 d, while Wellington proudly informed the Portuguese that the French asion was at an end.

he first phase was over; and it remained to batter in the gates of tugal. For the French still held Almeida (which guards the vestibule Ciudad Rodrigo) and Badajoz; and Wellington directed simultaneous vs at both. Leaving Almeida in the grip of an investing force, he : south to survey Badajoz, covering 135 miles in three April days, ng two horses, writing endless letters on the road, and losing two oons of his escort in a torrent. He reconnoitred Badajoz in person drew up a detailed code of instructions for Beresford, who was to ge the fortress; in case the French attempted to relieve it and Beres-

ford resolved to fight, he was recommended to concentrate at Albuera
Then Wellington returned to the north. The French were on the mov
again; for Masséna, his gaps repaired with fresh troops, came marchin
to the rescue of Almeida. They faced him one May morning at Fuente
de Oñoro on the upland which parts the high prairies of wester
Spain from the tumbled rocks of Beira. All that day and the next th
struggle swayed along the slopes. Then Masséna, groping round th
British right, launched his attack on May 5. French cavalry charge
British infantry in squares; the squares held (it was a lesson that Wel
ington observed); and whilst his infantry stood firm, his cavalry heavil
outnumbered were ridden off the field, and two British guns by th
supreme paradox of war charged and broke through a whirlpool
French horse. But, with his right in danger, Wellington swung it bac
with Frederician deliberation; and when the long day ended, his 37,0
men still lay between Almeida and its 47,000 rescuers. But he felt litt
pride in the achievement, writing to William that "Lord Liverpool w
quite right not to move thanks for the battle at Fuentes, though it w
the most difficult one I was ever concerned in. We had very nearly thr
to one against us engaged; above four to one of cavalry; and moreov
our cavalry had not a gallop in them; while some of that of the ener
was fresh and in excellent order. If Boney had been there, we shou
have been beaten." But Boney was not there; and in his absence
might be permissible to take occasional liberties with the art of war.

Its fate duly sealed by the battle at its gates, Almeida fell. But
Wellington's acute annoyance the garrison escaped, and he was l
reviling "the most disgraceful military event that has yet occurre
reaching the grim conclusion that "there is nothing on earth so stu
as a gallant officer." (Indeed, one unhappy object of his displeasure s
himself.) The spring campaign in the north had cleared the way
Ciudad Rodrigo and incidentally closed Masséna's career; for an
grateful Emperor rewarded him with summary retirement, and M
mont commanded in his place.

But news from Badajoz drew Wellington's attentions south ag
For Soult had pounded Beresford at Albuera—"a strange concern,"
Wellington wrote. "They were never determined to fight it; they
not occupy the ground as they ought; they were ready to run away

every moment from the time it commenced till the French retired."
Yet dogged gallantry prevailed; and Soult learned reluctantly, in Napier's
eloquent rhapsody, "with what a strength and majesty the British soldier
fights. . . . Nothing could stop that astonishing infantry . . . and fifteen
hundred unwounded men, the remnant of six thousand unconquerable
British soldiers, stood triumphant on the fatal hill!" But such heroic
exploits were not to Wellington's taste; and he was left writing grimly
that "another such battle would ruin us." Meanwhile, the summer was
before him; and he made a rush at Badajoz before the French could
return in force to relieve the fortress. But ample time is the essence of
successful sieges, and time was wanting. They were too quick for him;
and he drew off to safety, falling back once more to a strong position
just inside the Portuguese frontier. At midsummer the armies faced
one another in Estremadura. But the deadlock held; and the war drifted
north again along the frontier. For Wellington was still knocking at the
gates of Portugal; and having failed at Badajoz, he turned briskly to
Ciudad Rodrigo. That red-tiled fortress with its big brown church and
vaguely Mexican aspect was waiting in a broad green valley; and in
August he encircled it in preparation for a siege. But Marmont came up
in force to its relief; there was a scuffle on September 25 at El Bodon;
once more a British square held off the charging French; and Wellington again withdrew—without conspicuous assistance from the impulsive
Craufurd. He made a point of it on parade next morning.

"I am glad to see you safe, General Craufurd," he observed with
elaborate irony.

"I was never in danger," his rash subordinate replied.

"Oh! I was," said Wellington tartly.

"He's damned crusty this morning," muttered his unabashed lieutenant.

His designs on Ciudad Rodrigo postponed, Wellington fell back with
long deliberation to a strong position on the Coa; but Marmont lay
watchfully in front of him and made no attack. The war was over
for the season now; and 1811 went out upon Wellington among the
rocky hills of Beira. It had been a fruitful year. He had cleared Portugal
and broken Masséna, and the gates of Portugal gleamed hopefully before
him. His business now lay with the frontier fortresses; and whilst they

lay waiting for his onslaught, the initiative had passed to him. Bette
still, he had transformed the war; as he wrote to Liverpool, "we hav
certainly altered the nature of the war in Spain; it has become, to
certain degree, offensive on our part. The enemy are obliged to concer
trate large corps to defend their own acquisitions; they are obliged t
collect magazines to support their armies (Marmont says he can d
nothing without magazines, which is quite a new era in the moder
French military system); and I tnink it probable, from all that I hea
that they are either already reduced, or they must soon come, to th
resources of France for the payment of those expenses which must l
defrayed in money. As soon as this shall be the case, and as soon as th
war will not produce resources to carry itself on, your Lordship may l
certain that Buonaparte will be disposed to put an end to it, and w
submit to anything rather than draw from France the resources whi
must be supplied in order to keep together his armies. I think it n
unlikely, therefore, that peace is speculated upon in France."

Peace flushed the eastern sky, as he looked eastwards out of Portug
Spain lay before him now, and beyond Spain the long line of t
Pyrenees. That was the goal; his exclamation in a letter pointed it—

> "You appear to think it probable that Buonaparte would be inclined
> obliged to withdraw from the Peninsula; and you ask, what would I do
> that case? I answer, attack the most vulnerable frontier of France, that
> the Pyrenees. Oblige the French to maintain in that quarter 200,000 n
> for their defence; touch them vitally there, when it will certainly be
> possible to touch them elsewhere."

It was a lucid vision, and he followed it across his maps on a Decem
day in 1811. He was still in Portugal, and between him and a sight
the Pyrenees lay Marmont, Soult, King Joseph, the French armies, a
the long corridors of Spain; but the Pyrenees were waiting.

2

The war was forming him. Now he was nearly forty-three—h
nosed, clear-eyed, and confident. His nerves were always steady. T
was his secret; Lowry Cole had pierced it, when he termed his c

ander "a fine fellow with the best nerves of any one I ever met with." or the sharp gaze never wavered, and the upper lip drew tightly down ver the slightly prominent teeth without a quiver. His nerves were lmirable; exercise, long days in the saddle, and plain fare helped to eep them so. Did not Alava learn to dread his standing answer to the iestion at what o'clock the Staff would move and what there was to be r dinner? "At daylight," he invariably replied; and to the second in-rrogation, "Cold meat." "*J'en ai pris en horreur*," the anguished Span-rd moaned, "*les deux mots* daylight *et* cold meat." But Wellington rove on them. His night's rest varied between three hours and six; and r his first four years in the Peninsula, although he was Commander--Chief, he had reverted to the practice of his Indian campaigns and pt in his clothes. His days were regular; rising at six, he wrote steadily til breakfast at nine o'clock. Those quiet morning hours served to dis-se of his enormous correspondence with incredible punctuality; for y rule always was to do the business of the day in the day." Then he eakfasted and transacted military business with the Staff. This lasted all morning, except on hunting days when a gleeful Quartermaster-neral records that he "could get almost anything done, for Lord ellington stands whip in hand ready to start, and soon despatches all siness." Those were the days that startled Portuguese on lonely hill-es beheld an unprecedented cavalcade, heard view-halloos and the rp note of hounds, and marvelled at the strange proceedings of their omprehensible allies. "Here," as *Captain O'Malley* loved to recall, e shell-jacket of a heavy dragoon was seen storming the fence of a eyard. There the dark green of a rifleman was going the pace over plain. The unsportsmanlike figure of a staff officer might be observed erging from a drain, while some neck-or-nothing Irishman, with light ntry wings, was flying at every fence before him"—and the Peer self followed his hounds in the sky-blue and black of the Salisbury t. Such was the impressive apparatus with which Lord Wellington ed his nerves in winter-quarters.

is nerves, indeed, were admirable; and a becoming sense of who was and what he had achieved contributed to steady them—"I am mainspring of all the other operations, but it is because I am Lord lington; for I have neither influence nor support, nor the means

of acquiring influence, given to me by the government." Small wonde
that his correspondents never ventured upon a more familiar addres
than "My dear Lord." Even behind his back he was "the Peer" to Gen
erals and "our great Lord" to ardent subalterns; although an intoxicate
private once alluded (in the presence of a scandalised staff officer) t
"that long-nosed b——r that beats the French," and the army had bee
known to call him "Atty." But such diminutives were rare; for he kep
his distance.

Not that he kept it by conventional distinctions of uniform and en
tourage. Headquarters, as one observer noted, were "strikingly qui
and unostentatious. Had it not been known for a fact, no one woul
have suspected that he was quartered in the town. There was no thror
of scented staff officers with plumed hats, orders and stars, no ma
guard, no crowd of contractors, actors, cooks, valets, mistresses, equipage
horses, dogs, forage and baggage wagons, as there is at French
Russian headquarters! Just a few aides-de-camp, who went about t
streets alone and in their overcoats, a few guides, and a small staff guar
that was all! About a dozen bullock carts were to be seen in the lar
square of Fuente Guinaldo, which were used for bringing up stra
to headquarters; but apart from these no equipages or baggage trai
were visible." Perhaps he had seen quite enough of personal magnificen
in Richard's case to damp his taste for it. At any rate, his dress was u
pretentious. A harassed army might echo Micky Free's lyrical compla
to the Fourteenth Light Dragoons:

> Bad luck to this marching,
> Pipe-claying and starching;
> How neat one must be to be killed by the French!

But such niceties were scarcely to their commander's taste. One su
altern recorded that "provided we brought our men into the field w
appointed with their sixty rounds of ammunition each, he never look
to see whether trousers were black, blue, or grey. . . . The conseque
was that scarcely any two officers were dressed alike! Some wore g
braided coats, others brown: some again liked blue; many (from cho
or perhaps necessity) stuck to the 'old red rag.'" His own opinions w
plainly stated to the Horse Guards:

"I hear that measures are in contemplation to alter the clothing, caps, &c. of the army.

"There is no subject of which I understand so little; and, abstractedly speaking, I think it indifferent how a soldier is clothed, provided it is in a uniform manner; and that he is forced to keep himself clean and smart, as a soldier ought to be. But there is one thing I deprecate, and that is any imitation of the French in any manner.

"It is impossible to form an idea of the inconveniences and injury which result from having anything like them. . . . I only beg that *we* may be as different as possible from the French in everything."

his was severely practical. So was his own costume, which generally n to grey. His taste for personal reconnaissance inclined him to the conspicuous combination of a grey frock-coat worn with a low cocked-t in an oil skin cover. It bore no plume; and before long Europe arned to know that austere silhouette. He was not altogether innocent sartorial vanities, though, fancying the skirts of his coats a trifle orter than most men's in order (a Judge-Advocate conjectured) to set a trim figure; nor was he without strong and individual opinions on a novel cut of half-boots. But these effects were all contrived in the odest key of grey; and his entourage was equally inconspicuous. An pretentious Staff, designed for use rather than ornament, was put shame by the glory of gold lace and plumes that caracoled in the endid wake of any Marshal of the Empire. But Wellington had little petite for millinery. Besides, few Marshals shared his taste for solitary onnaissance. He had unbounded faith in a strong glass and a fast se, and often rode beyond his outposts, a lonely horseman in a cloak, h his perpetual desire to see things for himself—the French vedettes uld never suspect a single figure in grey. So he dressed modestly ow his military station, leaving the foppery of war to gaudier, if less :essful, Marshals. Indeed, their master did the same. For Europe l another *redingote grise*: he might be matched against it one day. rey-coated, spare, and trim, the bleak figure, sharply outlined against deep blue of Spanish skies, appears a shade incongruous. He never sed the part; indeed, he had little taste for drama. When his advance-d blundered into the whole French army, he greeted the alarming ligence with a casual, "Oh! they are all there, are they? Well, we

must mind a little what we are about then." And news that the French
were off, leaving Almeida in his grasp, reached him one morning early
whilst he was shaving. He lifted the razor from his cheek, remarking
"Ay, I thought they meant to be off; very well"; the shave resumed, and
nothing more was said. He specialised in a form of dry understatement
peculiarly unfriendly to heroics. Who else, addressing a charitable appeal
to the Prime Minister on behalf of a devastated ally, was capable of the
sublime exordium: "The village of Fuentes de Oñoro having been the
field of battle the other day, and not having been much improved by
this circumstance . . . ."? Few themes, indeed, moved him to eloquence
except the imperfections of his human instruments. But there his language often verged on the sublime. Unwearying himself, he was un-
merciful in his comments upon lack of energy in others; and exasperation frequently betrayed him into unpardonable generalisations. A fixed
belief that insufficient inducements were offered to recruits had led him
to the conclusion that "none but the worst description of men enter the
regular service"; and from this premise he proceeded to the gravest dis-
paragements of the men under his command. "The scum of the earth"
he termed them, "the mere scum of the earth. . . . The English soldiers
are fellows who have all enlisted for drink—that is the plain fact—
they have all enlisted for drink." This tone became habitual with him in
later years, as a congenial antidote to the prevailing cant. For Wellington
could not bear his hearers to be romantic about soldiers—"people talk
of their enlisting from their fine military feeling—all stuff—no such
thing. Some of our men enlist from having got bastard children—some
for minor offences—many more for drink; but you can hardly conceive
such a set brought together, and it really is wonderful that we should
have made them the fine fellows they are." They were fine fellows, then.
He was prepared to admit as much; and for seven years in the Peninsula he toiled to make them so. Seven volumes of General Orders, drawn
in his own handwriting and traced endlessly across the paper with
"the short glazed pens" from Tabart's in New Bond Street, testify to his
parental care. "Crime" is duly present; the crackle of illicit pig-shooting
is heard; bee-hives are purloined; and the misdeeds peculiar to military
operations in wine-producing countries stalk through his pages. His
camp-kettles, shirts, and brushes haunted him; his dreams were full

rmy biscuit; and his housekeeping anxieties are in strange contrast
vith the grave ablatives absolute of Cæsar or Napoleon's baroque elo-
uence. Supply was still the burden of his severely humdrum song. He
ill insisted that "it is very necessary to attend to all this detail, and to
ace a biscuit from Lisbon into the man's mouth on the frontier, and
) provide for its removal from place to place, by land or by water, or
o military operations can be carried on, and the troops must starve."
ven his strategy was dominated by the practical consideration that
a soldier with a musket could not fight without ammunition, and that
. two hours he can expend all he can carry."

This was admirably unheroic. But in one particular he found his gal-
nt subordinates more unheroic than himself. Uniformly indifferent to
e risks of battle,

> "When, squadron square,
> We'll all be there,
> To meet the French in the morning,"

ey failed to share his taste for uneventful winters in the discomfort of
-country billets in the hill villages of Beira. Moved with a simul-
neous passion for the immediate transaction of urgent business at
me, they applied for leave. Such unanimity was touching. But their
nmander was untouched; for leave was one of Wellington's blind
ots. Lisbon leave was one thing. He could be positively debonair on
 subject of Lisbon leave, recording in a sardonic postscript that a
ordinate "wants to go to Lisbon, and I have told him that he may
y there 48 hours which is as long as any reasonable man can wish
stay in bed with the same woman." But why gentlemen who had
ne all the way to the Peninsula in order, he presumed, to fight the
nch should wish to go home again entirely passed his comprehension.
ealth might form a valid reason; but business grounds left him
kly incredulous. Even Craufurd was grudgingly informed that "Of-
rs (General Officers in particular) are the best judges of their own
ate concerns; and, although my own opinion is that there is no
ate concern that cannot be settled by instruction and power of
rney, and that after all is not settled in this manner, I cannot refuse
e of absence to those who come to say that their business is of a

nature that requires their personal superintendence. But entertainin
these opinions, it is rather too much that I should not only give lea
of absence, but approve of the absence of any, particularly a Gener
Officer, from the army. . . . I may be obliged to consent to the absen
of an Officer, but I cannot approve of it. I repeat that you know th
situation of affairs as well as I do, and you have my leave to go
England if you think proper." He could contrive a kindly refusal—"
always feel much concern in being obliged to refuse officers who wi
to quit the army; indeed it is the most painful duty I have to perform
But is must be performed; otherwise, between those absent on accou
of wounds and sickness, and those absent on account of business
pleasure, I should have no officers left." Indeed, he ultimately mov
the Horse Guards to confine Peninsular appointments to Generals p
pared to make a declaration in advance that they had no private busin
likely to recall them to England. More romantic reasons moved him
irony, although a hint from home that one young lady's continued sepa
tion from a love-lorn Major might be followed by fatal consequen
elicited a kindly, though terrifying, lecture on the course of love:

"It appears to me that I should be guilty of a breach of discretion i
were to send for the fortunate object of this young lady's affections, and
apprise him of the pressing necessity for his early return to England:
application for permission ought to come from himself; and, at all eve
the offer ought not to be made by me, and particularly not founded on
secret of this interesting young lady.

"But this fortunate Major now commands his battalion, and I am
apprehensive that he could not with propriety quit it at present, even tho
the life of this female should depend upon it; and, therefore, I think
he will not ask for leave.

"We read, occasionally, of desperate cases of this description, but I
not say that I have ever yet known of a young lady dying of love. T
contrive, in some manner to live, and look tolerably well, notwithstand
their despair and the continued absence of their lover; and some even I
been known to recover so far as to be inclined to take another lover, if
absence of the first has lasted too long. I don't suppose that your *prot*
can ever recover so far, but I do hope that she will survive the conti
necessary absence of the Major, and enjoy with him hereafter many h
days."

This was not unkindly. After all, Lord Wellington himself had the best reasons for believing in the capacity for survival of young ladies in love. Had not Kitty borne his own absence for nine years (and very nearly married Lowry Cole in the course of her vigil)? That, perhaps, was why he was a shade unsympathetic about leave. He had left so little behind him (his brother William was informed that "as for private concerns, I never trouble my head about them"), that home meant little to him; and why should it mean more to others?

Not that he was inhuman. He even had his moments of weakness. The day after Somers Cocks was killed at Burgos he came into someone's room, paced it for some time in silence, opened the door to go, and as he left exclaimed abruptly, "Cocks was killed last night." But his emotion was dry-eyed; how, with his work to do, could it be otherwise? High command is a supremely lonely business. Yet there were moments when he needed company. At four o'clock on winter afternoons he left his room "and then, for an hour or two, parades with any one whom he wants to talk to, up and down the little square of Frenada (amidst the chattering Portuguese) in his grey great coat." The talk ran on everything—on India, on Ireland, on Mr. Canning's views about the Catholics—and the trim figure in grey paced up and down the little square among the staring drovers. He could be affable; and the Head-quarters mess grew familiar with his laugh—a terrifying cachinnation very loud and long, like the whoop of the whooping cough often repeated."

The Peer kept his distance, though. For was it not almost his duty as Commander-in-Chief to be a shade aloof? Perhaps aloofness came natural to him. At any rate, it was his fate, his rather lonely fate, always to be a little different from his surroundings, his head held a trifle higher than his neighbours'. Had he not been an Englishman in Ireland, an Anglo-Indian in India, a soldier among politicians, and finally a politician among soldiers? He was invariably in contrast, never in perfect harmony with his assorted backgrounds; and the spare figure, tightly buttoned in its grey beneath a black cocked-hat, contrasted oddly with the life of Spain. It was a lonely *rôle* to be Lord Wellington.

VI

THE worst was over now. For it was 1812, and the slow tide
war began to ebb. They had withstood the full force of it sin
1810, bearing up against the whole weight of the Empire. In those cruci
years—the years of Busaco, of Torres Vedras, Masséna's retreat, ar
Fuentes de Oñoro—all Europe beyond the Pyrenees had been at peac
its Emperor at leisure to pour the flood-tide of his armies into Spai
But now the tide checked and, called by its unrestful luminary, beg
to ebb away towards the north, where the French faced about to me
another enemy. For Russian drums were tapping in the mist beyo
the edge of Germany; the Czar's tall grenadiers were stiffly aligne
and the little Cossack ponies trotted smartly beneath the long lances
their bearded riders. Soon there would be more than Spain to think
Spain must be held, of course; but now the Guard had gone, the Po
were going, and there would be no more reinforcements for Ki
Joseph and the fretful Marshals. The tide was ebbing now. The Fren
evicted three times in four years from Portugal, were scarcely likely
return; although the Emperor seven hundred miles away in Paris s
appeared to regard Lisbon as their objective, and pelted his Marshals w
a succession of fantastic orders. These documents, in which Napol
appears at his least impressive, were uniformly unhelpful, since
facts on which he founded his instructions originated almost exclusi
in that powerful imagination, and the resulting orders (which bore
relation to Peninsular conditions) were invariably out of date when
arrived. Indeed, the least harmful to their recipients' chances of suc
were those which failed to arrive at all.

A fair proportion of these missives were diverted from their la
destinations by the kindly forethought of *guerrilleros*; for the mil
genius of Spain, which had hitherto found infelicitous expression
disastrous series of pitched battles, was admirably suited to the steal
operations of the *petite guerre*—the *guerrilla*. Cloaked figures hau
Spanish defiles; French despatch-riders, ambling inattentively into

roat of some dreadful gully, failed to emerge into the sunlight; and
the empty road beyond wound dustily across the plain, eager knives
ere slitting French saddlery in search of correspondence, to be for-
arded by faithful hands and lonely tracks and patiently deciphered at
ord Wellington's headquarters. (If official Spain left much to be
sired as an ally, few armies have found more effective friends than
e Spanish *guerrillero*, who effaced the long French line of com-
unications with grim persistence, rounding up the rumbling convoys,
shing incautious posts, and imposing an escort of 1,800 men upon a
ench General who wished to reach his destination.) From his perusal
intercepted despatches Wellington might pardonably conclude that,
an adversary at long range, the Emperor was fallible, and from the
he which he habitually employed towards inferiors that Napoleon was
stinctly not a gentleman. This, indeed, became one of his fixed con-
ctions. Did he not once inform a houseparty of Lord Hertford's that
uonaparte's mind was, in its details, low and ungentleman-like," a
fect which he charitably attributed to "the narrowness of his early
ospects and habits"? His fastidious taste was equally repelled by the
peror's frequent use of deception—"Buonaparte's whole life, civil,
itical, and military was a fraud. There was not a transaction, great
small, in which lying and fraud were not introduced. . . . Buon-
arte's foreign policy was force and menace, aided by fraud and corrup-
n. If the fraud was discovered, force and menace succeeded." Not that
was convinced of their success—"I never was a believer in him,
I I always thought that in the long-run we should overturn him. He
er seemed himself at his ease, and even in the boldest things he did
re was always a mixture of apprehension and meanness. I used to
him *Jonathan Wild the Great*, and at each new *coup* he made I
I to cry out 'Well done, Jonathan'." . . . As he read his papers
Headquarters, this rich distaste, the full fruit of later years, was
vly ripening.

ut a more valuable discovery which emerged from the Emperor's
gential dealings with King Joseph and the bewildered Marshals was
Napoleon could err. Lord Wellington sat in his Portuguese head-
rters above a village street and learned that serviceable lesson. Other
ersaries encountered the Emperor for the first time on battlefields,

and were appropriately awed into helpless immobility. But Wellingto
first came upon him in the more reassuring form of palpably absur
instructions to his deputies in Spain. "The habit of Napoleon," as Wel
ington wrote of him later, "had been to astonish and deceive mankin
and he had come at last to deceive himself." He did not fall into th
vulgar error of underrating him, retaining a salutary belief that "h
presence on the field made the difference of forty thousand men." B
no student of his interventions in Peninsular affairs could retain in i
full perfection the awe in which Europe held the white-breeched, gree
coated figure. That, if Wellington was ever to meet him in the fiel
would be something gained.

Meanwhile, his problem waited. The French were still at large
Spain, and the strong places of the frontier barred his way. But
Ciudad Rodrigo and Badajoz awaited his attack, he enjoyed the ra
advantage that he could choose his own moment for attacking the
For the initiative had passed to Wellington. He was at perfect libe
to move his pieces up and down the board, while the French could
little more than pant after him, parrying his blows. The cause v
simple: Spain was a desert, and in desert warfare supply and transp
are the only wings upon which armies can rise into motion. The Sej
General had both; the French had neither.

Endowed with this superior mobility, he made a winter thrust
Ciudad Rodrigo. The January snow was deep in Leon as they mo
against the fortress; and after twelve days in open trenches they storn
it on January 19—"in half the time" (as he wrote Liverpool with
rare note of triumph) "that I told you it would take, and in less t
half that which the French spent in taking the same place from
Spaniards." His speed was costly, though; for the siege cost heavily
casualties, including Robert Craufurd, whose last words of reconcilia
evoked the wondering comment that "Craufurd talked to me as t
do in a novel." But speed was vital, if they were to snatch Ciu
Rodrigo before Marmont could return to its relief; and the sudden c
secured the northern gate of Portugal, eliciting for Wellington a Spa
dukedom from the grateful Cortes, a marquisate from Portugal,
earldom from the Prince Regent, and an annuity of £2,000 f
Parliament.

The new Earl of Wellington and Duque de Ciudad Rodrigo surveyed the frontier with half the winter still before him. Badajoz remained, a rich prize to be seized before Soult from the south or Marmont from the north could intervene to rescue it. Time is the essence of siege-warfare—ample time for the slow ritual of investment, opening trenches, racing parallels, saps, sorties, siting batteries, mining and countermining, and breaching scarps, the whole culminating in the triumphant *finale* of an assault and escalade. When conducted in due form, it had something of the grave decorum of a minuet (had not the Eighteenth Century once opened trenches to the sound of violins?); or it might be viewed under the guise of courtship—of a singularly formal courtship in which the gallant besieger drew a reluctant fortress with exquisite deliberation into the embraces of his parallels and saps. But time was the essence of this lingering procedure; and when time presses, besiegers are of necessity crude, hasty, and ungraceful. Wellington's approach to Badajoz was sadly lacking in the graces of unhurried siege-warfare, since his problem was to batter down the last remaining gate of Portugal before its guardians could return to save it. He moved south in February, with an agreeable pretence for the benefit of the French that he was "going to hunt . . . and you might even have a house arranged for the hounds at Aldea de Yeltes." Whilst his exceedingly impromptu siege-train jolted slowly forward towards Badajoz, he corresponded on the agreeable theme of his latest honours, even finding time for lengthy expositions on French finance and Indian army problems. News reached him that his brother Richard, whom the passing years rendered increasingly intractable, had resigned the Foreign Office and elicited the judicious comment that "in truth the republic of a cabinet is but little suited to any man of rule or of large views"—a sentiment of which he was himself to experience the justice later. Richard, indeed, was scarcely suited to republics; even a not too constitutional monarchy cramped him unduly. But his defection left Arthur as the leading Wellesley, though Henry still toiled patiently as British Ambassador at Cadiz—had laboured there, indeed, since Richard's translation to Downing Street—and now received the recognition of knighthood.

Meanwhile, the French still mounted guard in Badajoz. The siege began in March; the parallels crept closer; Easter went by; and on a

dark spring night (it was April 6) the attack was launched. For tw
interminable hours it swayed round the fortress in a glare of port-fire
as each storming column went roaring forward into failure. When th
news came to Wellington, the colour left his face and his jaw fell; bu
he turned to give an order in that calm way of his, and even apologise
with formal courtesy for giving it to the wrong person. Then a repo
arrived that Picton's men were in the fortress; the Staff hallooed; bu
Wellington was still giving orders in his level voice. Badajoz was hi
Yet, for the moment, it was not Lord Wellington's, but his army's; an
for three nights and days of unprecedented riot they celebrated the
capture. Discipline dissolved in floods of wine; locks were shot ope
looting was universal; and scared nymphs (in comb and *mantilla*) fl
shrieking down the winding alleys before reeling fauns (in scarlet tunic
Even the gaunt silhouette of gallows in the Plaza failed to check t
saturnalia, though their formidable master "fulminates orders and w
hardly thank the troops, so angry is he." But he was sad as well
angry. For he had purchased Badajoz at a cruel price; and when
saw the casualty returns, Wellington (for once not dry-eyed) we
bitterly.

The first phase of 1812 was over. Badajoz and Ciudad Rodrigo
cured, the gates of Portugal swung open; and in June they march
eastwards into Spain, having the red earth underfoot and on th
right a line of snow mountains, until they saw the heaped brown cupc
of Salamanca piled up against the eastern sky. That was the first sta
on the long road from Portugal to the Pyrenees. His blow was aimed
Marmont in Leon rather than at Soult further to the south in Andalu
for the simple reason that French movements would be cramped
starvation (had not hunger just recalled Marmont from a raid i
Portugal?) until the harvest ripened; and "the harvest in all the count
north of the Tagus . . . is much later than it is to the southward.
shall retain our advantages for a longer period of time in these co
tries than we should do to the southward." This was the applicatio
supply to strategy with a vengeance; and obedient to its dictates Well
ton marched on Salamanca.

The French fell back, leaving a garrison to hold some forts; and e
one June morning Wellington rode in. The town was roaring; and

ode slowly through the press, deafened with shrill *vivas*. Excited women rowded round him with tears, with kisses, with hoarse Spanish voices; nd the still figure, writing orders on a sabretache, was almost pulled rom his saddle. Three armies in four years had jingled spurs under the rown arcades of the Plaza Mayor—Moore's hurried redcoats racing gainst the Emperor in 1808, then an interminable succession of French- nen in blue, and now the redcoats once again. Some of them marched ff to besiege the French remnant in the forts; the rest took post to the orth of the city on the ridge of San Christoval, where Wellington hoped gainst hope that Marmont would attack him. That position, where e deliberately offered battle on two occasions in the course of 1812, as never fought over. But as the ideal is always more exquisitely ounded than the real, Wellington's conception of a defensive action is erfectly revealed in the unfought battle of San Christoval.

Exposing to the French a long and easy slope of innocent aspect nd a blind skyline, the ridge dropped steeply on its inner face, affording erfect concealment to the defenders until the moment came to reveal em. For the Wellingtonian defensive had the splendid simplicity of a oby-trap. Its modest object was to spring unsuspected forces upon sur- ised attackers; and San Christoval (like Busaco before it and Waterloo few years later) was admirably suited to this simple pleasantry. The ackers would pant uphill towards the blind skyline; somewhere behind e crest a line of British infantry would crouch, completely sheltered om artillery and waiting happily to fire its volley, utter its huzza, and p forward with the bayonet. This game, if only Marmont would lige with an attack, could be repeated three times on three successive ges of identical conformation, before the French offensive could pierce rough to Salamanca. One afternoon they came quite close to the posi- n; and Wellington was heard muttering, "Damned tempting! I have great mind to attack 'em." The French guns opened, and the round t began to fall among his Staff quite close to where Wellington was nding with a map. He "moved a few paces, and continued his direc- ns." But the moment passed; Marmont thought better of it, and drew towards the north; and the battle of San Christoval—the perfect llingtonian battle—was never fought.

'welve hundred miles away the Emperor, a squat figure in a great-

coat, whistled *Malbrouck s'en va't en guerre* and watched his long
columns wind slowly across a Polish river into Russia. Their bayonets
gleamed in the June sunshine, as the loaded caissons rumbled across
the bridges and the *Grande Armée* took the long road for Moscow. Then
the dust settled in the plain, and silence fell again behind them. In Spain
Marmont and Wellington were groping for one another outside Salamanca. At one moment the deadlock seemed complete, and the Peer
miraculously gave leave to a Staff officer, conjecturing that "you have
seen the end of it. . . . I shan't fight him without an advantage, nor h
me, I believe." There was an interlude of countermarching, in which
each followed suit with the precision of chess-players in the opening
moves. Marmont was edging round Salamanca towards the road t
Portugal. If that were threatened, Wellington must fall back; and th
two armies wheeled against the distant and unchanging background
a tall sierra across a sort of dusty Wiltshire with long, marine horizons
a reddish Wiltshire with tiled villages built of adobe—and this blen
of Mexico and Salisbury Plain appropriately evoked a series of preci
manœuvres. For they wheeled in full sight of one another, the tw
armies racing southward side by side for the faint line of trees th
marked the Tormes. The air, oddly enough (since it was the third we
of July), was fresh, chilled by a biting wind off the sierra; and We
ington "never suffered more from cold." The focus shifted rou
the city, as Marmont felt for the road behind his adversary; and as th
swung south of Salamanca, the French seemed to be leading in t
race. They could not be quite sure, though, how much of Wellingto
command was on the ground; for he had interposed a slope—one
his favourite long slopes with a blind skyline—and three divisions w
concealed behind it. As the French headed for the west, they were stru
out a little in the race, gaily unaware that they were marching acr
the front of Wellington's entire command. The morning of July
passed in this agreeable manner, Marmont "manœuvring" (as Welli
ton wrote) "in the usual French style, nobody knew with what obje
But about lunch-time the French lapse became manifest. Wellington
"stumping about and munching" in a little farmyard among the bro
cottages of Los Arapiles, lunching apparently off alternate bites of chic
and glances at the French through a telescope. (The occasion ling

in Alava's memory because, for once, there was not cold meat.) The Peer's lunch was interrupted by a final look towards the French. "By God," he suddenly exclaimed, "that will do"—and scandalised Alava by flinging far over his shoulder the leg of chicken which he had been eating in his fingers. Then he cantered up the hill for a more comprehensive view, and the whole field was spread before him—the red masses of his own command, the still country, and the marching French. The game was in his hands: "*Mon cher Alava,*" he said cheerfully, "*Marmont est perdu,*" and rode off to launch the attack. For it was not his way to entrust such vital missions to subordinates; and when he left the stony hill, he galloped across level fields with one companion to give his orders. Edward Pakenham, Kitty's brother, commanded the leading column of attack.

"Ned," said his formidable brother-in-law, "move on with the Third Division; take the heights on your front; and drive everything before you."

"I will, my lord," he dutifully answered, "if you will give me your hand."

There was a handshake; and the attack developed which "beat forty thousand men in forty minutes." In the later phases he presided lovingly over each turn of his battle; as Pakenham informed his mother, "our Chief was every where and Sadly Exposed himself." For he was often riding forward with the advancing lines of his own infantry; and when the heavy cavalry went thundering against the French (it was a favourite hallucination of the Prince Regent in later years that he had charged with them), Wellington was close enough to remark to their commander, "By God, Cotton, I never saw anything so beautiful in my life; the day is *yours.*" The day, at any rate, was England's. For Wellington had launched twenty-eight battalions against seventy-eight and sent them reeling eastwards into Castile; Marmont and Clausel, his second in command and successor, were both wounded; and the Army of Portugal hurried to shelter with a loss of fifteen thousand men and twenty guns, a solid testimony to Wellington's ability to do something more than defend strong positions of his own choice. Foy termed the battle Frederician; and there were traces of the King of Prussia's "oblique order" in the slanting thrust of Wellington's attack.

Indeed, the victory might have been still more crushing if a Spanish force, which he had posted at a ford behind the French, had been capable of simple obedience. But Carlos de España had decamped from Alba de Tormes, and the French slipped by. Spain was at Alba, though —the sinister, uncomprehended Spain of macabre *Caprichos* and sardonic portraits of egregious Bourbons and preposterous grandees—watching through the sharp eyes of Francisco Goya y Lucientes. For Goya watched him, as he rode in that night from Salamanca, if the note appended to his sketch can be believed; and the strange drawing with its unavoidable suggestion of an ascetic interrupted in his cell or a drowning man restored unexpectedly to the surface, records the exhausted victor—unshaven, hollow-eyed, the damp hair plastered to his forehead, a little shaken by the spent bullet which had bruised his thigh—a wild-eyed, unfamiliar Wellington, as Goya saw him on the summer night in a Spanish village.

The long corridors of Spain lay open to him now; and the French scurried wildly in all directions. Clausel drew off the wreckage of Salamanca towards the north; King Joseph hung disconsolately round Madrid; and Soult with infinite deliberation moved out of Andalusia to the rescue. Wellington, whose *forte* was not pursuit, shepherded Clausel warily towards Valladolid and the great road to France. A little artifice framed to delude King Joseph's outposts, employed legitimate deception —"I shall stay here all day," he advised an officer in command of Portuguese cavalry, "and will act according to the Intelligence which I shall receive from you"; but an ingenious postscript enclosed "a letter which I beg you to send to the French advanced posts by an officer of the German Cavalry well-mounted with a well-mounted Escort. . . . Tell him to answer no questions and give no information excepting that Marmont's army is totally annihilated as a Military Body; and to get the information he can. Desire him to say he does not know where I am, and that I move every day."

A choice, it would appear, was open to him between pressing farther to the north, where Burgos beckoned at the angle of the road to France, and evicting Joseph from his capital. He chose the latter, largely for the reason that "I could not go farther north without great inconvenience, and I could at that moment do nothing else." Besides, to send King Joseph scampering out of Madrid would deprive his government of all air of permanence; and the threat would almost certainly draw the French armies out of southern Spain. (Far beyond hearing now, behind the silence in the north, the long columns of the *Grande Armée* wound through the summer haze across the endless Russian plain. Napoleon was half inclined to reach Smolensk and halt, to check his senseless march deeper and deeper into Russia. But, as Wellington said of him later, "a conqueror, like a cannon-ball, must go on. If he rebounds, his career is over." So he went on into the silence.)

Bound for Madrid, Lord Wellington rode southward from Valladolid under the wide skies of Old Castile. Segovia watched him go by, the Roman arches of its aqueduct stepping serenely across the prostrate town; he passed the bald Guadarrama in the blazing August days; and within three weeks of Salamanca he was in the dusty plain below Madrid. King Joseph, a reluctant harbinger, scuttled before him into his capital and out again, bound for the distant security of Valencia with a retreating army and a vast convoy. For that unhappy monarch moved southward like a tribal migration in the choking dust of two thousand vehicles, whilst his capital made cheerful preparations to welcome the approaching British. They marched in on August 12, and found a city in the grip of the splendid dementia of which Southern capitals are occasionally capable. Bells pealed; the road ran wine and lemonade by turns, became a forest of waving palm-branches, and changed with dream-like ease into a *ballet* of young ladies pirouetting alongside the marching redcoats with offerings of grapes, of sticky sweets, of laurel leaves, and treating their impassive chief to worship that bordered perilously on the divine. For Wellington, high-nosed and silent, rode at the centre of the mass with wild brunettes covering his hands, his sword, his boots, even his horse with Spanish kisses, and picked his cautious way across a bright sea of flowered shawls, until King Joseph's palace walls shut out the roaring city; and the new master of Madrid after this violent apotheosis resumed his problems.

Far behind him a grateful England, ringing with the news of Salamanca, poured out fresh honours. Official England was a little changed that summer, since a crazy pistol-shot had accounted for the inoffensive Perceval. But Liverpool assumed his place, Castlereagh returned to

office, and the Government was still in friendly hands. The Peer was to
be a Marquess now; and from his retirement Lord Wellesley, whose
sumptuous mind was always apt to run on heraldry, offered the generous suggestion that his victorious younger brother should be permitted
to augment his coat of arms with the French eagle. Ministers, consulted
on this vital problem, preferred the Union Jack; and Lord Wellington,
who felt that the French emblem "carries with it an appearance of
ostentation, of which I hope I am not guilty," concurred in their opinion. The Prime Minister was busy with the purchase of the manor of
Wellington on his behalf; and though cheerfully indifferent to his step
in the peerage (he asked someone, "What the devil is the use of making
me a Marquess?"), he took some interest in his new estates, and was not
above indicating that his allowances were quite inadequate to his expenses in the field. It was still raining Spanish honours, and his splendid
jewellery was augmented by the Golden Fleece.

Meanwhile, there were the French. He hoped to keep them busy in
the south with minor operations, whilst he secured the road to France
at Burgos. His tone was quite light-hearted—"Matters go on well, and
I hope before Christmas, if matters turn out as they ought, and Bone
requires all the reinforcements in the North, to have all the gentlemen
safe on the other side of the Ebro." (That day the swelling domes of
Moscow gleamed under a pale northern sky, and the French dead were
piled high round the Great Redoubt at Borodino.) Wellington turned
northwards now. Madrid was left behind; the blind windows of the
Escorial stared at the British columns, as they went by towards the
north; the French fell back before them; and one September day that
saw the spires of Burgos and the long saddle of the Castle. That obstacle
remained; and as Wellington saw it rising in tiers above the brown
roofs of the town to the crowning defiance of its embrasures, he was
inclined to "doubt . . . that I have means to take the castle, which is
very strong." (Doubt hung on the autumn air of 1812; for while the
Peer stared doubtfully at Burgos through his glass, a dreadful doubt
hung over Moscow. The bright domes were veiled in smoke; and as
the French marched away, they turned to stare over their shoulders at
the red glare on the sky behind them.) He was at Burgos for a month
until the distant mountains were dusted with the October snows. Snow

ell in Russia, too—the first drifting flakes that fluttered harmlessly on the
till air, then powdered the interminable plain, until the winter skies
were dark above them, and they toiled endlessly through the white
ilence. Wellington's three siege-guns—"Thunder," "Lightning," and
Nelson" (who had lost a trunnion)—were banging bravely at the Castle.
He was still hopeful, though his hopes were chastened now—"Time is
wearing apace, and Soult is moving from the south; and I should not
e surprised if I were obliged to discontinue this operation in order to
ollect the army." Headquarters were enlivened by an opinionated
Marine, whom the senior service had consigned to Burgos to enlighten
Wellington with demonstrations of "a new exercise of the bayonet, which
s to render a British soldier equal to 12 Frenchmen." This bright pros-
ect opened one morning after breakfast; whereupon "after Lord W.
ad looked and listened with some impatience, he gave his orders for
ae day to the Adjutant-General, mounted his horse, and galloped to the
enches." Marines, it would appear, were prodigal of bright ideas.
ne had contrived an "artificial hill" for facilitating reconnaissance; but
s ingenuity faded before that of the learned Portuguese who "proposed
o burn the French army by means of convex glasses."

Burgos still barred the way; and impatient men stared from their
atteries at the brown roofs, the pointed spires, the trees along the
ver, and the distant roads that wound across the plain like ribbons.
he autumn weeks were passing, and the French were gathering to
orth and south of him. His parallels crept slowly forward; but the
in drove down, flooding his trenches. He could not storm the place,
aving but little musket ammunition." Besides, he would not willingly
peat the slaughter of Badajoz; when he stood at Cocks' graveside that
atumn, his face was wrung with pain. So he resolved to treat Burgos
trifle summarily, as he had treated hill-forts in India, and resorted to
alf-measures. But in war no half-measure succeeds. For mining, inade-
uate bombardment, and small storming-parties were no substitute for
e sustained exertions which had forced the gates of Portugal; and the
ge failed. As he wrote later in the year, "I played a game which might
cceed (the only one which could succeed), and pushed it to the last;
d the parts having failed, as I admit was to be expected," he faced the
asequences. He blamed no one else—"the Government had nothing to

say to the siege. It was entirely my own act. . . . That which was want ing . . . was means of transporting ordnance and military stores to the place where it was desirable to use them." Transport, for once, had failed him.

Regretfully he turned to go. Soult and the fluttered Joseph were work ing north towards Toledo; Madrid was threatened; and Wellington could not maintain himself in his advanced position. They must turn back from Burgos, as John Moore had once turned back from Sahagun on the Burgos road; but (unlike Moore) they would not need to run for their transports, since Portugal was safely held behind them. A great cathedral watched them file through the silent streets under the moon; their wheels were muffled; but the Castle guns were silent. Within a week they were behind the Douro at Valladolid, and November found them on the familiar heights of San Christoval. The Peer breathed again, having reassembled his forces without misadventure and "got clear in a handsome manner from the worst scrape that he ever was in." Bare countries are like ladders with few rungs; and having lost the rung of Burgos, Wellington was forced to drop to the rung of Salamanca. He hoped to hold it, though he had scarcely more than fifty thousand men against ninety thousand. But once more the battle of San Christoval re mained unfought. The French manœuvred round his flank. Once again the armies wheeled round Salamanca. But, unlike Marmont, Soult gave no opening; the rain came driving down; and Wellington marched his men off to Portugal.

The four final days of retreat were miserable. Supplies went astray; starving men ate acorns and shot uncovenanted pigs; it rained incessantly and an exasperated chief presided over awkward moments in the rear, confessing that, by God, it was too serious to say anything. Yet, serious indeed, it was never dangerous; and he brought off his army "in face of a superior enemy, with the deliberation of an ordinary march . . . and the casualties from the sword under 850"—a lively contrast with the long agony of the *Grande Armée*. For Wellington incurred no Beresina, and did not require a Ney to fight heroic rearguard actions. He brought his army off; and long before a pale, furred man in a sleigh drove hurriedly from Smorgoni towards Paris, he had them safe in Portugal.

Not that he was content. An angry circular informed subordinates that discipline was lax, that "the officers lost all command over their men" in the retreat, and that this lapse was solely attributable "to the habitual inattention of the Officers of the regiments to their duty." This ungentle document found its way into newspapers, and left a wholly false impression of a grim martinet. His irritation was excusable. For at some points on the long road from Burgos wine had been as plentiful—and almost as destructive—as snow in the retreat from Moscow. But it was all over now; and they were safe on the windy hills which look down into Portugal after a year in which British arms had secured two vital fortresses, taken twenty thousand prisoners, and cleared southern Spain of the French. Small wonder that the Marquess wrote, "I believe that I have done right"; while Pakenham reported him "in good health and temper, satisfied with himself." For 1812 was over. The South, the peerless South was free. The Frenchmen with their clanging bands were gone at last; and Seville throbbed with innumerable strings, while the soft wail of its own music stole through Granada. For the South was free, and Andalusia sang in the sunlight. Twelve hundred miles away the *Grande Armée* was dead.

VII

THE pace was quickening, as 1812 passed into 1813. All Europ
was on the move that winter—France falling back across German
Russia in ponderous pursuit, the Prussians drilling hopefully, and eve
Italy stirring a little. The Emperor in Paris created, improvised, decree
and threatened. He must have fresh armies; and French drafts wer
northwards now up the long road towards the Pyrenees. Valladolid ar
Burgos, long accustomed to their south-bound convoys, watched t
changing tide and felt the wind of war set from a new quarter.

Not that Spain was to be left bare; for 200,000 men remained,
whom nearly 100,000 faced Wellington. Once that winter he left l
village street in Beira to visit his allies. His first call was on the Spa
iards, who had at last appointed him Commander-in-Chief. This hono
was delayed until the Spanish armies had exhausted the possibilities
defeat under their own commanders; and the Peer accepted the co
mand without enthusiasm. But it might be made to serve as a mea
of co-ordination and control, and he defined his new authority ir
series of precise demands. Then he rode off through winter floods
Cadiz and, enlivened by lumbago on the road, pressed his points
person. This visit has inspired romantic guesses. But his main purs
during the sixteen days of its duration were far from Capuan; for
negotiated with the Spanish Regency, addressed the Cortes in bad
energetic Spanish, and wrote stately letters in rather stilted French to
new subordinates. His task, as he defined it to a correspondent, was
try 'to organise the Poles,' which appears to be a work something of
same kind with that which Dumouriez describes so well in his Li
he had used the same comparison fourteen years earlier, when he
organising the Nizam's army before Seringapatam—a testimonial to
thorough reading of a book that had travelled from his Dublin lodg
to Madras in Colonel Wesley's baggage. He judged that he had "n
some progress; but the libellers have set to work, and I am appreher
that the Cortes will take the alarm." For he found journalists and Pa

nentarians almost uniformly unhelpful. He was prepared, of course, to fight for Spain as long as she is the enemy of France, whatever may e her system of government." But a constitution created "very much on he principle that a painter paints a picture, viz., to be looked at" failed o compel his admiration; and he was frankly derisive of "a sovereign opular assembly, calling itself 'Majesty' . . . and of an executive govern- ent called 'Highness' acting under the control of 'His Majesty' the as- embly." He could see the menace.

"The theory of all legislation is founded in justice; and, if we could be certain that all legislative assemblies would on all occasions act according to the principles of justice, there would be no occasion for those checks and guards which we have seen established under the best systems. Unfor- tunately, however, we have seen that legislative assemblies are swayed by the fears and passions of individuals; when unchecked, they are tyrannical and unjust; nay more: it unfortunately happens too frequently that the most tyrannical and unjust measures are the most popular. Those measures are particularly popular which deprive rich and powerful individuals of their properties under the pretence of the public advantage; and I tremble for a country in which, as in Spain, there is no barrier for the preservation of private property, excepting the justice of a legislative assembly possessing supreme powers."

he proposed a House of Lords for Spain. Meanwhile, he "could wish t some of our reformers would go to Cadiz"; the lesson, he appeared feel, might be salutary for Mr. Cobbett. For Cadiz marked a stage in llington's political education, serving to deepen his distaste for popular emblies. Apart from Westminster, he had only known two legislative lies intimately—the Irish House of Commons and the Cortes—and ther was calculated to make a democrat of him.

One ally grounded in the elements of military organisation, he passed to his next pupil and rode off to Lisbon. Business was almost wholly cluded by four days of strenuous celebration. The anniversary of dad Rodrigo was honoured with a banquet; Captain Gurwood, who commanded the "forlorn hope," arrived a trifle late and was exalted he skies when his excuses were greeted with a genial "You were not late this time last year." They all went to the Opera, where (for some on buried deep in the Portuguese intelligence) doves fluttered in the

cheering auditorium, and one perched on the Peer's box. These arduou
festivities concluded, he rode back to his village in the hills.

Life at Headquarters was not without its compensations. A buttone
figure still bent above its papers or tramped the little square on winte
afternoons among the drovers. His hounds still hunted, and his tal
was quite as varied as ever—how Ireland must be held by force, an
what a blunder his brother Richard and Mr. Canning made in takin
up the Catholic question; how he meant to have twenty-five couples (
hounds to hunt next winter; and how admirably the Peninsula was suite
to warfare, because there was nothing in it for anyone to damage—"a
for instance, what is this village worth? burn it, and a few hundre
would make it as good as ever with a little labour"—but that he shou
be almost sorry to see such a war in Germany. Sometimes it was pla
night in the Light Division, and he rode over to Gallegos for the
theatricals. The programme (printed on War Department paper by t
army press at Freneda) announced *The Rivals* with a cast of Riflemen,
pink subaltern as *Lydia Languish*, and a small part for Havelock's eld
brother—"after which a Variety of Comic Songs," the whole loyally co
cluding *Vivat Wellington*. For the Light Division Theatre was w
aware of its position. But the great occasion was the ball at Rodri
That afternoon he had been working at Headquarters until half-p
three; but he rode the seventeen miles in two hours, dined in his deco
tions, danced, took supper, and set off at half-past three for a gall
home by moonlight. They sat down sixty-five to dinner, and two hu
dred guests came to the dance. The ball-room was a trifle draughty,
the siege had left a large gap in the roof. But they danced with spi
though the floor left much to be desired, and a sentry had to be pos
near a hole. Two Spanish couples obliged with the whirl and flutter o
fandango and a *bolero*; and a disapproving Judge-Advocate, who fai
to relish

> "Fandango's wriggle, or Bolero's bound,"

observed that his allies twirled and handled their partners "a li
more . . . than our fair ones would like at first," but was incline
think that on the whole the English practice was for the best. T
drank innumerable toasts—"The next campaign," "Death to all Frer

men," and "King Ferdinand VII"—and when the ladies had retired, they taught the Spaniards how to say "Hip, hip, hip hurra" instead of "Viva," and chaired one another freely until someone dropped a General. Outside the moon was shining; it was freezing hard; a thoroughbred was clattering up mountain roads at a hand-gallop; and before dawn came to Ciudad Rodrigo, Lord Wellington was back at Headquarters.

He could be genial, though a snub could still be administered at need; and a bewhiskered aide-de-camp of the Prince Regent, appearing on parade in the full glory of a Hussar uniform, received no more from him than two fingers raised to a cocked hat at full gallop, followed by a resounding "Grant, if you will dine with me, I dine at six o'clock." But dinner at Headquarters had been known to end in a song; and he was apt to call without undue modesty for the song made in his honour by the Spaniards after Salamanca. The guitar spoke softly; long fingers plucked the strings; and, "*Ahe Marmont,*" the singer gloated, "*onde vai, Marmont?*" Wellington sat listening with composure to the lift and wail of the *copla*. Indeed, they noticed that he "hears his own praises in Spanish with considerable coolness"; and someone termed the song "Lord Wellington's favourite."

But life at Headquarters was not all dinners and fox-hunting. For there were still his endless papers—letters from ministers, from grandees of Spain, from half the Army List—all answered in his swift handwriting. His letters to the Spaniards were a complete correspondence-course in elementary administration, enlivened by sardonic comments to his brother Henry on the unsatisfactory progress of their backward pupils at Cadiz. Then there were endless courts-martial to be written upon or discussed with Mr. Larpent, departmental queries from young Lord Palmerston on the inspiring theme of regimental accounts, friendly notes from the Prime Minister about his new estate at Wellington, the eternal problem of cash payments, his regular report to the Secretary of State, and supplies to be collected for the spring campaign. A more agreeable category related to the fresh honours which came crowding on him. The Portuguese, not to be outdone by Spain, made him a Duke under the splendid title of Duque da Victoria; he became Colonel of the Blues and expressed his rapture in the shy confession that "there was never so fortunate or favoured a man"; the Garter was conferred on him, and he wrote home

an anxious query over which shoulder he should wear the blue ribbon
An enticing offer of Russian troops for the Peninsula flits through h
papers; but Spanish pride was, for some occult reason, offended by th
thought; the offer turned out to be unauthorised; and, true to the
invariable tradition, the phantom Russians never came.

There was no limit to the size, large or small, of the topics sub
mitted to the Commander-in-Chief. He advised the Cabinet upo
European strategy; and when Lieutenant Kelly of the Fortieth elope
with a young lady, the case received his best attention. He even inte
viewed the angry mother and undertook (in Portuguese) to restore th
erring child on condition that she should not be ill-treated or consigne
to a convent. Then he directed Lowry Cole to part the lovers. But Co
impressed by the mother's menacing aspect, pointed out to the Cor
mander-in-Chief the probable nature of the fair prodigal's welcom
Besides, the impulsive Kelly (as he reported) was quite prepared
make amends by marriage. Lord Wellington, more sceptical, could "n
but observe that he has it in his power, whenever he pleases, to co
pensate in that manner the injury which he has done to the family"
and improved the occasion by an impressive homily upon the lamental
tendency of officers and men abroad to commit such outrages as th
individually thought fit. But that very day the knot was tied by
army chaplain of Portuguese *Caçadores*. Propriety had received its d
tribute and when the outraged parent called at Headquarters, she fou
a disobliging Wellington who declined to intervene and left his sh
visitor vociferating threats of sudden death for her offspring and tra
portation for the obliging chaplain. So romance was satisfied; and o
more frontal attack upon a Wellington position had failed.

England was very far away; and the distance served to modify
attitude to politics. He had come out to Portugal as Chief Secretary i
Tory administration, returning from Vimeiro to dispense party ar
ments from the Treasury Bench without a conscious effort. But now
view of his position had changed; and when a Whig correspond
seemed to emphasise the party difference between them, he wrote
"as I have long ceased to think of home politics, it cannot be said
I am of a party different from that to which any other person belo
I serve the country to the best of my ability abroad, leaving the Gov

ent at home to be contended for by the different parties as they may
ink proper." In fine, he was Lord Wellington and knew his duty.

Besides, the Peninsula still claimed his full attention. The French were
ow uneasily aligned on the great road to France; and the French mon-
chy in Spain was little more than a field-army. The South was up; the
atalans persisted bravely; *guerrilleros* went freely up and down the land;
d the shaggy hills behind Bilbao were loud with drumming, as the
orth marched out to war behind its pipes. A French rearguard still
cupied Madrid; but the King's headquarters were already far to the
rth in Valladolid; and his modest hope was to hold the line of the
ouro against the British, who were bound to come marching up from
rtugal by way of Salamanca. But were they? Lord Wellington had
er views. For he was disinclined to force a passage of the Douro in face
a French army in strong prepared positions. He preferred to cross the
er lower down its course, far behind the Portuguese frontier, and to
pear in disagreeable force on the French bank. That, he surmised,
uld be an inexpensive method of dislodging them. So early as the third
ek of April his design was confided to Beresford:

"I propose to put the troops in motion in the first days of May. My in-
ention is to make them cross the Douro in general within the Portuguese
rontier, covering the movement of the left by the right of the army towards
he Tormes. . . ."

is was simplicity itself. At the same time he chose a bold expedient to
elerate his spring towards the north. His base was now at Lisbon; and
ilst it might be satisfactory to draw supplies thence so long as he was
rating in Leon and Castile, his line of communications would be in-
rably lengthened (and the resulting delays increased), if he succeeded
dvancing further to the north. So he resolved upon the unusual meas-
of transferring his base to the north coast of Spain as soon as he
uld reach the northern sphere of operations. (The same conception
ears in the transfer of his base in 1803 from Mysore to the west coast
ndia.) Before his march began, the Admiral commanding on the sta-
was advised that Wellington thought it "not impossible that we may
after have to communicate with the shipping in one of the ports in
North of Spain"; and at a later stage his supply ships were definitely

ordered to the great bay of Santander, a striking instance of the superio
elasticity conferred by sea-power on land operations.

Now they were ready to advance; and symptoms of the move began t
appear at Headquarters, where the Peer's claret was reported to be pack
ing. The date was fixed by the ripening of crops of forage for his horse
But the spring rains were late that year, and slight delays in the arriva
of the bridging-train (he infuriated the artillery by taking their gun-team
to draw pontoons) deferred his start—fortunately, perhaps, as Wellingto
was visited by a devastating cold. They moved before the end of May
and as they passed the frontier into Spain, he turned his horse and, wit
a rare concession to drama, flourished his hat towards the rear with th
apostrophe, "Farewell, Portugal! I shall never see you again." He neve
did.

For the hunt was up that sent the French behind the Pyrenees. Withi
a fortnight he had manœuvred them off the Douro; and the bells we
clashing in Zamora, as a cloaked, grey figure rode in. He waved away th
dishes of an endless lunch; and disappointed Spaniards asked, "Is th
Lord Wellington? The man who is sitting there so meekly in a grey coa
has only one officer at his side, and will not eat or drink anything? Goo
God!" Delighted villages thumped tambourines; nuns showered ros
leaves from the security of upper windows; but the advance went on,
they moved steadily northwards up the broad corridors of Old Casti
The Peer was on the move; and a hurried glimpse caught him pacing
village street with Beresford, whilst his tent was being pitched and t
Military Secretary sat writing orders on his knee under a wall. The Fren
continually fell back, as rung after rung of the long Spanish ladder slipp
from their hands. They stood at Burgos; but its works were still un
paired. He was outflanking them again; and they fell back once mo
leaving a rearguard to destroy the Castle (and blow out the glass of
cathedral). The roar of the explosion reached Wellington, who was
their heels and promptly resolved to "hustle them out of Spain." His f
design had contemplated a formal siege of Burgos. But the French
saved him the trouble; and his spirits mounted, as King Joseph's m
archy dwindled to an army in retreat. "Affairs are somewhat change
he wrote, "since the period when the frightened Leopard was to have b
driven into the sea. I think that if the Powers of Europe chuse it we n

now carry on a successful War, or may force the Tyrant to make a peace which shall give genuine tranquility to the World, & security to Independent States." (His spelling seemed to suffer slightly in the swift advance.) The French were waiting for him now in the hills south of Ebro. It was a strong position, approached precariously by a narrow road that crawled beneath the wicked spires of Pancorbo. But Wellington had little taste for frontal attacks on strong positions; and his columns slanted northwards away from the main road to France by which he was expected. For he would get behind the French again. He was still groping round their right; and their route lay by unlikely mountain paths, where he walked his horse and the guns were man-handled as the teams stepped gingerly over the boulders. The French were turned again and went disconsolately behind the Ebro, the Peer shepherding them; and his method of command was neatly illustrated by three notes written in a single afternoon to Lowry Cole:

"On the heights near Poder June 19th 1813 $\frac{1}{2}$ past 12 at Noon.

"I have ordered the Light Division to cross the River, & to get possession of the Ridge on the Enemy's left; and you will advance, & cannonade them in front, & push your Light Infantry across supporting it by Cavalry & Heavy Infantry.

"There is a Bridge at the Village, & I understand several fords."

The affair developed, and a second note conveyed his further wishes:

"I will make the Light Division continue its march till the Ridge on your right ends; & do you follow them up the valley to the same point.

"$\frac{1}{4}$ before two P.M.

"Let the Cavalry go with you."

A final scrap torn from his notebook warned the advancing Cole and left him with a discretion that, from such a source, was both flattering and rare:

                                      2 P.M. June 19th.

"Since I wrote to you a quarter of an hour ago I have heard that the Enemy are in strength on the great Road; you had better therefore halt when you will have crossed the River; & taken up such Posts as you may think proper."

His great sweep to the north had sent the French behind the Ebro and placed his own forces between Santander and the enemy. Now he could draw supplies by a short road from his new base; and if the French would fight, he was prepared to fight them.

He had come up with them at last; and their meeting-place was the great amphitheatre of Vitoria, where the last foothills of the Pyrenees look out across Castile. The hunted French—an army fifty thousand strong encumbered with a King, a Court, large portions of a Civil Service, and an extensive *smala* (someone irreverently remarked, "*Nous étions un bordel ambulant*")—lay across the great road to France. Somewhere behind the hills Lord Wellington was waiting to attack. It was all a little like the last phase of a *corrida*, when the trim *matador* steps briskly sword in hand into the silent ring, watched by a weary bull. The French waited for the blow, watched by the distant circle of the hills. The blow prepared by Wellington was a miniature of the whole campaign, in which he had continually groped round the French right to place himself between them and their road to France. His groping left should swing behind them once again, cut the great road to Bayonne, and encircle them or (at the worst) deflect them from their natural line of retreat, leaving them to stumble towards Pamplona and the high passes of the Pyrenees. That was his plain design, and on June 21 he executed it. His sole uncertainty was the whereabouts of Clausel's command, which had been hunting *guerrilleros* in the north; but an obliging innkeeper rode twenty miles to tell him that Clausel was safely lodged in his *posada*. Lord Wellington had ridden over the ground; his troops were up; and as the guns began to speak in the mist of a June morning, Vitoria watched from all belfries. The Peer, as usual, was everywhere, placing the troops and riding behind his infantry, as Picton led them into action in a cloud of blasphemy and a top-hat. Perhaps the full perfection of his scheme was slightly impaired by Wellington's practice of ubiquitous intervention, as an orchestral rendering would scarcely be improved by a conductor able to restrain his virtuosity from playing half the parts himself. But the blow fell, though Graham on his left had failed to get behind them; and as the shadows lengthened, the French went reeling off towards the Pyrenees. They had lost all their guns but two, the loot of Spain, and (worse still) the great road by which they might have marched back ayonne. Behind them in Vitoria excited redcoats were breaking open oxes full of Spanish dollars; while Portuguese capered in French Generals' uniforms, and by the light of flares a great fair was held where the whole *débris* of King Joseph's monarchy—pictures, books, currency, hurch-plate, and tapestry—was auctioned to perspiring men by bawling omrades. Wellington gave dinner to General Gazan's wife, who had een left behind. They asked her if another lady in the same plight was ot a General's wife as well. *"Ah, pour cela—non,"* she answered brightly, *lle est seulement sa femme de campagne."* The lure of loot was almost resistible; and the pursuit left something to be desired, though a Light ragoon suggested that the cause was rather Wellington's reluctance "to atrust officers with detachments to act according to circumstances, and am not quite clear if he approves of much success, excepting under his vn immediate eye."

But the blow had fallen. In just a month from his adieu to Portugal the rench monarchy in Spain had ceased to exist; and the news rang through urope. The *Gazette* with Wellington's despatch was printed in French, utch, and German and distributed broadcast; the unwelcome news was rust upon French fishermen in the English Channel; a Russian *Te eum*—the first ever sung for a foreign victory—greeted it; and the ws sent Stadion running at midnight down the corridors of a Silesian âteau, knocking at doors and greeting ruffled kings and ministers with e glad tidings that *"Le roi Joseph est —— en Espagne."* The tall Czar s radiant at the news; the dismal King of Prussia brightened; Berna- tte was a more loyal ally now; and even Austria veered towards action. r the guns of Vitoria echoed across the Continent, and Wellington had pped from the Spanish to the European stage.

VIII

I T W A S midsummer, 1813; and as they went forward, a long line ᴏ
mountains climbed slowly up the sky, where all the folded Pyrene
stood ranged in order. Beyond them lay the fields of France. For the lor
road from Lisbon had brought the marching redcoats all the way froɪ
Portugal, across the bare Castilian uplands, until they saw the last
Spain and the curved skyline of the Pyrenees. Spain was behind the
now with its wide skies and crumbling cities; and their road wou
upwards, past the brown belfries of Pyrenean villages and the anfr
tuosities of Basque nomenclature, towards the gates of France. Kɪ
Joseph was a dejected phantom flitting through the passes to St. Jean
Luz, his armies a receding line of bayonets winding beneath the drippɪ
trees through driving rain towards the frontier. Lord Wellington ro
irritably behind them, reviling the indiscipline of his own troops—"ᵥ
have in the service the scum of the earth as common soldiers; and
late years we have been doing every thing in our power, both by law a
by publications, to relax the discipline by which alone such men can
kept in order. . . . As to the non-commissioned officers, as I have
peatedly stated, they are as bad as the men. . . ." This angry mᴏ
inspired the summary arrest of an unlucky gunner for disobedience. ɪ
it soon subsided; and Pakenham reported him "vastly well and in hɪ
spirits," whilst his indignation grumbled in the distance like a recedɪ
storm as he reported to the Horse Guards that nobody in his army e
thought of obeying an order, with the rare and generous admission t
it was "an unrivalled army for fighting, if the soldiers can only be kepᵗ
their ranks during the battle."

The march went on towards the frontier. They heard the sea at lasᵗ
San Sebastian bay and saw the slow tide draw through the narrowₛ
Pasajes. France lay before them now. For there was nothing in their ᵖ
except the garrisons of San Sebastian and Pamplona; and they swept ᵖ
the fortresses, until they stared through the passes into France
watched the smoke of French villages across the gleaming Bidassoa.

was six months before any other European army came in sight of
France.) But the Peer was cautious, though civilian correspondents
might expect an immediate invasion of France and began to count the
days until he should ride into Paris; yet, as he drily pointed out, "none
appear to have taken a correct view of our situation on the frontier, of
which the enemy still possess all the strongholds within Spain itself; of
which strongholds, or at least some of them, we must get possession
before the season closes, or we shall have no communication whatever
with the interior of Spain." Facile ministers might write smooth things
about the prospects of his elevation to supreme command of the Allies in
Germany (eliciting a dutiful statement that he was the Prince Regent's
servant, would do what his masters pleased, but was far better where he
was); and Prinny himself, to whom he had despatched Marshal Jourdan's
bâton after Vitoria, responded in a slightly gushing letter that "you have
sent me, among the trophies of your unrivalled fame, the staff of a
French Marshal, and I send you in return that of England"—a gesture
which caused some embarrassment to his advisers, since there was no
such thing. But while the Horse Guards did their very best to design one
for the occasion—with some misgivings lest the Prince, whom an official
boldly denominated "the fountain of taste," might do it for himself—the
new Field Marshal, raised at last to the very top of the military tree,
obstinately declined to lose his head.

His sole objective, as he saw, was to prevent the French from reaching
their isolated garrisons in San Sebastian and Pamplona. Soult was in
front of him, selected by the Emperor (who was somewhere in Saxony
at grips with half the Continent) as *"la seule tête militaire qu'il y eût en
Espagne"*—a warier Soult than the light-hearted Marshal who had waited
for Sir Arthur Wellesley at Oporto in 1809. A chastened order now directed all his smaller units to send their eagles back to the depots for
safe custody; for now he had Lord Wellington to deal with. British guns
were banging in the sunshine at the roofs of San Sebastian huddled beneath the slopes of Urgull; and Pamplona would be starving soon. It was
time for the French to provide a distraction; and one morning in the
third week of July (the Peer had a slight touch of rheumatism) sharp
firing on the bare hills behind Pamplona brought him to Sorauren. For
Soult was thrusting southwards into Spain through Roncesvalles.

(Strange how that year's fighting hung about old scenes; for the Black
Prince's men had drawn their bows at Vitoria, and now French bayonets
wound through the pass where Charles the King had ridden and the last
despairing echoes of Roland's horn once died away.) The French advance
was sharply pressed; and Wellington came up at a gallop, stopping to
scrawl a hasty order on the stone parapet of a bridge with the Staff
muttering all round him, "The French are coming." But he was off again
before they came, the grey figure jolting in the saddle round corners and
up mountain paths, until its trim silhouette was seen at the very summit
—cocked-hat, frock-coat, and thoroughbred outlined against the summer
sky. The Portuguese caught sight of him first; and their hoarse cries of
"Douro" set the whole army roaring, until the cheers ran like a flame
along the hillsides and far out of sight. Erect and silent, a trim figure sat
its horse above the cheering, as the whole army roared its recognition of
"our great Lord," in "that stern and appalling shout" (as Napier termed
it in a famous rhapsody) "which the British soldier is wont to give upon
the edge of battle." Since Vitoria they called him "the hero of Britain."
They knew him now; and as he said that summer, "they will do for me
what perhaps no one else can make them do." He could see the blue and
gold of Soult and his staff across the narrow valley; and the wary Marshal
deferred the French attack, spread out his maps, took lunch, and went to
sleep, leaving a spirited junior to lean against a tree and positively beat
his brow with blind exasperation at the thought of sleep at such a junc-
ture. The attack followed on the morrow; but by now Wellington's
command was comfortably aligned upon a ridge; and though he termed
it "fair *bludgeon* work," the results were satisfactory. It had been a risky
business, though (he told someone afterwards that "at one time it was
rather alarming certainly, and it was a close-run thing"); and he had
little taste for mountain warfare, where the nature of the ground prevented him from being everywhere at once—"It is a great disadvantage
when the Officer Commanding in Chief must be absent, and probably at
a distance. For this reason there is nothing I dislike so much as these
extended operations, which I cannot direct myself."

There was an interval, while they were battering San Sebastian into
readiness for an assault. The Peer was limping with lumbago (his health
gave him unusual trouble that year, with a spring catarrh, his rheu-

sm, and now his back; and a misadventure when a chimney at Head-
uarters caught fire and sent him out to shout directions in the rain with
silk handkerchief over his head had scarcely helped). So when they
ned in state for the Prince Regent's birthday, he rose with difficulty for
e toasts, though a Spanish commissary rendered his favourite *Ahe Mar-*
ont. His correspondence now was full of politics—of *haute politique*
om Central Europe where a galaxy of Allied monarchs performed a
ghly complicated dance, and of the usual vexations from Cadiz where
accomplished troupe of Spanish politicians continued to exasperate
s long-suffering brother Henry by striking progressive attitudes, when
that the situation called for was a single-minded prosecution of the
r. The last evoked from Wellington a promise that he would not
iss a fair opportunity that may offer to give the democratical party a
ke"; he was slightly favourable to an offer of royalist support in
nce by the plump Duc de Berry; but he was frankly disrespectful
the Allied sovereigns, whose endeavours to concert a plan of campaign
re cheerfully dismissed as "loose conversations among Princes. For
part, I would not march even a corporal's guard upon such a system."
clear intelligence discerned that Allied war-aims must be harmon-
before combined Allied strategy could be dreamt of, and he summed
n up:

"The object of each should be to diminish the power and influence of
rance, by which alone the peace of the world can be restored and main-
ined: and although the aggrandizement and security of the power of one's
vn country is the duty of every man, all nations may depend upon it
at the best security for power, and for every advantage now possessed,
to be acquired, is to be found in the reduction of the power and in-
ence of the grand disturber."

nwhile, he entrenched himself securely at the gates of France. The
of San Sebastian still boomed; but on the very day that Soult made
her thrust a little nearer to the sea, the place fell. Flames licked its
bling houses, and the sea swung idly in the bay beneath the silent
el. The road to France was clear—the long road that they had
ped, mile after mile, since they first heard the thunder of the surf
the beaches and the first creak of loaded ox-waggons in Portugal,

six years behind them now. They had seen Lisbon with its straight an
sheltered streets, the brown forts along the Tagus, cool hospitals in Belen
and the big hills that guard Torres Vedras, as they tramped throug
Portugal in the dusty sunshine and watched the cactus writhe silentl
along the roads. The tall sierras of the frontier, where chilly rivers win
through deep, slaty gorges, had seen them on the march; and they ha
passed the empty distances of Spain, until they heard the torrents racir
through the shaggy Pyrenees. For those perspiring redcoats in the
black shakoes had tramped half the length and breadth of the Peninsu
Choking inside their stocks and loaded with sixty pounds of kit an
rations and nine pounds of Brown Bess, they had marched all the w
from Portugal to France in scarlet faced with yellow, white, and blu
and heavily cross-belted, through the blinding sunlight of six Peninsu
summers. Lord Wellington had formed them, corresponding endles
about their needs and husbanding them carefully; for when a Fren
adviser volunteered a wild strategical design, he opined that it "mig
answer well enough if I could afford, or the British Government or
tion would allow of my being as prodigal of men as every Frer
General is. They forget, however, that we have but one army, and t
the same men who fought at Vimeiro and Talavera fought the other
at Sorauren; and that, if I am to preserve that army, I must proc
with caution." Now he was almost proud of them. Army orders mi
abound with his customary fulminations against irregularity, and
could still ingeminate that "there is no crime recorded in the New
Calendar that is not committed by these soldiers, who quit their ra
in search of plunder." But in the privacy of his despatches he inforr
the Cabinet that "it is probably the most complete machine for its n
bers now existing in Europe," adding in a letter to Dumouriez that
command was *"plus en état de faire une campagne d'hiver qu'auc
armée que j'aie jamais vu"*; and in later years he said proudly tha
could have done *anything* with that army: it was in such splendid orc
For he was proud of them; and they responded with more warmth
he was quite accustomed to, cheering his silent figure for miles alon
line at Sorauren and even in camp acclaiming him "not with three t
three, or nine times nine, but as long as they could see him."

Now he had brought them to the edge of France; and in the aut weeks of 1813 the invasion was ready to begin. France had not been invaded since the wild days of the Republic, when the heads fell in Paris and Colonel Wesley of the Thirty-third beat his disconsolate retreat from the northern fortresses. But now his glass was busy among the red roofs and white walls of Basque villages; and in the first week of October they slipped across the river below the brown church-tower of Fuenterabia. (Before the month was out, the Emperor faced a great ring of enemies in front of Leipzig, fought for three days, and trailed off in defeat towards the Rhine.) The strict exigencies of strategy, perhaps, demanded that Wellington, once comfortably established astride of the western Pyrenees, should turn eastwards and drive Suchet from Catalonia. He confessed as much to Dumouriez:

"*La Catalogne m'a donné bien des mauvais momens pendant l'automne, et j'ai bien souvent pensé a y aller.*

"*Peut-être que, si je regardais seulement l'Espagne, ou même si je voyais les affaires sous un aspect militaire seulement, j' aurais du y aller, parcequ'il n'y a pas de doute que Buonaparte tient en Catalogne et tiendra les facilités pour rentrer en Espagne. Je dis peut-être, parceque, dans ce diable de pays, où j' ai fait la guerre pendant cinq ans, j'ai toujours trouvé, comme votre Henri Quatre, qu'avec des petits armées on ne faisait rien, et qu'avec des grandes armées on mourait de faim. . . . D'ailleurs il faut que la vue purement militaire cède à la politique. J'ai vu la marche des affaires en Allemagne, et, malgré les revers très graves qui sont arrivés; j'ai cru voir des germes des succès très considerables qui sont depuis arrivés.*

"*Si je ne me suis pas trompé, il est bien plus important aux alliés, et à l'Espagne même, que je me porte en avant en France, au lieu de faire une guerre de forteresse en Catalogne. . . .*"

His steady reasoning gleams through the imperfect French; and he went forward into France. Pamplona fell behind them, and in November they drove the French from the Nivelle, where Soult had hoped to stand behind a miniature version of Torres Vedras. Now they were closing in on Bayonne, and Headquarters moved to St. Jean de Luz, between the blue Biscayan rollers and the carved hills behind. A conversation with a captured Colonel, to whom Wellington gave dinner, informed him of the Imperial *Götterdämmerung*. The Staff plied their unhappy guest with questions; but the discreet Peer "interfered quietly and whispered to them to let him alone, and that after a good dinner and a few glasses of Madeira our friend would mend." The treatment answered; and his host adroitly brought the conversation round to comforts at Headquarters— to the Emperor's recent experiences in that respect—and then, with the most casual air in the world, he launched a question.

"*Où était le quartier-général de l'Empereur,*" he innocently enquired, "*d'après les dernières nouvelles?*"

"*Nulle part,*" the Colonel answered gloomily, "*il n'y a plus de quartier-général.*"

"*Comment plus de quartier-général?*"

"*Monseigneur, il n'y a point de quartier-général, et point d'armée, l'affaire est finie.*"

But Soult was still in front of him, and the fortress of Bayonne wa formidable. Besides, he had all the novel problems of an invasion—o French feelings to be handled with his invariable discretion, angry depu tations to be soothed, and proclamations posted up in Basque. Perfec discipline became more necessary than ever, and the pardonable inclina tion of his Spanish troops to avenge the long French occupation by carnival of theft and destruction caused him endless trouble. Indeed, h Peninsular allies were more than usually trying that season, and he wro bitterly that "*le Démon de la discorde se plaît à mêler des affaires a la Péninsule.*" Wellington was rarely figurative; but the outbreak wa not surprising, since he was afflicted with a Minister of War at Cad whom he stigmatised as "that greatest of all blackguards," and he w unusually sensitive to the attacks of Spanish journalists upon allege atrocities at San Sebastian.

A new complication threatened his peace, as he faced in his clear-head way the problem of the future government of France. He had be thinking of it ever since he read a *Quarterly* review by Croker in 1811 a book by some exiled royalist; he read the book itself (it was Fabe *Notices sur l'Intérieur de la France*) and found it highly instructive; a when two rainy days confined him with the *curé* at St. Pé and his int locutor confirmed his previous impressions of French opinion, promptly advised the Government that France was weary, that the p vailing hunger was for peace—peace, probably, without the Emper But he found no positive revival of royalist sentiment and advised pe with Napoleon, if he was inclined to moderation. At the same time he hinted broadly that "if I were a Prince of the House of Bourbon, nothing should prevent me from now coming forward, not in a good house in London, but in the field in France; and if Great Britain would stand by him, I am certain he would succeed." He even sent a message to the same effect to Monsieur; and the majestic processes of the Bourbon mind, assisted by Wellington's report of his conversations with a village *curé*, evolved the project of despatching the Duc d'Angoulême to San Sebastian. A grateful letter to Headquarters from Hartwell House even compared Wellington to Marlborough—strange praise from a great-great-grandson of Louis XIV—and advised him of the satisfaction with which Louis XVIII observed his entry into France.

There was a pause in drenching Pyrenean rain; and two brigades of Guards in scarlet tunics and white pantaloons attended divine worship on the sands at St. Jean de Luz, whilst Lord Wellington in full uniform stood near the drum-head. Then they attacked again, driving the French behind the Nive. But Soult struggled hard, and 1813 went out upon a week of stubborn fighting in the hills behind Biarritz. This year there could be no interlude of peaceful winter-quarters in his village street at Freneda. For the war scarcely halted except for a few weeks of leisure at St. Jean de Luz, when everybody strolled on the sea-wall from four o'clock till six "at a true twopenny postman's long trot," whilst languid guardsmen (recently arrived and a shade exhausted by their unaccustomed activities) lounged on the parapet, and Lord Wellington himself was seen outraging military sensibilities with his frock-coat and top-hat of the sky-blue and black, no less civilian, of the Salisbury hunt. For he lost in his hunting. The little streets were full of vociferating Spanish muleteers and the long strings of jingling mules; the little shop-windows offered the unaccustomed delights of butter and sardines; and obliging Frenchmen ran the blockade of their own sentries with poultry for their country's foes. For they preferred the invader's ready money (helped out with bags of sugar to which they had been strangers, thanks to the blockade, for seven years) to the less profitable traffic of Soult's requisitions. It had been the invariable practice of French armies to live upon the country; but when the country happened to be French as well, the practice failed to commend itself, and a shrewd countryside preferred to sell to Wellington's commissaries.

The French prince and his suite arrived, and nobody was much impressed—"Lord Wellington was in his manner droll towards them . . . they bowed and scraped right and left so oddly, and so actively, that he followed with a face much nearer a grin than a smile." There were balls at the *Mairie* (where an adventurous *gendarme* essayed a horn-pipe) and church parade on Sundays with the Guards in hollow square on the sands against a sunny background of blue sky and crowded shipping in the smooth blue bay—"quite," as a rapturous Judge-Advocate remarked "a Vernet." But work crowded on the Peer. His next enterprise was to encircle Bayonne by bridging the wide Adour below the town while the February gales were still blowing; and someone saw him studying th sea from the sea-wall at halfpast seven one winter morning. The bol throw succeeded; and whilst they made it, Soult was distracted by a attack far inland, which drove him beyond Orthez on February 27. Bu for the first time Wellington was very nearly one of his own casualtie He was standing under fire with Alava, when a wounded Portugues limped past, explaining that he was *"ofendido."* Something knocked ov Alava; and Wellington was laughing at him, when he was hit himsel He fell and scrambled to his feet, remarking with cheerful blasphem "By God! I am *ofendido* this time." For a stray shot had driven h sword-hilt against his hip, bruising it and breaking the skin; but, thoug stiff, he was well enough to ride on the next day.

The French drew off along the Pyrenees; and the war rolled eastwar across France. The spring was bitter; and Lord Wellington rode aft them with the snow driving in his face (that day his taste for inco spicuous costume selected a white cloak). In the north the Emperor w fencing desperately, as the net slowly tightened round him. The end w coming now; and hopeful kings revisited their kingdoms. King Fer nand of Spain, more like a Goya than ever, lifted the questionable light his unpleasing countenance upon Gerona; and Wellington remembe that he had got some pictures of King Joseph's after Vitoria, which mi belong to Ferdinand. They had not impressed him at the time—not, t is to say, so much as the Raphaels which they had shewn him in Mad —and he had "thought more of the prints and drawings, all of

Italian school, which induced me to believe that the whole collection was robbed in Italy rather than in Spain." He sent them home for cleaning, but was now concerned to learn that they were finer than he had supposed. So Henry Wellesley was instructed to ascertain if they were Spanish royal property, as "I am desirous of restoring them to His Majesty." But he had Bourbons nearer home; and Wellington, now a convinced royalist on strictly military grounds, pressed the Prime Minister to take a stronger line in favour of the dynasty:

"Any declaration from us would, I am convinced, raise such a flame in the country as would soon spread from one end of it to the other, and would infallibly overturn him.

"I cannot discover the policy of not hitting one's enemy as hard as one can, and in the most vulnerable place. I am certain that he would not so act by us, if he had the opportunity. He would certainly overturn the British authority in Ireland if it was in his power. . . ."

Then Angoulême, *incognito* discarded and a Royal Highness once again, rode into Bordeaux in the wake of Marshal Beresford; and the white cockades came out.

The war rolled slowly east; and Wellington's paper-work was more than usually exacting. Diplomacy absorbed him now; he was in the saddle all day long; and correspondence was reserved for after dinner. But the French were still in front of him. He had a brush with them at Tarbes, a slightly tangled affair with Soult in front and a town amicably bawling *"Vive le roi"* behind. Then he was facing Toulouse in the last week of March, with Soult comfortably ensconced behind the broad Garonne. There was endless trouble with the bridging-train; and he went reconnoitring in his usual fashion, riding down to the river with an oilskin cover over his cocked-hat and positively chatting with a French vedette. Then he dismounted, strolled about, and having seen the ground rode off. (That week the heavy footsteps echoed in the deserted galleries of Fontainebleau, as Marshals came and went, until a lonely man sat saddled in an empty palace.) An excited note was on its way from Paris, acquainting Wellington that "Glory to God and to yourself, the great man has fallen." But Soult was still in Toulouse; and on April 10

Wellington's attack was launched. It took liberties that in other circumstances would have been scarcely pardonable, and there were grave vicissitudes. But it succeeded; Wellington, for once, was playing high for victory; and Soult, driven from his stronghold, trailed off towards Carcassonne, while the Peer rode into Toulouse. They cheered him in the streets; and he had not been in the place an hour before a Colonel came riding in with news from Bordeaux.

"I have extraordinary news for you."

"Ay," said the Peer, whom nothing could surprise, "I thought so. I knew we should have peace; I've long expected it."

"No," said the Colonel, "Napoleon has abdicated."

"How abdicated?" Wellington replied with cheerful incredulity. "Ay, 'tis time indeed. You don't say so, upon my honour! Hurrah!" And the Colonel enjoyed the unprecedented spectacle of Lord Wellington without his coat on spinning round and snapping his fingers.

He gave a ball at the *Préfecture* that night; and they sat down about forty to dinner. He gave them a new toast as well—"Louis XVIII"—and someone served out white cockades for them to wear. Then Alava stood up and gave them *"El Liberador de España,"* whilst all the foreigners—French, Germans, Portuguese, and Spanish—toasted him in their own languages—*"Liberateur de la France," "Liberador da Portugal," "Liberateu de l'Europe."* They shouted for ten minutes; and then the embarrasse hero "bowed, confused, and immediately called for coffee." After tha they all went to the play. Their white cockades were stared at; but whe Wellington (who was in the stagebox with Picton and the Spaniards laid his hat on the front of the box to shew the royal colours, the hous roared. They played the royal anthem, too; and someone recited the ne constitution from a box. The piece was admirably chosen. For it wa Grétry's *Richard Cœur de Lion;* and when the band struck up the air, vocalist sang the appeal of his devoted Queen disguised as Blondel—

"Ô Richard, ô mon roi, l'univers t'abandonne . . ."

and those excited soldiers heard the very air once sung to other soldie as a young Queen at Versailles walked graciously among them with sleepy Dauphin in her arms. Dauphin and Queen were gone; but t wheel had come full circle. For King Louis reigned once more in France. Peace came within a week; Lord Wellington signed a Convention of Toulouse with less unhappy consequences than that of Cintra; and as the firing died away, the marching columns halted. There was a sudden silence, and the war was over.

"—— and then all the people cheered again." For it was 1814—"the year of revelry," as someone called it, with Allied sovereigns bowing graciously in all directions, and Lord Byron writing *Lara* whilst undressing after balls and masquerades, and oxen roasting whole in country market-places, and mail-coaches bowling along every road in England trimmed with laurel leaves and rousing sentiments about "the Downfall of the Tyrant" and bright with transparencies of Lord Wellington. But Wellington was still at Toulouse. Army business kept him there a few weeks longer, mitigated by more balls at the *Préfecture* and a little hunting, for within a week of the armistice he was riding to hounds at five o'clock one morning, and a distinguished soldier enquiring for his whereabouts was scandalised to learn the the Commander-in-Chief was believed to be somewhere in a forest about eighteen miles away. But his top-hat and blue frock-coat were seen about the streets, as he slipped unobtrusively out of Angoulême's *levée* on his way back to the *Hôtel de France*; arch whispers even hinted that his residence was rendered more attractive by the Spanish belle wedded to its proprietor—"I do not mean to be scandalous," as the Judge-Advocate primly observed, "but this, perhaps, may have decided the choice of the house." After all, the war was over. Now they were all discussing who goes to America; for "the government," as someone at the Horse Guards wrote, "have determined to give Jonathan a good drubbing," and a large detachment of that incomparable army was to see the shining spaces of the Great Lakes, the flames of Washington, and the endless cane-brakes of Louisiana. But Wellington did not go with them. Another duty called. For Castlereagh invited him to take the British Embassy in Paris, and he accepted with a sober conviction that he "must serve the public in some manner or other; and as, under existing circumstances, I could not well do so at home, I must do so abroad." His acceptance alluded modestly to "a situation for which I should never have thought myself qualified." But he was not too old to learn a new trade at forty-five; besides, six years of dealing with the

Spaniards and Portuguese were a respectable apprenticeship in diplomacy, and Henry wrote cheerfully from Madrid that he would find it "very pretty amusement."

Then he was off to Paris in the first week of May, arriving just in time to see the Russians march past the Allied sovereigns on the *Quai*. Those exalted personages watched from a window in the Louvre; and King Louis XVIII sat composedly in an armchair, while the lean Emperor of Austria stood just behind him with the dismal King of Prussia, and the tight-waisted Czar did the honours. Lord Wellington saw the spectacle on horseback, riding between Castlereagh and his brother Charles. But he was quite a spectacle himself; for all the monarchs craned forward for a sight of him, where he sat his horse almost defiantly civilian in his blue frock-coat and top-hat. They introduced him to old Platow the Cossack; and when he saw the Russian cavalry, he said in his plain way, "Well, to be sure, we can't turn out anything like this." The Czar called on him that evening, and he looked in at a ball where the company was sublimely mixed—a *galimatias* of reigning princes, Blücher's moustaches, the red head of Ney, and the watchful eyes of Metternich. The Czar waltzed with Maréchale Ney, and Blücher kissed Lady Castlereagh's hand with gusto. Then he was introduced to Wellington and, in default of conversation, "they held each other's hands, and there was a great deal of hearty smiling"; someone interpreted; but the old Hussar looked merely puzzled. Wellington was a week in Paris. Whilst he was there, the news arrived that Liverpool and the Prince Regent had given one last turn to the fountain of honour, and so he was to be a Duke. Kitty had it from the Prime Minister himself; and Richard, who was always strong upon such matters, was duly taken into counsel as to the proper title for him. So Arthur passed him in the race. For Richard was a Marquess still; but Arthur was to be a Duke—the Duke of Wellington. His hands were full; and it was three weeks before a brotherly postscript acquainted Henry that "I believe I forgot to tell you I was made a Duke."

Before May was out, he was back at Toulouse on the road to Spain, where Ferdinand was rapidly reducing his long-lost subjects to distraction. But it would never do to inaugurate the new golden age with a civil war; and hopes were entertained that Wellington's familiar tones might discipline the restive Spaniards and their unprepossessing king. Castlereagh had thought him looking well in Paris; but an observer at Toulouse found him a little thin and pulled down by a cold. Then he posted off to Spain at eight o'clock one morning. The long road was familiar; he saw Vitoria again, and the tall spires of Burgos; Valladolid went by, and once more he came in sight of Madrid. He saw the King, and thought him "by no means the idiot he is represented." But his ministers were quite deplorable; and Wellington discharged a heavy cargo of good advice—that promiscuous arrests should be followed up by trial or release, or, at the very least, by some kind of attempt to justify them; that England would expect an effort to govern "on liberal principles"; and that, in certain circumstances, she might even undertake "to discourage and discountenance, by every means in our power, the rebellion in the Spanish colonies." (For the time had not yet come for calling a New World into being to redress the balance of the Old; besides, the Duke of Wellington was not Mr. Canning.) This business was transacted to an accompaniment of etiquette that varied between the impressive and the imbecile. He stood with Ferdinand on a palace balcony and kept his hat on, because he was a Grandee of Spain; and when he had his audience, the simpering San Carlos asked him if he noticed how the guards had stamped their feet. "That is only done," he added, "for a Grandee of the first order—you must indeed be a happy man."

He was happy in his way; for he was fully occupied. His family displayed a tendency to share his happiness, since William had brought his household to the Continent and joined him in Madrid. Soon he would see them all; for he was on his way to England now. He stopped a few days in Bordeaux writing farewell epistles, and a final Order was issued to the army:

"1. The Commander of the Forces, being upon the point of returning to England, again takes this opportunity of congratulating the army upon the recent events which have restored peace to their country and to the world.

"2. The share which the British army has had in producing these events, and the high character with which the army will quit this country, must be especially satisfactory to every individual belonging to it, as they are the Commander of the Forces; and he trusts that the troops will continue the same good conduct to the last.

"3. The Commander of the Forces once more requests the army to accept his thanks.

"4. Although circumstances may alter the relations in which he has stood towards them, so much to his satisfaction, he assures them that he shall never cease to feel the warmest interest in their welfare and honor; and that he will be at all times happy to be of any service to those to whose conduct, discipline, and gallantry their country is so much indebted."

The debt was honourably acknowledged; and he was granted nearly forty years for its discharge—forty years of begging-letters and hats touched by eager fingers as his horse went by. There was a loose sovereign ready in his waistcoat pocket for any old soldier who had served under him. His letter-bag was filled for nearly half a century with applications for every kind of favour; and can he be reproached if his replies more often than not were in the negative? Harrowing anecdotes are preserved of hungry veterans who, dining at his table, filled their pockets with the broken meats for starving families at home. An angry officer who had served with him in the East, endorsed his courteous confession of inability to find him employment with the angry query, "Can this Man have a Heart!!" Yet the indignant applicant had voluntarily retired from the service in 1812; and now he was inclined to blame the Duke for not employing him in 1828. (Indeed, his notion of the Duke's utility was even more extensive; since a note survives in which "the Duke of Wellington presents his Compliments to Mr. Elers, and is much obliged to him for his Letter of this day. The Duke has no occasion for a Newfoundland Dog, and will not deprive Mr. Elers of him.")

Had he a heart? The contrary is scarcely proved by the circumstance that he did not grant every favour that was asked of him. How could he? It was easy enough for Byron to reel off indignant stanzas inciting him to

> "go, and dine from off the plate
> Presented by the Prince of the Brazils;
> And send the sentinel before your gate
> A slice or two from your luxurious meals:
> He fought, but has not fed so well of late."

but to become the almoner of fifty thousand men drawn from the least provident classes of his fellow-subjects, to forward the professional ambitions of half the officers in the Army List, and to prolong these services into the second generation was utterly impossible. Besides, his hands were often tied by a strong sense of orderly administration. For how could responsible Departments ever do their work if the Duke of Wellington perpetually intervened in favour of innumerable *protégés*? That was the reason why his correspondents often received an irritating *non possumus*, and concluded angrily that they were forgotten. True, he had every excuse for not remembering them. For whilst they had ample leisure for their reminiscences, Wellington had something more to do than to perfect his recollections of the breach at Badajoz. His life was crowded almost to the end with diplomacy and politics and army administration. New faces and fresh problems perpetually engaged him; and Larpent once diagnosed his apparent neglect of old associations.

> "You ask me if Lord Wellington has recollected——with regard? He seems to have had a great opinion of him, but scarcely ever mentioned him to me. In truth, I think Lord Wellington has an active, busy mind, always looking to the future, and is so used to lose a useful man, that as soon as gone he seldom thinks more of him. He would be always, no doubt, ready to serve any one who had been about him, or the friend of a deceased friend, but he seems not to think much about you when once out of the way. He has too much of everything and everybody always in his way to think much of the absent."

That was excusable; and if England omitted to make due provision for his soldiers, the fault was not Wellington's, but his country's.

France, from St. Jean de Luz to Calais, flowed past his carriage windows as he posted homewards through the summer days of 1814. He stopped long enough in Paris to transact some army business with the Ministry of War, where Bourbon tact had installed the sleek Dupont for that paladin reigned over the army of Austerlitz, wearing the withered laurels of Baylen—a defeat commanding twenty years of victory. Then Calais slipped behind him; and Wellington came in sight of England, last seen the gusty day he sailed for Portugal in 1809. The little streets of Dover rang with huzzas; and eager faces pressed against his carriage windows, as he drove through the cheering countryside. Kent and Surrey were one dusty, roaring lane of bawling Englishmen, and London was waiting to take out his horses. But he drove too fast;

them to Piccadilly, where he found Kitty and his boys in Hamilton Place —a smiling Kitty, more short-sighted than ever and a trifle breathless with her sudden rise from Countess to Marchioness, and now to the last dizzy empyrean of a Duchess. Besides, she had sustained exhausting conversations with foreign royalties. A crowd was cheering in the street; but he escaped by a back way into the Park, and slipped off to see his mother in Upper Brook Street, strolled down Oxford Street, met Richard in a cheering crowd, and went to see his married sister. Then he drove down to Portsmouth, where naval salutes were booming for the Allied sovereigns, and paid his respects to the Prince Regent. Next the protracted triumph—first popular, then royal—took a Parliamentary turn; and the new Peer put on his robes to take his seat in the House of Lords as Baron, Viscount, Earl, Marquess, and Duke. After the Lords it was the Commons' turn; and one afternoon he visited them. They had already voted money for the purchase of an estate; as Government proposed £300,000, the Opposition outbidding them, as Oppositions will, carried £400,000 with Mr. Canning and Mr. Whitbread (who had once charged him with exaggerating Talavera) among the loudest voices. Now he was coming to the House in person. His voice had not been heard there since a few words on Irish agriculture and canals five years before. But now a chair was set for him at the Bar; the House rose at his entry, and he sat "for some time covered." The House was full of uniforms; the very mace assumed a military pose, since the Serjeant-at-arms had grounded it and stood beside him at attention. Then he made them a little speech of thanks—first to the Commons for their compliment, and then to the nation for its war-effort.

He was five weeks in England; and his days were loud with ceremonial eloquence and bright with presentations, whilst his evenings were an unending *levée* in the new Field Marshal's uniform. He went down to Essex, and stayed with William's son at Wanstead. The Prince, the royal Dukes, and the whole Wellesley clan were there; and the adoring eyes of Lady Shelley were on him after dinner, when they drank to his father's memory and the Prince Regent proposed his health. The Duke rose, smiling broadly, and began:

"I want words to express . . ."

The Regent promptly interrupted him with royal geniality. "My dear fellow," said Prinny, in his easy way, "we know your *actions*, and we will excuse you your *words*, so sit down."

The Duke, always obedient to royalty, sat down "with all the delight of a schoolboy who has been given an unexpected holiday." Then they all drank to Richard, who replied (as might have been expected) at considerable length. After dinner the Duke polonaised; Blücher performed a country dance; and old Platow gave a Cossack performance, which convulsed the company and appeared to consist of nodding his head and stamping like a horse.

He was all smiles that summer, savouring his triumph and saying gaily to the lady on his arm, as the crowds outside the Opera parted respectfully before them, "It's a fine thing to be a great man, is not it?" He enjoyed the incense; and he could enjoy the general gaiety as well, watching his aides-de-camp all dancing hard at Carlton House and asking cheerfully, "How would society get on without all my boys"? And someone saw him "in great good humour apparently, and not squeezed to death" at the great masquerade in Burlington House, where Hobhouse went as an Albanian; Byron was there dressed as a monk, and Caroline Lamb was more outrageous than usual. A *Star* reporter grew rapturously classical, recording that "the company did not separate from the allurements of Terpsichore's court till Sol rose to light them to repose." But there was business to be done—prospective country houses to be viewed with Mr. Wyatt, letters to Henry about Spanish policy, and advice to ministers upon the American war. They consulted him about an expedition to New Orleans, inspired by Cochrane's appetite for prize money; but the Duke was full of practical objections. He stated his opinion plainly; and when the failure had cost heavily in casualties (including Edward Pakenham), he wrote bluntly to his brother-in-law:

"We have one consolation, that he fell as he lived, in the honourabl discharge of his duty: and distinguished as a soldier & as a man.

"I cannot but regret however that he was ever employed on such service or with such a colleague.

"The expedition to New Orleans originated with that colleague, & plu der was its object. I knew & stated in July that the transports could n approach within leagues of the landing place, & enquired what means we provided to enable a sufficient body of troops with their artillery provisio

& stores to land, & afterwards to communicate with them. Then as plunder was the object, the Admiral took care to be attended by a sufficient number of *sharks*, to carry the plunder off from a place at which he knew well that he could not remain. The secret of the expedition was thus communicated & in this manner this evil design defeated its own end. The Americans were prepared with an army in a fortified position which still would have been carried, if the duties of others, that is of the Admiral, had been as well performed as that of him whom we lament.

"But Providence performed it otherwise & we must submit. . . ."

Then the cheers died away behind him; and he was off to the Continent once more. He did not go direct to Paris, but performed a minor military duty *en route* by reporting upon the defences of Belgium. This territory was now incorporated in a single kingdom with the Netherlands; and it was manifestly desirable to render its southern frontier impervious to French invasions. He reconnoitred for a fortnight, riding round the Belgian villages with three Colonels of Engineers; and his conclusions were embodied in a memorandum favouring a return to the Barrier line of fortresses. A brief examination of the country scarcely enabled him to be precise upon the probable course of military operations. But he indicated "good positions for an army" at various points, of which the last was "the entrance of the *forêt de Soignies* by the high road which leads to Brussels from Binch, Charleroi, and Namur": it was the ridge of Waterloo.

His reconnaissance concluded, Wellington resumed his new profession and became a diplomat. It was a pleasant change to bombard the French with arguments about the slave trade and mild remonstrances upon the misdeeds of American privateers. The French conception of neutrality was frankly scandalous; and the activities of the *True Blooded Yankee* kept his pen busy. One ardent privateer, whose appetites appeared to extend to monumental masonary, had even captured a recumbent statue of Queen Louise of Prussia; and tearful representations were made to Wellington to assist in its recovery for the mausoleum at Charlottenburg. But a large proportion of his work related to the slave trade. He had been startled whilst in England by "the degree of frenzy" felt in this admirable cause, the Lord Mayor positively hesitating to propose the health of King Ferdinand in the solemn shades of Guildhall in case the company refused the toast. But Paris brought Wellington a closer acquaintance with the problem; for he was pelted with improving literature, interviewed by Zachary Macaulay and the virtuous Clarkson, and positively satisfied the latter that he had read through his *History of Abolition* and *Impolicy of the Slave Trade*, to say nothing of a little thing by Mr. Wilberforce and all the memoranda from the African Society—strange reading for a conqueror. But his interest was genuine; and he gave shrewd advice upon the management of French opinion, even volunteering to finance their publications out of public funds. Smaller matters occasionally diversified his work; once he applied for special library facilities on behalf of a Fellow of Trinity in uncertain health engaged on an edition of Demosthenes; he argued with some reason in the interests of scholarship that the *Archives* might reasonably raise their ban upon research into the reign of Louis XV; and that awful eye, before which Generals had shrunk, was turned upon an irritable oculist who had expected every facility for his scientific investigations in spite of a total ignorance of French. Courtesy suggested that he should offer to the King his pack of hounds—*"une meute des meilleures races d'Angleterre"*—a not unflattering description of the assorted hounds behind which he had hunted all the way from Portugal to Toulouse.

Life was a pleasant relaxation—a shade too pleasant, if hostile whisper were to be believed, since a Bonapartist lady circulated stories about *prima donna*. But Kitty was in Paris now; his boys were coming ou for Christmas; and if Grassini smiled, who could resist? Not that hi life in Paris was all triumphs and trivialities. Interminable papers brough him accounts of the negotiations at Vienna, and his advice was sough at every turn. He even advised upon the menace of the Regent's wif suggesting shrewdly that it might be "worth considering whether it not desirable that every facility should be given to the Princess of Wal to amuse herself abroad, in order that she may not be induced to retur to England"—a rich example of the Wellingtonian horse-sense that w requisitioned for the next half century upon every problem from th future of Europe to the disposal of Mrs. Fitzherbert's papers. His ow affairs were relatively calm, though a libel in *The Times* moved him unaccustomed wrath. He could be philosophical enough in general, minding sensitive acquaintances that "misrepresentation of facts is t

mmon practice of the writers of newspapers." But this time his pa-
ence failed; and William was instructed to set the Law Officers in
otion. His indignation was sublime—

"If I possess any advantages in point of character, I consider myself
bound to set the example to others of a determination to prevent the black-
guard editors of papers from depriving us of our reputation by their vulgar
insinuations.

"The truth is, I refused to employ a relation of the editor of the 'Times'
in my family, and that is the reason he has accused me of corruption; but
that is no reason why I should bear it."

at autumn ministers discovered a new cause for anxiety. The French
re restless; a stout King in an arm-chair formed an imperfect substitute
an incomparable Emperor on horseback; veterans were muttering in
ners; and there were grave fears for Wellington. His life was precious,
a military insurrection might endanger it—or at least detain him in
nce and deprive the Allies of his services. The official mind was busy
h pretexts for bringing him away. Could he not be sent for to advise
Congress? Once at Vienna, he need not return to Paris; and then he
ld be sent to take command in America. That was their real design.
e Regent felt that "nothing should be neglected to induce the Duke
Wellington to accept of the Chief Command in America as soon as
sible, as his name alone will reconcile the whole view & opinion of
Country, & at the same time be the means of obviating as well as
oving many difficulties which may afterwards arise." Lord Liverpool
curred, and put it tentatively to the Duke, who felt "no disinclination
undertake the American concern," but demurred on purely European
nds to leaving Paris at the moment. It might, he thought, be pos-
in March, 1815; but at the moment he was strongly inclined to stay.
re was no false modesty about his refusal—"I entertain a strong
ion that I *must* not be lost." But the very unrest, which was the
on for his recall, was in itself the strongest argument for retaining
in Europe—"In case of the occurrence of anything in Europe, there
body but myself in whom either yourselves or the country, or your
s would feel any confidence." Besides, his presence in America would
nake much difference, since "that which appears to me to be wanting

in America is not a General, or General officers and troops, but a na
superiority on the Lakes"; without it he could do little more than "si
a peace which might as well be signed now." Then he went on
advise them bluntly to make peace without annexations. The dashing :
of solemn Mr. Gallatin, who was negotiating at Ghent, even believ
that Wellington in his eagerness for peace with the United States, c
responded directly with the American delegate, urging him to come
terms and dwelling with some skill on Gallatin's Swiss origin. The eff
if James Gallatin can be believed, was admirable—"Father, I think, v
pleased. He is a foreigner and is proud of it." For the Duke's diploma
accomplishments even included the art of charming that unpleas
type of American whose chief pride is that he is not American. Once
was almost persuaded to leave Paris, though he was still reluctant–
confess that I don't see the necessity for being in a hurry. . . . I rea
don't like the way in which I am going away. . . . I don't like to
frightened away." But he admitted the necessity for his recall, thou
the American command had few attractions. A better plan was fou
when Castlereagh, recalled to England by his Parliamentary dut
invited Wellington to replace him at Vienna. This was respectable, a
he accepted.

The year went out upon a world at peace. For peace was positiv
signed on Christmas Eve at Ghent between Great Britain and the Uni
States (personified by the pertinacious Adams, Bayard, Henry Clay, a
Mr. Gallatin, always comfortably aware of the nobility of his Sv
blood). On the last day of the year Lord Liverpool wrote to the D
with evident relief about the mission to Vienna and a difficulty v
Murat at Naples and his own plans (the Prime Minister was hoping
get down to Bath). Then Europe slept, and midnight sounded from
steeples—from the tall spire above Vienna, from Ste. Gudule at Brus
and Notre Dame (where Paris stirred a little in its sleep) and from
little belfries, where a lonely man counted the hours on Elba—and as
echoes died away, it was 1815.

Waterloo! Waterloo! Waterloo! morne plaine!

LES CHÂTIMENTS.

EUROPE was under snow. Lord Castlereagh, with something less
than his customary tact, informed an after-dinner audience at
Vienna that *"il commence l'âge d'or"* and was generally understood to
have alluded to British subsidies; the Czar, acutely conscious of his
virtue, was full of noble sentiments and frankly covetous of Poland; even
the widowed King of Prussia forgot his mourning in a lively appetite
for Saxon territory; and M. de Talleyrand limped deferentially among
the gilded furniture with his thin smile. Two carriages rumbled along
the miry roads, one taking Byron and his bride to their uncomfortable
honeymoon; the Duke was in the other, rolling across the Continent
towards Vienna. Behind him in Whitehall the Horse Guards struggled
with the problem of Peninsular medals; the Prince Regent was at
Brighton reading official papers and contemplating the Pavilion domes;
and the Cabinet instructed Wellington upon the future of Corfu. He
had a heavy cold when he arrived, and found the hot rooms of Vienna
most exhausting. But it was winter still, and the hot rooms were full
of bowing gentlemen in decorations. He saw Prince Metternich; he saw
the Swedes; he saw the Poles. Life became an endless succession of
interviews and drafts—drafts about Switzerland and Frankfort and the
Valtelline. The Czar called one evening with a complicated grievance
about the Danes and Bernadotte and the purchase price of Guadaloupe.
He would be leaving soon for Russia; but Wellington seemed doomed
to sit for ever manipulating drafts in stifling rooms. Would the spring
never come?

It came that year a little early. For spring came with the violets in the
first week of March. Prince Metternich had gone to bed at three one
morning after a conference. He was not to be disturbed; but an officious
servant brought in an envelope at six o'clock. The Prince looked at it
and, observing without interest that it was merely from the Austrian
consul at Genoa, turned over again. But he failed to sleep; and about
half past seven he opened it and read that Napoleon was missing from

Elba. Within an hour he saw three sleepy sovereigns; the Duke, wh
had a letter to the same effect, was told at ten; and when Talleyrar
predicted that the Emperor would make for Switzerland, the Prince to
another view—"*Il ira droit à Paris*." Metternich was right: the spri
had come.

Spring

There was a sudden stir. The solemn exercises of Vienna were brok
off, and diplomacy subsided like an interrupted minuet. Once ag
there was a sudden rapping on the doors; the music stopped, the danc
huddled into corners, and angry gentlemen drew swords. The Du
three Princes, and fourteen assorted noblemen declared in the na
of eight governments that Napoleon Buonaparte had forfeited
human rights. It was the dreadful cry once heard from revolutionary
in Paris, when angry men with staring eyes bawled "*Hors la loi*" ;
dragged something shrinking to a scaffold. But it rang gravelier n
for it sounded from the solemn countenances of Wellington and Met
nich and Nesselrode and Talleyrand, still wearing his thin smile. '
Duke appeared to think at first that the King of France could do
business for himself; but he could see that Europe might have to in
vene, and he was hard at work among the excited Allies—"Here
are all zeal, and, I think, anxious to take the field. I moderate t
sentiments as much as possible, and get them on paper. . . ." T
was a notion of employing him as a courtly *attaché* to the Czar; but
I should have neither character nor occupation in such a situatio
should prefer to carry a musket." There would be ample opportu
with all Europe marching upon France in a great crescent from
Alps to the North Sea. They gave him the command of an asso
force of Allies, which was to take the right of the line in the
Countries. His tried battalions were largely in America or in
ocean; and his first instinct, in the absence of that incomparable a
was to call for a contingent of those Portuguese whom he had c
its "fighting cocks." A soldier once again, he turned briskly fron
plomacy and all its drafts—the protocol about the Swiss, the en
chicanery of the Dutch loan, and the Prince Regent's portrait

amond-mounted snuff-box to be presented to the Bavarian—and posted
ross Europe. He was at a party the night before he left Vienna; and
the women kissed him, saying gaily that he would conquer Paris
d that in that event he might include them in his conquests. Once
ore his carriage rumbled along miry roads; and at five o'clock one
orning in the first week of April he was in Brussels.

The city was not unfamiliar. He had passed through the country in
previous summer; but it was twenty years since Lady Mornington
d her ungainly son had lodged in Brussels, where he learned French
d played his violin. His French was readier now, and he had manlier
omplishments; but his mother was once more in Brussels. It was quite
aionable that winter. The *ton*, denied all opportunities of Continental
vel by twenty years of war, was glad to make a jaunt to Brussels.
e Guards were there; Mr. Creevey took his wife and girls (was not
ky Sharp seen chattering at the Opera?); and Lady Mornington,
ased from Upper Brook Street was there as well, until her anxious
arrived and packed her off to Antwerp. Then the town filled with
ated Frenchmen; the royalties were all at Ghent; but Brussels had
hare of Marshals—Marmont at the *Hôtel d'Angleterre*, Victor (with
easant echo of Talavera) at the *Hôtel Wellington*, and Berthier stay-
with friends. The Duke was seen at evening parties; and Mr.
evey, who had once crossed swords with him in Indian debates,
d him "very natural and good-humoured" and exceedingly com-
icative. For Wellington discussed the prospects freely, and Mr.
vey was not impressed. Opposition Whips are not easily im-
ed by military men; and when the Duke insisted that it would
r come to war, he left a poor impression of his perspicacity upon
politician. But there was something to be said for using peaceful
uage to members of an Opposition, which was busy denouncing
sters for hurling Europe wantonly into another war. So Wellington
d Mr. Creevey by his unintelligent insistence that the republicans
bound to prevail in Paris and that in all probability some Brutus
d soon make an end of Buonaparte. Not that he thought so; for
ae very morning after his tone of stupid confidence shocked Mr.
ey he wrote to Blücher, "*Je ne serais pas étonné si la partie se
ait remise pour quelque temps. Mais nous l'aurons sûrement un jour*

ou l'autre . . ." But it would never do to use that language in Bruss⟨e⟩
soirées, where every sentence would be promptly echoed from the O⟨p⟩
position benches. So a military man, for once, was one too many f⟨or⟩
an Opposition Whip; and Mr. Creevey went to his grave convinced th⟨at⟩
Wellington had failed to grasp the gravity of the position in April, 18⟨1⟩

He made a point of being cheerful, laughed when the *Champ*
Mai passed off successfully in Paris, and greeted any fresh deserti⟨on⟩
of the Emperor as evidence that his house was "tumbling about ⟨his⟩
ears." He gave innumerable balls and made everybody dance half t⟨he⟩
night. For the town was full of eyes; and it was just as well that Pa⟨ris⟩
should believe that confidence prevailed in Brussels. But Brussels, if t⟨he⟩
truth were known, was anything but confident. The Duke, inde⟨ed,⟩
could scarcely be expected to be in high spirits with a discouragi⟨ng⟩
command in which foreigners outnumbered British troops by m⟨ore⟩
than two to one. His dealings with allies in Spain had made him ⟨an⟩
expert in the lukewarm; but this time their temperature was m⟨ore⟩
discouraging than usual. His Dutch were poor, his Belgians unreliab⟨le,⟩
even his Hanoverians were hardly more than willing; and the Ki⟨ng's⟩
German Legion alone came up to British standards. Not that ⟨the⟩
British troops were an inspiring spectacle. For out of twenty-five ⟨ba⟩
talions only six had served in the Peninsula; the rest (except the Guar⟨ds)⟩
were neither up to strength nor standard. His cavalry was toler⟨ably⟩
abundant, since there had been no need for cavalry in America;
his demand for guns was answered by a grim intimation from ⟨the⟩
Ordnance that while guns abounded, "men and horses are the ⟨great⟩
difficulty I have." Even his Staff depressed him, since he inherited ⟨the⟩
Staff of a small army of occupation already in the Low Countries. ⟨His⟩
loud protests in his most emphatic manner gradually relieved hi⟨m of⟩
them; the authorities were most obliging, though he complained bitt⟨erly⟩
of being "overloaded with people I have never seen before; and it ⟨ap⟩
pears to be purposely intended to keep those out of my way who⟨m I⟩
wished to have"; and he ended with a Staff of thirty-three, of w⟨hom⟩
thirty-one had considerable Staff experience in the Peninsula. B⟨ut at⟩
the outset it was not surprising that his correspondence rang ⟨with⟩
indignant outcries. April found him complaining that the British tr⟨oops⟩

ere "not what they ought to be to enable us to maintain our military aracter in Europe. It appears to me that you have not taken in England clear view of your situation, that you do not think war certain, d that a great effort must be made, if it is hoped that it shall be ort." The month passed in a fever of preparations—of friendly cor-:pondence with the Prussians on his left, of visits to the French royalties Ghent, innumerable tangles of inter-Allied diplomacy, peculiar trans-:ions with foreign potentates for the supply of infantry at a flat rate £11 2s. a head, and ingenious rearrangements of the assorted nation-:ies in his command until the mosaic gave some promise of stability. t he could still write in May that he had "an infamous army, very ak and ill equipped, and a very inexperienced Staff." He was more :eful now—"for an action in Belgium I can now put 70,000 men into field, and Blücher 80,000; so that I hope we should give a good ount even of Buonaparte." Besides, the need might not arise, **since** was sometimes tempted to believe that internal politics might keep the peror in Paris. But he was haunted by his old desire for 40,000 British antry; with them "I should be satisfied, and take my chance for the , and engage that we should play our part in the game."

That thought was in his mind one day, when he met Mr. Creevey in Park at Brussels. The pert civilian asked a question.

Will you let me ask you, Duke, what you think you will make t?"

he blunt question stopped him in his walk. "By God," the Duke ied, "I think Blücher and myself can do the thing."

Do you calculate upon any desertion in Buonaparte's army?"

Not upon a man," said the Duke, "from the colonel to the private a regiment—both inclusive. We may pick up a Marshal or two, iaps; but not worth a damn."

hen Mr. Creevey asked him about the French royalists in Belgium. Dh!" said the Duke, "don't mention such fellows! No: I think :her and I can do the business."

t that moment his eye was caught by a British private in the green 's of the Park; and as he watched the little scarlet figure staring at foreign statues under the foreign trees, "There," said the Duke,

pointing a long forefinger, "it all depends upon that article whether v
do the business or not. Give me enough of it, and I am sure."

SUMMER

1. *Brussels*

Something was stirring behind the frontier. It was not altogetl
easy to say precisely what it was, though spies reported copiously a
French deserters trickled in with unlikely stories. But secret age
were lamentably apt to enrich the tedium of fact with those live.
circumstances which they wished to happen—or which (better still) t¹
felt that their employers would wish to happen; and the Duke's writi
table groaned under every form of voluminous misstatement. If his
telligence could be believed, the Empire was becoming momenta
more precarious and the Emperor had developed an uncanny fac
of being in several places at the same time—in Paris, in half
fortresses along the northern frontier, even in Cherbourg on his ¹
to the United States—whilst his regiments appeared to be involved ir
endless saraband. They flitted up and down the frontier, were ⁵
drilling in unlikely places, and passed on every road by watc
travellers. But they were plainly coming north. So much was evid
But it was hardly possible to learn more about their strength and m
ments, since war had not been declared; and Wellington compla
bitterly that "in the situation in which we are placed at present, nei
at war nor at peace, unable on that account to patrole up to the en
and ascertain his position by view, or to act offensively upon any
of his line, it is difficult, if not impossible, to combine an opera
because there are no data on which to found any combination. Al
can do is to put our troops in such a situation as, in case of su
attack by the enemy, to render it easy to assemble, and to pr
against the chance of any being cut off from the rest." (This di
half-measure was the tribute paid to appearances, to the susceptib.
of Opposition speakers who might otherwise have vituperated min
for being bellicose.) The army waited patiently in Belgian vil
grooming their horses, cleaning side-arms, and counting champaig

a bottle among their blessings. The Duke was busy with his papers,
changing memoranda with the Allies upon the impending march of
lignant Emperors on Paris timed for the end of June, studying
lky reports on the French army from the lucid pen of Marshal Clarke,
uc de Feltre (once the Emperor's, and now King Louis', Minister of
ar at Ghent), and reading fluttered notes from London about the
sdeeds of the Opposition which had now been joined, for some in-
utable reason of enlightened views or disappointed pride, by the
gential Richard. Then there were quantities of good advice, and
eful letters from the War Office promising to hire unemployed post-
s to drive his guns, and indications that it might be possible to call
the Militia by the end of June, a line from Kitty with the news
: Lowry Cole was getting married, and a helpful offer from a con-
tor who was prepared to manufacture howitzers of an entirely
/ pattern (grimly endorsed "Compliments; and I do not consider
to be a proper period to alter the equipments of the army or to
experiments"). Slightly inimical to innovations at the moment,
ordered the rocket troop to store its cherished weapons and use
nary guns instead; and when someone urged that the change would
k their Captain's heart, the implacable reply was, "Damn his heart,
let my order be obeyed."

metimes he was out reconnoitring in his usual fashion, riding alone
. an orderly dragoon and studying the rolling ground between
sels and the frontier. They would be moving soon, and he was
king about the siege of Maubeuge. But he still regretted his lost
nsular battalions, writing to Lowry Cole how much he wished that
could bring every thing together as I had it when I took leave
e army in Bordeaux, and I would engage that we should not be the
n the race; but, as it is, I must manage matters as well as I can."
was still cheerful, though, with an agreeable tendency to crawl
t the floor with children. The Duke of Richmond, under whom he
once served as Chief Secretary, had brought out his entire family;
in his circle Wellington revived old memories of the Viceregal
e and morning rides in Phœnix Park. One day he rode to Enghien
one of the girls to see a cricket match. But there is no need to
ose a sudden taste for cricket, since the Guards were billeted

at Enghien and the Duke could have a word with Maitland. For
pleasures were always apt to take a business turn, and the Pee
hounds in Portugal would often take him conveniently near a u
that stood in need of an inspection.

The June days went slowly by; and when he wrote to Graham
cepting membership of a new military club, he added comfortal
that the Emperor seemed unlikely to leave Paris at the moment—
think we are now too strong for him here." But the reports came
—French *feux de joie* were heard at Maubeuge; Valenciennes was f
of troops; the gates of Lille were closed; Soult was on the road; Grouc
had been seen reviewing cavalry; the Guard was on the march;
Emperor was everywhere at once. Something was stirring now beh
the frontier.

2. *Waterloo*

The June days went by in Brussels. Late one Thursday carria
were clattering over the cobbles, and a sound of dance-music dri
into the summer night. The Duke was there. He had been working
with Müffling and the Staff; for he had news that afternoon that
French had passed the frontier opposite the Prussians, and orders
been sent to move the army in the direction of Quatre Bras. But it
just as well to reassure the doubters by shewing up at the ball; and w
he made his bow, Mr. Creevey's girls found him looking as compo
as ever; though one young lady, who shared a sofa with him, thou
him quite preoccupied and noticed how he kept turning round
giving orders. More news arrived while they were all at supper; anc
desired the senior officers to leave unobtrusively. He said sometl
civil to his host and slipped off with him to look at a map, remar
when the door closed behind them that Napoleon had *humbugged*
by God! and gained twenty-four hours' march upon him. Asked
intentions, he replied that he proposed to concentrate at Quatre Br
"but we shall not stop him there, and if so, I must fight him"-
thumb nail traced a line on the map behind Hougoumont and La I
Sainte—"*here.*" Then he went off to bed. It was a little after two;

r. Creevey, who had stayed at home that evening and heard a deal
hammering on doors along his street, was writing in his Journal,

"*June* 16. *Friday morning* $\frac{1}{2}$ *past two.*—The girls just returned from a
ball at the Duke of Richmond's. . . ."

ae marching bayonets went down the empty streets, and in the sum-
er dawn the pipes went by.

He followed them next morning (a gleeful English maid, who
ight a glimpse of him as she was opening the shutters, cried, "O,
lady, get up quick; there he goes, God bless him, and he will not
ne back till he is King of France!"); and before noon he was staring
the woods beyond Quatre Bras. Then he rode over to the Prussians
l had a word with Blücher. Their dispositions did not impress him,
ce they were rather recklessly aligned (in contrast with his own
icious practice) upon an exposed slope; and he said grimly that if
y fought there, they would be damnably mauled. For his ally's bene-
he translated this uncompromising view into the milder sentiment
t every man, of course, knew his own troops, but that if his own
e so disposed, he should expect them to be beaten. His expectation
not disappointed, since the Emperor shattered them that evening
Ligny. But Wellington employed the afternoon at Quatre Bras,
re Ney flung four thousand men away in wild attacks. They heard
guns in Brussels; and the enquiring Creevey strolled on the ram-
s, while sixteen miles away the Duke was steadying a line which
often far from steady. It was a wild affair of French lancers
eling in the corn and redcoats hurrying up the long road from
ssels. Once Wellington was almost caught in a flurry of French
lry far out beyond his firing-line. The ditch behind him was lined
l Highlanders; and with a timely reminiscence of the hunting-field
shouted to them to lie still, put his horse at the unusual obstacle,
cleared it, resuming a less exciting position of command. And once
deep voice was heard calling, "Ninety-second, don't fire till I tell
" For he was everywhere as usual; while Ney, whose military talents
almost wholly pugilistic, raged up and down the line watching
cavalry surge vainly round the British squares. But the price paid
tolerably high, although a great lady in Brussels cooed consolingly

to a friend that poor Sir D. Pack is severely wounded, and the p
Duke of Brunswick died of his wounds. . . . The Scotch were chi
engaged, so there are no officers wounded that one knows."

But the reverse at Ligny served to nullify any advantage gained
the Duke at Quatre Bras; and he grimly observed that "old Blücher
had a damned good hiding, and has gone eighteen miles to the r
We must do the same. I suppose they'll say in England that we h
been licked; well, I can't help that." He took this unpalatable deci
early the next morning; but (it was typical of him) the retreat
deferred until his men had cooked a meal. With that inside them
would, he felt, be more equal to the perils of a retirement with Napo
at their heels. The red columns filed off towards Brussels; and as
went, the Duke remarked with obvious relief, "Well, there is the
of the infantry gone, and I don't care now." The cavalry, he kr
could look after themselves with a few guns to hold them. He watc
the perilous retreat, occasionally sitting in a field and laughing
some old English newspapers or turning his glass on the imm
French. The morning opened brightly; but as the day wore on, t
was a stillness, and a pile of leaden clouds climbed slowly up a s
sky. The storm broke in floods of rain, as his cavalry were drawing
and the thunder drowned the sharper note of guns, while the ro
(in fulfilment of the Duke's most sceptical anticipations) sputtered
fizzed and not infrequently exploded backwards. The rain drove d
and the long *pavé* gleamed before them, as they struggled back tow
the ridge in front of Waterloo, the French plodding after them a
the sodden fields.

There was a night of damp discomfort; but food was waiting in
British bivouacs. They lit fires, and Peninsular veterans dispensed der
consolations, observing cheerfully to newcomers, "Oho, my boy!
is but child's play to what *we* saw in Spain," and "Lord have m
upon your poor tender carcass. What would such as you have dor
the Pyrenees?" Uxbridge, his second-in-command, came to Wellin
and asked what he proposed to do. The Duke countered with a que

"Who will attack the first to-morrow—I or Buonaparte?"

"Buonaparte."

"Well," said the Duke, "Buonaparte has not given me any id

projects; and as my plans will depend upon his, how can you expect
to tell you what mine are?"

Then he rose and, laying a hand upon the other's shoulder, said
dly, "There is one thing certain, Uxbridge; that is, that whatever
opens you and I will do our duty."

For his belief in plans was never strong. He once said pityingly of
Marshals that "they planned their campaigns just as you might
ke a splendid set of harness. It looks very well, and answers very
ll, until it gets broken; and then you are done for. Now, I made my
mpaigns of ropes. If anything went wrong, I tied a knot; and went
' Blücher had fallen back from Ligny; so Wellington had tied a
t, conforming with his ally's retreat by falling back to Waterloo.
ow he was comfortably established on the ridge; but who could say
at would happen next? If they attacked him in position, it might
Busaco over again. Or they might know their business better and
e round his right. In that event they might give an opening—and
it would be Salamanca—or they might manœuvre him from Water-
without a battle. That would cost him Brussels and send the French
lties scampering from Ghent. It was too much to hope that Napoleon
ld choose a frontal attack, when the manœuvre round his flank
nised so richly; and Wellington inclined to think that he would
se the latter course. So he sat writing in the night—to warn the
lties at Ghent, to suggest that Lady Frances Webster would be wise
ave at once for Antwerp, and to beg someone in authority in Brussels
keep the English quiet if you can. Let them all prepare to move,
neither be in a hurry or a fright, as all will yet turn out well." And
ight long the summer rain drove down on sodden fields; the trees
ed at Hougoumont; gleaming pools stood in the little farmyard at
Haye Sainte; somewhere across the darkness a square figure in a
grey coat was straining eager eyes into the night for a glimpse of
ington's camp-fires; and two armies slept in the busy whisper of
ain.

pale dawn broke over Belgium. The Emperor was breakfasting by
o'clock. Soult was uneasy; Ney prophesied that Wellington would
way again; but Napoleon swept away all objections.

*"Il n'est plus temps. Wellington s'exposerait à une perte certain.
Il a jeté les dés, et ils sont pour nous."*

When Soult pressed him to call up reinforcements, he snapped co
temptuously, *"Parce que vous avez été battu par Wellington, vous
regardez comme un grand général. Et, moi je vous dis que Wellingto
est un mauvais général, que les Anglais sont de mauvaises troupes, et q
ce sera l'affaire d'un déjeuner."*

"Je le souhaite," replied the Marshal glumly.

The Emperor sailed before gusts of optimism that morning. Reil
who came in a little later, altogether failed to share his enthusiasm
a frontal attack on Wellington. But then Reille had served in Spai
even at Quatre Bras he shied nervously from an apparently unguard
position, because *"ce pourrait bien être une bataille d'Espagne—les trou
Anglaises se montreraient quand il en serait temps"*; and now the si
of a British line behind an easy slope made him uncomfortable—he l
seen something of the kind before. But the Emperor was rarely a g
listener.

Besides, he meant to have his victory. A victory would mean so m
—the road to Brussels open, France reassured by a familiar bulle
King Louis made ridiculous again by further flight, the British dri
into the sea at last, and (who knows?) a change of Government
London, the enlightened Whigs in office, and a world at peace with
tricolour floating peacefully above the Tuileries. The sky was clea
now; a breeze sprang up; the ground would soon be dry enough
guns to move. He would have his victory; and June 18 should tak
place among his anniversaries.

"Nous coucherons ce soir," he said, *"à Bruxelles."*

Across the little valley Wellington was waiting on that Sunday m
ing in his blue frock-coat and the low cocked-hat that bore the l
cockade of England with the colours of Spain, Portugal, and the Ne
lands. His mixed command was, if anything more mixed than ever,
he had left some of his British troops to guard his right flank an
road to Ostend; and his foreigners outnumbered them by two to
Still, he had got them in position on a ridge—one of his favourite r
with an easy slope towards the enemy and shelter for his men be
its crest. The French outnumbered them; the Emperor had 70,000

o the Duke's 63,000; and he had only 156 guns against 266 in the hands
f that incomparable artillerist. But if Blücher was to be believed, some
russians would be coming later. The old *sabreur* had been unhorsed
nd ridden over at Ligny; but he dosed himself with a deadly brew of
n and rhubarb (and apologised to a British officer whom he embraced,
bserving cheerfully, "*Ich stinke etwas*"); and somewhere across the sod-
en fields his dark columns wound towards the Emperor's unguarded
ank.

The Duke was waiting. As it was showery that morning, he kept put-
ng on a cloak, "because I never get wet when I can help it." He waited
r the French manœuvre to begin; had not Marmont manœuvred "in the
ual French style" at Salamanca? But the Emperor made no attempt
manœuvre. Then it was not to be another Salamanca. For they came
unging straight at the British line in columns of attack, just as he
d seen them when the French columns charged the heights above
meiro and Masséna's men struggled up the slope at Busaco. It was
be the old style of attack, to which he knew an answer that had never
led—the waiting line behind the crest, the volley long deferred, and
n the bayonet. (As he wrote afterwards to Beresford, the Emperor
d not manœuvre at all. He just moved forward in the old style, in
umns, and was driven off in the old style.") But there were variations;
the fighting surged round the outworks of his line at Hougoumont
l La Haye Sainte. Then, the columns foiled, a stranger variation
eared, as the French cavalry came thundering uphill against his line.
s infantry formed square to meet them, and the delighted gunners
zed into the advancing target, until they scampered off to safety in the
rest square bowling a wheel from each dismantled gun before them,
he bewildered horsemen rode helplessly among the bristling squares of
ospitable bayonets. It was a picturesque, but scarcely an alarming,
erience. "I had the infantry," as he wrote afterwards, "for some time
squares, and we had the French cavalry walking about us as if they
been our own. I never saw the British infantry behave so well."

he Duke, as usual, was everywhere, fighting his line along the ridge
commander fights his ship in action. He rode "Copenhagen"; and
lay long the chestnut carried him along the lanes of weary men. Each
: of the interminable battle elicited a gruff comment or an order

scrawled on a scrap of parchment. He saw the Nassauers pressed out c
Hougoumont and acidly observed to an Austrian General, *"Mais enfi*
c'est avec ces Messieurs là qu'il faut que nous gagnions la bataille," p
in the Guards to retake the position with "There, my lads, in with you
let me see no more of you," and watched Mercer's guns dash into pla
between two squares with an appreciative "Ah! that's the way I like
see horse-artillery move." When the Life Guards charged, a deep voi
was at hand to say, "Now, gentlemen, for the honour of the Househo
Troops"; and when they rode back, a low cocked-hat was raised wi
"Life Guards! I thank you." At one moment he formed a line of sha
infantry himself, like any company-commander, within twenty yards
the flash of an oncoming French column. And as the tide of cavalry w
ebbing down the trampled slope, he asked the Rifles in his quiet manr
to "drive those fellows away."

The light was failing now; and he rode down the line before t
Guard was launched in the last charge of the Empire. The shado
lengthened from the west, as the tall bearskins came slowly on behi
six Generals and a Marshal walking (for it was Ney) with a dra
sword. They were still coming on "in the old style"; and the waiting l
held back its fire in the Peninsular fashion until the Duke was he
calling, "Now, Maitland! Now's your time." The volley crashed; and
the smoke drifted into the sunset, the Guard broke—and with the Gu
the memory of Austerlitz, of Eylau, Friedland, Jena, Wagram, and B
dino melted upon the air. Then the Duke galloped off with a sir
officer to order the advance. The smoke thinned for an instant; an
trim, bare-headed figure was seen pointing a cocked-hat towards
French. Someone enquired (a shade superfluously) which way to go;
the Duke's voice answered him, "Right ahead, to be sure."

Late that night Blücher met him in the road on horseback and clas
a weary Duke, exclaiming *"Mein lieber Kamerad"* and exhausting
entire stock of French by adding a trifle inadequately, *"Quelle affa*
For the Emperor had shattered his last army in blind attacks upon
ridge and then crushed it between Wellington and the Prussian
lonely, white-faced man, he stood in the moonlight waiting in a
wood, waiting for troops that never came: his cheeks were wet with t

ar to the south the Prussian cavalry were sabring the last remnant of
ne *Grande Armée* under the moon. . . . "No more firing was heard at
russels—the pursuit rolled miles away. Darkness came down on the
eld and city; and Amelia was praying for George, who was lying on his
ce, dead, with a bullet through his heart."

The Duke rode slowly back to Waterloo. There was no feeling of
ation, and they were all exhausted. Besides, he had a solemn notion that,
here so many had fallen close to him, he had somehow been preserved
· Providence. "The finger of Providence was upon me," he wrote that
ght, "and I escaped unhurt"; and he repeated almost the same words
Paris later. Then they sat down to supper; the table had been laid for
e usual number, but the Staff had suffered cruelly, and there were so
any empty places. The Duke, who ate very little, kept looking at the
or; and Alava knew that he was watching for the absent faces. When
e meal was over, he left them. But as he rose, he lifted both hands
ing, "The hand of God has been over me this day." Then he went out
d began to write his despatch:

"MY LORD,
    "Buonaparte having collected the 1st, 2nd, 3rd, 4th, and 6th corps of
the French army, and the Imperial Guards . . ."

asked them to bring in the casualty returns, and slept for a few
urs. When he read them by the first morning light, he broke down.
ton, Ponsonby, De Lancey, Barnes, Gordon, Elley . . . it had been
·se than Badajoz. Then he took his tea and toast, finished his despatch,
rode sadly into Brussels. He saw Creevey from his hotel window and
·ed a signal to come in. He was quite solemn still and said that it had
· a damned serious business—a damned nice thing—the nearest run
g you ever saw in your life. His mind ran on the losses, and he added
·ly that Blücher got so damnably licked on Friday night that he
·d not find him on Saturday morning and was obliged to fall back to
· in touch with him. Then he walked up and down the room and
·sed his men. Creevey enquired if the French had fought better than
·l.

No," said the Duke, "they have always fought the same since I first

saw them at Vimeiro. By God! I don't think it would have been done i
I had not been there."

3. *Paris*

In twelve days they were in front of Paris. There was a spectral inte
lude, in which ghosts walked the Paris streets. For the long figure of L
Fayette, last seen when Marie Antoinette was Queen of France, leane
from the tribune; and men heard a voice of 1790 unmake the Empire.
was as though Mirabeau had spoken. The Emperor, almost a gho
already, haunted the green alleys of Malmaison like an uneasy spirit. T
little house among the trees filled with Imperial *revenants*. His broth
Joseph came, the shadow of a King of Spain, and Jerome, faint simu
crum of a King of Westphalia; less shadowy, the indomitable Madar
Mère took leave of him; Walewska came to sob out the last echoes
their love in Warsaw; and Hortense made a last home for him amo
her mother's flowers. His tired eyes watched round every corner for t
lost figure of an Empress bending over her roses; for the roses were
bloom at Malmaison.

Uneasy gentlemen flitted in all directions—to safety in the south,
make their peace with the returning King, to Wellington's headquart
with bewildering proposals for an armistice. He had one answer
them all, since in his clear way he discerned the objects of the war. L
before Waterloo he had stated them to Marmont:

> "*La France n'a pas d'ennemis que je connaisse. . . . Nous sommes
> ennemis d'un seul homme, et de ses adhérens. . . . La situation où n
> allons nous trouver ne peut pas donc s'appeler un état de guerre contr
> France, mais bien une guerre de la part de toute l'Europe, y inclus la Fra
> contre Buonaparte, et contre son armée, de laquelle la mauvaise condui
> donné occasion aux malheurs qui vont arriver, et que nous déplorons to*

With these opinions it was not surprising that he reminded the invac
army that "their respective Sovereigns are the Allies of His Majesty
King of France, and that France ought, therefore, to be treated a
friendly country." But these refinements were far beyond the sin
minded Prussians, who clung to the consoling thought that Fra

which had so recently dominated Germany, was now defenceless, and behaved accordingly. The Duke, on the other hand, burned with the chivalry peculiar to citizens of uninvaded countries. Even his troops were slightly irked by his tendency to side with the civil population; and ministers grew almost plaintive over his leniency. "It is quite right," wrote Liverpool, "to prevent plunder of every description, but France must bear a part of the expenses of the war. . . . We do not exactly know what course in this respect the Duke of Wellington has been following. . . I trust, however, that you will be able to satisfy him that the French nation ought to bear a part of the expense."

Not that his chivalry was mere knight-errantry. For it had a distinct and practical purpose, since he was determined to restore King Louis. His devotion to the Bourbons was anything but sentimental. Long before Waterloo he had described their restoration as "the measure most likely to insure the tranquillity of Europe for a short time." He recognised that their cause did not command unanimous enthusiasm, but wrote cheerfully to Henry Wellesley that "if we are stout we shall save the King, whose government affords the only chance of peace." After the victory he moved King Louis into the neighbourhood of Paris on his own authority because he "wished His Majesty should be on the spot, or as near it as circumstances would permit." He told the delegates from Paris that he conceived the best security for Europe was the restoration of the King, and that the establishment of any other government than the King's in France must inevitably lead to new and endless wars." With that in view it was vital to avoid anything that might render him distasteful to his subjects. It was unhappily inevitable that King Louis should return *dans les fourgons de l'ennemi*; but if that enemy were only reasonably well-behaved, his subjects might forgive his choice of a conveyance. So the Duke's army orders became a protracted correspondence-course in good manners, and his command found that its business with the French had been changed from winning battles to the more exacting task of winning Frenchmen opinions.

Since Blücher, a devoted partner in the field, was disinclined to enter the tournament of chivalry. Prussia had bitter memories (as well as several bad manners), which it was comforting to gratify by scaring French villagers and devastating French country houses. So Müffling,

duly installed as Governor of Paris, proposed to apply himself with gust
to the collection of a fine of 100,000,000 francs. And was it reasonable
Wellington to discover scruples about blowing up a Paris bridge, who
mere existence was an affront to his allies, since it was named *Po*
d'Iéna? Blücher was strong for it, although the French offered helpless
to rename the offensive structure *Pont Louis XVIII*; and when Wellin
ton still pleaded for the bridge, the old man tartly enquired what wou
have been the fate of any bridge in Washington named after Saratog
But the Duke summarily closed the discussion by the heroic measure
posting a British sentry on the bridge; the Prussians, it was thoug
would hesitate to blow up an Allied soldier. But this view was bas
upon an under-estimate of their distaste for ill-timed historical allusio
For, less sentimental, Blücher's engineers promptly set to work upon t
simple problem of destruction; but though thoroughly determined, th
did not know their business; and the bridge, which ultimately surviv
under the abject name of *Pont des Invalides*, was saved by their compl
incompetence rather than by British chivalry.

It was a reasoned chivalry; for the Duke insisted that "if one sho
fired in Paris, the whole country will rise against us." That would mea
war of conquest for the Allies and a civil war for Louis XVIII. If s
disasters were to be avoided, France must be reconciled to the new te
of peace. It was hardly customary to consider the feelings of defea
states; but the Duke's reasoning rendered this novel course inevitabl
followed that the terms must be of a character that would comm;
French consent; and this effectually precluded further annexations.
the Duke wrote, *"nous avons raison de croire que la France cédera ;*
grande difficulté sur le système qu'on veut adopter, et que la na
entière s'opposerait à son démembrement." The problem was not sim
since *ex hypothesi* France was still a European menace standing in g;
need of restraint; but the restraining measures must be such as woul
acceptable to France. Lord Castlereagh devised an ingenious expedi
but since its character was wholly military, it depended upon Wellingt
support. His views were as clear as ever:

"In my opinion . . . the Allies have no just right to make any mat
    inroad on the treaty of Paris, although that treaty leaves France too st
    in relation to other powers; but I think I can show that the real intere

the Allies should lead them to adopt the measures which justice in this instance requires from them. . . .

"My objection to the demand of a great cession from France upon this occasion is, that it will defeat the object which the Allies have held out to themselves in the present and the preceding wars.

"That which has been their object has been to put an end to the French Revolution, to obtain peace for themselves and their people, to have the power of reducing their overgrown military establishments, and the leisure to attend to the internal concerns of their several nations, and to improve the situation of their people. The Allies took up arms against Buonaparte because it was certain that the world could not be at peace as long as he should possess, or should be in a situation to attain, supreme power in France; and care must be taken, in making the arrangements consequent upon our success, that we do not leave the world in the same unfortunate situation respecting France that it would have been in if Buonaparte had continued in possession of his power. . . .

"If the King were to refuse to agree to the cession, and were to throw himself upon his people, there can be no doubt that those divisions would cease which have hitherto occasioned the weakness of France. The Allies might take the fortresses and provinces which might suit them, but there would be no genuine peace for the world, no nation could disarm, no Sovereign could turn his attention from the affairs of this country. . . . We must, on the contrary, if we take this large cession, consider the operations of the war as deferred till France shall find a suitable opportunity of endeavouring to regain what she has lost; and, after having wasted our resources in the maintenance of overgrown military establishments in time of peace, we shall find how little useful the cessions we shall have acquired will be against a national effort to regain them.

"In my opinion, then, we ought to continue to keep our great object, the genuine peace and tranquillity of the world, in our view, and shape our arrangement so as to provide for it.

"Revolutionary France is more likely to distress the world than France, however strong in her frontier, under a regular Government; and that is the situation in which we ought to endeavour to place her.

"With this view I prefer the temporary occupation of some of the strong places, and to maintain for a time a strong force in France, both at the expense of the French Government, and under strict regulation, to the permanent cession of even all the places which in my opinion ought to be occupied for a time. These measures will not only give us, during the

period of occupation, all the military security which could be expected fro
the permanent cession, but, if carried into execution in the spirit in whic
they are conceived, they are in themselves the bond of peace."

He added shrewdly that "the troops of those Sovereigns should be selecte
for this service who would have the least inclination to remain in posse
sion of the fortresses at the termination of the period."

A later paper neatly summarised the choice before the Allies:

"If the policy of the united powers of Europe is to weaken France,
them do so in reality. Let them take from that country its population a
resources as well as a few fortresses. If they are not prepared for th
decisive measure, if peace and tranquillity for a few years is their obje
they must make an arrangement which will suit the interests of all t
parties to it, and of which the justice and expediency will be so evident th
they will tend to carry it into execution."

Other Allies at the end of other wars have faced the choice between
negotiated and a dictated peace; but the alternatives were not so clea
stated, and the statement did not emanate from their leading soldier.

The Allied policy of moderation in 1815 owed its main driving-force
Wellington. His lucid reasoning served largely to impose it on a reluct
Cabinet and unenthusiastic Allies; but his reasoning prevailed less
cause it was lucid than because it was his. For the Prime Minister refer
to it respectfully as "the Duke of Wellington's projet," and its reasonab
ness was gilded by the prestige of Waterloo. Other problems faced h
as the Allies mounted guard in Paris and irreverent Parisians enjoyed
unwanted spectacle of redcoats in the Bois and bewildered Cossacks s
ing at the Palais Royal, of "Prussian and Russian officers in blue or gr
uniforms, waists drawn in like a wasp's, breasts sticking out lik
pigeon's; long sashes, with huge tassels of gold or silver, hanging h
way down their legs—pretty red and white boyish faces, with an enorm
bush of hair over each ear; lancers in square-topped caps and wav
plumes; hussars in various rich uniforms . . . Austrian officers in p
white uniforms, turned up with red." Whilst Europe strolled on the bo
vards in every colour of the rainbow, the Emperor, in Europe still,
mired the coast of Devonshire from *Bellerophon*; and the Prime Min
discussed his destination with the First Lord of the Admiralty. His

nce was embarrassing; but Lord Liverpool, stifling a hearty wish that
'the King of France would hang or shoot Buonaparte as the best termina-
ion of the business," was prepared, if necessary, to take him into custody.
The Duke, for once, was not consulted; he had already expressed a strong
istaste for Blücher's bloodthirsty opinions on the subject, stating firmly
hat "if the Sovereigns wished to put him to death they should appoint an
xecutioner which should not be me." And when Napoleon's surrender
as announced in Paris, they heard the Duke say that he must have an
iterview with him, and that he ought to be imprisoned at Madras. But
Ir. Barrow, of the Admiralty, recommended St. Helena; Sir Hudson
owe accepted the appointment; and Lord Bathurst anticipated com-
rtably that "Bonaparte's existence will soon be forgotten." Charged with
is hopeful mission, *Northumberland* sailed through the summer days
to the south, until the roar of Europe sank to a distant murmur and
e Western Ocean fell silent round them.

In France the Duke of Wellington attended conferences, inspected
ops, and drafted inexhaustibly. It was still raining decorations; his
iform became a gallery of European orders of chivalry, as the long
ocession of saints and heraldic monsters resumed with St. Andrew of
ssia, the Black Eagle of Prussia, and the Elephant of Denmark. The
ut King of France detached the ribbon of the Saint-Esprit from his own
red person, hung it on the Duke, and offered him a park; though
ellington's good sense preserved him from the *gaucherie* of celebrating
French defeat with an estate in France. The grateful Netherlands,
ng one better than the rest of Europe, made him a Prince—the Prince
Waterloo. But his own country was a shade embarrassed by the prob-
of its gratitude, since he had everything already. He was a Duke;
had the Garter; so they were reduced to voting him a further
0,000 towards the purchase of an estate. But though the fountain of
our had run dry, the Regent could still gush; and that royal hand
uainted his dear Wellington that even the consummate skill of the
sican could not withstand the superior genius of our own hero, and
England once more fulfilled a glorious destiny under the auspices of
transcendent General, adding with condescension that his most sin-
friend was George, P.R.

he Duke went cheerfully about his business. The worst was over now.

The King of France was on his throne again; and Wellington, more tha
any other man, had seated him there. For the second Restoration was th
outcome of his prompt initiative after Waterloo and those endless co
ferences in the Paris suburbs, when Wellington, watched by the narro
eyes of Fouché, imposed the King and (stranger still) imposed a mi
ister upon him who had sent his brother to the guillotine in '93. He h
kept uncongenial company, with Talleyrand limping beside him a
Fouché's whisper in his ear; and clever Count Molé thought him
innocent. But Wellington was a deft match-maker; the King's relucta
hand lodged safely in the old regicide's, the peculiar *mariage de co*
venance was successfully contrived; and King Louis, to the Duke's in
nite relief, reigned in France once more. Not that his troubles end
there. For the peace-treaty was still on the anvil. He knew his own min
which was in complete agreement with Castlereagh; but there was st
the Cabinet to be persuaded, and the Allies had strong opinions of th
own. For Allies, once wooed (like Danaë) in a shower of gold, gr
sadly independent with no further British subsidies in prospect. T
Prussians were stiff-necked by nature; Metternich was sly; and the C
was torn as usual between Russian interests and the Sermon on t
Mount. But Russia being largely satisfied, his better self prevailed.
sides, the Duke required a counterpoise to the dead weight of Cent
European reaction; and there was less than usual to fear from what
used to term Alexander's "Jacobinical flights."

There were distractions, though; for the Paris season of 1815 was
endless whirl of balls and reviews. Half London was in Paris to re
the glorious emotions of that unforgettable June evening when a ch
drove up Whitehall with the Waterloo despatch and a French ea
sticking out of each window. Croker was there, rejoiced by the spect
of "the old Life Guards patrolling the Boulevard last night, as they u
to do Charing Cross during the Corn riots"; Walter Scott came, thril
with patriotic fire; and Palmerston prepared to leave the War Departm
(and Lady Cowper's smiles) for a lounge round Paris. They stro
about the conquered streets, linked arms with friends in uniform,
filled the theatres every night. Not that Paris minded; for that mercu
city was in raptures over a ballet in which Waterloo was positively mir
and a grateful *ballerina* received her wounded lover from the hands

noble-hearted Briton. Britons were quite the mode, and kilted Highlanders the rage. But though gentlemen abounded, the town seemed to be
fuller still of ladies. All the world was there; white shoulders gleamed in
all directions and curls shook at every turn, though Kitty lingered in
England, mildly astonished by the accuracy of her own presentiment
(confided to Scott long before the battle) that when her hero met Buonaparte, he would destroy him at *one* blow. But the bright eyes of half the
Continent followed the Duke, as he went briskly about Paris in his blue
frock-coat. None followed him more closely than the adoring gaze of
Lady Shelley. That devotee was among the earliest arrivals; and as Lady
Granville acidly observed, she and her husband "ran after the great Duke
in a very disgusting way, but as they were together, '*sans peur et sans
reproche.*'" Expanding slightly in the sunshine of her simple-minded
worship, he talked to her about the battle, said solemnly, "The finger of
God was upon me," and let her cut off a lock of his hair in the reassuring
presence of her husband. Her sensibility was quite prodigious; for a *tête-
à-tête* with the Duke was almost too much for her; and (as she told
someone) it was positively sacrilegious to degrade her adoration with the
coarse name of love. But she drew him out. One day he shewed her all
his gold boxes with the portraits of European monarchs, and let her watch
him answering his letters. He liked to talk to her about the battle, and
told her what he said to Uxbridge and how experience gave him a pull
over other soldiers. Not that he struck martial attitudes before her. "I
hope to God," he said, "that I have fought my last battle. It is a bad
thing to be always fighting. While in the thick of it, I am too much
occupied to feel anything; but it is wretched just after." He told her that
next to a battle lost the greatest misery was a battle gained, and that he
was only just recovering his spirits. (He could write more cheerfully
about the losses now—"Never did I see such a pounding match. Both
were what the boxers call gluttons. . . .") Now he looked forward to a
cheerful life—"I must always have my house full. For sixteen years I
have always been at the head of our army, and I must have these gay
fellows round me." Flushed with these confidences, she glowed with pride
at being born an Englishwoman and living in the same age with this
great being, though the sharp eye of Lady Granville observed the Duke
be a trifle inattentive to her strenuous pursuit.

The bright round continued, with reviews by day and parties almos
every night. Lady Castlereagh's were dull (though she did her best t
enliven them by wearing her husband's Garter as a hair-ornament); an
Wellington preferred more cheerful company. So he was sometimes to b
found in a livelier *milieu* than the grave-eyed world of monarchs an
diplomatists. Caroline Lamb (who startled Paris with a purple riding
habit) amused him with her outbursts; and French ladies were a littl
apt to express their royalist opinions by embracing him in public. Ha
not a roomful of beauty in Vienna offered him a vista of conquests b
yond the dreams of Alexander? The world whispered (and even wrote
unseemly things about his friendship with Lady Frances Webster, thoug
the world knew nothing of the hurried note which he had scrawled to h
in the rainy darkness of the night before Waterloo advising her to remo
from Brussels. But Lady Shelley, whose devoted gaze rarely left hir
remained quite convinced of their perfect innocence. He seemed so simp
and so fatherly. But then Lady Shelley was a goose.

He was the saviour of Europe, just forty-six, with a trim figure an
a handsome face. He dressed the part at last; and an admiring wor
crowded to watch him bow by candlelight or sit his horse in Field Ma
shal's uniform with his sword drawn as the long lines of infantry we
stiffly by. In the Peninsula they had sometimes called him "the Dandy
now he was "the Beau"; and what is a Beau without his due accompa
ment of belles? Sometimes he rode with Lady Shelley; and how
thrilled her to hear him say, "Stick close to me." Once she was actua
close enough to hear him order an aide-de-camp to "tell that damn
adjutant he can't ride: tell him to get off his horse." It positively ma
her feel as though she could have charged up to the cannon's mo
under her hero's orders. He shewed her how the infantry formed squ
at Waterloo, and once he told her how much he disliked cheering in
ranks—"I hate that cheering. If once you allow soldiers to express
opinion, they may on some other occasion hiss instead of cheer." T
dined at Malmaison one night; and after dinner she walked in the d
garden with him and explored Josephine's conservatory by the uncert
light of a few candles. Not that their evenings were invariably so rest
since he once polonaised with her all through the house. He let her
on "Copenhagen"; and one hot afternoon, as they were sitting i

garden, she watched him playing with a grubby little child—he positively took a bite out of its apple and sat the urchin on his knee. Then they all went off to a fair and rode on the merry-go-round, the ladies circulating gaily upon swans and the Duke more suitably accommodated with a wooden horse.

But there were statelier occasions, when he received his guests. All Europe came; and the Duke bowed them in—sovereigns, Field Marshals, allies, Frenchmen, diplomats, and Cossacks. M. de Talleyrand limped up the stairs; Fouché was there; and the big double doors flew open, as the footmen bawled, *"Sa Majesté le Roi de Prusse."* Walter Scott was there as well; and his eyes filled with tears as he saw Wellington shake hands with Blücher. Paris was full of thrills for Scott; did not old Platow discount and kiss him in the Rue de la Paix? Besides, he had been presented to the Czar, wearing his blue and scarlet Selkirkshire uniform; and royalty, eyeing his lame leg, floored him at once by asking in what affair he had been wounded. The Duke awed him; he told someone that he had never felt abashed except before the Duke, because Wellington—the greatest living soldier and statesman—possessed every mighty quality of the mind in a higher degree than any other man did or had ever done. That evening Walter Scott sat down to supper with him and two ladies. The royalties were supping somewhere; but the Duke apparently preferred the company of Scott and Lady Caroline Lamb, who punctuated their repast "by an occasional scream." There was a bust above his head, which displayed (the house had once belonged to Junot) the marble features of the Emperor; and two thousand miles away *Northumberland* sailed on into the South Atlantic.

AUTUMN

The ship sailed on below the horizon; and the leaves fell in Europe. Waterloo was fading into retrospect, and the Duke wrote polite discouragements to eager historians. For he was quite convinced that no true account of it could be written, and that it was just as well.

"The object which you propose to yourself is very difficult of attainment, and, if really attained, is not a little invidious. The history of a battle is not unlike the history of a ball. Some individuals may recollect all the little

events of which the great result is the battle won or lost; but no individual
can recollect the order in which, or the exact moment at which, they oc
curred, which makes all the difference as to their value or importance.

"Then the faults or the misbehaviour of some gave occasion for the
distinction of others, and perhaps were the cause of material losses; and
you cannot write a true history of a battle without including the faults and
misbehaviour of part at least of those engaged.

"Believe me that every man you see in a military uniform is not a hero
and that, although in the account given of a general action, such as that
of Waterloo, many instances of individual heroism must be passed over
unrelated, it is better for the general interests to leave those parts of the
story untold, than to tell the whole truth."

He was prepared to help, but added ominously "Remember, I recom
mend you to leave the battle of Waterloo as it is." For he was grimly
positive that "if it is to be a history, it must be the truth. . . . But if
true history is written, what will become of the reputation of half of those
who have acquired reputation, and who deserve it for their gallantry, but
who, if their mistakes and casual misconduct were made public, would
not be so well thought of?" With these opinions it was not surprising that
in later years "the Duke entertains no hopes of ever seeing an account
all its details which shall be true." Truth, he believed, might well be
damaging; and he was disinclined to expose brave men to undiluted
truth. Besides, he was more indulgent now and even pleaded with the
Horse Guards for a delinquent, whom a later age would have diagnosed
unhesitatingly as a case of shell-shock:

"Many a brave man, and I believe even some very great men, have been
found a little terrified by such a battle as that, and have behaved after
wards remarkably well."

(Had he, one wonders, any recollection of the distant night when a
scared young Colonel staggered into camp from Sultanpettah Tope?
His diagnosis was sympathetic:

"From what I have heard of the case since I received your letter, it ap
pears that, —— —— having left the field as wounded, the surgeon of the
regiment could not return him in the list of wounded. It will turn, fir
upon whether the surgeon was right or wrong; and, secondly, whether

was not so stunned as to be obliged to quit the field, although not in such a state afterwards as that the surgeon ought to have returned him as wounded."

But now the Duke was busy with a fresh problem. For the Allies, denied any further opportunities of territorial gain, developed a wholly unexpected passion for the fine arts. There were excuses, since France under the Empire had been a connoisseur of comprehensive tastes, appropriating every major work of art from The Hague to Rome, until the Paris galleries came to resemble less a national collection than a complete history of European painting and sculpture. Laocoon writhed in the Louvre; the horses of St. Mark's stepped decorously on the arch outside the Tuileries; Apollo Belvedere posed in his niche; and, far from her native Florence, Venus dei Medici simpered in exile. Art had indubitably followed the eagles, though in the opposite direction; and the liquidation of this sumptuous collection promised the Allies all the delights of a gigantic jumble-sale where there was nothing to pay. Vast inventories were prepared; military working-parties took pictures down from walls and handled unaccustomed packages; Canova came from Rome with an interminable list of Papal property; there were the Hessian pictures at Malmaison, the Dutch pictures in the Louvre, and the Pope's statuary everywhere; and Prussia developed a wholly unsuspected wealth of art-treasures. The Venetian horses gave endless trouble, since they were now Austrian property; but the Austrians, who had no tools, were quite incapable of moving them. They requisitioned British Engineers, lined the Place du Carrousel with a guard of white-coats, and slung the horses down under the watchful eye of Lord Palmerston, who clambered up the arch himself. These exercises somewhat dimmed the lustre of the Duke's popularity in Paris, since the recovery of stolen property is rarely popular among receivers.

Major and minor diplomacy absorbed him; and he corresponded vigorously upon the composition of the Allied army of occupation for northern France. The Duke was to command it in the name of the Allied monarchs; and he was full of cares about the British contingent. Ministers, in sudden access of post-war economy, were demolishing the army, and advised them gravely that "my opinion is that the best troops we have, probably the best in the world, are the British infantry, particularly the old infantry that has served in Spain. This is what we ought to keep up; and what I wish above all others to retain." He had his fill of troops that summer; for it was the season of the great reviews in Paris, when the streets were lined with every colour of the Allied rainbow, and Wellington took the salute in the Place Louis XV beside a King and two Emperors. He watched the Prussians at Grenelle, the Russian Guard at Neuilly, and expounded the superiority of line over column to Palmerston, a fresh-faced young gentleman who had figured in his correspondence as the source of irritating departmental queries. He told the attentive Secretary at War that he had started in the last campaign with the very worst army that was ever got together, fortunately leavened by four or five of his Peninsular regiments. Nothing, he thought, could equal British soldiers in the field. They might not look quite so well as others at reviews, because appearance was, he felt, a trifle underrated. But in the field he was always confident that a detachment would maintain its post against any force until they dropped. So he was proud of them, as he shewed off their paces in the fields beyond Montmartre. It was a replica of Salamanca, faultlessly performed without rehearsals. The Prussians were apt to require two days of preparation for such performances and to peg the ground with finger-posts. But Wellington, who saw the *terrain* for the first time that morning, took it impromptu; and the watching foreigners were vastly impressed as the long scarlet lines wheeled and deployed with the added (and, in Paris, wholly irresistible) fascination of swinging kilts.

Diplomacy recurred in an unusual form that autumn. For while negotiations for the peace-treaty followed a comparatively normal course, the Czar soared beyond protocols into a region inhabited by the sublime platitudes of revealed religion. This revelation was principally vouchsafed through the ecstatic agency of Baroness von Krüdener, whom Castlereagh described irreverently as "an old fanatic, who has a considerable reputation amongst the few highflyers in religion that are to be found at Paris. Her vein was highly mystical; she had a Swiss disciple, a private entrance to the Elysée, and a flow of words by which the Czar was frequently reduced to tears. But tears were not enough; for action was required of a repentant Czar. His noble attitudes had already inspired disrespect

British to term him "the Magnanimous Dandy"; but refreshed by nightly draughts from her apocalyptic well, his magnanimity dilated to more than Wilsonian proportions. Not that she led him towards a novel idea; since he had been vaguely haunted for more than ten years by the nebulous conception of a European union of Christian states, which now emerged, wreathed in sanctimonious garlands of Scriptural allusion. Diplomacy raised polite eyebrows. Prince Metternich concluded that the Romanoff "mind was affected"; Lord Castlereagh agreed that it was "not completely sound"; the Duke was present when the plan was mooted by its Imperial patentee, and experienced some difficulty in keeping a straight face. The Foreign Secretary thought it a "piece of sublime mysticism," and its proposal "what may be called a scrape." But if the Czar derived satisfaction from addressing autograph letters to the Prince Regent inviting him to conduct his policy upon the principles of Holy Writ, was not easy to refuse him; and as the October days drew in, they signed the blameless articles of the Holy Alliance in Paris, Alexander glowing with a slightly evangelical pride at the circumstance of their signature in that godless capital.

Far to the south the ship sailed on into silence. South of the Line an island waited. It was the island where Sir Arthur Wellesley had stayed ten years before on his way home from India. Fate had transposed them now; for he commanded on the soil of France, while the Emperor descended at the very house where he had stopped on St. Helena in 1805.

In those October days a lonely figure paced the garden of The Briars, while kings and emperors in Paris subscribed their august signatures to the Holy Alliance. Europe was growing chilly now; the year was almost over; winter had come again.

Nations are never so grateful as their benefactors expect.—WELLINGTON TO CANNING, DEC. 15, 1814.

Was this the summit? Field Marshal, Duke—three times a Duke and once a Prince—he had dethroned an emperor and restored king. His victories had saved Europe, as he had heard Pitt prophesy ten years before, when he sat unrecognised at a long table in Guildhall; and the greatest soldier in the world had fled before him. Monarchs accepted his rebuke, and respectful nations did as he told them. Cheers were the least part of his incense, although he savoured them. For one summer evening he had stood beside King Louis at a palace window; candles were set to light their faces; and when the sea of waiting Frenchmen outside the Tuileries saw their sovereign smiling beside the foreign Duke, they cheered and cheered. The cheers found softer echoes, where adoring ladies flocked after him at evening parties. Aloof from cheering crowds, he was rarely indifferent to ladies' homage; and it was generously offered. He liked to talk to them about himself; they listened prettily; though if they were inclined (like de Staël) to unwomanly accomplishments, he took a manly pleasure in alarming them. For while the wide-eyed Lady Shelly might ask favours freely, he wrote with wicked glee that "I am on proper terms with the Staël—that is, she is confoundedly afraid of me." So the indulgent hero mounted them on "Copenhagen," rode with them in the Bois, took them to boxes at the Opera; and a skirt generally fluttered among his staff at a review. It was a cheerful picture, though Kitty was not in it. His Duchess was detained in England, since a brief experience of her in the year before had left him disinclined to expose her to the risks of Paris. For her accounts were always in inextricable confusion, and a big establishment was sure to be too much for her. Besides, there were his boys to be looked after. And she was so short-sighted, too; his vast international parties called for arts of management that lay far beyond her Dublin range. Did not Miss Edgeworth, of Edgeworthstown, write appreciatively, when she called on St. Patrick's Day and found a plate of shamrocks on her table, that "nothing could be more like Kitty Pakenham" than the Duchess of Wellington? So she was in England; and he kept house for himself. Almost a widower already, he tasted bachelor delights, was free to choose his own companions, and walked briskly down the long avenue of smiling faces. He was the Duke. Indeed, he was something more, since an impressive protocol signed by four Powers appointed him Commander-in-Chief of an international army of occupation. Russians, Austrians, Germans, and British presented arms at his approach; he reigned in seven Departments from Calais down to Bâle with 150,000 men; and an Ambassadors' Conference sat in Paris to be the vehicle of his communications. Small wonder that Miss Berry found that when "talking of the allied sovereigns . . . he says *we* found so-and-so—*we* intend such-and-such thing—quite treating *de Couronne à Couronne.*" For the Duke of Wellington had positively become a European Power with his own army, territory, and diplomatic relations. Was this the summit?

I

Unpleasant problems faced him before 1815 was out, since Ney, always injudicious, contrived to get arrested. A frantic wife besieged the Duke with prayers to intercede with the King, and Ney added something soldierly relying on the general amnesty embodied in the capitulation of Paris after Waterloo. The Duke was disinclined to help, since Ney's treachery to King Louis in the spring had been exceptionally gross, and settled government would become wholly impossible in France if such treason went unpunished. Besides, the Cabinet were pressing with civilian sternness for an example to be made in the interests of public order, and Wellington concurred; for he was unlikely to lag behind Liverpool and Castlereagh upon a question of elementary discipline. The King apparently expected him to intervene on behalf of the Marshal, and avoided giving him an audience. Wellington, who had no such intention, resented the discourtesy with a tremendous intimation that, as commanding troops, he should remain and do whatever was officially required of him, but that he was likewise an English gentleman, that the King of France had insulted him, and that until the insult was atoned for he should never go near him except on public business. Meanwhile he made no move in favour of the Marshal, who fell to a French firing-party; and angry Bonapartists were convinced that he was a victim to Wellington's jealousy of his military achievement, while lively Radicals in England embraced the martyr's cause and lampooned the Duke for a cold-hearted refusal to interfere with the course of French justice, *Don Juan* ingeminating

> "Glory like yours should any dare gainsay,
> Humanity would rise and thunder, 'Nay!'"

and adding in a footnote with a grin, "Query, *Ney?—Printer's Devil.*"

Now it was 1816, and the world began to settle down. The Duke left Paris in the spring and installed his headquarters at Cambrai. There were as many papers as ever on his table—papers about mad Englishmen in Paris who got themselves into scrapes by plotting against the King, complaints from Zieten about the treatment of the Prussians, a polite request that Fouché would discourage the French authorities from their enterprising plan of opening gaming-houses in occupied territory for the benefit of the Allied troops, and a note from Hill who had gone home and found his family in some embarrassment (eliciting the kindly answer that the Duke possessed "a large sum of money which is entirely at my command, and . . . I could not apply it in a manner more satisfactory to me than in accommodating you, my dear Hill, to whom I am under so many obligations"). He wrote judicious letters on French politics to Louis and his ministers, pleaded for General Mouton (whose conduct in the Hundred Days, though he commanded a corps at Ligny, had not been actively treasonable), and positively prolonged his residence in Paris at the King's request. How many conquerors have been invited to extend their stay in a conquered capital? Small wonder that he wrote that "there is not much confidence in anybody either here or in England, excepting myself." Then he was off to The Hague; the Netherlands were full of problems—French refugees in Brussels, the new fortresses along the frontier, and a growing tendency in Belgian quarters to resent Dutch preeminence. In June he was brought back to Paris for a French royal wedding. The Shelleys were there; and he told her that he was not well and had been recommended to try Cheltenham. He took them to the play and carried her off to drink tea in his favourite social haunts. One evening he gave dinner to the Spaniards, and she saw him in his Spanish uniform. She had been going on to a reception at the Duchesse de Berry's; but he pressed her to stay; and as the royal invitation was for ladies only,

she "felt that it would be monstrous dull" and stayed. After the guests
had gone, she heard him talking about Spain and about the blunder they
had made in abolishing the Inquisition; someone, it seemed, had proposed it in his time, but he had told them shrewdly, "*Quoi, vous voulez
me donner un autre ennemi à combattre! J'aurai tous les curés de la
Castille contre moi. L'Inquisition se meurt d'elle même. Voyez le Portugal; nous ne l'avons pas aboli là, et cependant elle n'existe plus. Ce sera de
même ici. Si vous l'abolissez, elle existera toujours.*" Reformers of abuses
have received worse advice.

He gave a ball of his own; and Lady Shelley, who came a little early,
found him by himself moving the chairs about; for he was always strong
on detail. That evening he took in Marmont's wife to supper; but afterwards he sat with Lady Shelley until he went off to bed at four o'clock in
the morning. He told her that he should be going home in a few days—
"You must dine with me every day until I go." They rode together, and
she talked about her husband's political affairs. "What," said the Duke,
"are quarrels to be eternal? I hate these party squabbles." For he was a
indifferent partisan; and when an injudicious letter from Lord Grey
an arrested Englishman fell into his hands, he returned it unopened
the Whig leader. They had their last ride, and Lady Shelley felt quite
sad; indeed, she was completely overcome that evening by the delicacy
of Biggotini's dancing in the affecting ballet of *Nina*. Then he was off—
three o'clock one morning, jolting along the road to Calais. The roads
1816 were full of travellers. That summer Lord Byron swept the Continent again with his sombre regard. It was just seven years since he had
meditated on the quays of Lisbon, while Sir Arthur waited for the
French at Talavera. Still faithful to Sir Arthur's footsteps, he meditated
now in Brussels. He was a trifle patronising with Waterloo (though he
compared it favourably with Troy, Mantinea, Leuctra, Marathon, and
several other sites of his acquaintance) and, having noted the rare lyric
possibilities of a sound of revelry by night, passed on to meditate
elsewhere.

II

IT WAS past midsummer, 1816, when he saw England once again. The cliffs of Dover gleamed, onlookers cheered, and he drove off to Richard's house not far from Ramsgate. Richard, an enigmatic figure in these days with the air of an imperfectly extinct volcano that is inseparable from a career of Empire-building, was getting on for sixty now. Once a master of the art of resignation, he had nothing left to resign; but he was still prepared to favour correspondents and the House of Lords with his unnaturally progressive opinions upon the Catholics and fiscal policy. Besides, there was his toilet; for Richard was arranged with care. When Lawrence painted him a few years earlier, he noticed that his sitter's lips already owed something to art; and some years later a malicious eye observed his blackened eyebrows, rouged cheeks, and awful brow whose lofty pallor, alas! was not innocent of artificial aid. The Duke called on this ageing Cæsar and posted on to London. But London in July was hardly restful. The Regent claimed him for dinner; he dined out assiduously and took a hand in a feminine cabal at Almack's against the autocracy of Lady Jersey. The London round seemed to revive him. Then he was off to Cheltenham for his cure. The spa received him with triumphal arches and illuminations; he sipped his water in Well Walk, gossiped with a few Peninsular acquaintances, and strolled with Kitty and his boys. She wrote off delighted bulletins, informing the anxious ladies at Llangollen that

"he for whom all the world is so justly anxious is considerably better both in looks and spirits since his arrival in England.

"I think I perceive an amendment every day. This happens to be the time of the holidays of our Boys, and I say with delight they are as fond of and as familiar with their noble and beloved Father as if they had never been separated from him. They accompany him in his walks, *chat* with him, play with him. In short they are the chosen companions of each other. . . ."

He had always got on well with children, and could get on with these, even if they were his own. Kitty might have her faults; her trick of admiring him in public was particularly trying. But that summer he was at his gentlest. When someone hinted that he sometimes failed his friends, he defended himself with warmth—"The truth is that for fifteen or sixteen years I have been at the head of armies with but little intermission; and I have long found it necessary to lay aside all private motives in considering publick affairs. I hope that this practice does not make me cold hearted, or feel a diminished interest for those I am inclined to love. I I may judge by what I feel, I should say it does not. . . ." And judged by what he did, it did not either. For ne was busying himself to obtain public aid for Sheridan's impoverished family. His benefactions were often gruff; and a formal manner sometimes left a suitor under the impression that his petition had been dismissed, when it was generously granted. Thus, he reported to a friend of Indian days in search of an appointment that he had spoken for him without success and "I now recommend you to let the matter drop. . . . You may be quite certain that great situations are not obtained in this country by personal exertion and interest. Let a man show that he has talents, integrity, and enlarged views, and he may depend upon it that if employment abroad is h object, he is more likely to obtain it without solicitation than by making the most active exertions." The recipient of this homily might be excused for concluding that the Duke had done with his affairs. But without his knowledge Wellington wrote the same day to urge his claims upon t Company, dilating on his zeal, integrity, and talents, and concluding th they could not do better than employ him in a great situation, such as t governorship of Bombay. He always hated to raise hopes or to parade h services; and they were often rendered under cover of a curt reply.

Another suitor haunted him that season; for the French were pressi for a reduction of the army of occupation, and its commander was felt be the likeliest person to view their request with favour. M. de Richel had seen him on the subject before he came home on leave; he advi Castlereagh that there was no danger in the proposed reduction, and g the French the benefit of his guidance as to the best moment to put f ward their demand. His leave was ending now; the walks with his t boys at Cheltenham were over; and he was back in London. One af noon he rode as far as Kensington. For Graham took him out to Wilk studio in Lower Phillimore Place, and he called on the respectful painter with Lady Argyll and the Duke and Duchess of Bedford. The painter had been warned, his mother and sister posted to watch the great arrival from behind the parlour curtains, and his works judiciously disposed about the studio. The Duke surveyed them and approved, remarking in his decided tone "Very good" and "Capital." Then he sat down to study one of them; and Lady Argyll began to tell the artist that Wellington wished him to paint a picture. The Duke tilted his chair back and proposed a group of old soldiers outside a public-house chewing tobacco and telling stories; he should not be particular about their uniforms and suggested that the public-house might be located in the King's Road, Chelsea. Wilkie concurred with rapture, adding that the picture only wanted a story. Wellington said that perhaps it would do if they were playing skittles. Wilkie proposed a reading from a newspaper, to which the Duke was perfectly agreeable and added that the sketch might be sent to him abroad. Then he stood up, took out his watch, and informed the company that he was dining with the Duke of Cambridge. He turned to Wilkie with a bow and asked when he should hear from him. The artist answered that he could not get the picture done for two years. "Very well," replied the art patron, "that will be soon enough for me." He went downstairs, bowed once more to his host, saw old Mrs. Wilkie at the parlour window and bowed to her, mounted his horse, and then rode off. The little windows were all full of faces; two Guardsmen watched him from the corner; and as the sound of hoofs died away down Lower Phillimore Place, they were tying ribbons on the historic chair which he had honoured. His leave was over now; and before August was out, he was in France again.

III

BACK once more in his little kingdom, Wellington resumed the endless correspondence about his troops, about the new Barrier fortresses on the Belgian frontier, about Bonapartist exiles who misbehaved themselves in Brussels, and British officers who misbehaved nearer home in the theatre at Boulogne. Canning passed through on his way back to Lisbon and the Duke, whose enthusiasm for abolition had manifestly waned since the days when he discussed slavery with Clarkson in the Paris embassy, disliked his notion of awarding British support to Portugal o Spain according to their respective display of abolitionist virtue—"nonsense and folly" was his brief description of the philanthropic policy Then he had his autumn reviews, graced by the royal Dukes of Kent and Cambridge and a due accompaniment of evening parties. The Dukes wer hardly to his taste; as he told Creevey afterwards, "they are the damnede millstone about the necks of any Government that can be imagined. The have insulted—*personally* insulted—two-thirds of the gentlemen of England." But he had more congenial guests; for the Duchess of Richmon brought out her girls to stay with him at Cambrai. He had writte charmingly to Lady Shelley, telling her how much he missed his "absen A.D.C." at the reviews. But she was far away in Vienna, and now oth belles rode "Copenhagen." Georgy Lenox found him a rather tryin mount from an unpleasing mannerism of neighing violently at the sig of troops (an authentic instance of a war-horse laughing "ha-ha" to t trumpeters); and one day when she found herself inside a square wi him, she overheard the ranks remarking, "Take care of that 'ere hors he kicks out; we knew him well in Spain." The house at Mont Martin was crowded and cheerful with incessant amateur theatricals a a more violent diversion known as "riding in the coach," which appear to consist of dragging ladies down interminable corridors on rugs. T gentlemen were harnessed; even the Duke did not disdain this hum office, though he occasionally mounted the rug himself, and Wellingt drove through Headquarters behind a team of ladies. A bulletin from his own hand describes the romping:

"We are going on here as usual—'Riding in the coach,' dancing the Mazurka, &c., &c. The house is as full as it can hold. Yesterday was a very bad day, and I went to Cambray, and I understand that they hunted Lord C—— through all the corridors, even that in the roof. At night we had an improvement on the coach. Two goats were brought in and harnessed, but instead of being horses and assisting to draw, they chose to lie down and be drawn. The night before, the ladies drew me the *petty* tour, and afterwards Lord Hill the *grand* tour, but the 'fat, fair and forty,' and M—— were so knocked up that some of us were obliged to go into the harness, although we had already run many stages."

This cheerful horseplay filled his evenings. For he could romp with his own circle, though the outer world found him less oncoming, the indomitable de Staël concluding bitterly that as she had done everything to fascinate him without success, the glacial Duke must be devoid of all "*cœur pour l'amour.*" But he had little taste for clever women. His days were rendered quite sufficiently exhausting by clever men; and in the evenings he might be excused for preferring something a trifle less exacting.

His days, indeed, were full of problems. He did not spare much attention for the gathering storm at home (which he was inclined to attribute to the sudden "reduction of our war establishments . . . the rage for travelling of all our gentry, which have deprived some of our people of employment, and lastly and principally . . . the idleness, dissipation and improvidence of all the middling and lower classes in England, produced by a long course of prosperity and of flattery of their vices by the higher orders and the government"). His interests were, of necessity, almost purely Continental; but in that sphere no problem, however civilian, lay beyond his range. He was the guardian of the peace-treaties; and finance, the inseparable (though often insubordinate) hand-maid of peace-treaties, came within his survey. The French were bound by treaty to pay an indemnity of 700 million francs in five annuities, in addition to the costs of the Allied occupation; and the Duke picked his way through a morass of foreign loans, of rates of interest, of scrip, of currency, of interviews with Mr. Baring. He favoured the financing of France by an

issue of *Rentes* to leading houses in London and Amsterdam, and ex
pressed his view that "unless some arrangement of the description pro
posed is adopted, France will be aground this year, and our settlement o
last year will be entirely destroyed." That degree of common sense i
post-war settlements was not reached by later generations without year
of blundering and controversy. But Wellington could grasp the poin
Embodying the wisdom vainly sought by his successors in endless Con
ferences at unnumbered health-resorts, he saw the bankers for himse
and faced the still more tangled problem of French Reparations. He ha
some experience of finance, since remittances to his army in the Peninsu
had always involved complicated banking transactions. But the Repar
tions question in 1817 was worse than financial, since it included t
awkward problem of distribution between hungry Allies as well as th
of French ability to pay; and Wellington was finally enthroned, on t
proposal of the Czar, as supreme arbiter of all Allied claims. How ma
men would rather deal with Napoleon than with Reparations? But W
lington faced both; and what is more, he faced Reparations single-hand

Not that the French were grateful. For nations rarely are; and Pa
theatres rang with denunciations of *"le tyran de Cambrai"* and little jo
on *"Vilainton,"* whilst he took care never to "go into any blackgu
mob or place in which a fellow might insult me with impunity."
went about his business, as the months slipped by, reviewing troops
specting Belgian counterscarps, discussing Mr. Rothschild's dealing
exchange, and maintaining order in occupied territory. His own aff
scarcely engaged him, though he was still at the Spaniards for a decis
about the royal pictures which he had captured at Vitoria; and whe
was suggested that his boys should be educated at the Military Coll
he was strong for "the education usually given to English gentlemen"
preference to anything more technical. He ran across to England n
than once in the course of 1817. On one visit he attended the Prince
gent's inauguration of Mr. Rennie's new Strand bridge; and once he
besieged by James Ward, the Academician, who had just won a p
with his design for an "Allegory of Waterloo." This masterpiece, a t
fying composition in which mythology predominated, involved a si
from the Duke, whose lifelong servitude to painters was just begin
He saw Mr. Ward and, stifling his objection to being painted by an

whose leading triumphs had hitherto been achieved in the depiction of
ulls, made the valid excuse that he was just off to the Continent.
"My lord," said the determined painter, "I will follow you there."
"Ah, Mr. Ward," the deep voice replied, " a man that has five thousand
oops under his command knows not where he may be one day after
other. But I will sit to you on my return."

He was back again before the year was out to view another country
ouse. This time it was Lord Rivers' place near Reading; the splendid
venue of trees found favour in his eyes; and the purchase of Stratfield
ye for £263,000 was approved. But his concerns were still wholly Con-
ental; and as 1817 wore on, he was kept busy with a tour of inspection
Alsace, his autumn reviews, and the absorbing business of checking
sporting and pugilistic proclivities of his command in France. Kitty
ne out to him that autumn; and he wrote sternly to complain that
neone had been using in her carriage horses belonging to the pon-
n train. He had other pets as well; since a Foreign Office messenger
s once charged with a "black and tan dog of the Duke of Norfolk's
ed" for the Commander-in-Chief, and Lady Castlereagh recruited his
nels with two boar-hound puppies. But life at Cambrai was not all
ting and house-parties. For French politics were far from reassuring
he first weeks of 1818, and the Duke feared gravely for the dynasty—
ntertain no doubt how this contest will end. The descendants of Louis
will not reign in France; and I must say, that it is the fault of Mon-
r and his adherents. . . . I wish Monsieur would read the histories of
Restoration and subsequent Revolution, or that he would recollect
t passed under his own view, probably at his own instigation, in the
olution." Besides, there was the endless wrangle over Reparations;
Wellington reported that "since Baring left me, as I generally spend
greatest part of every morning now with money-changers, Roths-
has been with me." It was not simple to assess the damages result-
rom twenty years of European war; and the Duke struggled bravely
the appetites of half the Continent. As he wrote, "my plan is first
certain what will really and ought to satisfy each nation. . . . I will
secondly, negotiate with the French government to obtain that sum
e mode which will be most advantageous to the Allies, and least
ous to the other operations of the French government." The goal

was plain enough, though it was less readily accessible; for the interven
ing region was inextricably tangled with tales of ancient outrages com
mitted by the armies of the First Republic and every exaction of th
Empire in its career of conquest. But he laboured on untiringly, and th
Allied claims were ultimately reduced by his industry to 240 millio
francs.

One February night these labours were almost interrupted, as he wa
driving home in Paris after a party. A shot rang out; he saw the flas
himself and suspected nothing, though he was perfectly aware that h
life was threatened; a sound of running footsteps died away down th
dark street, as he got out at his own door and asked the coachman wi
some heat what he had meant by driving in at such a pace. The coac
man answered that he had seen a man fire at his Grace. The news affect
Europe variously. Prinny was shocked beyond belief, writing in alm
tearful terms to his "dear Friend" and eliciting the courtly answer th
if anything could reconcile a man to such attempts upon his life, it w
the reception of such letters from one to whom he owed all his succe
old soldiers in French *cafés* muttered in deep moustaches that Water
had been avenged; King Louis fluttered, and his ministers entered w
gusto on a series of promiscuous arrests in the best manner of Continen
justice; while poor Kitty sobbed out her relief at his escape in a note
Richard—

"I cannot bear that you should run the hazard of hearing reports
alarming whilst I have the blessing of knowing that he is safe. Thank G
thank God, my dear Lord Wellesley, my Husband is perfectly safe but
life has been attempted as he returned home on Wednesday night at
own door a pistol was fired at him, but he ever was he still continued
special charge of Heaven tho' so close he was not touched neither is th
the smallest mark on the carriage why did not the footman seize the va
for it appears that he stood near the sentry box and that they must h
seen him, but he has none but French footmen. . . . My next wish
thanking God for the preservation of the most precious life, is to save
from anxiety."

She was still fluttering, when she wrote to him again:

"Tho' still far from well I am so anxious to see you for many rea
. . . I wish to rejoice with you on the success of my dear and exce

husband, his very narrow escape which I am not yet warrior enough (tho'
I have thought myself very valiant) to think of it without agitation. . . ."

While the French police stirred muddy waters by haphazard arrests
f Bonapartist malcontents, his own Government ordered the Duke to
ave Paris forthwith and withdraw to Cambrai. He did not relish the
treat and fenced with their command, complaining that he had not
een consulted in a matter in which he was "principally and personally
ncerned," and politely deploring the necessity for disobeying orders.
ut he disobeyed them; and Wellington's one act of mutiny was con-
aled in a blandly phrased expectation that "the Prince Regent and his
vernment will agree with me in thinking that I ought to delay to
ey His Royal Highness's commands." He even took the unusual
erty of examining the desirability of such commands being given at
. For why should he be any safer at Cambrai? And if not at Cambrai,
y anywhere on the Continent? In that event he would become "the
icule of the world, and I should by this very act deprive myself of
means of serving you in future in any capacity." This was unanswer-
le; and the Duke stayed in Paris.

There was so much for him to do—French Reparations to be settled,
nch politics to be supervised, and the Allied occupation to be brought
nehow to an end. His own affair was soon disposed of, when they
ested a Bonapartist *bravo* of the name of Cantillon, who was manifestly
lty (though a French jury subsequently acquitted him). The news
ched St. Helena, where an ageing, lonely man noted Cantillon's
ne. Paris echoed this unpleasing temper, though King Louis was
ost tender now, sending the Duke a little present of old Sèvres with
y intimation that he felt himself *"encouragé dans cette démarche par*
vieux proverbe que je vais tâcher de rendre dans votre langue: Do
e gifts—keep friendship alive." Friendship, alas! was sadly strained
Reparations in 1818. But the Duke persisted, revising Allied claims,
ferring endlessly with bankers, and running backwards and forwards
veen Paris, Cambrai, and London. He had a new address in town;
that spring he dated his first letter from Apsley House, which he had
ght from Richard. He had a fresh problem, too. For Spain and
ugal were drifting into war over the rebellious Spanish colonies in

South America. The Duke, it was believed, might intervene in the com
manding character of uncle to the Peninsula; but this view reckone
without the towering altitude of Spanish pride; and his interventior
when it came, rather resembled the tentative intrusion of a nephev
between two punctilious uncles. His views were plain enough. No notio
of calling a New World into being to redress the balance of the Ol
had crossed his mind; he was not Canning, and he disapproved o
revolutions. Besides, his main anxiety was lest the United States mig
seize the opportunity of recognising infant nations struggling to be fr
in South America; and he pressed the Spaniards to prompt action i
the River Plate before this calamity could supervene.

His hands were full that summer, though life at Cambrai was st
cheerful. Creevey came over and found him riding out to see a crick
match with two belles from Baltimore. Wellington talked freely aft
dinner about the royal Dukes and their bad manners, and how t
House of Commons could not be blamed for making difficulties abo
their allowances, as it was their only opportunity of revenge, and
thought, by God! they were quite right to use it. This was strange la
guage from a pillar of the throne to a former Opposition Whip. B
the Duke did not see himself as a strict Tory, and he enquired wi
friendly interest about the problem of Whig leadership; Tierney mi
do, he thought, though Romilly was strange to him—but then, t
House of Commons never cared for lawyers. He was less Tory than ev
when he discussed the Regent—"By God! you never saw such a figu
in your life as he is. Then he speaks and swears so like old Falstaff, t
damn me if I was not ashamed to walk into a room with him." Th
dined together again in a French provincial inn; and Creevey was qu
shocked when two grubby maids brought in two partridges, a fowl, a
a fricasse to set before six hungry gentlemen. The Duke, who had dri
from Paris on the meagre support of a cold chicken eaten in his carri
seemed to enjoy it all. The champagne was poor; the tea at break
the next morning came out of an enormous coffee-pot; there were
saucers; but when Creevey opined that this formidable brew was a cre
able product for Vitry, Wellington remarked "with that curious simpli
of his" that he had brought it all the way from Paris. Then Cree
saw his coach driving away at breakneck speed; for Wellington had

wind of the approaching Duke of Kent, and incontinently bolted. But the
royal Duke caught him up at Valenciennes. His troubles multiplied,
since the new Duchess of Kent accompanied him, to say nothing of a
German lady-in-waiting of the most austere appearance. There was a
dinner-party, and Wellington went grumbling round the Staff, enquiring
who the devil was to take out the maid of honour. An anxious silence
ended in a flash of inspiration—"Damme, Fremantle, find out the Mayor
and let him do it." After all, the French had lost the war; they were in
occupied territory; and the invitation was a mild, but pardonable, *væ
victis*. They dined; they danced; the Duke of Kent amused them all by
his new-found solicitude about his lady's health (he positively stroked
her cheek after a waltz in order to ascertain if she was overheated);
and Creevey regaled his host with a sanctimonious saying of the Duke
of Kent's about his aged mother's illness. The delighted Wellington
took Creevey by the button and, remarking "God damme! d'ye know
what his sisters call him? By God! they call him Joseph Surface," exploded into one of his tremendous laughs which startled the entire ball-
room. But the Duke of Kent always amused him. Wellington called
him "the Corporal," from an untidy habit of appearing in undress uniform; and he could never forget the broad comedy of his confessions
to Creevey about his royal sacrifices of domestic happiness on the altar
of dynastic duty. He relished simple fun; and the Duke of Kent afforded
ample opportunities, especially when he got them all up at dawn for an
inspection, and kept poor Creevey waiting for his breakfast until the
shower of royal interrogations had rained itself out. Wellington advised
the starving gossip that it was always wise on such occasions to take
his breakfast first and went chuckling round the Staff, pointing at
Creevey and repeating with wicked glee, *"Voilà, le monsieur qui n'a pas
déjeuné."* He liked the little man, savoured his anecdotes, and spoke
freely to him about the Whigs, praising Grey and Lansdowne, and
deploring the fact that they were buried in the House of Lords—"Nobody
cares a damn for the House of Lords; the House of Commons is everything in England, and the House of Lords nothing." And Creevey liked
him in return: the Duke's simplicity impressed him—"that curious simplicity of his . . . his comical simplicity . . . the uniform frankness and
simplicity of Wellington in all the conversations I have heard him

engaged in, coupled with the unparalleled situation he holds in the world,
for an English subject, make him to me the most interesting object I
have ever seen in my life."

His reign at Cambrai was ending now. For the world met once more
in conference that autumn to resettle the peace of Europe and to end
the Allied occupation. Lord Castlereagh passed through *en route* for Aix-
la-Chapelle; the Czar descended from his distant Sinai; and the statesmen furbished up their decorations, polished their protocols, and prepared
themselves for the invigorating processes of another Congress. He was
in Brussels just before it opened, and once more Creevey met him strolling
in the Park.

"Well now, Duke, let me ask you, don't you think Lowe a very unnecessarily harsh gaoler of Buonaparte at St. Helena?"

"By God! I don't know. Buonaparte is so damned intractable a fellow
there is no knowing how to deal with him. To be sure, as to the means
employed to keep him there, there never was anything so damned absurd.
I know the island of St. Helena well. . . ."

His view of Lowe was simple—"as for Lowe, he is a damned fool."
But one evening when Creevey was at him again at Lady Charlotte
Greville's about a newspaper report that he was to join the Cabinet, he
answered with a grunt.

Then he was off to Aix-la-Chapelle for the Congress. He and Castlereagh formed the British delegation and he played his part in the
agreeable charade of Continental unity. The Foreign Secretary was
"quite convinced that past habits, common glory, and these occasional
meetings, displays, and repledges, are among the best securities Europe
has now for a durable peace"; and if the common past of the Allies
was to be recalled, the Duke was a notable exhibit. He gave the Czar
a great review, composing for the occasion the libretto of a sham fight,
which made him feel as if he had been "writing a Harlequin Farce."
The ceremonial round began once more—review, ball, dinner, play—
Palmerston was vastly impressed by the perfection of his manners, "the
extreme respect and deference paid by all to the Duke, and, on the other
hand, the manly but respectful manner with which he treats all
sovereigns." The Prussians, by an odd twist of fate, gave their display at
Donchery, outside Sedan, where Prussia was to wait in spiked helmet

for the sword of another Emperor. The Duke talked a good deal to Palmerston, telling him all about line and column and how it was his practice to meet French attacks behind the shelter of a little ridge. He pointed at a Prussian column.

"Look how formidable that looks; and yet I defy the French" (the Duke clapped his hands) "to mention any one instance in the whole war in which these masses had made the least impression on our lines."

Then he described the process in detail—the British volley and the scattered reply of the advancing French, the wavering of the attackers, and the odd way in which their columns always frayed out from the rear—"As the French column ran from the rear, one used to see the men huddling together and running to the right and left, just as they saw the means of sheltering themselves behind a body of fellow-fugitives, so that at a little distance they went waddling like ducks." That was his simple picture of the tactics by which the Empire had been broken.

The business of Europe was transacted at Aix-la-Chappelle: the Allied occupation was to end, and Wellington was liberated from his duties in a fresh shower of military honours. For he became a Marshal of the Russian, Austrian, and Prussian armies. At one moment his functions were almost extended beyond Europe, since it was proposed that Wellington should mediate in the name of the Great Powers between Spain and her colonies. But he replied judiciously from the depth of *"mon expérience et ma connaissance intime du caractère Espagnol"* that *"il n'y a pas sur la terre une nation si jalouse que l'Espagne de l'intervention dans les affaires des Puissances Etrangères."* Had he not fought a war in the Peninsula to convince the French of that simple truth? The notion dropped; and he was left with the less exacting duty of evacuating France. The last time-tables were prepared; the Allies who had brought down Napoleon parted for the last time; the bayonets wound homewards across France in opposite directions; the British sailed; the Russians and the Germans marched; and before 1818 was out, Wellington was left alone in Paris. He went home by way of Brussels, and by Christmas he was safe at Apsley House.

The long task was over; but it was unthinkable that Wellington should fade discreetly into private life. He was far too useful; and ministers, who had found him a judicious colleague since 1814, still desired his

company. Now there was nothing for it but the Cabinet. They had a
notion that he might join without portfolio; but it was felt to be more
appropriate to bring him in as Master-General of the Ordnance. Lord
Liverpool made him the offer, and he accepted on slightly peculiar terms.
Accustomed to the public service, he was prepared to serve. But he was
at pains to divest his acceptance of all party connotations:

> "I don't doubt that the party of which the present government are the
> head will give me credit for being sincerely attached to them and to their
> interests; but I hope that, in case any circumstances should occur to remove
> them from power, they will allow me to consider myself at liberty to take
> any line I may at the time think proper. The experience which I have ac-
> quired during my long service abroad has convinced me that a factious op-
> position to the government is highly injurious to the interests of the country;
> and thinking as I do now I could not become a party to such an opposition;
> and I wish that this may be clearly understood by those persons with whom
> I am now about to engage as a colleague in government."

In other words, he was prepared to sit with them in Cabinet, but by no
means to go out of office with them, as a good Tory should. For it was
possible that some other Prime Minister might require his services; and
Wellington plainly viewed himself as a public servant, not as a Tory politician. It was his sense of public duty, not party affiliations, that brought
the Duke home from France in 1818 to be a Cabinet minister. For he
was still "*nimmukwallah*"; he had eaten the King's salt and would serve
him still, even among the politicians.

The Cabinet

And what is a great man? Is it a Minister of State? Is it a victorious General? A gentleman in the Windsor uniform? A Field-Marshal covered with stars?—CONINGSBY.

I

IT WAS 1819, and this handsome, greying man of fifty was home again. Home would be quite a novelty, since he had been a wanderer for twenty years. Indeed, it was not easy to recall a time when he had lived at home. School, Brussels, Angers, Dublin lodgings, freezing camps in Holland, Dublin once more, eight years of Indian cantonments, his Irish interlude divided between the Lodge in Phœnix Park and Harley Street, an endless succession of Peninsular billets, the Paris embassy, a hotel at Brussels, Paris again, and then headquarters at Cambrai—it was a gipsy record; and home would be a new experience for Wellington. Not that he was unfitted for home life. Quite the reverse; since all his inclinations appeared to lie in that direction. For he liked nothing better than a house full of guests and cheerful evenings in society where all the men were well-connected and nearly all the women pretty. How he had enjoyed watching his "boys" dancing, and confessed to Lady Shelley that he must always have his house full—"for sixteen years I have always been at the head of our army, and I must have these gay fellows round me." The mood recurred with him; and his house-parties at Cambrai were an attempt to satisfy it. Perhaps it had been easier for him to play the smiling host abroad than it would be in his new mansion at Hyde Park Corner and the big house in Hampshire. For Kitty would be there as well; and Kitty seemed to fail him somehow. Sadly deficient in the arts of house-hold management (her finances on his return from the Peninsula had been as involved as a French loan), she was afraid of him; and her fears were often hidden in an irritating trick of gushing over him in public. Besides, her eyes were always weak; and she was quite unequal to the exacting duty of recognising all London and half Europe. The Duke could always manage a nod at the right moment; but his short-sighted Duchess hid her embarrassment behind an open book when she drove out. And was she quite so beautiful as all the smiling faces that had shone like stars on him in Paris? Or so intelligent? He had no taste for bluestockings; but when he talked, he liked to be understood. He once defined feminine ability as "anticipating one's meaning; that is what a clever woman does—she sees what you mean." Poor Kitty was not clever though; she never knew what Arthur meant; and it was more than doubtful how far home would disappoint him.

But his own part, if he had leisure, could be played to perfection. Trim handsome, and mature, he was "the Beau" indeed, a figure made for admiration. Not that his countrymen outside Society were particularly ready to admire. For the first rapture of public worship that succeeded Waterloo had evaporated; he had not banked its fires by public appearances in England; and England, in its odd way, had grown slightly indifferent to the man who won the war. But the wanderer returned to cheerful scene; for London in the last year of the Regency was nothing if not cheerful. It was the gay arena of *Tom and Jerry*, where Vestris danced, Grimaldi clowned, the Regent's tilbury spun through the Park and Almack's was a nightly galaxy where the Lieven looked sharply about her and Lord Palmerston quadrilled with Lady Cowper. The town quoted *Don Juan*; Corinthians in vast top-hats boxed uncomplaining watchmen or strolled through Piccadilly in the tightest garments; there was a pleasant buzz about the turf, the masquerade, the ring, and Tattersall's; and the *ton* gathered nightly in opera boxes to talk in Frenchified slang and to exchange the latest wisdom of George Brummell for the last impudence of Harriette Wilson. Somewhere beyond the town angry provincials tramped to mass-meetings and stood in rows to stare at banners with exciting mottoes and listen to the most disturbing speeches. There was a new stir in the air that alarmed the Cabinet and left county magistrates bewildered. For misguided men appeared unable to appreciate that change was anathema, that Waterloo had been a final victory over change, that change had been exiled to St. Helena. Why had King George fought the Revolution to a finish, if his victorious subjects were to be gnawed by revolutionary cravings? Small wonder that his ministers looked anxious. For their endless talk about the Sinking Fund and currency reform concealed deeper misgivings. The Whigs might be too strong for them. But was that the worst? Something graver menace stirred in the shadows behind the Whigs. No Whig avowed it; it was remote from Ricardo's blameless calculations; and in their wildest moments Hunt and Cobbett refrained from naming

But it hung on the dusty air above the lines of sullen Yorkshiremen ramping to meetings. Half seen in the grey skies over Manchester, it struck a distant spark where Shelley, writing by an Italian bay, mouthed his unforgettable

> "I met Murder on the way—
> He had a mask like Castlereagh—
> Very smooth he looked, yet grim;
> Seven blood-hounds followed him,"

and as his voice rose in the direct appeal of

> "Men of England, wherefore plough
> For the lords who lay ye low?
> Wherefore weave with toil and care
> The rich robes your tyrants wear?"

he broke into the marching-song of the English revolution.

Such prospects rendered Wellington a welcome recruit to the harassed cabinet which, having won the war, found peace a trifle baffling. The glowing memory of *Coningsby* recalled the event—"a Mediocrity, not without repugnance, was induced to withdraw, and the great name of Wellington supplied his place in council. The talents of the Duke, as they were then understood, were not exactly of the kind most required in the cabinet, and his colleagues were careful that he should not occupy too prominent a post; but still it was an impressive acquisition, and imparted to the ministry a semblance of renown." There was no trace as yet of that pre-eminence which inspired Disraeli's later comment on "the aquiline supremacy of the Cæsars." But the Duke was a valued colleague with interests extending far beyond the somewhat limited concerns of the Ordnance Office; and it was unlikely that he would be left in peace to rearrange his Paris furniture at Apsley House, stare at King Joseph's pictures on the walls, and hang his latest purchases of the Dutch school. His Parliamentary appearances were, with one exception, slight. But foreign diplomats corresponded freely with him on the prospects of European stability (eliciting the shrewd advice, *"Soyez sûr qu'en politique il n'y a rien de stable que ce qui convient aux intérêts de tout le monde; qu'il faut regarder un peu plus loin que soi-même"*); and upon foreign policy he was treated by Liverpool and Castlereagh as a member of the inner Cabinet.

His grasp of home affairs was more intermittent, since they came before
him mainly in the form of applications by local commanders for Ordnance stores with a view to maintaining public order. He had no doubts
upon the subject, since nothing in his previous experience had led him
to believe in the divine nature of *vox populi*. Had he not governed Ireland
from a room in Dublin Castle? Few Chief Secretaries are democrats.
His long professional career had been an uninterrupted war against
French democracy. He was the natural enemy of Jacobins; and nothing
that he had seen of the Spanish Cortes modified his distaste for democrats. His contempt for governments founded upon *"la popularité vul-
gaire"* was unconcealed. He watched this lamentable tendency abroad—
*"Le grand mal en France est, qu'on croit pouvoir gouverner par la popu-
larité, et gagner la popularité en flattant les viles passions de la classe l
plus avilie et la plus corrompue de la nation."* Ignoble abroad, was then
the slightest reason to believe that popular appetites in England wer
any more exalted? He could see none; and the Duke diagnosed th
objective of the democratic movement as "neither more nor less tha
the Radical plunder of the rich towns and houses which will fall
their way." This simplified the question. If robbery and arson were
prospect, the Duke knew where he stood. It was just possible, of cours
that he misjudged the movement, that it derived its impetus from som
thing nobler than an ill-regulated impulse for destruction. England w
deeply moved that autumn; for 1819 saw the first stirrings of democra
But democracy was hardly likely to be more congenial to Wellingt
than arson. For the sanctity of numbers made no particular appeal
him. Less interested in the numerical support for any policy than
its merits, he was no democrat. How could he be? He had passed
lifetime in the constant endeavour to act wisely; and in almost ev
case wise action had been diametrically opposed to a crowd's desi
Indian administration in 1802 was a poor school for democrats; Dub
Castle was an embodied denial of democracy; and he was unlikely
absorb its tenets in the Peninsula, since generals in the field are
dependent on securing a majority of votes in favour of next seaso
plan of operations. Besides, the crowds of his experience had been alm
invariably wrong. A London mob had hooted him for the Convention
Cintra; and as he bled the French Empire to death in the Peninsula,

had been pursued by Opposition invectives. It was French mobs that had infected Paris with the Terror and inflicted upon Europe the long nightmare of the Empire; even now their sudden fevers were a constant menace to European peace. Spanish mobs had inspired the ignoble babble of the Cortes and deepened their country's peril in its darkest hour. And was there any ground for hope that English mobs would be wiser?

With these convictions he was single-minded in his resolve to check the English revolution. Not that he had the slightest taste for military rule. That might do well enough for France—he told Decazes as much, but added that "*il faut envisager l'armée en France sous un point de vue tout à fait différent de celui où nous envisageons l'armée dans ce pays-ci.*" England, so far as he could see, was well served by its civilian institutions; and he was stout in their defence. His advice was practical. Local commanders should keep their forces concentrated and quarter them outside the towns; their health should be considered, and it would be as well to attach a field-gun to each column. The law must be administered—"Don't let us be reproached again with having omitted to carry into execution the laws. . . . Rely upon it that, in the circumstances in which we are placed, impression on either side is everything." The ship rocked a little after Peterloo; but the country came safely through the autumn of 1819, and the Duke was writing cheerfully to friends abroad that the crisis had passed. The return to firm government in the Six Acts raised his spirits. For he had been thoroughly uneasy in the intervening months before the strong hand was brought into play, writing almost feverishly to Lady Shelley that "if our wise laws allow 50,000 people to assemble to deliberate, what Government can prevent it? If they allow secret societies, having for their professed object the overthrow of the Establishments, the forging of pikes, and the training of the people to the use of them, I am sure there is no Opposition member's wife . . . who would wish the Government to overstep the law in order to prevent the people from the exercise of these valuable and useful privileges. Then every man who attends one of these meetings—whether for the purpose of deliberation or crime, or for that of secret conspiracy thinks, and boasts, that he is performing a public duty; and it would be a sin to deprive the people of this gratification." His irony had the metallic ring of an impatient man who found himself a little out of sympathy with his surroundings. But he was heartened in the autumn by a general rally of the propertied classes to the existing order. For he was convinced that the palladium of English liberty reposed mysteriously in the alliance of property with ordered freedom—a blend too subtle for its Continental imitators. As he wrote to Alava,

"*On veut notre constitution en Europe; mais ce qu'on ne veut pas c'est la sûreté, la conservation des propriétés, que chez nous en fait la base et la force. Observez aussi que c'est cette conservation que nous faisons marcher de front avec nos libertés, et qui en est le garant qui nous rend ennemis toute la classe soi-disant Libérale en France, dans les Pays-Bas, et en Allemagne. Pourquoi? Parce qu'ils ne veulent que voler, ils ne parlent de liberté qu'avec l'objet d'empocher le bien d'autrui; et ils ne peuvent pas souffrir un pays où la liberté est établie et fondée sur l'ordre, et sur la sécurité des propriétés.*"

His estimate of democratic motives might be unduly low; but there could be no doubt of his belief in the British compound of private property and freedom. Indeed, his faith in it was almost mystic—and there are few states of mind more perilous than a mystical attachment to any set of institutions. For his fervour inspired him ten years later an untimely intimation that the human mind could scarcely attain such excellence as the unreformed constitution—a saying which served to precipitate Reform. His faith was stated in the first week of 1820, when he informed a foreign correspondent that "*grâces à Dieu et à nos Institutions miraculeuses*" the danger was, for the moment over, adding shrewdly that "*se qu'on appelle içi les anciens abus, ce dont les Reformateurs modernes voudraient se defaire et ce que nos voisins et imitateurs liberaux ne veulent pas imiter, sont les circonstances qui nous donnent un appui notable dans toutes nos difficultés.*"

That month

> An old, mad, blind, despised, and dying king

faded out of his long dream at Windsor into eternity; and his kingdom passed to George IV. The change was far from sedative, since domestic infelicity supplied a grateful country with a new form of sport. There was a carnival of indecorum; and the Queen's virtue became

a party question, the Crown challenging and Whigs defending that
somewhat battered fortress. Prinny appeared in the unusual *rôle* of an
injured husband; and Opposition speakers, long accustomed to baiting
the Prince Regent, found themselves denouncing the sovereign. Attacks
upon the monarch were barely distinguishable from attacks upon the
monarchy; and as the coarse fun of the Queen's divorce proceeded,
Whiggery itself drifted perilously near to republicanism. The Duke's
alignment was inevitable. He was a minister; he viewed his sovereign
(since he was a gentleman) without enthusiasm; but he kept official
company. He had spent Christmas at Stratfield Saye with the Castle-
reaghs, two foreign diplomats, Mr. Arbuthnot of the Treasury (and his
handsome wife), and Mr. Planta of the Foreign Office. Kitty was there,
of course; but an observant Austrian found the house "not very comfortable, the park ugly, the living mediocre, the whole indeed indicating
the lack of sympathy existing between the Duke and his Duchess." Poor
Kitty's tragedy was known already; and the Duke went his social rounds
without her. Wellington went on to Woburn, where he found the
Lievens and the Duke of York. Such company was scarcely likely to
make him a *frondeur*.

Besides, the dark forces of disorder were more menacing than ever.
There was a plot to murder the Cabinet one night at the Spanish
Embassy; but Life Guards cleared the street, and a constable secured
a halter thoughtfully provided for hanging Castlereagh on a lamp-post.
One evening someone hung about outside the Ordnance Office to stab
the Duke, as he walked home across the Park to Apsley House. But that
night Fitzroy Somerset happened to meet him in the street; the two
men strolled along arm in arm; and the pair of friendly backs alarmed
the unheroic murderer. Then there were whispers of a dark design to
invade the Cabinet at dinner in Grosvenor Square, murder them all,
parade Castlereagh's head on a pike down Oxford Street, attack the
Bank, break open Newgate, and finish up a crowded evening after the
best French precedents by proclaiming the Republic at the Mansion
House. Few things are more depressing than the exaggerated deference
of English revolutionaries to foreign models; but their sense of detail
was creditable, since a thoughtful butcher had provided two bags for the
heads (though the defence contended later that they were destined for

the gentler office of carrying off Lord Harrowby's plate). The Cabinet was warned in time; and the Duke, true to his usual tactics, proposed to await the attack in a favourable defensive position. Ministers, he thought, should take pistols in to dinner with them and await developments. But his civilian colleagues found the proposal unattractive. Indeed, from the civilian point of view it had its flaws; and they preferred to dine elsewhere, while the Bow Street magistrate rounded up Thistlewood and his associates in a back-street off Edgeware Road.

It was a dark, tumultuous time, when Castlereagh carried pocket pistols at the dinner-table; and the Duke's distaste for democrats deepened excusably. So, it must be confessed, did theirs for him. For the first ecstasy of public admiration had faded before he joined the Cabinet; he had been cheered at the opening of Parliament the year before; but in the restive mood of 1820 opinion involved all persons in authority in a common unpopularity. Its manifestations were occasionally harmless, as when the roadmenders in Grosvenor Place shouldered their pickaxes and stopped his horse on the way home to Apsley House, insisting that he should say "God save the Queen." The Duke complied.

"Well, gentlemen," he said obligingly "since you will have it so God save the Queen—and may all your wives be like her."

In a year of breaking glass his windows were respected. But he was hooted by an English crowd for the first time since 1808. For that autumn Creevey heard them booing him in the Park, though they scattered hurriedly as the Duke reined in. Not that it embittered him against the Opposition, since he could manage a good-humoured nod to the little Whig above the hooting mob and strolled up to him in the Argyle Rooms with a genial "Well, Creevey; so you gave us a black last night. . . ." But his contempt for crowds was scored a little deeper. "The mob are too contemptible to be thought about for a moment. About thirty of them ran away from me in the Park this morning, because I pulled up my horse when they were *hooting*! They thought I was going to fall upon them and give them what they deserved!" As the unpleasing scuffle of the Queen's divorce proceeded with its long procession of preposterous and perjured foreigners, his sense of public dignity was gravely offended. His shrewd advice at the beginning of the affair had been to avert the danger by selecting a handsome young diplomat (Fred Lamb, a favourite of Miss Harriette Wilson, struck him as being suitable) and sending him to the Queen's hangers-on abroad with the judicious warning, "You are going to lose your golden eggs—you are going to kill your goose! Once in England, and you will not be able to live with her on your present footing and retain your present allowances." But the moment passed; the monumental farce of the royal trial was mounted in the House of Lords; and when somebody objected to its effects upon the Crown's prestige, Wellington replied bitterly that the King was degraded as low as he could be already.

The constant threat to public order filled his mind. He settled routes for cavalry patrols through West End streets with the detail appropriate to the march of armies, sending six men to Portman Square, twelve more to Cavendish Square by way of Wigmore Street, and posting a vedette in Brooks Street as though Soult and all his men had been expected from the direction of Park Lane; and when the Guards alarmed them all that summer with dangerous symptoms of mutiny, his common-sense evolved the first proposal of a separate police-force. Not that he had become a frozen pillar of reaction. For he was quite prepared to recognise inevitable changes, insisting that the Spaniards could not hope to recover their rebellious colonies—"One would suppose that the reconquest of their colonies by force of arms would be out of the question even to them . . . Considering that their colonies must now considered as lost. . . ." He was no less positive upon a policy of non-interference in Spain itself, adducing the whole course of the Penin-sular War as evidence that Spain would never tolerate foreign inter-vention, and adding generously that "this result of the war may in part be attributed to the operations of the Allied Armies in the Peninsula; but those would form a very erroneous notion of the fact who should not attribute a fair proportion of it to the effects of the enmity of the people of Spain." Even the settlement of 1815 seemed to lose something of its sanctity for him at times, since he confessed one night at Almack's that he was beginning to doubt how long the restored dynasties would last; though when Naples rose, he urged the Austrians to act promptly, since they could do with 80,000 men now what they might fail to do with 200,000 later. For he had a constitutional distaste for revolutions. He saw a good deal of the Lievens. It was a time when London society

seemed to be full of foreigners; Allies abounded in all directions; Ester
hazy and Palmella were seen everywhere; Alava told his stories; and
tame cossacks chattered in opera boxes. The Duke met the Lieven
everywhere, and seemed to find the unwearied Dorothea agreeable
There was no accounting for her triumphs, since a meagre throat sur
mounted by an indifferent profile formed an inadequate equipment
and malicious rhymesters were inclined to dwell upon her accessories:

> *"Des broderies, des bouderies,*
> *Des garnitures—comme quatre—*
> *Voilà l'Ambassadrice à la façon de Barbarie."*

But there was no denying her success; for those curls were shaken a
every magnifico in Europe; Metternich himself succumbed at Aix-la
Chapelle; and lively malice termed her latest child *"l'enfant du Congrès*
This *vivandière* of diplomacy set her snares for Wellington; and h
yielded so far as to act in country-house charades with her. Indeed, h
lifelong renunciation of musical performances were momentarily relaxe
when she played the latest waltzes on the pianoforte; for the Duke a
companied her on the blameless triangle. He talked freely to her an
(greatest test of all) answered politely when she asked him which
his battles he liked best.

Not that he lived entirely in a world of foreigners. For he had l
English friends. Lady Shelley, home from her travels, conversed wi
him at evening parties and found him a little scared by thoughts of t
old age of Marlborough. They rode together in the Green Park, whe
he passed an hour most afternoons between office and the House
Lords; she dined at Apsley House, where she found Caroline Lamb a
Mrs. Arbuthnot, and they saw all his treasures. She loved to hear h
talk; his friendship was discreet; and they never knew what dread
things "my husband's young kinsman, Percy Shelley, who seems c
posed to become a poet" was writing about the Government. The gr
day arrived when he came to stay with them in the country. Her de
tion had roused the countryside, and forty mounted farmers rode bes
his carriage; they took out the horses and dragged it up the hill; a
as his hostess heard the cheers, she very nearly fainted. But the Duk
smile revived her; even her nervous headache vanished; and she c

harged her social duties. He was quite wonderful at dinner, scrawling
plan of Toulouse upon a scrap of paper (carefully preserved) and
ketching Orthez on the knee of his evening breeches (which were not
vailable as a souvenir) "with an eagerness and intentness which were
uite delightful." She showed him a French account, which he dis-
uissed as "all a lie. The French were much superior to us in force."
His enemies, it may be observed, began about this time to shew a
riking tendency to grow in numbers when he discussed his battles.)
hey talked till midnight, and he entertained them with a full descrip-
on of the new breakwater at Plymouth and its dimensions. At breakfast
e next morning he was quite delightful with her children; and every-
ing was going *à merveille*. Then they went off to shoot, and Lady
elley breathed again. Not that she breathed for long; for as a marks-
an the Duke was anything but commonplace. The terror of his
untry's foes, he terrified her little girl by letting off his gun in all
rections. "What's this, Fanny?" cried Lady Shelley. "Fear in the
esence of the Lord of Waterloo! Fie! Stand close behind the Duke
Wellington: he will protect you." Indeed, it was the safest place.
He shot a dog, then a keeper, and finally an aged cottager who had
en rash enough to do her washing near an open window.

"I'm wounded, Milady," cried his victim.

"My good woman," she replied, "this ought to be the proudest moment
your life. You have had the distinction of being shot by the great
ke of Wellington!"

An embarrassed Duke assisted her sense of history with a guinea.
t she was not his only bag, since he positively shot a pheasant which
pious hostess had stuffed and added to the museum of Wellingtoniana
her dressing-room, where it stared glassily down upon the coffee-cup
ich he had used before Waterloo and the chair on which he dined
h her in 1814.

hey shared a rather schoolgirl joke about Mrs. Arbuthnot and her
ninion over him, giggling together over "*La Tyranna*" and her un-
ain temper, and keeping up the agreeable legend that he lived in
ct terror of her and was under the necessity of seizing favourable
ortunities to get her leave to visit Lady Shelley. The Duke vastly
yed his mythical subordination and was almost kittenish—"I have

325

taken advantage of a favourable moment and have obtained *permission*
. . . *When the cat's away the mice go and play*, and as she is at her
brother's in Lincolnshire, and at her mother's, I have taken leave to ask
you to Stratfield Saye. . . ." So Mrs. Arbuthnot's leave, not Kitty's, was
the requisite. Kitty wrote dutifully, sending Lady Shelley news about
her boys and farmyard fatalities, and was "quite sorry we are deprived
of your company." But Mrs. Arbuthnot played her part according to
their standing joke, writing to Frances Shelley in her most commanding
tones that "the slave (poor creature!) has asked my leave to invite you
to dinner next Saturday, and, in order to bribe me into compliance, has
invited me to meet you and keep watch, in order to prevent any attack
being made upon my legitimate authority. I have been very magnanimous
about it, and I beg you will return me your best thanks. I have given
permission. . . ." It was a mild diversion; and the Duke supported his
rôle admirably with nervous bulletins about his tyrant's moods. Other
news sometimes crept in; his shooting was improving; Charterhouse was
a better school than Eton (strenuously denied by Kitty); he had known
so many instances of boys going through Eton without learning anything;
Free Trade in 1821 would mean free, irretrievable ruin; Buonaparte was
printing lies about Waterloo; but "supposing I *was* surprised: I won the
battle; and what could you have had more even if I had not been
surprised?"

They prattled pleasantly enough, as he went his rounds among the
country houses. Once he was near his mother's old friends at Llangollen,
but not near enough to call, though he sent a charming note. House-
parties and official papers filled his life; and he still had leisure sometimes to give sittings to an artist. Lawrence painted him that year for
Robert Peel's collection of notabilities, and he sat without undue protest.
For he was not overwhelmed with business, though he took his position
in public life seriously enough. He was, he knew he was more than
Master-General of the Ordnance with a seat in the Cabinet. For he was
the Duke of Wellington; and when the King displayed an awkward
tendency to dismiss the Government, the Duke favoured him with a
long memorandum of personal advice. He had been accustomed to deal
with Continental kings and emperors, as someone said of him in Paris

de Couronne à Couronne"; and having managed Louis and Alexander
s equals, why should he shrink from George IV?

Politics were still lively in 1821, though the ferment was dying down.
The ground-swell of revolution, which had menaced 1819, was sub-
ding now. But there were still breakers on the surface. For one evening
arly in the year, when the King risked himself at Drury Lane, a disrespectful playgoer in the gallery addressed the royal box with the
entorian enquiry, "Where's your wife, Georgy?" But a loyal audience
ng *Rule Britannia* and positively rendered *God Save the King* three
mes. The crowds outside the theatre were immense. A slightly officious
yalist insisted upon making a lane for Wellington, returned into the
owd, performed the same kind of office for Lord Palmerton, felt in
s fob, and then made the disastrous discovery that his seals were
issing. As he had made four journeys through a crowd within five
inutes' walk of Seven Dials, this was not surprising. But he appeared
think that his loss established some claim upon the Duke. The Duke,
ith slightly chilling courtesy, disabused him of the notion. Admitting
at he perfectly recollected the incident, he pointed out that "this
rvice, if it can be so called, was purely voluntary on the part of this
ntleman. The Duke is as well able as any other man to make his
ay through a crowd even if there existed any disposition to impede
s progress, which did not appear, and therefore the assistance of this
ntleman was not necessary; and, moreover, the Duke's footman at-
ded him." This was unkind; although the next paragraph expressed
grateful thanks for the stranger's courtesy. His sole objection was
the resulting claim for compensation, which he met with a denial
liability that would have done credit to a solicitor, pointing out that
loss was not discovered until after the journey with Lord Palmerston
d, alternatively, that even if it had been suffered on his journey with
Duke, the journey was itself wholly superfluous—*volenti*, in fact, *non
injuria*. But the Duke did not rest wholly upon his Common Law
hts; for as the claimant "may be a gentleman in circumstances not
e to bear the expense of such a loss, and as the Duke certainly con-
red his conduct towards him as very polite, the Duke feels no objec-
n to assist him to replace the loss he has sustained," adding the
ellent advice "in future to omit to render these acts of unsolicited

and unnecessary politeness unless he should be in a situation to bear the
probable or possible consequences." The whole effect, it must be confessed, was chilling; and the result upon his unknown benefactor's politics
remains unknown. How long did he remain a Tory? Or did he go
straight home, stopping on the way to buy a pike, and join a secret
society? Yet Wellington had granted his request for compensation. Only
the kindness had been done, as usual, a trifle gruffly. For the Duke had
been at pains not to create a precedent. It was a wise precaution, since
after all, he passed his life in crowds; he had numerous admirers; and
if it were known that he was willing to replace all missing jewellery,
where would it end?

The year wore on with preparations for the Coronation, and the King
plunged with gusto into the details of that sartorial apotheosis. His ministers struggled with the unholy forces of economics and the more sanc-
tified obstacle provided by the claims of Roman Catholics to citizenship.
The Duke appeared to hold a somewhat Dublin Castle view. In former
days he used to tell the Duke of Richmond that "it was nonsense to talk
of the Church and State being in danger; English influence and connection were in danger if the Catholic Emancipation were ever carried."
But he had spoken on the question in the House of Lords in 1810,
arguing with simple-minded emphasis that the whole question turned
upon how far the Protestant Church could be safeguarded in Ireland,
and that in view of the fact that it had been established "at the point
of the sword and by means of confiscations," the Roman Catholics were
quite certain to be inspired "by the remembrance of the events to which
I have alluded and the idea of unmerited and mutual suffering." These
were generous admissions. But the Duke's conclusion, though he appeared to realise the whole tragedy of Ireland, was that it was wholly
unsafe to leave the future of Protestantism in the hands of men who
had passed through such fires. For Protestantism must, in his view, come
first. Not that he was a bigot, since he declined to become an Orangeman
upon the ground that Roman Catholics were excluded and that, their
faith apart, he had always found them loyal subjects. Besides, that year
he began to press Lord Liverpool to take Canning back into the Cabinet;
and Canning's views on that and other questions were more advanced.
The Duke discerned a useful colleague, though his own convictions

not incline him further towards respect for democracy, since he shocked
politicians in 1821 by his blunt statement that, after getting 9,000 signatures to a petition, it was superfluous "to go through the farce of a
county meeting." The Whigs were deeply pained; but as he regarded
as a national calamity to "give up the Government to the Whigs and
Radicals, or, in other words, the country in all its relations to irretriev-
ble ruin," he did not greatly care. This was a very different tone from
his non-partisan acceptance of office three years before. But the disorders
of 1819, followed by the addiction of democrats in 1820 to the meaner
forms of murder, had changed his views; and he was a Tory now.

One day that spring a lonely, dying man was making his will seven
thousand miles away. He left 10,000 francs to the *sous-officier* Cantillon,
acquitted by a French jury on a charge of attempting to murder Wellington three years before: the Duke had always been convinced that
Napoleon was not a gentleman. But Providence designed one of its
latest repartees. For at his funeral (he died within the month) the
battle-honours on the colours dipped at the Emperor's grave-side were
"Talavera" and "Pyrenees": the last word, one feels, was Wellington's.
The news came to London in the summer days when the town was
buzzing with the Coronation. The great day arrived at last; and Wellington fitted on his coronet, while Benjamin Robert Haydon hurried
round London in an ecstasy of patriotism borrowing the items of his
court suit. The Abbey was a sea of ermine, swayed by the stately tides
of the Coronation Service; although the streets outside witnessed a
slight, but farcical, recrudescence of the Queen. Westminster Hall moved
Haydon to a page of perfect prose. The royal epiphany was comparable
to the sun's—"There are indications which announce the luminary's
approach; a streak of light—the tipping of a cloud—the singing of the
lark—the brilliance of the sky, till the cloud edges get brighter and
brighter, and he rises majestically into the heavens." Cast for this splendid
rôle, George IV enraptured his beholder—"A whisper of mystery turns
all eyes to the throne. . . . Then three or four of high rank appear
from behind the throne; an interval is left; the crowds scarce breathe.
Something rustles, and a being buried in satin, feathers, and diamonds
sinks gracefully into his seat. The room rises with a sort of feathered,
silken thunder. . . . As he looked towards the peeresses and foreign

ambassadors he shewed like some gorgeous bird of the East." Wellington in his brightest plumage, figured in this ornamental aviary. As th banquet opened, he walked down the Hall in his coronet, cheered b the Guards, and returned on horseback. He rode up to the throne an (oh, miracle) backed his horse to the door and out of it. Next he w seen beside the armoured figure of the King's Champion. He saw a goo deal of the King that summer, since he was commanded to go with hi as far as Brussels, when he went abroad. Privileged to escort his sovereig to Waterloo, the Duke explained the action; and the lucidity of h explanations doubtless contributed to the King's lifelong belief that had fought himself, though Wellington recalled that "His Majesty to it very coolly; indeed, never asked me a single question, nor said o word, till I showed him where Lord Anglesey's leg was buried, a then he burst into tears."

The year went out upon an increase of Irish anxieties; and early 1822 they had a notion of sending him to Dublin as Lord-Lieutena But his reply was shrewd—"I am ready to go anywhere you please, b remember my going will attract notice not only in England but Europe. Take care that you don't let off your great gun agains sparrow! What is it you want me to do for you? If you want me put down *the row*, I will do that easily enough; but if afterwards I merely to continue the divided system—a Lord-Lieutenant one way a Secretary the other—I tell you fairly I don't expect any good from So Richard went instead. He had subsided now into the shadow of junior, murmuring to Wyatt, the architect, "Aye! Arthur is a m cleverer fellow than I am, you may depend upon it." Was there a to of irony? If so, it might be forgiven; for Arthur had passed him in race. He was the greatest Wellesley of them all, with Richard's plac head of the family, the dukedom Richard might have had, and e Richard's house at Hyde Park Corner; and now Richard went to Viceregal Lodge because Arthur would not go. It is a slightly melanc part to play Quintus Cicero.

Not that Arthur was devoid of opinions upon Irish matters. He pressed a healthy appetite for Coercion in the House of Lords, tho he was equally emphatic on the dereliction of absentee landlords, ought to have "gone over to look at their properties instead of *brau*

nd *balling* in London. . . . A population of seven millions, increasing
an immense proportion, without employment, . . . getting in fact
othing for the produce of their country . . . appears to be a dangerous
henomenon in political economy. I believe we have not yet seen the last
ll of the Irish population on the charity of their English countrymen;
nd we shall yet have something more to do for them than give charity
lls and brawl upon distress. We want in Ireland the influence of man-
rs as well as laws. How we are to get the former in the absence of
arly all the landed proprietors is more than I can tell." This was
nsible; and it shewed a laudable desire to do something more with
-land than repress it. Other problems faced them, as the summer
onths of 1822 stole by—resurgent Greece, insurgent Mexico, a restless
ood in Italy, Spain ringing with Riego's hymn, and the ferment of
olution working wherever Metternich turned his uneasy eye. There
s another Conference in prospect. For the perambulating Areopagus
s to meet at Vienna in the autumn and disolve these menaces by the
gic of collective wisdom. Castlereagh (he was Lord Londonderry now)
s busy on his own Instructions; and no clouds as yet obscured that
lendid summit of bright and polished frost which, like the travellers
Switzerland, we all admire; but no one can hope, and few would
h to reach." The Duke took delivery of Wilkie's pictures, ordered six
rs before and now astonishing the Academy with the diversity and
liness of its Chelsea pensioners. The painter asked £1,260; and as the
ke counted out the notes himself, Wilkie suggested that a cheque
ht be more convenient.

Do you think," replied his patron, "I like Coutts' clerks always to
w how foolishly I spend my money?"

hat summer the Park wall was breached not far from Apsley House;
rouded figure trundled through; workmen were busy on the mound
ss the road; and on the anniversary of Waterloo "Achilles" was un-
d just outside his library windows. Midsummer passed; and the
les on Castlereagh's table burned low, as the bowed figure wrote
wrote his inexhaustible despatches, conjuring an ordered world out
e tumult of 1822. The burden weighed him down; and the dying
flickered suddenly. For at his farewell audience before leaving
he Continent he scared the King by talking wildly; his mind was

an unhappy whirl of plots; he started at chance words; and when th
Duke observed it, he warned him with terrible lucidity. The two me
were alone. Wellington looked into the white face of Castlereagh an
spoke.

"From what you have said, I am bound to warn you that you cann
be in your right mind."

This must be the truth. The Duke would not deceive him. The u
happy man covered his tortured face and answered from the sofa.

"Since you say so, I fear it must be so."

Castlereagh was sobbing bitterly. Wellington offered kindly to st
with him; but he declined, since the world must not suspect. The Du
warned the doctors—those sagacious doctors whose sole specific was
bleed and bleed. But Castlereagh escaped them all one summer mornir
clutching a little knife. A gloating mob outside the abbey cheered his cof
(the mourners took it to be a cheer for Wellington, since crowds cheer
him still); and Lord Byron exclaimed with his customary felicity,

> "So *He* has cut his throat at last!—He! Who?
> The man who cut his country's long ago."

But Wellington was deeply grieved; for he had lost his oldest friend
politics.

HE age of Castlereagh was over. Who was to succeed him at the Foreign Office? But there was a more immediate question. Who as to take his place at the impending Conference? They settled that ithin a week. For Wellington received the King's command to attend and he was writing to assure Metternich *"de ma bonne volonté, et de on zèle pour consolider l'alliance générale, et le système de l'Europe."* e choice was natural, since the Duke was now the sole survivor of the plomatic campaigns of Vienna, Paris, and Aix-la-Chapelle. Besides, he ew everyone in Europe, and everyone knew him; and Europe, it was be hoped, had retained its habit of attending to the Duke.

But the main problem still confronted them. Who was to take the reign Office? The choice was difficult, since it was complicated by liamentary considerations. For the Government was lamentably weak the House of Commons, and it was vital to reinforce the Treasury ach, where Mr. Peel, Home Secretary at thirty-four, withstood the htly onslaught of the Whigs almost unaided. If they promoted Peel ead the House, were his lieutenants adequate? The best was Palmers- ; and Palmerston, in the thirteenth year of his uneventful tenure of War Department, was scarcely an exciting figure. He had been oducing Army estimates since 1809; he wrote a sound official letter; defence of flogging was an annual event; and he had earned from Croker the doubtful compliment of being judged "as powerful ntellect as Robinson, and much more to be relied on in readiness nerve." But he was no Rupert of debate; and, Palmerston apart, rest was silence. For ability in its more glaring forms was hardly atenanced in Lord Liverpool's administration. There was one possi- , since the first orator in England was Canning; and Canning was iverpool, waiting for his passage to India as Governor-General. It been a strange career. The favourite disciple, as he liked to think, of he had proved a sad embarrassment to Pitt's successors. For he highly unaccountable. A splendid flourish had proclaimed that his

political allegiance lay buried in Pitt's grave; and it was undeniable th
his loyalty resided in no very accessible spot. His course had always bee
uncertain. Resigning on a deadly feud (and an exchange of pistol-shot
with Castlereagh in 1810, he had hung insecurely in the Parliamenta
firmament, until he dropped suddenly like an erratic meteor towar
the west. For in 1814 he demobilised his few supporters and departed
the British embassy at Lisbon, content apparently to serve Castlerea;
as an official subordinate at an augmented salary of £14,400. Then
returned, rejoined the Cabinet, and administered Indian affairs ur
his second resignation—this time upon the treatment of Queen Caroli
After an interlude he had accepted the Governor-Generalship of Inc
consenting, it would seem, to abandon his political ambitions for t
opulence which is the last refuge of disappointed politicians. His c
appointment was not surprising, since every avenue was closed
Canning in 1822. The King could not forgive his attitude of chiva
towards the Queen, even professing to regard him as her accepted lov
the Whigs bore too many scars of his corrosive wit; and Tories
donically wished him "very well whatever part of the world he mi
go to." This was a melancholy harvest to reap at fifty-two; and
summer Canning waited disconsolately for his passage to the East.

The scene was changed suddenly by the tragedy at Cray; and
was waiting now for Castlereagh's succession. He would take notl
less; his mind was quite made up; it must be "the whole heritag
the Foreign Office with the leadership of the House of Commo
or nothing. Embarrassed Tories hoped to see Peel lead the Comm
and the Duke at the Foreign Office. But the Duke had other vi
For he had favoured Canning's readmission to the Cabinet since
although it was not easy for him to control the situation now, s
he was seriously indisposed. A light-hearted aurist, in a bold atte
to cure his ear-ache, had inserted caustic in the ear, destroyed its l
ing, and very nearly destroyed his patient at the same time—a no
achievement for British medicine, which already numbered Castler
among its victims for the year. But the King waited on the D
opinion. Each found the other slightly trying; for the King's exuber
jarred on the Duke, and the Duke was apt to differ from George I
military topics, forcing his sovereign to the painful avowal that "it i

·r me to dispute on such a subject with your Grace." But the King knew loyal adviser, and the Duke knew his duty. Wellington was still in ·d; but a royal emissary was assiduous at his bedside, and the King ·en deferred his interview with the Prime Minister until he knew the ·uke's opinion. Wellington expressed it plainly; Canning, he felt, was necessary reinforcement and would prove a loyal minister in spite · his eccentric views upon the Roman Catholic question. As to the ·ng's personal objections, did not the sovereign's honour consist in ·ing acts of mercy? This was the height of tact; and the King's self-·eem expanded in the sunshine of conscious virtue. He positively ·elled in his own magnanimity. Indeed, the Duke had almost over-·ne it; since the King, borrowing his line from Wellington, sum-·med Canning to office with an unduly gracious intimation that "the ·ng is aware that the brightest ornament of his crown is the power ·extending grace and favour to a subject who may have incurred his ·pleasure." This was too much for Canning, who was narrowly re-·ined by Wellington from making a reply. But the Duke, always ·ctical, advised him that "as he intended to accept, he had better take · further notice of the paper." The King and Canning were not his ·y charges, since his Tory colleagues were a trifle fretful, and he was ·n compelled to pacify Castlereagh's reproachful widow with a lengthy ·ument, in which he urged shrewdly that "nothing can be so erroneous ·o place any individual of great activity and talents in a situation in ·ch there is no scope for his activity, and in which he must feel that ·talents are thrown away. His views must always be directed to dis-· rather than to preserve the existing order of things, in order that · of a new arrangement he may find himself in a position better ·d to him." This danger was averted now; Canning was safely in-·ed as Castlereagh's successor; and the Prime Minister wrote grate-·· that without Wellington's assistance "it never might have been ·ght to such a result."

2

·ithin a fortnight he was on the Continent, bound for Vienna. ·stopped in Paris to confer with French ministers, resumed his

journey, and plunged into the latest Congress. For a melancholy iror
compelled Mr. Canning, who had once gleefully announced that "v
shall have no more congresses, thank God!" to direct British policy
a Congress. But events had an unpleasant trick of following a cour
precisely opposite to that laid down for them by Mr. Canning. T
business before the Congress was highly variegated—the Greek insu
rection, Spanish colonies, the Austrians in Italy, and an awkwa
tendency on the part of Russia to claim the coast of British Columb
They were to meet at Vienna; but the Congress was transferred to Veror
and Byron welcomed them to Italy with elaborate raillery at

> "Proud Wellington, with eagle beak so curl'd,
> That nose, the hook where he suspends the world!
> And Waterloo—and trade—and—(hush! not yet
> A syllable of imports or of debt)—
> And ne'er (enough) lamented Castlereagh,
> Whose penknife slit a goose-quill t'other day—
> And 'pilots who have weathered every storm,'—
> (But, no, not even for rhyme's sake name Reform).

>   .   .   .   .   .

> "Strange sight this Congress! destined to unite
> All that's incongruous, all that's opposite.
> I speak not of the sovereigns—they're alike,
> As common coin as ever mint could strike;
> But those who sway the puppets, pull the strings,
> Have more of motley than their kings.
> Jews, authors, generals, charlatans, combine,
> While Europe wonders at the vast design:
> There Metternich, power's foremost parasite,
> Cajoles; there Wellington forgets to fight;
> There Chateaubriand forms new books of martyrs;
> And subtle Gauls intrigue for stupid Tartars;
> There Montmorenci. . . ."

The French delegate played a leading part. For the chief item
the agenda was Spain, where the French were shewing awkward s
of intervening in a civil war. There was no doubt of British views u
foreign intervention; the Duke had made them clear to Castlereagl
months before; Castlereagh concurred in his disapproval; and Can
followed suit after knocking impressively at the open door and inst
ing Wellington "frankly and peremptorily to declare, that to any

terference, come what may, his Majesty will not be a party." There
as no difference between them, and the Duke did not feel the slightest
fficulty in conveying that "we had insuperable objections to interfere
the internal concerns of any country" and, more formally, that "to
imadvert upon the internal transactions of an independent State, unless
ch transactions affect the essential interests of his Majesty's subjects,
inconsistent with those principles on which his Majesty has invariably
ted in all questions relating to the internal concerns of other countries;
it such animadversions, if made, must involve his Majesty in serious
ponsibility if they should produce any effect, and must irritate if
y should not." The doctrine of non-intervention in Spain was quite
igenial to Wellington, since he had argued it at length before Canning
ne to the Foreign Office; and now he argued it once more before
ighly unsympathetic audience of foreign diplomats. The French were
iling for a fight against a paralytic enemy; and the Czar was haunted
a disturbing dream of marching Russian armies across Europe in the
red name of counter-revolution. The Duke, who diagnosed him
ewdly—"The Emperor would have no objection to a war, but it
st be on a stage on which he would have the eyes of all Europe upon
t and the applause of the world"—laboured steadily to damp the uni-
al ardour in a modest hope "that we shall get through these difficulties
a creditable manner, and that we may be able to maintain the
:e of the world." He had no difficulty in enlisting Austrian appre-
:ions of the Russian design; and the danger of a general conflagra-
was averted by his downright dissociation of Great Britain from
mon action at Madrid, which immobilised the Alliance. This dis-
d of Alexander's vision of 150,000 Russians tramping through Austria
lilan *en route* for the Pyrenees. But the uneasy possibility remained
France might intervene alone. Wellington had preached reason on
vay through Paris; but when Villèle disclosed the military details of
'rench plan for invading Spain, he had not refrained from practical
nents. It was his vanity, as a sharp woman guessed, to know "how
) everything, and to do it better than anyone else." The problem
vading Spain interested him professionally. After all, he was the
:st living expert on Peninsular wars; and he could scarcely be
ted to pass by in silence such alluring topics as the line of the

Ebro and the military effects of occupying Madrid. Always a stron
believer in the virtues of prompt action for the suppression of revolutio
(had he not prescribed it unofficially in the case of Naples two yea
before?), he was perfectly convinced that "the French will meet wi
no more resistance in marching to Madrid than he does in going to t'
Ordnance Office." But it scarcely follows that he told them so. There
no evidence that Wellington encouraged them to try the experiment a:
that, as a learned fantasy suggests, he was deliberately false to Cannin
policy by privately inciting France to intervene in Spain. Such treach(
was not in his manner. Besides, he had just been at considerable pa:
to instal Canning at the Foreign Office; and, in any case, the policy
opposing intervention in Spain was Wellington's as well as Cannin;
In reality he laboured to avert the war; and if he failed, at least he l
succeeded in preventing a general explosion.

On minor matters he was still more successful. Russia was chec'
in North America; Austria was pressed discreetly to repay war-ti
loans; and he made some progress with the abolition of the slave tr:
Upon the question of the Spanish colonies he served Canning a
loyal mouthpiece—"I shall of course follow what is laid down in y
despatch." But he followed it with evident distaste, finding the re
uncongenial company and deploring undue haste—"I know that we n
at last recognise all these governments, but I would recognise them w
necessary, and only when really constituted and become powers, ins*
of seeking for reasons for recognizing them, and by recognizing t'
constitute them." This was rational; and he restated his position
consider it a point of honour that we should not be in a hurry to re
nise that independence, and that the measure should be forced upo:
by circumstances rather than we should seek for occasions to adopt it.
I therefore have always been for going as far as was necessary,
never further." Canning recognised his fairness in a final tribute t(
work at Verona—"You have done, in respect to that question
Spanish America), all that could be desired; and upon the slave t
more than could have been expected."

It had been a strange affair. The Congress of Verona with its *par*
de rois—two emperors, three kings, a cardinal, three grand-dukes, tv
ambassadors, twelve ministers, and three foreign secretaries—had

ie last parade of a vanishing Europe, where Metternich whispered his
narp asides and the Duke moved in splendid profile through a lane of
owing gentlemen in stars. They had their relaxations too. There was
.e great Roman amphitheatre for their plays, and for lighter entertain-
.ent Dorothea Lieven and the Récamier with her echoes of Directoire
lons and the distant days when Josephine was gay and General Bona-
arte an awkward lover. A stranger echo hung about a stout and smiling
chduchess, where Marie Louise, Duchess of Parma, played écarté
ith Wellington. As the cards fell between them, they settled their
counts in *napoléons*; and when he dined with her, she told the Duke
w sorry she was that she had failed to get his favourite roast mutton
him. For Napoleon's widow studied Wellington's tastes. He saw
nething of her son as well, finding him "a fine lad, educated just
e the archdukes"; and the Duke told someone later that "he was
y civil to me." Then he was off to Paris by way of Milan and Lyon,
ving loyally applied the policy which enabled Canning to write
imphantly "For 'Alliance' read 'England.' "

Ie had business in Paris, where he still hoped to check the French.
anning instructed him to offer British mediation; the Duke, fearing a
uff in Paris, delayed the offer; Canning insisted; and the Duke pre-
ed gloomily that "the government have mistaken this case, and that
mediation will be rejected on the ground on which it was rejected
Verona." The Duke was right; and Canning's insistence got nothing
e for his country than "a parting blow." But Wellington had done
duty in Paris. Indeed, he had done more, since Lady Shelley had
usted him with an important mission concerning a blouse. Less
ious than Mr. Canning's, he discharged it to a nicety and could
rt in triumph that "your blouse goes to you by the stage tomorrow.
mind! You are to wear it the first time you dine with me, with the
nna!" He took the road again and was at Apsley House for Christ-
1822.

3

e new year opened pleasantly enough with house-parties at Stratfield
The Duke of York came to shoot with the lugubrious Leopold;

he asked the Shelleys; but their meeting was delayed, since a week lat
he was still pressing her to come with the Liverpools and Madame Lieve
—and "mind you bring the blouse!"—and when Neumann came,
found the Arbuthnots there with the Lievens and Prince Esterhazy. B
Spain still filled his horizon, and he loyally seconded Canning's efforts
deter the French from intervention, even adding the unique resourc
of his personal position to the exiguous armoury of the Foreign Offi
For in his character as a Grandee of Spain he sent Fitzroy Somerset
Madrid with sedative advice. Canning struck martial attitudes (he h
already written gaily that the French tone "really stirs one's blood
in the good old constitutional way in which France and England u
to hate and provoke each other") and flung his thunderbolts about w
a fine carelessness. He talked of his own "itch for war," made dash
speeches in the House of Commons, increased the Navy, and laid pap
—the normal prelude of a declaration of war. In Canning's case, h
ever, the free publication of diplomatic correspondence formed part c
design for invoking public opinion on matters of high policy and, perh
owed a little to the pardonable pride which literary men feel in t
own compositions. These proceedings were unspeakably distastefu
the Duke, though they were still on friendly terms, Canning beg
him expansively never to stand on ceremony in volunteering comm
upon policy. But though Wellington defended his own action in
longest speech that he had yet delivered in the House of Lords, it
unpleasing to be dragged in Mr. Canning's foaming wake. He had
givings now, warning Lord Liverpool that a draft of Canning's "w
go to a break up of the Alliance; and I don't believe that any of us
even Mr. Canning himself, thinks that the affairs of Europe are in
a state that the Alliance provided in the Second Article of the Trea
1815 may not be necessary." Canning's pyrotechnics failed to exhil
him:

> "We have given the Spaniards reason to believe that we should
> them, and we have shaken the confidence of France in our desire of
> taining peace for her sake as well as our own. Then at home, nobody l
> what the policy of the Government is, and it will turn out at last th
> country and Parliament will declare for neutrality before the governmer
> have an opportunity of doing so; and it will be believed that the g

ment have been forced by the country to be neutral, their intentions having been to interfere in favour of Spain."

series of false positions, however brilliant, was distasteful to the uke. He disliked the promiscuous publication of official documents; d it was disconcerting to encounter the pitying regard of his Contintal associates. For the French ambassador wrote patronisingly that he us *"guerrier peu redoutable sur les champs de l'intrigue"*; and Metter- ch, deep in Vienna, recorded with regret, *"Quel dommage que Welgton soit si craintif, lui qui a un cœur si droit et une si honnête figure!"* So he went the round of country houses in 1823, while Canning issued challenges. The Duke moved from Stratfield Saye to Wherstead, from herstead to Maresfield, on to the Pavilion, and from Beaudesert to tfield. It was a stately progress; and the red boxes followed him with ir depressing tale of Canning's extravagances. There was no war with ance; no one had ever meant to have one; and if they had, there was time, since Spain collapsed before the French invasion with the most concerting suddenness and left Mr. Canning thundering in spite of rything to delighted crowds about the might of England. It was far asanter to sit to Hayter in his cloak; for Mrs. Arbuthnot had consented Lady Shelley having a portrait of him, "provided the picture is not nted by Sir Thomas Lawrence, and is not so good as hers." So the ke went his social rounds and made a charming offer to Alava, exiled he turmoil of Spanish politics, of a home with him in England.

ut 1824 renewed his cares. He still maintained a correspondence upon ign affairs with Metternich and with those embassies abroad where he a brother or a friend; and early in the year he confessed to Henry lesley that "we are radically defective in our diplomatic head-quarters :." He disliked the hail of Blue-books, with which Canning sought aptivate his countrymen; for such publications seemed to lead inevi- y to the renunciation of Cabinet control of foreign policy. Mr. Canning ht prefer to have his policy debated in a wider circle than the *champ* of Downing Street, where ageing Tories sat round the table with pproving faces; but the Duke did not. Trained in an older school, alued secrecy—hardly for its own sake (though Madame Lieven d that he loved a secret), but for the greater freedom of manœuvre

which secrecy confers. He was not greatly interested in evoking cheers
Besides, he disapproved the drift of Canning's policy, writing to Metter
nich that "I feel as you do the *isolement* of the British government; and
am equally aware with you of the mischief which it does to us as we
as to the world; probably more to the world than to us." Canning migh
proclaim the dissolution of the Alliance in the gloating formula, "Ever
nation for itself, and God for us all." But was it reasonable to expect th
Duke to part from it without a pang? The Allied ministers were me
with whom he had worked in close confidence since the great days
1815. They had shared common dangers, won wars together, and settle
Europe in agreement. The endless conferences that followed Waterl
had left a certain *camaraderie* among them, which Wellington could n
easily forget; and, slow to make new friends, he was as slow at losi
old ones. But his Continental ties were something more than person
He had his principles, though they were less articulate than Mr. Canning
and it was wholly inevitable that his point of view should be m
European. It was scarcely possible to be a Duke in four countries and
Marshal of every Continental army, to have served two emperors a
half a dozen kings in command of an international army of occupati
to make an annual tour of inspection of the new Belgian fortresses—a
to retain in its perfection that insularity which was now Mr. Cannir
pride. Besides, the settlement of 1815 owed so much to his work. He
won Waterloo; his diplomacy restored Louis XVIII; the peace-treaty b
his signature; the Reparations settlement was his personal achievem
and if Canning could intimate in a celebrated flourish that he had ca
a New World into existence, it was almost as true that Wellington
called the Old.

The two were bound to clash. Canning owed his promotion alr
wholly to the Duke's intervention; but even gratitude will not enabl
to mix with water. Their views were poles apart; their methods
discordant; and what soldier relishes the sight of a civilian flourishi
sword? Viewed by the Duke, the Foreign Secretary was hasty
advised, and quite unbearably dramatic; his popular appeals were
distasteful; and—the uneasy question rose in Wellington—was he
a gentleman? These discontents found a sympathetic audience at V
sor, where his sovereign fished disconsolately in Virginia Water. H

ot fish alone; for Lady Conyngham was there, and they had week-end
arties at the Cottage. The life was not conspicuously gay. The King
reakfasted alone, the Duke with Lady Conyngham; they met at three;
haetons were at the door; the guests paired off and drove—a gentleman
d lady between each spinning pair of wheels—till five; sometimes the
yal drive was diversified by brandy and water at a park lodge; then
nner in the pagoda, conversation until ten, and cards till midnight.
t the "Cottage Coterie"—a pair of Austrians, two Lievens, and the
ench ambassador—was anything but favourable to Mr. Canning; and
e Duke was admitted to their circle. He talked freely to them, though
was hardly a party to their drawing-room conspiracy "*de faire sauter
. Canning.*" But that autumn he involved himself in a dispute with
nning on the latter's plan of visiting Paris; Canning suspected royal
rigues and retorted sharply that "it is high time to look about me,
d to beware of what Burke calls 'traps and mines.'" The Duke was
: a plotter; but it was comforting to pour his views into receptive
s. He was distressed by Canning's eagerness to sanctify South
nerican revolutionaries with British recognition, pleading in vain
t "considering what is passing in Ireland, and what all expect will
ur in that country before long, the bad with hope, the good with
prehension and dread, we must take care not to give additional
mples in these times of the encouragement of insurrection, and we
st not be induced by clamour, by self-interested views, by stock-
bing, or by faction, to give the sanction of our approbation to what
called the governments of these insurgent provinces." The analogy of
and haunted him: how could Dublin Castle extend a hand to Buenos
es? He reasoned lucidly that "if you hold that the people of Colombia
e been guilty of no crime, and that Bolivar is a hero and no rebel,
you ought not to prosecute O'Connell." This was logical; and in
last weeks of 1824 he carried his objections to the length of offering
esign. There were struggles in the Cabinet; the King almost mutinied;
Canning got his way. Lord Liverpool was on his side, and the
e ultimately acquiesced, admitting to a foreign diplomat that he
etted having introduced Canning to the Cabinet, but that it was
ossible to dismiss him. So the New World was duly conjured into
g. Not that Canning's policy was a romantic gesture towards the

great open spaces, since in its later phases it was partly inspired b
a legitimate anxiety to forestall the United States; "Spanish America," a
he wrote gaily, "is free, and if we do not mismanage our affairs sadl
she is English. The Yankees will shout in triumph, but it is they wh
lose most by our decision."

The Duke's skies were darkening. Madame Lieven wrote that "M
Canning poses as a Radical to please the populace—the other Ministe
smile approvingly to keep their places. The Duke of Wellington alo
is prepared to break a lance for the good cause." Ireland was full
menace, and the Roman Catholic question began to loom with u
pleasant urgency. His shooting was improving, though; and he cou
report a bag of fourteen rabbits, a dozen hares, a brace of pheasants, a
a partridge. One theme alone seemed to inspire him with no misgivin
for national defence found him as calm as ever—"I confess that I a
one of those who do not much apprehend invasion. I think ste
navigation has in some degree altered that question to our disadvanta
. . . But I confess that I think a solid invasion of the country . . . is
of the question." His nerves were always steady, and the soldier in h
was still reassured; but as he went to Windsor for Christmas, 1824,
statesman was distinctly uneasy. For the world was full of awkw
problems. Portugal was in an uproar; Byron had died at Missolong
and British sympathy seemed to be solicited on behalf of revolutiona
in every hemisphere. Nearer home the Irish situation increased
gravity; and the Duke corresponded copiously with Peel, who was
the guardian of public order at the Home Office. The two men d
together. Their convergence, as *Coningsby* diagnosed it, "was the s
pathetic result of superior minds placed among inferior intellige
and was, doubtless, assisted by a then mutual conviction, that the
ference of age, the circumstance of sitting in different houses, and
general contrast of their previous pursuits and accomplishments, rend
personal rivalry out of the question." Besides, they both distrusted
ning. As 1825 wore on, the King surrendered to his Foreign Secre
but his colleagues surrendered none of their misgivings.

The Duke passed the year among his customary employments.
Ordnance Office kept him busy with revetments, counterscarps,
barracks at Bermuda; he was consulted upon Indian affairs; an

iews about the Greeks were plainly expressed. "The establishment of new Power in Europe, which must be founded on the principles of modern democracy, and therefore inimical to this country," filled him with no enthusiasm. Not that he loved the Turk, admitting frankly that the Turkish government is so oppressive and odious to all mankind, that we could scarcely expect to carry the country with us in a course of policy . . . the result of which is to be to maintain by the exercise of our power that government at Constantinople." But he viewed the expansion of Russian influence with genuine concern. His minor interests were less absorbing. He defended spring guns in the House of Lords for the simple reason that they checked poachers, and he favoured Lady Shelley with a discourse on education:

"As for John, you must impress upon his mind, first, that he is coming into the world at an age at which he who knows nothing will be nothing. . . .

"If he means to rise in the military profession—I don't mean as high as I am, as that is very rare—he must be master of languages, of the mathematics, of military tactics of course, and of all the duties of an officer in all situations.

"He will not be able to converse or write like a gentleman . . . unless he understands the classics; and by neglecting them, moreover, he will lose much gratification which the perusal of them will always afford him; and a great deal of professional information and instruction.

"He must be master of history and geography, and the laws of his country and of nations. . . .

"Impress all this upon his mind; and moreover tell him that there is nothing like never having an idle moment. . . ."

he was still the young Colonel with a habit of private reading, who many years before had filled his trunk for India with improving books, took his Blackstone with him and learned from Cæsar how to cross river.

As he sat to Hayter, the tide of his patience mounted. For portrait-painters were rapidly becoming one of the burdens of his life. They talked; they borrowed all his clothes; and, what was worse, they would not paint. Even Lawrence kept him standing for three hours with folded arms, and then produced a complete travesty of his sword. This

must plainly be put right at once. The painter made excuses; but th
Duke insisted.

"Do it now."

"I must go to the Princess Augusta's."

"Oh no; you must put my sword right. It is really bad."

After all, he had more experience of swords—and of portraits—th
most men.

In the last days of 1825 a diversion offered itself. For Alexander di
at Taganrog, and the King and Canning tentatively suggested (w
profuse expressions of anxiety for the Duke's health) that he should
to Russia on a special mission to the new Emperor. The prospect v
uninviting, since he was far from well and the road from London
St. Petersburg in mid-winter was long. Besides, it was proposed that
should do his best to stop the Russians from going to war with Tur
in the cause of Greek independence. Preventing wars was his *métier*;
this war could only be prevented if the Porte could be prevailed on
make concessions to the Greeks; and it was doubtful how far the D
would relish being made an instrument of Greek emancipation. Mada
Lieven gleefully proclaimed that his mission was "*une idée bouffo*
et grande . . . side by side with the salaam the Duke is to make sho
he come to an understanding on the question of Greece." '
ingenious Canning, she thought, would thus contrive to "compror
him and mock him at the same time—a double pleasure." But how cc
he refuse? "I don't see how I, who have always been preaching
doctrine of going wherever we are desired to go, who had conser
to go and command in Canada, could decline to accept the offer
this mission." So he announced himself "at all times ready and wil
to serve your Majesty in any station" and accepted. Indeed, if Can
told the truth, he "not only accepted but *jumped* at the proposal."
his alacrity is doubtful, since the world whispered that Canning w
not be inconsolable if this Arctic journey proved too much for him;
the Duke seemed to share the world's misgivings. Rarely emotiona
took leave of his friends with unusual tenderness; Alava had never
him so profoundly moved; he parted from his mother with emo
and the tears streamed down his cheeks, as he left Lady Burghersh

346

4

Wellington entered upon his Russian campaign in February, 1826. The journey was to take three weeks; and to elude the minor irritants of Polish inns he adopted the ingenious expedient of a silk mattress; silk, was hoped, would be impenetrable to invaders; and he had chosen a ght material, upon which they would be more conspicuous. Such ingenuity was not unworthy of a great tactician. Besides, there was a strong ement of the White Knight in the Duke's composition. A lifetime in the field will often implant a taste for minor ingenuities; for the igencies of campaigning tend to stimulate such proclivities; and the turning veteran will sometimes carry them into the less exacting conditions of civilian life. Was he not the inventor of a patent finger-ndage, which he demonstrated incessantly? Were not his later years lighted by the dual precaution of a sword-umbrella? So the ingenuity his travelling bed (explained with pride to Lady Shelley after his urn) was quite in character.

He went by way of Berlin, where he called upon the King of Prussia d wrote to Canning five times in one day. He was frankly sceptical his prospects of success in Russia; if the Russians chose to go to war h Turkey, he should not be able to stop them. But his major object s to localise the conflict to prevent a scuffle in the Balkans from eloping into a European war. "The question of Greek and Turk rifling in comparison"; and he was infinitely less concerned with the talities of Pashas and the indomitable Ypsilanti than with the major blem of European peace. As to the Greeks, he was prepared for "an ngement short of independence." But peace must be preserved in ope; and he agreed with Canning in believing that another Congress the last way to preserve it. His carriage rumbled across Poland and sad Livonian levels, and he reached St. Petersburg in the first week March. That evening he saw Nesselrode and called upon the Emperor holas on the next day. The Czar seemed eminently reasonable about Greeks; and Wellington plunged into a vortex of diplomacy, miti-d by that Russian official hospitality which consisted of "pallid ragus and fœtid oysters." His nights, as someone wrote, were

"nothing but blow-outs for the Duke," his days all "politics and pipe-
clay." Stiff Russian guardsmen in tall shakoes and tight tunics presented
arms; stiffer generals raised fingers to preposterous cocked-hats; the
Czar gave him a regiment of infantry on the anniversary of the Allies'
entry to Paris; and he visited a stupendous girls' school, where he watched
young ladies curtsey by platoons and heard twenty-five pianos in simultaneous action. He managed to survive it somehow, without even getting
one of his customary colds. Indeed, the chief thing that impressed the
Duke in Russia was that no one seemed to have a cold. He drafted
endless protocols and spoke his mind to Nicholas, warning him "that
he can fix the moment when, and the point at which the first shot
will be fired; but that he may as well talk of stopping the course of the
Neva as of fixing the limits of his operations if once he goes to war."
The Russians listened blandly; but it is doubtful how far his presence
in St. Petersburg modified their course. Indeed, he was a shade perplexed
by the Byzantine complications of palace politics, confessing to his
brother that "it is difficult to judge of matters here, and whether there
is any Minister or not, and who is the adviser. We have some great
diplomatic characters here, but I believe they are all as much in the
dark as I am." He worked assiduously to avert a Russo-Turkish war
or, at the worst, to localise it. That was his main objective, and he succeeded in attaining it; for there was no European war. As to the Greeks
he was already reconciled to seeing them with something short of
independence; and when the persuasive Lievens represented that Russian policy was not aimed at abetting revolutionaries, but at the
establishment of order in Greece—"a regular state of things, a hierarchy,
discipline"—the Duke was charmed. His pen grew busy with more
drafts; and a Protocol emerged which guaranteed to Greece a qualified
degree of independence under Anglo-Russian auspices. Canning was
slightly rueful, since the Protocol committed England to Greek independence far beyond his original instructions to the Duke. But Wellington was three weeks distant from the Foreign Office and acted on his
own discretion. Canning could have no grievance, since the Duke followed lines that were perfectly consistent with a disinterested support of
Greek emancipation. Peace was preserved; the world was spared the
horrors of another Congress; and a ray of hope fell across Greece.

Duke was moving with the times (though his critics have preferred to think that he was unaware of what he was doing); and if the Russians rejoiced, it does not follow that British interests had been betrayed. Imperial gratitude expressed itself, as always, in terms of sables and malachite vases; and at four o'clock one April morning Wellington started for home again. He might have stayed in Russia for the coronation; but he preferred to leave. The work was over; and Peel, who had acted as his Cabinet correspondent, was pressing him not to delay his return "a single day beyond absolute necessity." Once again duty called; this time it was his duty to the Tories. For his Tory colleagues were uncomfortable without him. He travelled by Warsaw and Berlin, where he stopped long enough to receive the honour of a Prussian infantry regiment; and before the month was out, he was in Apsley House once more.

5

Wellington's Russian campaign was over. It had been a picturesque interlude, and the walls of Stratfield Saye bore traces of it in the form of innumerable engravings of high-collared autocrats, of sleighs, of snowy scenes, of angry bears, of the tall buildings of St. Petersburg. But no musical composer was ever moved to celebrate his *1812*, no painter to depict him in the snow. Yet, like Napoleon, he had returned without his army; but, unlike the Emperor, he had left home without it too.

Home was a trifle unattractive in April, 1826. Canning was high in the ascendant, and the skies were darkened by "the three C's," as Croker called them, "Corn, Currency, and Catholics." The eager Huskisson must really be restrained from committing ministers to repeal the Corn Laws. The Duke would go no further than an undertaking that they should be "fairly considered" in the next session; while the Government's nice equipoise upon the Catholic question must be maintained. That summer he found greater comfort in the past—in dining at the Admiralty with Croker and the Duke of York and recalling how the French cavalry at Waterloo in their cuirasses and jack-boots "lay sprawling and kicking like so many turned turtles," and regaling a house-party of Lord Hertford's with reminiscences of Spain and Paris and the distant days of his campaign in Denmark. But the unpleasing present still persisted; red boxes

followed him with their distasteful reminders of the world of 1826; and
at sight of them he grew almost peevish. Canning was worse than ever—
"a most extraordinary man. Either his mind does not seize a case ac
curately; or he forgets the impressions which ought to be received from
what he reads, or is stated to him; or knowing and remembering th
accurate state of the case, he distorts and misrepresents facts in his instruc
tions to his ministers with a view to entrap the consent of the Cabinet t
some principle on which he would found a new-fangled system." Th
Foreign Office papers failed to circulate for Cabinet approval; and whe
the British minister was suddenly withdrawn from Spain without notic
to the Cabinet, Wellington complained bitterly to the Prime Minister:

> "Here we are with a step taken which will be considered as a signal
> war throughout Europe . . . without any one of the ministers being awa
> of the existence even of discussion.
>
> "I am certain that Mr. Canning would not consent to such a proceedin
> by any other man. There is no person who (with propriety, in my opinio
> reserves to himself more frequently the right of judging for himself of t
> cases for which he is to be held responsible. I am certain, likewise, that y
> will admit that this is not the mode in which the business of this coun
> ever has been, or can be carried on."

But Canning was incorrigible. His latest escapade was the defence
Portugal—of Portugal lately turned constitutional and acidly describ
by the Duke as "Constitutional Portugal, I mean in the modern ser
with licentious Chambers sitting in Lisbon and publishing their deba
and a licentious press." This victim of repression failed to stir his sy
pathies. It had been one thing to rescue decorous Braganza Portugal a
Bourbon Spain from the revolutionary legions of the French; but
was quite another matter. However, Mr. Canning and the Cabi
thought otherwise. A splendid declamation was pronounced in the Ho
of Commons—"We go to plant the Standard of England on the w
known heights of Lisbon. Where that Standard is planted, foreign
minion shall not come . . ."—and while Mr. Canning stirred memb
pulses, the Duke conveyed the same intelligence to the Lords in
sentences. Even the prospect of a new war in the Peninsula failed to m
him to eloquence. For Great Britain intervened at last—in the sa

name of non-intervention—and when a brigade sailed for the Tagus, Wellington dutifully acquiesced with notes for the commanding officer on the familiar topic of bullock-carts.

The year ended with a menace of still further change. For the Duke of York was dying, mourned by the tearful King in the congruous lament, "Alas! my poor brother!" He had commanded the army (with a brief interruption due to the vivacious Mrs. Clarke) since the distant days when Arthur Wesley was a Colonel; and his broad figure formed an unchanging part of the architecture of the Horse Guards. He died in the first week of 1827, and the world waited for a new Commander-in-Chief. There was one soldier with transcendent claims. But Peel warned the Duke that his sovereign contemplated taking the command in person. Was it not a royal hallucination that he had charged with the heavy cavalry at Salamanca? Besides, the post-war exercises of the British army had been mainly sartorial; and the King played a splendid part in military tailoring. Wellington received the warning with a bitter intimation that he had been promised the succession, but that he always viewed the royal promise, "like many others, as so many empty and unmeaning words and phrases." The fancy passed, however; and Wellington was duly installed as Commander-in-Chief, taking command in a General Order consisting of a single sentence.

Now there could be no more promotion. For he had reached the very summit of his profession. How could he rise further? There were still politics, of course; in civil life he was no more than a mere minister; but if a vacancy occurred, could a Commander-in-Chief hope to become Prime Minister? Croker, at any rate, thought not; the way, he felt, was clear for Canning now. The vacancy occurred within a month. For the Prime Minister collapsed in February; and the age, the interminable age of Liverpool was over.

6

Who was to be Prime Minister? There was an eager scurry; and the Duke spoke his mind at the breakfast-table at Apsley House. The present Government, he said, must be kept together for everybody's sakes— "after them comes chaos." Croker agreed, adding that it would all have been so simple if he had not become Commander-in-Chief, but that put him out of the question as Prime Minister.

"Yes, yes, I am in my proper place, in the place to which I was destined by my trade. I am a soldier, and I am in my place at the head of the army, as the Chancellor, who is a lawyer, is in his place on the woolsack. We have each of us a trade, and are in our proper position when we are exercising it."

This was admirable; but who was to be Prime Minister? Canning felt no uncertainties: his moment had arrived. But even Canning required colleagues; and his Tory colleagues were frankly hostile to the notion of a Canning administration. For, all else apart, his Catholic opinions scared them. They scared the Duke as well, who could not bear his methods at the Foreign Office and confessed to Arbuthnot (who passed it on to Peel) that he detected "much of trickery; he sees that the sons and relations of our most vehement opponents are taken into employ; and he cannot divest himself of the idea that, directly or indirectly, there has been an understanding with some of the leaders of the Opposition." Canning was in league with the Whigs, it was quite impossible for the Duke to serve under him. At any rate, he did not mean to. Four years Canning had made him a Tory of the strictest sect. But he played scrupulously fair; and when the King summoned him to Brighton, Wellington sent word that "he had nothing to say to him, and that it would not be fair to his colleagues that he should see the King at such a moment." But his own opinions were developing. For the ardent Protestants besieged him with suggestions that he should manœuvre Canning out of the new Cabinet; the Duke, however, favouring a continuance of the status quo, repelled them. They even proposed that he should take the Premiership himself; but Wellington put by the crown, though he confessed that "circumstances might be conceived under which it would be his duty to accept the situation if he was called upon by the King to do so." His views inclined, however, to the substitution of Mr. Robinson as Prime Minister; Canning, he thought, would be content to serve under Mr. Robinson. Canning, however, was indisposed to become the main ornament of a Robinson administration, suspecting that "the Protestant part of the Government wished to have me as *cheap* as possible, to use me to the utmost for their support in the House of Commons and in

Foreign Office . . . but to repress all higher aspirations as strictly as if
were of another species than their Lordships." Perhaps he was.

The tension lasted from mid-February to the second week of April.
London buzzed with rumours; Taper and Tadpole were on tip-toe; and
Mr. Croker lived in an ecstasy of exclusive information. But perhaps
George IV enjoyed this interlude more than any of his subjects, except
when agitated Tory magnates addressed him in the most unbecoming
terms. For the King presided over the *imbroglio* in a mood that was
positively Puckish. He had suffered much from his ministers, and it was
treat for him to keep them dangling. Once, indeed, he asked the leading
characters in the official comedy to Windsor. It was an uncomfortable
house-party; and when Wellington passed the whole morning with the
King, Canning aged visibly. Besides, the royal mood at lunch was plainly
favourable to the Duke. After lunch the customary phaetons came. The
royal Puck, with perfect malice, sent the Duke for a drive with Princess
Lieven, a fervent Canningite, and kept Canning at home for a talk. The
drive was trying; and it was painfully significant to find on their return
that the impartial King had passed the entire afternoon with Canning.
But nothing came of it. For when the rival statesmen met, each asked
the other if he knew anything; but their elusive sovereign, deep in his
delicious game of hide-and-seek, had said precisely nothing.

Yet even royal games must end at last; and Canning's firm refusal of
any compromise won the trick. No Government could live without him;
and if he could not have Tory colleagues, he should bring in the Whigs.
A cold exchange of letters with the Duke ensued. His Grace's sincere
and faithful servant, George Canning, advised him that he had his
Majesty's commands to reconstruct the administration, that it was his
wish to adhere to the principles on which Lord Liverpool's had so long
acted together, and that his Grace's continuance as a colleague was essential. The Duke replied with a polite enquiry of his dear Mr. Canning
who was to be Prime Minister. Canning responded in a didactic vein
that he had believed it to be generally understood that the person charged
with the formation of a Government was apt to be Prime Minister, that
his course would be followed in the present instance, and that the King
approved. The letters rang like pistol-shots on a frosty morning. The
Duke was winged. One shot remained, however, and he fired it. Writing

in a cold fury, he expressed his inability to believe that any Government of Canning's could follow the ancient ways of Lord Liverpool's, or that anyone would ever think so, or that its policy could serve either King or country. So he resigned. His resignation of the Ordnance, which was a Cabinet office, was natural. But he declined to serve Canning as Commander-in-Chief and resigned the Horse Guards too; and for the first time in forty years the Duke was out of place.

354

THE Duke was out; and gleeful caricatures depicted *Achilles in the Sulks,* or the *Great Captain on the Stool of Repentance,* with a ~~figure~~, angry and aquiline, sitting in Apsley House and exclaiming ~~bitterly~~,

> "Here for brutal courage far renowned,
> I live an idle burden to the ground.
> (*Others* in *counsel* fam'd for nobler skill
> More useful to *preserve* than I to *kill*.)"

~~La~~tely Commander-in-Chief and Master-General of the Ordnance, he ~~wa~~s now a comparatively private individual, a mere Field Marshal with ~~ma~~rked Tory leanings. Opinion was a trifle shocked, although strict ~~Pr~~otestants nodded approval when he resigned. A file of Tory colleagues ~~fol~~lowed. For the Duke's resignation was a signal to Peel and the older ~~To~~ries. He was a party-leader now; Peel was his aide-de-camp; and the ~~a~~ged nobility awaited his commands. For he had travelled far in the ~~eig~~ht years since he accepted office from Lord Liverpool on an express ~~un~~derstanding that he should not be bound to go into Opposition with ~~his~~ colleagues. That reservation had once served to mark him as a public ~~ser~~vant still, to distinguish him from the humbler breed of politicians. ~~Bu~~t he was a politician now; and, like any politician, he resigned. ~~T~~he Duke was out; and the King was left almost alone with Mr. Can~~nin~~g and the Whigs. This was a shade alarming, since the royal con~~scie~~nce was firmly opposed to Catholic Emancipation, and the sovereign ~~wa~~s left feeling "very sore at his notion of desertion by those who forced ~~Mr.~~ Canning on him originally." The royal irritation was expressed in ~~cu~~rt acceptance of the Duke's double resignation. But how could he ~~com~~plain? Wellington could scarcely be expected to serve in Mr. Can~~nin~~g's Cabinet. That disposed of the Ordnance. Could he retain the ~~Hor~~se Guards? The office of Commander-in-Chief was not political. But ~~Wel~~lington chose to view Canning's second letter as "a rebuke for which ~~I ha~~d given no provocation, and in which the authority of the King's

name was very unnecessarily introduced." His honour, the last refuge o
an angry statesman, was involved. Besides, there would have to be fre
quent consultation between Prime Minister and Commander-in-Chie
questions were bound to arise on pay, on garrisons, on the troops i
Portugal; and manifestly he did not possess the Prime Minister's co
fidence. The fact was that his dislike of Canning was too strong for ar
form of official co-operation. For he was writing vehemently of "th
charlatan" and the "foolish, insulting and indecent manner of his b
haviour to me." Yet Wellington was not the man to act impulsive
from motives of merely personal distaste. He saw a larger issue, to whi
his quarrel with Canning was only incidental. Was not the world of 18
full of threats to the existing order?

> "Rely upon it, my dear Charles, the object of the great aristocracy, a
> of the *parti conservateur* of this country, is to secure the Crown from
> mischief with which it is threatened, by moderation, by consistency, by fir
> ness and good temper. Matters have been brought to the state in which th
> are by a man (for after all there is but one man) who does not posses
> particle of any one of those qualities. The aristocracy must not aid
> views. They must not render perpetual the unfortunate separation betwe
> the Crown and the party to which I have above referred. I earnestly reco
> mend, then, moderation and temper, and above all, respect for the Cro
> and for the person of the King."

This had the firm tone of a party-leader—of the new leader of the p
conservateur and its natural allies, the aristocracy. For though M
Arbuthnot could still describe him as "of *no party*," Wellington was n
the rising hope of the stern, unbending Tories.

The spring passed in irritable explanations, while the army lived un
a confused interregnum with Lord Palmerston, that hermit of the V
Department, for its temporary and civilian Commander-in-Chief. '
Duke made a reasoned statement on his resignation in the House
Lords, which compelled the praises of Lord Ashley for its manly vir
How could their Lordships have supposed him capable of a desire to
Prime Minister—"a station, to the duties of which I was unaccuston
in which I was not wished, and for which I was not qualified; as it n
be obvious to your Lordships, that not being in the habit of addres
your Lordships, I should have been found, besides other qualificati

ncapable of displaying, as they ought to be displayed, or of defending the
measures of government as they ought to be defended in this House, by
the person thus honoured by his Majesty's confidence? My Lords, I
should have been worse than mad if I had thought of such a thing."
This was putting it a trifle high. Besides, his disclaimer gave awkward
hostages to the enemy if an opportunity of office should recur. (*"En
politique,"* as a judicious Emperor remarked to an impulsive politician,
il ne faut point dire 'Jamais.'") But statesmen are frequently carried
away by their own abnegation, when they disclaim their own ambitions.
There was an awkward interchange of correspondence with Canning,
discontinued by the latter from an anxiety (which seemed a shade be-
lated) that it might not "degenerate into controversy." The King, a little
nervous now, intimated that the command of the new army was still
open; but the Duke's frowns persisted. His brother William was the
bearer of a furtive invitation (promptly disavowed to Canning by the
courageous monarch) to call at Windsor. The Duke went at duty's summons; and London buzzed again. The irrepressible Creevey met him
one afternoon coming out of Arbuthnot's front-door in Parliament Street
and promptly buttonholed him with "Curious times these, Duke." The
Duke agreed, put his arm through the inquisitive Whig's, swung him
right round, and marched him off towards the House of Lords. He sent
a civil message through Creevey to Lord Grey and spoke with heat of
Canning, stopping at intervals to emphasise his points and very nearly
pulling the button off Creevey's coat in the process. No one, he said,
could act with Canning; and his temper was quite sure to blow him up.
Others noticed it as well that summer, a sharp American observer recording that "Mr. Canning's temper has become most uncertain." Canning, it seemed, was growing odd; office had broken stronger men; and
the Duke watched him with genuine concern. One evening the Prime
Minister bore down upon the American ambassador with an unprovoked
tirade against the aristocracy; and Wellington drew up a chair between
Gallatin and Humboldt, looked anxious, and asked suddenly if they
found anything odd in Mr. Canning's manner. He had seen such things
before; could it be possible that Canning might be going the same way
as Castlereagh? While the Duke looked on, he did not play an active
part in Parliament, though he spoke once or twice on the Corn Bill with

a clear repudiation of "any feeling of party or of faction, or of the lea
desire to embarrass His Majesty's Government." For he had not learnt-
perhaps he never mastered—the ways of Opposition. He had served th
State far too long to distinguish readily between Opposition and seditio
He might resign: that was permissible. But the Duke could rarely brir
himself to oppose a Government, even if it was Mr. Canning's.

The House rose in July; and the Prime Minister was far from we
He had never managed to throw off a cold contracted at the Duke
York's funeral in the previous winter, when they were all kept standi
on cold pavements; he had persuaded Eldon to stand on the Lord Cha
cellor's cocked hat and written gaily to the Duke that "Mr. Mash,
whoever filched the cloth or the matting from under our feet in the ais
had bets or insurances against the lives of the Cabinet." He had been a
ing all the summer; and now the bet was almost won. For "it was a ri
warm night at the beginning of August, when a gentleman enveloped
a cloak, for he was in evening dress, emerged from a club-house at t
top of St. James' Street, and descended that celebrated eminence."
paused, as readers of *Endymion* know, to impart the news that M
Canning was *in extremis*. That brief reign was over now; it had las
for three months. Strange how the Duke's customary allowance of pow
to his opponents was a Hundred Days.

His epitaph on Canning was laconic—"I hear that Dr. Farr says t
it was Canning's temper that killed him." This was unkind; but he sp
kindly of him in company, admiring his rare gifts of speech and writ
and the patience with which Canning had permitted him to "cut a
hack" his drafts. But he deplored the ungovernable rages with which
often greeted differences in council; and Canning impressed him as "
of the idlest of men." For industry of the Duke's order often susp
more rapid methods. Idle or not, Canning was gone; and the King
left to find a new Prime Minister. There was a flutter among the
pectant Tories. Would the Duke be sent for? He was not; for b
pleasing irony the King, averse to further changes and dreading
humiliation of a summons to the evicted Tories, summoned the shad
presence of Mr. Robinson, now ennobled as Lord Goderich, to
Canning's Government together. That "transient and embarrassed ph
tom" reigned without distinction and with a growing personal disc

rt, until he vanished like an uneasy spirit at cockcrow. To steer a course
with a mixed crew of Whigs and Tory Canningites might have tasked
ronger nerves than his; and his nerves were anything but strong. A
ter age views nervous ailments with an indulgent eye. But to the full-
looded world of 1827 an intermittently lachrymose Prime Minister was
erely comic. Lord Goderich whimpered through five months of office;
d when he made his final exit behind a borrowed royal handkerchief,
heartless world guffawed. Not much had been accomplished, though
Wellington had been induced to resume his post as Commander-in-Chief.
e took command "as of an Army in the Field" without political con-
derations, although his action was submitted for approval to his Tory
ends; for the Duke felt his new position as a party-leader with respon-
bilities towards his political associates.

The reign of Goderich was a conscious interlude; and Wellington
atched from his Tory fastness. One day before the summer ended he
olled in to the "Social Day" of a new sculptor's exhibition. A respectful
cle in the gallery marked the majestic presence of Mrs. Siddons in tow
an Academician. The Duke's air was less sublime; Haydon, indeed,
s positively disappointed and "never saw one whose air and presence
re so unlike genius or heroism." But, thanks to the Elgin Marbles,
aydon's standards of the heroic were unduly elevated. He thought that
ellington "seemed embarrassed, and as if he felt he was unpopular."
at was quite possible in a year in which he had endured distinct re-
fs. But he was not too embarrassed to admire the sculpture, stepping
he order-book and inscribing himself for a *Milo* and a *Samson*. One
he artist's friends came up to thank him. "He should go abroad," said
 clear military voice. This sentence of exile sounding a little unpro-
ous, he added hastily, "Not to stay, but to see—eh—the—eh—great
ks as others have done." Then he wheeled briskly round, lifted a
tial finger to his hat, and left the gallery, his duty to the arts accom-
hed. In the autumn he paid a round of visits in the north, and was
mphantly received, even Grey recording that his "course has been
 continued scene of rejoicing." The cheers melted his diffidence. He
 a coming man once more, though he shot worse than ever. They
 all at Stratfield Saye; the Duchess was unwell and kept her room,
re Mrs. Arbuthnot bore with fortitude the tedium of her conversa-

tion. Downstairs Alava told his stories and Lady Jersey aired her charm while the gentlemen expressed their sympathies with Turkey at the out rageous violence of Navarino. The Duke was in the grip of one of h tremendous colds; the subject of catarrh appeared to fascinate him, an he was apt to send detailed directions for its treatment to his relation confiding sovereign remedies to diplomatic bags. They had lent Apsl House to the Shelleys; and poor Kitty wrote from Stratfield Saye beggin Lady Shelley to stay on in London, adding, "I hope you like my Dou upon further acquaintance! Is he not the living image of his father For she was still devoted to her alarming Duke.

Then he was back in London, while Lord Goderich, a tearful Sisyph administered his country. Wellington's infrequent sense of family loya impelled him to press his brother Henry's claims to a peerage; Henr ambition was to figure as Lord Cowley, if that spelling of their form name was correct, although he had "a decided aversion to the name Colley." His wish was gratified, and Lord Cowley joined the Duke, Lc Wellesley, and Lord Maryborough in the family peerage; for with sole exception of Gerald, who was in the Church, they were all pe now. The weeks went by; Lord Goderich's outcries became more audib and as his tears flowed faster, he resigned.

The question, the eternal question which had haunted 1827, was rai again in the first week of 1828. Who was to be Prime Minister? Th had been a notion of Lord Harrowby; but he refused. Richard was e spoken of. But the King knew his own mind at last; for nine months keeping company with Whigs had roused his sleeping fervour for Reformation, and he was now an ardent Protestant. That meant a T Government; a Tory Government meant Wellington; and the Duke sent for. His audience was highly unusual; for the King was ill. A ch ful voice, owned by an unbecoming figure in a dirty silk jacket, exclair from the recesses of a royal bed, "Arthur, the Cabinet is defunct." royal head was crowned by a singularly greasy turban; and royal proceeded to enliven the occasion with a perfect rendering of the dep ment of his late ministers. His visitor was then requested to form a C ernment upon the understanding that Catholic Emancipation sh form no part of Cabinet policy. The Duke was guarded. In view of position as Commander-in-Chief, he must consult his friends. He a

or time, but went so far as to elicit royal wishes for and against individ-
als. The King had no objections except to Lord Grey; the Government,
he thought, should be composed of persons of both opinions upon the
Catholic question; and he repeated frequently that he desired nothing
more than a strong Government. The Duke returned to town and sent
for Peel—Peel was his second-in-command—and he would speak to nobody till Peel had been consulted. Peel's advice was plain. Their course,
he felt, would be anything but simple, since the Tories had been split by
Canning and the tide of Catholic Emancipation was rising. But he was
content to serve under Wellington in a reunited Tory administration, and
was decidedly of opinion that the Duke should be Prime Minister. Canning had once objected to "the union of the whole power of the State,
civil and military, in the same hands" as being "a station too great for
any subject, however eminent, or however meritorious, and one incom-
patible with the practice of a free constitution." The Duke himself had
termed it madness. But his view was changed. He could do better than
Goderich. Besides, the Tories looked to him; the King was quite subdued; and was it not his duty to accept public situations? So the Duke,
at fifty-eight, became Prime Minister.

The man of the age is clearly the Duke, the saviour of Europe, in the perfection of manhood, and with an iron constitution.—ENDYMION.

I

H E W A S to govern England now; and an expectant world took his success for granted. Wellington had never failed; his long career had been a mere procession of success; and what civilian task could find him wanting? After all, he was no stranger to administration. Eight years in the Cabinet were a respectable apprenticeship; he had once governed Ireland, to say nothing of his administrative experience in Portugal, Mysore, and France. Diplomacy could hold no mysteries for him, since he had attended Congresses with Castlereagh, conferred with kings and emperors on equal terms, and corresponded with half the Continent. It was an adequate equipment; and the world was not in the least surprised that, in *Endymion's* phrase, "England should be ruled by the most eminent man of the age, and the most illustrious of her citizens."

The task was formidable, though. The auguries were good—"the conviction that the Duke's government would only cease with the termination of his public career was so general, that, the moment he was installed in office, the Whigs smiled on him; political conciliation became the slang of the day, and the fusion of parties the babble of clubs and the tattle of boudoirs." But the task was formidable. Could he perform the duties of Prime Minister? Pure administration had no terrors, since he knew his mind, could make decisions, and always answered letters. A slightly excessive sense of detail might, perhaps, encumber him. Soldiers are bred to detail, since there is nothing in the world (as Napoleon III once wrote of a War Minister) with so much detail about it as an army; and the Duke's passion for exactitude was sometimes lost among *minutiæ*, as when he accompanied an offer to keep an appointment in Westminster Hall with the somewhat exaggerated caution that "it will take me a quarter of an hour to go from the Ordnance to Westminster Hall; and as much for the Man who is to go for me." He could face all the paperwork, since Wellington had been writing State papers for as long as his countrymen could remember. There would be public speaking to be done, of course, and he was not a speaker. But the House of Lords must

put up with his plain manner of debating, once described by Walte
Scott as "slicing the argument into two or three parts and helping him
self to the best." That would suffice; for the world did not expect him t
give performances like Mr. Canning's. His colleagues could do all th
talking. But could he manage them? That was, perhaps, more doubtfu
since he was accustomed to the simple compliance of a staff; and a sta:
is not a Cabinet. Staff officers can be trusted not to resign at awkwar
moments. But Cabinets require arts of management that are wholl
unfamiliar to commanders in the field. Generals of division act upo
instructions; the Quartermaster-General is rarely troubled by his co:
science in performing simple departmental duties; but would Secretari
of State be equally reliable? As he complained later, "One man wan
one thing and one another; they agree to what I say in the morning, ar
then in the evening up they start with some crotchet which deranges tl
whole plan. I have not been used to that in all the early part of my li!
I have been accustomed to carry on things in quite a different manne
I assembled my officers and laid down my plan, and it was carried in
effect without any more words."

But Cabinets work upon different lines. For Cabinets consist of c
leagues; and the Duke was more accustomed to subordinates. Would
be happy as the head of such a republic? There was his party, too.
lifetime in the field had trained him to expect obedience in the ranl
they were not called on to concur, but merely to obey; and he appli
the same simple canons of duty to his political followers. "The party!"
exclaimed with irritable emphasis. "What is the meaning of a party
they don't follow their leaders? Damn 'em! let 'em go!" And it is har
to be wondered at that they occasionally went. For even party men h:
been known to require something more than to be led.

These were the limitations of his splendid equipment for civilian off
Mechanically perfect, he was defective in the minor art of persuasi
The defect was inherent in his nature and aggravated by his traini
For he was anything but pliant; and there had been no need for him
persuade anyone at Headquarters. If *Endymion's* glowing forecast of
dictatorship of patriotism" was correct, all would be well. Few men w
better qualified to be dictator. But if dictation failed, if a need arose
persuade colleagues or fellow-citizens that he was in the right, his p:

ects of success were questionable. He might, perhaps, succeed so long as
perations were confined to the familiar political *terrain* over which he
ad manœuvred with Lord Liverpool and Mr. Canning. So long as poli-
cs remained a highly complicated game played by well-connected per-
ns within the limits of the Parliamentary board, he played with tolerable
ill. But when the board was suddenly enlarged and new pieces with
range moves appeared upon it, he was baffled. This was not politics as
had learnt them. For politics according to the rules were a genteel
fair in which residents in Mayfair governed England by the simple
ocess of making speeches to one another in Westminster. That was the
d *terrain*, on which he could manœuvre with fair proficiency. But now
e ground was unfamiliar; Westminster had ceased to be the sole battle-
ld of politics, and operations were in progress all over England; strange,
authorised belligerents had elbowed the recognised players into cor-
rs; and where once the game of politics had turned upon the evolu-
ns of competing groups, it now depended on the incalculable appetites
crowds. The Duke was never at his best with crowds; he had no
te for them, whether they cheered or hooted him; besides, the best
rs of his life had been devoted to obstructing their desires. For a Chief
retary learns to be indifferent to Irish crowds; and the long war
inst the French was little more than an attempt to discipline the Paris
b. He had learnt a deep distaste for democracy in the dark, tumultu-
years when murder was its leading argument and Thistlewood its
ef apostle; and if crowds were to be the arbiters of politics, the Duke
uld stand his ground. He was a shade bewildered, as he faced the
y attack. There was no precedent (outside the unpleasing precedents
France) for politics on such a scale. For this was something wholly
erent from the orderly manœuvres of political parties. The rules of
were openly defied, and the *terrain* had been transformed out of all
ognition. It seemed to have no limits now; and where were the fa-
ar mountain-ranges, which had once prescribed the course of opera-
s? He could not have been more at sea, if fate had suddenly trans-
d Headquarters from the Lines of Torres Vedras, where he could
see with precision the direction of the next French offensive, to
son's quarter-deck surrounded by a shifting element and exposed to
k from every point of the compass.

But the Duke stood his ground. Indeed, resistance was his main con
ception of a statesman's duty. Not that his mind was purely negative
But he had not been the chosen swordsman of the *ancien régime* fo
nothing. What had he fought the French for, if not to check the tid
of change? He had resisted change at Busaco and Salamanca an
Waterloo; and it was too much to hope that he would welcome
in England. He had lived half a lifetime with the sound of the Frenc
guns in his ears; he was the saviour of Europe; and was it reasonab
to expect him to applaud the principles from which he had saved it
His country must be saved again. The need to save it from the Frenc
had passed; but there were still the Whigs. For those misguided me
were on the path which led direct to the French Revolution; and
was vital at all costs to bar them out of office. So early as 1821 he ha
urged Liverpool to pocket his official pride for the compelling reaso
that the dread alternative was to "give up the government to the Whi
and Radicals, or, in other words, the country in all its relations to ir
trievable ruin"; in 1827, when Liverpool collapsed and the Tory dai
began to break, he had told Croker that "after them comes chaos"; a
now the Whigs were at the gates.

How to exclude them? He was too intelligent to oppose a front
mere negation. That was the Tory system; but the Duke was more th
a mere "pig-tail" Tory. A master of defensive strategy, he was well aw
that at a certain stage resistance becomes dangerous to the defenders.
had never been his habit to defend positions after they had become in
fensible. That was the moment for a neat withdrawal to his next positi
When he commanded the last army of England in the Peninsula,
stood to fight at Busaco, fell back to Torres Vedras, and stood to fi
again; and he proposed to execute the same manœuvre in defence
social order. He always said that the best test of a great general was
know when to retreat, and to dare to do it"; and statesmen might
worse than learn the lesson. It would be madness to risk the safety of
constitution in an affair of outposts; that had always been poor Craufu
weakness, and the Duke found Tory braves almost as uncontrollable.
they must choose their ground with care, defend a strong position as l
as it could be defended, and then, if circumstances unfortunately tu

t, fall back to the next. For a judicious strategy of retreat might, if persisted in, keep the Whigs perpetually in Opposition and save the State.

That was his design. It would require a mobile force for its successful execution; and his Cabinet, the Tory party, and the King were anything but mobile. Politicians had an awkward weakness for consistency, which inclined them to defend positions long after a retreat had become imperative; and the King was now afflicted with an exceptionally trying conscience upon religious questions. But the Duke took command. He had led highly miscellaneous armies in his time; and in 1828 he led another.

II

H is methods of recruitment were simple but effective. All the wee
he sat in Apsley House with Arbuthnot at his elbow interviewin
candidates for office and writing briefly to likely recruits. Croker foun
him one day in the later stages, when his patience was wearing a litt
thin. The Duke compared himself to a dog with a can tied to its ta
and pointed irritably to a formidable mountain of red boxes and gree
bags. "There," he explained, "is the business of the country, which I ha
not time to look at—all my time being employed in assuaging what ge
tlemen call their feelings." This was a novelty; staff officers had had
feelings. But politicians were less reasonable; and he assumed with e
dent distaste the unfamiliar task of persuading these unmanageal
creatures. His object was to repair the damage done by Mr. Canning,
reunite the Tory party by retaining Canning's misguided followers ir
Tory administration. They gave him endless trouble, since Mr. Huskiss
who led the little group, was full of stipulations. First there were
leanings towards fiscal freedom. Then, if he was to stay at the Color
Office, Lamb must remain Chief Secretary; that would be a guaran
that strict neutrality would be observed upon the Catholic question. 1
cheerful Palmerston must be promoted to the Cabinet. And was
Duke prepared to apply the principles of Mr. Canning in foreign affai
His recent treaty about Greece went further than the Duke's Proto
of 1826. But Wellington satisfied their scruples by declaring that '
King's treaties must be observed" and appointing one of the group
the Foreign Office. The Canningites were duly enlisted; but their in
sion involved sacrifices. For Tories of the older school were droppe
order to make room for them; but as he banished them, Wellington w
ruefully that "the King's service must be carried on." He was less te
with the normal appetites which beset Prime Ministers, informing
persistent applicant for a peerage that as there had been twenty-six
tions in the last two years, it was his duty "to discourage and pr
against any more being created unless some public service of magni

r public emergency should require it. If this duty is not performed, ither the House of Lords will become a democratic body and a nuisance, r contemptible and useless. In either case the constitution of the country ill be overturned." Few party-leaders can afford to tell their followers aat the House of Lords will be unduly adulterated by their ennoble-aent; but the Duke was never a master of the soft answer. He was pre-ared to govern England and, for that purpose, to enlist a Government; ut minor arts of management were far beyond him, and he totally dis-ained the latest mode of popular conciliation. Canning had always aown a weakness for the Press; but the Duke was frankly hostile. aurnalists, in his experience, existed for the propagation of falsehoods; ad he asked helplessly, "What can we do with these sort of fellows? We ave no power over them, and, for my part, I will have no communica-an with any of them."

The voyage opened with a further sacrifice. Pressure was put on the ime Minister to resign the office of Commander-in-Chief, and he reluc-atly acceded. Work crowded on him; as he wrote grimly to an apolo-tic correspondent, "If you were to see the number of plans which I ceive every day upon every description of subject, all of which I am liged to peruse, you would admit there was no necessity for having y scruple about sending me your plan for diminishing the pay of the ny." Stray callers were occasionally informed a shade ungraciously by cer that the Prime Minister, having learnt the object of their unsuc-sful visit, did not regret not having seen them and must be acquitted, ver having heard of them, of any disrespect. But Creevey found him sing most rapidly in the market as a practical man of business. All the utations come away charmed with him. But woe to them that are too e! He is punctual to a second himself, and waits for no man." He nd little pleasure in his situation, writing to the Prince of Orange t he was involved in duties for which he was "not qualified, and they very disagreeable to me"; but he added in a more cheerful tone that Government was an unqualified success.

"There is in fact but little, if any, opposition to it. This state of things annot last, I know. But as the whole of the landed and great commercial ad monied interests of the country are decidedly with us, I hope that, if the existing state of tranquillity in this country should terminate, we shall remain still with a strong government.

"Your Royal Highness would scarcely recognise England again if you were now to come here. There is no party remaining. The ladies and the youth of the country in particular are with us, and I could almost count upon my fingers those who are hostile to the government."

This was a glowing picture. But though beauty smiled upon the Government, his colleagues did not always smile on one another. The Canningites were fretful from the first; groups of bereaved politicians attached to statesmen recently deceased are rarely enlivening companions. He was prepared to make concessions about Corn; but they found him unhelpful towards Greece. This was embarrassing, since Greek independence was prominent in the political testament of Mr. Canning; Wellington had assured the House of Lords that he must claim "the right of not being included in the number of Mr. Canning's enemies," and introduced a Bill pensioning his family. But it was more questionable how far the Duke could be regarded as Mr. Canning's intellectual heir, since he displayed a strong distaste for the Greek legacy. For Mr. Canning, they felt sure, would never have termed Navarino an "untoward event" in the King's Speech. The watchful Palmerston diagnosed strong and Russian leanings, which he was inclined to attribute to the Duke's p— encounters with the Lievens and some imagined slight at St. Petersburg; besides, the energetic Dorothea was unpopular with Lady Jersey and Mrs. Arbuthnot, the twin stars of the Duke's firmament. There we— endless Cabinets on Greece with "much discussion and entire difference of opinion." Spring turned to summer, and they continued uncomfortably "differing upon almost every question . . . meeting to debate and dispute, and separating without deciding." For the leaven of Mr. Canning's principles was having difficulty with the Tory lump. His followers grew still more restive. The Duke found them uneasy bedfellows, confessing to Arbuthnot that he regretted their inclusion, and complained of "the manner in which the *four* hang together" to Ellenborough, who confirmed his view with an unpleasing panorama of the Canningite revolt—Palmerston "always *pecking*," Grant "obstinate and useless," the innocuous Dudley incited to rebellion by the more active Huskisson. Huskisson was always trying; Lord Palmerston was bad enough—

exasperated Prime Minister had once termed him a mutineer; but Huskisson was quite unbearable. Persons who believe themselves possessed of an economic gospel are frequently distinguished by an offensive air of conscious superiority. Besides, he was the leader of the little group; and as the vicar of Mr. Canning upon earth he could scarcely hope to engage the Duke's affections.

Relief came from an unexpected quarter, as the long shadow of Reform fell across the scene. That rock was, to all appearances, one of the few on which the Cabinet was unlikely to split. For Mr. Canning had opposed Reform; the Duke was no Reformer; and, however they might disagree upon Corn, Portugal, and Greece, they might reasonably be expected to maintain a united front upon Reform. Indeed, the problem of Reform itself appeared to be in a fair way towards solution by simpler methods in the best English manner, since they were extremely practical and quite devoid of logic. Thorough-paced Reformers argued that the whole system of representation stood in need of drastic overhaul; but reasonable men, unwilling to admit the need, met it unobtrusively. For as the more outrageous boroughs disqualified themselves by electoral misdeeds, their members were inconspicuously transferred to the new industrial towns, a practical device which robbed Reformers of their grievance whilst enabling Tories to admire the incomparable outline of the existing constitution. In the spring of 1828 East Retford was available for redistribution, and the inheritance was disputed between industry and agriculture; for the Whigs wished to transfer its member to Birmingham, while Tory ministers preferred to add him to the county members. The matter was discussed in Cabinet, where Huskisson regarded himself as committed by a previous utterance to the Opposition view, and it appeared to be agreed to leave it as an open question. Accordingly (not without pressure from the enterprising Palmerston) he voted with the Opposition. That night, seized with a pardonable scruple after voting against his colleagues, Huskisson wrote to the Duke offering his resignation and expecting that the offer would be gracefully refused. But the Duke thought otherwise. Fine shades were never to his taste; and it was quite beyond him that there were degrees of resignation. If a gentleman resigned, Wellington assumed that he meant it. Besides, a resignation from Huskisson was too good to be overlooked. Marmont had once

exposed a flank to him at Salamanca; and now Huskisson had done th
same, and with similar results. For the Duke positively swooped.

After a decent interval he hurried to the King; and the startled Hus
kisson, expecting to be pressed to stay, received instead a curt intimatio
that the sovereign had been made aware of his intentions. There was
flutter among the Canningites. Lord Dudley saw the Duke, who wa
blandly unaware that there could be any mistake. Palmerston pursue
him to the House of Lords and had half an hour's conversation. The
paced up and down the Long Gallery, as Palmerston unfolded Huski
son's slightly involved apologia and Wellington stared at the groun
But the Duke insisted that the letter meant what it said; that Peel ha
thought the same; that this had been coming for some time; and th
such behaviour would soon bring him into as much discredit as Lo
Goderich. Besides, he could not go upon all fours to Mr. Huskisson ar
ask him to remain. (That was his ruling thought: if Canningites cho
to resign, why should the Duke prevent them?) Lord Palmerston w
still plying him with arguments; and when he intimated that he shou
feel bound to go out with Huskisson, the Duke raised his eyes, look
sharply at him, and resumed their walk. But they reached no conclusi

Then Palmerston returned to his colleague; and they concocted a s
ond letter to the Duke, endeavouring to make him responsible if Hus
son left office. A brief reply from Apsley House informed them tha
was better to lose Huskisson than to submit to the humiliation of begg
him to stay. For the Duke's *amour propre* was stirred. As he said af
wards, "I told Dudley and Palmerston that I had no objection, nay
wished, that they and Huskisson could get out of the scrape, but t
I begged on my own part to decline taking a roll in the mud with th
This was not a very elegant expression, but it was a sincere one."
imbroglio dragged on to an accompaniment of protracted explanati
But Wellington could not escape from his initial belief that a man n
be taken to mean what he said. There was no difference of princip
"There is not the idea of a principle in all these papers. . . . We he
great deal of Whig principles, and Tory principles, and Liberal princi
and Mr. Canning's principles; but I confess that I have never se
definition of any of them, and cannot make to myself a clear ide
what any of them mean." Political ideas were wholly irrelevant;

simple point was that Huskisson had providentially resigned, and the Duke meant to hold him to it.

He was victorious, although the victory gave him a little trouble; and in the middle of it all he had to dine at the Mansion House. A colleague found him looking "ill, and as if he had been annoyed; but he was quite in good spirits with his reception, *elated.*" He rather enjoyed the duel and was quite determined not to submit to Huskisson; as for Palmerston, he "did not choose to fire great guns at sparrows"; and, to Ellenborough's eye, he was "completely roused, and seems to feel as he did at Waterloo." In the last days of May silence descended on the field; the Canningites resigned; and *Endymion's* lovely mother heard a Tory hostess exclaim in triumph, "They are all four out. . . . The only mistake was ever to have admitted them. I think now we have got rid of Liberalism for ever." It was a sweeping forecast.

III

H is forces had begun to shrink. For the little group had been hi
Light Division, whose agility would have been of value if he de
sired to manœuvre towards the Left. Henceforward he was left wit
a residue of solid Tories, whose inclinations lay all towards the Righ
The Canningites were gone, each to his destiny—for Palmerston a dri
towards the Whigs, the Foreign Office, and a reign (nearly thirty yea
away) over Victorian England; for Lamb his father's coronet and th
unaccustomed exercise of Melbourne's endless conversations with
schoolgirl Queen; and for Huskisson the fatal locomotive. Their simu
taneous departure left the Duke undismayed. He was not sorry to h
rid of them. Their presence had endangered Cabinet discipline; and i
replacing them he took steps to remedy the defect. For two of the vaca
cies were filled by military men. Sir George Murray, a Peninsular vetera
went to the Colonial Office in succession to the fretful Huskisson; ar
Sir Henry Hardinge, who had been his *liaison* officer with Blücher, r
placed Lord Palmerston. The Prime Minister found the change co
genial, as his late Quartermaster-General was unlikely to waste valual
time in unnecessary disputation, though the Opposition found derisi
things to say about a "military and aide-de-campish" Government; ar
when a minister said that their minds were a blank sheet upon sor
question, a House of Commons wit remarked that it must be c
tridge-paper.

But their prestige was unimpaired. For there was no effective Op
sition; and the Duke exasperated Princess Lieven by saying, "I am t
most popular Minister that England has ever seen; take my word for
I am very strong." It was not like him to be boastful; but when he s
Dorothea, he seemed to harp upon his popularity. She was a soundi
board; and it was just as well for St. Petersburg to understand that W
lington was firmly seated in office. For his policy had a distinctly a
Russian flavour; and the Russians would be more respectful if t
realised that his reign was more than a passing episode of politics.

reigned securely now. His brother Henry, to whom he was unlikely to exaggerate, was informed that "we are going on well here. The government is very popular; and indeed there is but little opposition." His Chancellor found him an admirable man of business, and Aberdeen, the new Foreign Secretary, worked under his direction; "for almost every despatch of the following years there is a draft memorandum, preserved in Wellington's correspondence, and often embodied with just the necessary diplomatic wrappings from which his own peculiar telegraphic style was so refreshingly free." Foreign affairs were a shade trying, as he found the legacies of Canning's policy distinctly embarrassing. Russia was at war with Turkey in spite of all his efforts; the French were straining at the leash; and the territorial claims of Greece were growing every day. The Eastern Question had passed momentarily beyond control; and the Duke was limited by circumstances to a glum acquiescence in the inevitable. In Portugal he was compelled to witness the exact reverse of what Mr. Canning had intended. The Portuguese declined to rally to the constitution in defence of which Canning had struck his splendid attitude. For the British standard had been duly planted on the heights of Lisbon; but no one seemed to mind. This was a shade humiliating. Indeed, a flavour of humiliation seemed to infect foreign affairs, as the other ruffled birds of Mr. Canning's policy came home to roost. But Mr. Canning, *felix opportunitate mortis,* was not there to smooth them; and it was left to Wellington to put the best face upon a series of unpleasing situations.

His hands were full that summer, and his friends found him looking white and overworked. His days were arduous—the Treasury at noon, business till five, and then the House of Lords, followed by a dull dinner and more papers until bed. Even when he dined with Mrs. Arbuthnot, "poor fellow! the moment he had some coffee he sat down and read, and wrote papers till past twelve o'clock at night! I told him he would soon have no eyes left." But he got away to Cheltenham, when the House rose, and recuperated in those decorous alleys. He sipped his water every morning early and strolled in the Montpellier Gardens. Each afternoon he took his bath; this relaxation lasted an hour, and he mitigated its tedium with an armful of newspapers. (Always the White Knight, he had a frame put across the bath to support his paper, thus solving a

problem that has often baffled meaner intellects.) The summer passed;
and the autumn Cabinets came round with his autumn colds, though
Mrs. Arbuthnot found that he was "wonderfully improved by Cheltenham, has got a *brown*, healthy colour, and seems to have got his head and
stomach quite right"; and he was well enough to wing a keeper of
Lord Hertford's. They were still busy with the Eastern Question; and
William, Duke of Clarence, afforded occasional diversion by his vagaries
as Lord High Admiral. For this elderly eccentric, flown (as royal personages sometimes are) by a titular dignity, endangered naval discipline
by irregular exercises of authority. He was a royal duke and, what was
more, the next King of England; but Wellington had faced more formidable foes and checked him with such firmness that his future sove-
eign resigned. Indeed, he simultaneously refused a favour asked by the
Duchess of Kent, now Queen-mother presumptive, who was anxious to
instal Sir John Conroy in an Ordnance job. For Wellington was rarely
prone to seek royal smiles.

The Prime Minister drafted indefatigably on every subject; as Dorothea
Lieven bitterly observed, he was "the universal man." His pen was busy
with the problems of both hemispheres—with the next war in North
America, with the Persian Gulf (where Bagdad and Persia should, he
felt, be strengthened as outworks of India against Russian aggression),
with an offensive classical quotation by which a legal luminary had once
annoyed the King, with a fantastic allegation in *The Times* that he was
selling gunpowder to Russia, and the vast burden of a correspondence
affording him "the advantage which I possess in the proffered assistance
of nearly every gentleman in England, who has nothing to do but
amuse himself, and is tired of his usual amusements, and of reading
newspapers." The indomitable Haydon, in the thick of "Eucles arriving
with the news of Marathon," wrote asking leave to dedicate a pamphlet
upon State encouragement of the nobler forms of art, and received a
prompt refusal "in his own immortal hand." A more detailed proposal
for the embellishment of the House of Lords with scenes illustrative of
constitutional principles alternating with portraits of King Alfred, Bacon,
Nelson, and the Duke failed to excite him, since he responded with a
bare acknowledgment and left Haydon with a suspicion that he was
"innately modest." Haydon, quite undeterred, sent him a copy of

amphlet (duly acknowledged), and proposed a public grant of £4,000
r historical paintings. The Duke's attitude was highly unpromising;
r he first asked for details and, when he got them, objected that the
heme was not officially before him and that, in any case, he was opposed
o the grant of any public money for the object." He read everything
d wrote voluminously; even Marie Louise received a civil message
om the Duke condoling with her on the illness of Count Neipperg (her
st husband's death at St. Helena had caused him less concern); and, to
ake all things worse, his London house was full of workmen. For they
ere reconstructing Apsley House upon a more majestic scale; and in
e midst of the confusion the Duke's mind was busy with the Catholics.

The problem had been looming for a generation, ever since Mr. Pitt
l back defeated by the conscience of George III. That was a formidable
tress; and until it fell, the road to Catholic Emancipation was effectu-
y blocked. Time had removed it now. But, strange to record, the royal
nscience was inherited by George IV; and those rococo battlements still
rred the way. Would the Duke succeed where Pitt had failed? It was
t certain that he would make the attempt, since he had little taste for
perfluous reforms; though Creevey wrote at the very outset of his term
office that "my sincere opinion is—and I beg to record it thus early—
t the Beau *will* do something for the Catholics of Ireland." He knew
Beau; the Beau knew his Ireland; and if Catholic Emancipation be-
ne a practical necessity, he was quite capable of acting. The obstacles
re grave, since the royal conscience and the Tory faith were equally
posed to it. But could Wellington be seriously asked to respect the
uples of a king who fished all day at Virginia Water and came to
uncil meetings in a blue surtout covered with gold frogs in order to
hange racing tips with Greville behind a royal hand? If he did not
pect the royal person, he was unlikely to respect the royal scruples.
e Tories were a graver obstacle, since the Government had been
med upon an express understanding that "the Roman Catholic ques-
1 should be considered as one not to be brought forward by the
inet." But troops embarked for one objective had very frequently
n transferred to another; after all, he had begun the war in the Penin-
 (and won Vimeiro) with a force designed to operate in Venezuela.
 only doubt was how far his present command would be capable of

this manœuvre. The Tory mind was not adaptable; besides, there was the Tory past upon the Catholic question. But the last thing that the Duke thought of was his army's mind; they were not asked to have one; he did not invite the rank and file to make his plans; that was his duty. It might be awkward for them to have to contradict their former speeches; civilian politicians were apt to over-value consistency. But a retreat was sometimes the soundest strategy; he knew the value of a well-timed retreat; and if the situation called for one, they must abandon the position.

His mind was quickened by the events of 1828. The air was full of toleration. For the Whigs secured relief for Dissenters by the repeal of the Test and Corporation Acts. The Duke had little taste for Nonconformists; Methodist conventicles in the Peninsula had evoked the slightly grudging comment that "the meeting of soldiers in their cantonments to sing psalms, or to hear a sermon read by one of their comrades is, in the abstract, perfectly innocent." But when the House of Commons chose to emancipate them, he urged the Lords to concur, though his mind was still adverse to the Catholic claims. That was in April. Events moved swiftly in the summer, since the House of Commons positively carried a motion in favour of Catholic Emancipation by six votes, and an Irish by-election resulted in the impressive march of regimented voters headed by their parish priests to return a Catholic for County Clare. O'Connell, though ineligible, was elected; and the Catholic claims became an urgent problem, if Ireland was to be governed. Wellington spoke on the question in June. His tone was guarded, and his sympathies were carefully extended to both sides. Disclaiming all doctrinal objections, he proclaimed the issue "to be a question entirely of expediency," an intimation with which politicians frequently preface a change of front. He concentrated on the practical difficulties of devising a *Concordat*, and hinted that something might be managed, if only an arrangement could be found whereby "the King shall have the power to control the appointment of the hierarchy, and their intercourse with the See of Rome, and which shall connect the Roman Catholic Church in Ireland with the Government." His peroration was a *staccato* plea for calm reflection:

"If the public mind was suffered to rest; if the agitators of Ireland would only be quiet; if the difficulties of this question were not aggravated these perpetual discussions; and if men could have time to reflect upon the state of this question, they might become more satisfied, and it might then become more possible to discover the means of doing something."

So Mr. Creevey had been right. The Beau was perfectly prepared to do something for the Catholics, if only they would let him alone. It was a conversion as momentous (and far swifter in its consequences) than Mr. Gladstone's to Home Rule.

In August he approached the King for leave "to take into consideration the whole case of Ireland, with a view to the adoption of some measure to be proposed to Parliament for the pacification of that country." He faced the facts in his plain fashion:

"The influence and the powers of Government in that country are no longer in the hands of the officers of the government, but have been usurped by the demagogues of the Roman Catholic Association; who, acting through the influence of the Roman Catholic clergy, direct the country as they think proper. . . .

"We have a rebellion impending over us in Ireland . . . and we have in England a Parliament which we cannot dissolve, the majority of which is of opinion, with many wise and able men, that the remedy is to be found in Roman Catholic emancipation, and they would unwillingly enter into the contest without making such an endeavour to pacify the country."

That was his notion. If the citadel of public order was to be defended, the advanced position from which Eldonian Tories still defied the Catholics must be abandoned. Peel had reached the same conclusion, although he felt compelled by his own record as an uncompromising Protestant to warn the Duke "that it would not conduce to the satisfactory adjustment of the question, that the charge of it in the House of Commons should be committed to my hands." A reluctant convert, he proposed to announce his own conversion and resign. The Duke wrestled stoutly with his scruples. He had lost his Light Division, when the Canningites resigned; in all probability his next step would cost him a brigade of Tories; Peel was his chief ally; and his ally must be retained at all costs. But his next objective was the royal conscience; and all through the autumn his guns played upon that flimsy fortress. His policy was formulated in detail, though he still maintained silence in public; for secrecy must be maintained on the eve of a retreat. He proposed to enfranchise the Catholics and admit them to public life in exchange for a few formal safeguards and the dissolution of their Association. A hint of his intentions crept into a letter, which startled a Catholic correspondent with an intimation that if the question could be sunk "in oblivion for a short time . . . I should not despair of seeing a satisfactory remedy," though he still professed to "see no prospect of such a settlement." Such Delphic utterances brought indignant charges of duplicity from angry Protestants when the mine was fired in the next year; and Wellington was afterwards reduced to a blunt admission in debate that his letter "had been better let alone. Indeed, I shall take care not to write such a letter again to such an individual." But could he help himself? He was not yet authorised to formulate—much less to announce—a policy; and until the King released him, he was bound to work on in silence.

A new year opened; and in the first days of 1829 the Duke was busy sounding Bishops, coaxing Peel, and managing the King. He was successful in persuading Peel not to abandon the ship in heavy weather. But if persuasion was a new art to him, George IV gave him ample opportunities for learning it. The Duke's system was simplicity itself—"make it a rule never to interrupt him, and when in this way he tries to get rid of a subject in the way of business which he does not like, I let him talk himself out, and then quietly put before him the matter in question, so that he cannot escape from it." For George IV, no more amenable than Burgos to surprise attacks, required a siege *en règle*; and the Duke laid siege to him with infinite patience. His parallels crept slowly towards the doomed fortress; and one by one the royal outworks fell, until the last remnant of the King's conscience sought refuge in the citadel itself. It was Ciudad Rodrigo over again; for the unhappy King, whose favourite delusion was that he had fought in Spain, at least enjoyed the rare distinction of a siege by Wellington. His pressure was relentless. In January he broke down the embargo on Cabinet consideration of the problem. That month the King assented gloomily—"Damn you mean to let them into Parliament?"—to a plain announcement of Catholic Emancipation in the Speech from the Throne; and in February the murder was out. The Whigs, robbed of their leading grievance, were sulky; for the Duke had outmanœuvred them by falling back from

382

untenable position. But his Tory forces had little relish for the manœuvre. He spoke almost nightly in the House of Lords; and though a derisive Whig conjectured that his utterances could be summarised as "My Lords! Attention! Right about face! Quick march!" he grew positively persuasive. It was a new experience for him; there had been no need to persuade his army to fall back to Torres Vedras; but the Tories were more troublesome, and even Mrs. Arbuthnot shewed signs of mutiny. The storm broke in March. Peel, who had honourably resigned his seat at Oxford, was defeated by wild clergymen; the King was breathing treason to his circle; but Wellington persisted grimly. As he told Arbuthnot, "I have undertaken this business, and I am determined to go through with it. . . . I will succeed, but I am as in a field of battle, and I must fight it out in my own way." His royal master whimpered about abdication, though the audience was ended by a royal kiss (not, one feels, the least distasteful of the Duke's official duties). But a final plunge of his galled charger almost unseated him. For the King, positively frantic with Protestant apprehension, refused the final jump. He had been drinking brandy and water, when the Duke arrived with Peel and Lyndhurst. Their audience was painful, as the King talked for six hours. At intervals he took more brandy; at intervals they made an interjection. But the racing stream of royal indignation poured over their attentive heads. He should postpone the Bill—the Bishops must advise him—besides, there was his oath. He was not sure precisely what it was; but he had taken one; and so the Bill must go. They intimated that the Government went with it. But the interminable harangue proceeded with an uncomfortable echo of the dreadful garrulity which had marked the onset of his father's madness. The Duke was quite convinced that he was mad; he hated to be cruel to a monarch in distress; but resignation was the only course that might restore the royal senses. So they resigned. Three rigid backs were turned on Windsor, and three gentlemen returned to London. The cure was efficacious, as a prompt recantation followed them, with the affecting postscript, "God knows what pain it costs me to write these words. G.R." The careful Premier extracted a more specific statement of the royal approval, and the King complied. The long siege was over; and the Duke's flag fluttered on the captured citadel.

It remained to pass the Bill. The King would march with him; but

could he discipline the Tory peers into a wise retreat? His own authority
was sadly shaken by the violence of Protestant attacks—"If my physician
called upon me, it was for treasonable purposes. If I said a word whether
in Parliament or elsewhere, it was misrepresented for the purpose of fixing upon me some gross delusion or falsehood." In fine, there was a
distinct danger that the Duke himself would be discredited; and if his
name lost its magic, who would remain to give orders to a distracted
nation? Something must be done in order to restore his credit; and in
his sober way he made up his mind to do it. Among the most vociferous
of his opponents was Lord Winchilsea, an unimportant peer distinguished
by a loud voice, a mannerism of flourishing a large white handkerchief
when making speeches, and the *abandon* of his Protestant invective. This
zealot in an ecstasy of indignation composed a letter to the Press, in
which he charged the Duke with a mean subterfuge contrived in order
that he "might the more effectually, under the cloak of some outward
show of zeal for the Protestant religion, carry on his insidious design
for the infringement of our liberties, and the introduction of Popery in
every department of the State." This was too much. He had resolved to
make an example, and Lord Winchilsea would serve. The imputation of
dishonest motives must be stopped—if necessary, by a challenge. Duelling
was never to his taste; he had discountenanced it strongly in the Peninsula, since he disapproved of officers on active service running unnecessary
risks in private quarrels. He was on active service now; but he reflected
with complete detachment that a quarrel with Lord Winchilsea would
serve a public end, since it might dispel the prevailing "atmosphere of
calumny" and restore his personal authority. Then the Prime Minister
proceeded to pick his quarrel. Lord Winchilsea was asked in a curt note
if he was the author of the offending letter. When he admitted it, the
Duke demanded an apology. The Secretary at War acted for him, thus
demonstrating the utility of staff officers in a Government, when the
Prime Minister proposes to indulge in affairs of honour. The correspondence followed its appointed course: stiff gentlemen waited on one another; solemn memoranda were drawn up; the Duke demanded "that
satisfaction . . . which a gentleman has a right to require, and which
a gentleman never refuses to give"; and in the mist of a March morning
he rode out to Battersea. The Duke was punctual, and his opponent kept

him waiting. A round-eyed doctor, fetched early out of bed, recognised his formidable patient, who cheerfully remarked, "Well, I dare say you little expected it was I who wanted you to be here." Then they rode up and down till Winchilsea arrived; and the little party—four gentlemen, a doctor, and a case of pistols—proceeded on foot to a quiet corner. The Duke turned to his second.

"Now then, Hardinge, look sharp and step out the ground. I have no time to waste. Damn it! don't stick him up so near the ditch. If I hit him, he will tumble in."

There was a pause. The seconds had a final conference; and the Duke waited with a smile. Then Hardinge handed him a pistol. He had been wondering all the morning whether to shoot his man. It would be awkward if he killed him; he supposed he would have to go to prison until he could be tried; so he resolved to shoot him in the leg. A steady voice said "Fire"; and the Duke raised his pistol. But Winchilsea's was still pointing at the ground. The Duke paused for an instant, fired, and hit his coat. Then Winchilsea fired in the air. His second flourished a paper, which contained a withdrawal of the offensive charge. The Duke listened carefully. "This won't do," he said, "it is no apology." Then someone pencilled in the mystic word; the Duke distributed a chilly bow to each of his adversaries, lifted two fingers to his hat, and rode away. He went straight to Mrs. Arbuthnot's; walked in upon her at breakfast, and startled her by asking what she thought of a gentleman who had been fighting a duel; and later in the day he told the King at Windsor. "I have another subject," he remarked, "to mention to your Majesty, personal to myself. I have been fighting a duel this morning." His sovereign graciously replied that he was glad of it. That mirror of deportment told someone that he was delighted with the Duke's conduct, that gentlemen must not stand upon their privileges, and that he would have done the same himself (and malice added that he would soon believe he had). But it elicited a wail of horror from Jeremy Bentham, who favoured Wellington with a strange effusion beginning "Ill-advised Man!" dwelling in gratifying terms on the disastrous consequences of his removal from public life, and bleakly endorsed by the recipient, "Compliments. The Duke has received his letter." This prompt reply stirred Bentham's gratitude, and evoked further warnings against the perils of assassination, with slightly rambling reminiscences of Aaron Burr, John Wilkes, and Nelson's signal at Trafalgar.

The duel served its purpose. His motives were unquestioned now: "the system of calumny was discontinued. Men were ashamed of repeating what had been told to them. . . . I am afraid that the event itself shocked many good men. But I am certain that the public interests at the moment required I should do what I did." The House of Lords resumed the Bill; and he argued manfully. They listened, and a respectful House heard Wellington warn the extremists:

> "I am one of those who have probably passed a longer period of my life engaged in war than most men, and principally in civil war; and I must say this, that if I could avoid, by any sacrifice whatever, even one month of civil war in the country to which I was attached, I would sacrifice my life in order to do it. . . ."

This was far more impressive than all his laboured disquisitions on the Bill of Rights, the House of Stuart, and the *Concordat* of Rhenish Prussia. But he debated endlessly against the sullen legions of outraged Protestantism, until the Bill passed its final stage. Then he allowed himself a modest *Te Deum* in the House of Lords.

It was thirty-six years since Captain Wesley in a maiden speech counselled the Irish House of Commons to use the Catholics with moderation. The encyclopædic Croker disinterred the speech; but the Duke had quite forgotten it. For he was always more anxious to be right than to be consistent; though in the present case he happened to be both.

IV

THE campaign of Catholic Emancipation was over. Its strategy—
the swift recognition that Ireland had become ungovernable, the
abandonment of an untenable position, and the bold retreat—was eminently characteristic; and it had ended, as the Duke's campaigns were
apt to end, in victory. Wellington had never failed. Indeed, he was almost
coming to believe in his own luck; for one day when Croker called, the
Duke cheerfully remarked, "Yes, 'tis all my good luck, my Fortunatus's
cap," lifting a finger to the small red Cossack cap that he wore indoors
in cold weather. Where Pitt had failed, where Canning had not even
summoned up courage for an attempt, Wellington had achieved success.
The Whigs were dished; the House of Lords was silenced; and the King
had been outflanked. The siege of Windsor was, perhaps, the most
brilliant of Wellington's campaigns; for the victory was single-handed.
His personal authority had been his only weapon; and when the fortress
of the King's elusive conscience fell, it capitulated to one besieger. Small
wonder that his sovereign remarked sulkily that "Arthur is King of
England, O'Connell King of Ireland, and myself Canon of Windsor."
The teasing Guelph had done his best to irritate King George against the
Duke by terming him "King Arthur"; and there was something in the
accusation. For in his lonely mastery of King and Lords the Duke of
Wellington came near to being a fourth estate of the realm in his own
person.

Successful in its outcome, his Catholic campaign had been less satisfactory in its effect upon his followers. For discipline is always strained
in a retreat; and the Tory squadrons had found the retreat anything but
enjoyable. Mobility was not their *forte*; designed by nature for the fixed
defence of suitable positions, they were as unhandy as fortress artillery
in a sudden evacuation; and it was not surprising that some of the
heavier pieces had been left behind in the Duke's swift retreat. This was
distinctly awkward. Guns can be spiked; but it is not so easy to silence
politicians; and there was an uncomfortable possibility that some of

his Tory artillery, fallen into the enemy's hands, would be turned agai
his lines. For High Tories were now leagued with Whigs in Oppositic
The Duke's apostasy had roused them to excesses of bitterness; duri
the debates some humorist imported a rat into the House of Lords; a
the Duchess of Richmond adorned her drawing-room with an arr
of stuffed rats under glass labelled with the names of leading Protesta
apostates. In such a mood there was not much prospect of Tory uni
and the Duke's Parliamentary forces were sadly diminished. He h
already lost the Canningites; the solid Tories were departing no
there was still Peel, of course. Peel was an invaluable ally. But with
Light Division gone and his main body wavering, could the Duke ho
to win the war with the Portuguese?

Precarious in Parliament, the Duke's position was not greatly streng
ened in the country. Peel's adherence was an indication that Welli
ton was allied with the new forces of industrial progress. But the
liance had not yet borne fruit in progressive legislation. Besides,
main achievement was scarcely of a nature to evoke English gratitu
He had emancipated the Catholics, and grateful Irishmen passed glowi
resolutions; O'Connell himself sat with a Catholic committee to ra
funds and decorate the Phœnix Park with a towering Wellington Te
monial. But Irish gratitude is an uncertain passport to British affectic
Few statesmen have survived after rendering a service to Ireland. 1
bare attempt cost Mr. Gladstone his career, and subsequently an
powerful dictator fell from the summit of his Coalition within a y
of making peace in Ireland. It would almost seem that acts of just
towards Ireland must be their own reward; for English politics h
no other.

2

He was just sixty now, a trim frock-coated figure with a h
growing frosty and the profile that political cartoonists loved to dr
Coloured or plain, his eye was always sharp; the splendid hatchet
his nose was etched upon the background; and his tight-lipped sr
was visible in whatever disguise the caricaturist's fancy had suggeste
a mute's, a rat-catcher's, an Egyptian mummy's, or the sporting hat

multitudinous capes of *The Man wot drives the Sovereign.* The gentler
pencil of H. B. began its work with him that year; and the Duke, always
recognisable, took the centre of the political stage. Even the grateful
Edinburgh exclaimed "A greater than Cæsar is here, one who has not
destroyed in peace the country he had saved by his sword."

The effort had been great. He had endured torrents of abuse, and
done more public speaking on the Relief Bill than in the previous twenty
years of his life. Abuse was a small matter; but he found oratory an
uncongenial exercise and derived little pleasure from addressing the
House of Lords with a bad cold, to sink back into his seat and wrap
his cloak tightly round him. It was some satisfaction to compose a lengthy
memorandum on army discipline and to confront reformers with the
grim apophthegm, "I know the British army, and I dare not." The old
martinet had "always considered this desire to alter the system of
discipline of the army as one of the morbid symptoms of the times. It
is like the notion that thieves ought not to be punished . . ."; and his
conviction, that "the man who enlists into the British army is, in general,
the most drunken and probably the worst man of the trade or profession
to which he belongs, or of the village or town in which he lives," still
burned as brightly as though Badajoz had been sacked a week before.
But his real pride in the army appeared when he informed a correspondent that "its conduct in the field is unrivalled. Its officers are
gentlemen, and moreover the gentlemen of England. . . ." His military
duties cost him a fall that summer, when his horse threw him at a
review in the Park. He was unhurt; and as he rode off the ground,
they cheered him to the echo, crowding round to shake his hand. The
ubiquitous Creevey met him the same afternoon riding down a side
street in the West End, and congratulated him upon his Irish achievement.

"You must have had tough work," said the pert little Whig, "to get
it."

"Oh, terrible, I assure you," replied the unruffled Duke, and rode off
down the street.

He could return to business now; and, in all conscience, there was
quite enough of it, with Ireland and the Russo-Turkish war and currency and Portugal and the London traffic problem. It was a relief for

him to manage a Civil List pension for Miss Ponsonby, the Lady
Llangollen and his mother's friend; for he was capable of a friendly j₀
at need. Indeed, he took endless trouble to do something for Georg
Brummell. That exquisite, a stranger to the Duke, was languishing
Calais; and Wellington had done his best to provide him with a po
in the consular service. But his Foreign Secretaries were uniform
unhelpful; Dudley objected that the King would not like it; the Du
appealed to Cæsar, who remarked without sympathy that Brumm
was a damned fellow and had behaved very ill to him; but Wellingt
persisted, and his sovereign acquiesced. Then Dudley was obstructive; a
after him Aberdeen was nervous, until the Duke assured him that
would take full responsibility. So, thanks to Wellington, George Bru
mell got his post, though with a final gesture of dandyism he sub
quently recommended that it should be suppressed as a sinecure.

He went his autumn rounds among the country houses, and someo
engineered a meeting with Huskisson at Lord Hertford's. Would he ta
back the Canningites? That was an intriguing question. There was so
evidence besides that the Whigs themselves might join his forces; a
Arbuthnot, his intelligence officer, was out taking soundings. But,
the moment, he continued with his force of Tories, though the appoi
ment of a Whig as Privy Seal indicated that he was prepared for
manœuvre towards the Left. No party man, the Duke had stro
prejudices in favour of a national administration. Indeed, his Cathc
policy had been undertaken with the sole object of uniting all part
in support of firm government in Ireland. But politicians were unreas
able, and he found the King more trying than ever. The royal intell
was busy with alterations in the Guards' uniform; deep in the myster
of tailoring, George held a daily review of pattern coats. His mind
full of collars; but it was not too full to make difficulties for the Pri
Minister. The Duke retained his confidence that "nobody can man
him but me," though once a bitter cry escaped him:

"If I had known in January 1828 one tithe of what I do now, and
what I discovered in one month after I was in office, I should have n
been the King's minister, and should have avoided loads of misery! H
ever, I trust that God Almighty will soon determine that I have been
ficiently punished for my sins, and will relieve me from the unhappy

which has befallen me! I believe there never was a man suffered so much; and for so little purpose!"

The mood, which was unlike him, passed; but whilst it lasted, he found less pleasure in his public duties than in going to the play to see Fanny Kemble as *Juliet*. Foreign affairs were uninviting, since Canning's gay commitments had destroyed in advance the positions from which he might have made some resistance to the advancing tide of Russia; as he wrote ruefully, "Mr. Canning and Madame de Lieven have much to answer for!" His mood was irritable, and his Greek policy was little more than a bad-tempered rearguard action; though a sudden gleam from Mr. Canning illumined him when a hint of a French monarchy in Colombia elicited from Wellington an unexpected echo of the Monroe Doctrine, with a sardonic reservation in favour of the exportation of the Duke of Cumberland. His diplomacy was firmly based upon the principle of non-intervention, by which (unlike its other exponents) he meant what he said, and not—in Talleyrand's malicious phrase— "*un mot métaphysique et politique qui signifie à peu près la même chose qu'intervention.*" So the Duke kept the peace of Europe; and as the year went out, the world passed into 1830.

3

The year 1830 opened uneventfully. The calendars announced a new decade; but calendars were often wrong. The world, to all appearances, was very much what it had been since Waterloo. Canning and Castlereagh were gone; but the Duke and Metternich remained. Europe was still a symphony in white—in France a white ground sprinkled with the lilies of the Most Christian King; in Russia the white silence, mile after mile, where the Czar reigned behind the winter mists; in Italy the white gleam of Austrian uniforms, as Uhlans jingled by and *Kaiserlicks* hummed airs from Schubert. England was chilled that winter; and as it moved, the Duke sat answering his letters. Because he answered them at country houses, there was unkind comment about "gadding about, visiting, and shooting while the country is in difficulty, and it is argued that he must be very unfeeling and indifferent to it all to amuse himself in this manner." But Greville, who noted it, termed the impression "most

false and unjust," allowing that Wellington needed a little relaxation
and that, "all things considered, it is not extraordinary he should prefer
other people's houses to his own." Besides, he never missed his work
opening every letter and answering them all himself. The miscellany was
amazing—currency, a king for Greece, screw steamers, agricultural di
tress, West Indians complaining that they could no longer supply run
to the United States, French designs on Algiers, low wages at Birming
ham (with a sample bag of assorted hardware), and a proposal th
Buckinghamshire lace should be made compulsory at Court, eliciting th
grim reply that "if the use of lace is the fashion it will be worn wheth
the King orders the use of it or not. If it is not the fashion it will not I
worn, though the King might order the use of it." He seemed to ha
an eye for everything—even for the exasperating swarm of invento
"who speculate upon inventing plans and projects for government wh
they have nothing else to do. There are thousands of them at present
England; as well as I believe elsewhere; the offspring of the march
intellect. Their object is money; which, please God, they shall not
from the Public Treasury."

The King's health was failing now; and party politics were in
extricable confusion. For the Duke had split the Tories; the Wh
were split already; and the Canningites hung impartially on the fla
of either army. Bewildered groups steered intersecting courses in
endless saraband, and the Duke might have his choice of partners
the Parliamentary dance. He could recall the Canningites; but Huskis
was a distasteful colleague. Or he might beckon to Lord Grey
strengthen his depleted ranks with a Whig reinforcement. But he gues
that "all these parties prefer the Government to any other," and made
sign. For, if the truth were known, he was not greatly interested
colleagues. His Catholic campaign had shewn him that he could n
age the House of Lords; and he was quite content to leave the C
mons to Peel. The Government's position there was frankly precari
since Peel's majority depended upon casual support; and a der
Opposition said scornful things about "a good weak Government."
what risk was there in an unguarded flank in the absence of any en
strong enough to take advantage of it? That spring they were defe
twice on unimportant questions, of which a Jews' Relief Bill

...oked Wellington to write that "this Christian community will not ...uch like to have Jewish magistrates and rulers. . . . It besides gives ...false colouring, and throws ridicule upon the great measures of 1828 ...nd 1829, which it resembles only in name." For he was no friend of ...mancipation for its own sake. He had been perfectly prepared to ...nancipate the Catholics in order to ensure strong government in Ire- ...nd; but Jews were quite another matter.

Spring turned to summer; and the King, "very nervous but very brave," ...as dying by inches. Once he called for the *Racing Calendar*, and almost ...the last he talked of horses. The Duke was often at his bedside; and ...e prospect of a new sovereign filled him with misgivings, since King ...illiam would probably suggest that they should take in Lord Grey. But ...ellington was not inclined to admit him as a colleague—"I would ...initely prefer that he should be at the head of the Government to ...onging to a Government of which he was a member." For he had ...le taste for Coalitions. He would not find it more congenial to sit ...Cabinet with the Canningites. So it was probable that Whigs, Radicals, ...l Canningites would unite in Opposition under Grey. What would ...ppen then? The House of Commons would plainly be the main theatre ...war; and the Duke and Peel "must look not to what is personal to ...selves, but what is necessary for the King's service, and we must ...ke sacrifices to provide for its security. I have long been of opinion ...it it is desirable that the power of the government should be con- ...rated in one hand, and that hand that of the leader of the House of ...mons." So he pressed Peel to take his place, and offered to serve ...er him. Such abnegation was uncommon; but nothing came of it.

...King died in June—"poor Prinney," as Creevey wrote, "is really ...d"—and the Duke saw a faded ribbon round his neck tied to a ...ature. The portrait was a woman's, and he recognised Mrs. Fitz- ...ert.

...e world was changing now; and he watched King William with ... apprehension, as he launched into a little speech at his accession ...cil. But it turned out to be nothing worse than a becoming epitaph ...his brother. The Duke breathed again. Perhaps his new master ...d prove more reasonable than his antecedents gave any grounds to ...The streets, at any rate, were still for Wellington, since he was

"much cheered by the people"; and King William seemed to share thei
views. For the Duke told Greville that he found him both reasonabl
and tractable, and that he could do more business with him in te
minutes than with George IV in ten days. He had his weaknesses, (
course. For it was highly disturbing to receive twelve hours' notice tha
the King proposed to bring the King and Queen of Wurtemberg
dine at Apsley House. And the festivity itself was more disturbing sti
The royal guests were late, to start with; but, once at Apsley Hous
King William threw himself into the entertainment with terrifying ze
For an unsuspected appetite for after-dinner speaking developed und
the Duke's hospitality. The least felicitous of his allusions was a wan
panegyric on the married virtues, highly flattering to the Queen
Wurtemberg but inappropriate to Wellington. Then he desired the ba
to play, *See the conquering hero comes*, and addressed himself to
embarrassed host. The theme inspired him. He spoke of Marlborou
Queen Anne, Vimeiro, and the defeated French; then, with a sudd
memory that the French ambassador was present he argued w
creditable ingenuity that the Duke's victories were not over the arm
of his ally and friend, the King of France, but over those of a usurp
Refreshed by this excess of royal tact (quite wasted on the French a
bassador, who did not know a word of English and was restrai
with difficulty from bowing his acknowledgments), he returned to
main theme, spoke once more of Marlborough, and closed with
expansive vote of royal confidence in the present administration, wh
had been, he thought, and would be highly beneficial to the country,
should retain his confidence as long as he was on the throne. S
tributes were unusual from such a quarter; and the Duke's reply
brief. A startled company dispersed to set the clubs buzzing with
story. Happy the nation with an impromptu speaker for its king;
less happy its Prime Minister.

Things might have been far worse, though. For the eccentric mon
gave no sign of Whig opinions, and the Duke was left undistu
in office. But his Parliamentary weakness persisted; and before
summer ended, he signalled to the Canningites for reinforcem
Lord Melbourne was approached, and intimated that he could
join without Grey and Huckisson. This was too much for Wellin

uskisson might be endured, but he declined to swallow Grey. So there
ere no Canningite recruits. A demise of the Crown involved a General
ection, and he faced the contest with undiminished confidence. His
am was weak enough (even Greville wrote contemptuously of "the
uke's awkard squad"); but the issues were unexciting. For it was
probable that feelings would run high upon economy and slavery.
e contest opened quietly; but as it proceeded, a long shadow fell
ross the hustings. For strange news began to come from France. The
ris streets had risen in the last days of July; the troops were helpless;
armont tasted the flavour of defeat once more; and Charles X was
to England. This was revolution. All its familiar badges reappeared
he National Guard, M. de La Fayette, and the tricolour. Was 1830
revisit the familiar scenes of 1789? One thing was certain: the world
s changing fast.

4

he Duke still went about his business in a changing world. He
ognised the change, writing quietly to the Prince of Orange that
will be scarcely possible that we can all feel the same confidence
he duration of peace hereafter, as we have done heretofore from the
r 1815 up to the 25th of last month." The age of Waterloo was ending;
he kept his head. The last revolution in Paris had cost Europe
nty years of war. But Wellington had no wish to see another. A
d from him might have set armies on the move from Poland to the
ne. Louis Philippe had made his revolution; and Europe, if its
ers chose, might oblige him with his Valmy, his campaign of
nce, his Waterloo. The Duke need only raise a finger. Metternich
ld not be unwilling; for Metternich lived in the age of Waterloo.
Wellington, oddly enough, had quite outlived it.

or his main desire was to preserve the peace of Europe, and he
prepared to do so at any reasonable cost. The chastisement of
ace, which had once been his leading accomplishment, had no
ctions for him now. In consequence the Duke was rigidly opposed
tervention, informing Greville that "we should not take any part,
that no other Government ought or could." There must be no war;

he wrote to Aberdeen that "there are some bitter pills to swallow. .
However, the best chance of peace is to swallow them all." For he w
disinclined to treat the settlement of 1815 as sacrosanct, concluding th
"good policy requires that we should recognize the Duc d'Orléans
King at an early period." Few men are reconciled so easily to the d
truction of their own handiwork; and his self-control endured a furth
strain in August, when a Brussels mob streamed out of a theatre a
rioted against the Dutch connection. For the waves of revolutie
spreading beyond France, threatened the counter-revolutionary dyl
erected in 1815. If anything was the Duke's own creation, it was t
Kingdom of the Netherlands, the child of Waterloo. Its armies h
served under him; its Barrier fortresses along the French frontier h
been his own peculiar charge; and now its southern province was
insurrection. There was every temptation to rush to the rescue. I
the Duke resisted it. For his belief in peace was still stronger than
belief in the peace-treaties of Vienna.

Europe was changing round him, and he kept his head. But
change in Europe found an uncomfortable echo nearer home. Engla
was polling in those summer weeks; and as the news came in fr
France, the tone of the elections changed. There was a sudden se
that the old order was passing away; Reform, of which little had b
heard in the opening phases, became a leading issue; and Palmers
wrote gleefully that "this event is decisive of the ascendancy of Lib
Principles throughout Europe. . . . The reign of Metternich over
the days of the Duke's policy might be measured by algebra, if no
arithmetic." Besides, there was an odd belief that Wellington was sc
how identified with the fallen Polignac, whose crude efforts at read
had provoked the July Revolution. Progressive persons whispered
the Duke had caused Charles X to appoint him, and had even wr
to prescribe the due reactionary lines which he should follow. But (
doubted the story; Wellington told Lady Jersey that he had not wr
to King Charles since his accession; and his denial in a letter to A
was explicit.

"Por lo que toca á mi nombramiento del ministerio de Polignac, creo
no está en Europa hombre político que tiene ménos que yo á decir
asunto. Jamas me habló Polignac sobre sus intenciones. Jamas le he es

*ni al Rey, despues del nascimiento del Duque de Bordeaux, ni al Duque
d'Angoulême; ni he comunicado can ninguno en Francia sobre las cosas
internas."*

⟶is was plain enough; but an untrue belief is frequently as influential
the truth itself. Besides, the fact remained that a Paris mob had chal-
⟶ged law and order with undeniable success and reversed the im-
⟶table decrees of 1815. The Duke was the embodiment of law and
⟶ler; he was 1815 incarnate; and if these things could be done in
⟶nce, why not in England?

⟶The fall of Polignac was promptly echoed beyond the Channel in an
⟶leasing change of temper. The impassive Place recorded that "the
⟶ression the events in Paris made on even the least intelligent of the
⟶ple was such as will never either be effaced or to any extent forgotten
⟶them"; an *Edinburgh* reviewer cried that "the battle of English
⟶rty has really been fought and won at Paris"; Cobbett was in *staccato*
⟶ures; and Brougham thundered before Yorkshire crowds. If 1830 was
⟶e a year of revolutions, English Radicals would not be left behind;
⟶the Whigs followed at a more becoming pace. For the near pros-
⟶of office had its customary effect on a divided Opposition, and the
⟶g party was reforming its disunited ranks. The skies began to
⟶en, and the gloomy Eldon predicted "a storm for changes here,
⟶ially for Reform in Parliament." If there was to be an English
⟶lution, that was its most likely theme.

⟶form was looming nearer now. Detained for years upon the fringe
⟶litics, it had been a topic for occasional declamations by Parlia-
⟶ary faddists and a dangerous toy for Radicals to play with. But in
⟶it took the centre of the stage, and every candidate who had a
⟶constituency was forced to talk Reform. How would the Duke
⟶d it? Canning had opposed Reform: that was one thing in its
⟶r. But Wellington was hardly likely to tamper with the consti-
⟶. Democracy, even in the comparatively blameless form of a pro-
⟶to enfranchise the middle class, was not to his taste. He had small
⟶ct for elected persons, and was not greatly interested in the con-
⟶ncies by which they might be elected. He had seen Parliamentary
⟶cracy at close range in Cadiz; and the example of Spain was not

encouraging. For her colonies had gone, and he was inclined to think th
"no country in what is now called a modern constitutional state can ke
a dependency." This was unpromising for England. Besides, the tim
were scarcely propitious for constitutional experiments, with open revo
tion in the streets of Paris and Brussels in a heady uproar. Indeed, t
troubles on the Continent hardened his inclination to resist Reform a
induced a fatal mood of complacency. For in a document suspiciou
resembling a draft for a newspaper article he painted an unpleasing p
ture of events abroad, concluding that these facts, "if viewed in th
true light, will give the people of this country fresh reason every day
be satisfied with their own institutions." This comfortable temper v
unfriendly to Reform; and an ugly stir among the agricultural labour
sent him still further to the Right. For there was rioting that autumn
sixteen counties; the invisible "Captain Swing" summoned his ru
followers; the Oldham colliers were out; and the new cotton towns w
seething. Was it a moment for concessions? The Duke thought r
Misled by Catholic Emancipation, his critics have enquired why
did not concede Reform. But he never made concessions for their o
sake. Catholic Relief had been undertaken in order to unite respons
opinion in support of strong government in Ireland. His whole admi
tration was a campaign in defence of social order; and the concess
to the Catholics had been no more than a deft withdrawal to a stror
position in rear. But if his troops fell back before Reform and admi
democracy to Parliament, what would remain? There was no furt
retreat possible, and he resolved to hold his ground. For 1829 had b
his Busaco. Now he had reached Torres Vedras. The sea was at
back; and he must stand to fight.

He took his own decision in his own solitary fashion. There were
Cabinets upon Reform, and Peel was not consulted. Peel, indeed,
understood to complain that the Prime Minister was never influer
by men—only by women, and those invariably silly. The Duke's
camarilla, whom Greville impolitely termed "the women and the t
eaters," were not Reformers; and no influences checked his drift tow
the Right. His mind was thoroughly made up, and a later letter
colleague shews how impossible it was for him to repeat the bril
manœuvre of Catholic Emancipation:

"I have not leisure to discuss Parliamentary Reform either in writing or in conversation. I confess that I doubt whether it will be carried in Parliament.

"If it should be carried it must occasion a total change in the whole system of that society called the British Empire; and I don't see how I could be a party to such changes, entertaining the opinions that I do.

"To tell you the truth I must add that I feel no strength excepting in my character for plain manly dealing. I could not pretend that I wished sincerely well to the measures, which I should become not merely a party but the principal in recommending.

"I shall sincerely lament if I should be mistaken, and that Parliament hould adopt the new course proposed. I foresee nothing but a series of misfortunes for the country in all its interests, and even affecting its safety. cannot be a party in inflicting those misfortunes."

s impossible to say that he misjudged the moment for retreat, since would have regarded the retreat itself as an inadmissible surrender. Reform in 1830 was a subject on which he was incapable of commise. The brilliant opportunism of Catholic Emancipation could not epeated; and there was no alternative to resistance.

Vhat other course was open? Crowds were on the move, and he inctively resisted crowds. Gentlemen could be bargained with; but wds must be resisted. He had resisted them before. The age of tlereagh had been a generous education in resistance, and the Duke served his apprenticeship as a Cabinet minister under the beneficient of the Six Acts. If it was to be 1819 over again, he knew the method; he was soon provisioning his garrisons and warning officers against narrow streets of Manchester as though he were still Lord Liver-'s Master-General of the Ordnance. The age of Cato Street seemed to rn, as warnings reached him of plots against his life. He informed ung colleague that "I never neglect and never believe these things," had bolts put inside his carriage doors. Quite undeterred, he went to unruly North. It might have a good effect if the Duke shewed him- in Lancashire. There was a railway to be opened between Liver- and Manchester; and Huskisson, who was the local member, was are resentful that "the Great Captain is to be there with all his Of course, one object is to throw me into the background." But kisson, alas! retained the centre of the stage. The Duke's train

was a sumptuous affair, crowned with a canopy that could be lower
for tunnels. Wellington arrived wearing his Spanish cloak, entrained
Liverpool, and laughed heartily at his unusual situation. A vast co
pany rose to receive him; the band played *See the conquering h
comes*; a gun boomed; and his strange conveyance rumbled majestic
into the tunnel. After a dreadful interval the train emerged, and anxi
multitudes observed its progress through the cuttings until "the fly
machines sped through the awful chasm at the speed of 24 miles
hour." (Even the Duke with his sharp eyes could not read the m
stones.) This breathless flight could scarcely be maintained; and t
halted at Parkside for water. The halt was pleasingly diversified
a march-past of trains, which were reviewed by Wellington from
state carriage. Gentlemen got down to stretch their legs, and the Pr
Minister shook hands with Huskisson from his door. They were b
talking to Mrs. Arbuthnot, when there was a sudden cry. The "Roc
was approaching. Men ran to safety from the monster; but the unha
Huskisson, who lost his head, limped helplessly all ways at once
clung to a carriage door in panic. The engine swept him off; and a
pirited procession reached Manchester, where they feasted in a dis
hush. But the Duke was cheered to the echo, and both his hands v
nearly shaken off.

So Huskisson was gone; and within a fortnight Wellington rene
his signals to the Canningites. For the elections had increased his w
ness in the House of Commons. The Whigs appeared to be united r
and it was no longer safe to leave his Parliamentary flank uncove
Peel was clamouring for reinforcements. Besides, the Canningites w
be more palatable without poor Huskisson. So he sent somebod
Palmerston with a direct offer; but Palmerston refused to join wit
his Canningite associates and the Whig leaders. This was too much
Wellington, and Palmerston went off to Paris. For the Duke, o
prepared to re-enlist his Light Division, could scarcely be expecte
take in the enemy as well. A final effort was no more successful, v
Lord Palmerston spent six minutes at Apsley House, insisted o
thorough reconstruction of the Government, and was bowed out.

The Duke was still busy with the peace of Europe, insisting th
Conference about the Netherlands should meet in London; and

ter-bag still yielded a fair number of communications from Mr.
aydon, who was pressing indomitably for a State subsidy for art.
ellington responded bleakly that "no minister could go to Parlia-
nt with a proposition for a vote for a picture to be painted," and
poor Haydon (who was quite overwhelmed by tradesmen, babies,
d a colossal canvas of Xenophon arriving in sight of the sea) con-
ced that "impossibility, from Wellington's mouth, must be impos-
lity indeed." As for Reform, he spoke his mind upon it in the House
Lords:

"I never read or heard of any measure up to the present moment which in
ny degree satisfies my mind that the state of the representation can be
nproved. . . . I am fully convinced that the country possesses at the pres-
nt moment a Legislature which answers all the good purposes of legisla-
on, and this to a greater degree than any Legislature ever has answered
a any country whatever. I will go further, and say, that the Legislature and
he system of representation possess the full and entire confidence of the
untry. . . . I will go still further, and say, that if at the present moment
had imposed upon me the duty of forming a Legislature for any country,
d particularly for a country like this, in possession of great property of
rious descriptions,—I do not mean to assert that I could form such a
gislature as we possess now, for the nature of man is incapable of reach-
g such excellence at once,—but my great endeavor would be, to form
me description of Legislature which would produce the same results.
he representation of the people at present contains a large body of the
operty of the country, and in which the landed interest has a prepon-
rating influence. Under these circumstances, I am not prepared to bring
ward any measure of the description alluded to by the noble Lord. And
m not only not prepared to bring forward any measure of this nature,
t I will at once declare that, as far as I am concerned, as long as I hold
y station in the government of the country, I shall always feel it my duty
resist such measures when proposed by others."

was plain speaking. As he sat down, the Duke turned to Aber-

have not said too much, have I?"

s colleague guardedly replied that he would hear of it. But the

cautious Foreign Secretary gave a more significant summary of th
Duke's speech to an enquirer—"*He said that we are going out.*"

Their weakness in the House of Commons was a real menace no
For he had openly defied Reform, and Reformers were in a majori
there. He still professed to think that things might do, and said to La
Jersey, "Lord, I shall not go out—you will see we shall go on very wel
while Mrs. Arbuthnot echoed him faithfully. He trusted that his enem
—Whigs, Radicals, High Tories, and Canningites—were too divided
combine against him. Besides, the country gave him something m
serious to think about than Parliamentary manœuvres. Tempers w
rising now, and London did its best to behave like Paris. Excited me
ings roared every evening in the Rotunda, Blackfriars; informers scraw
their apprehensions to the Home Office; and the new Police, with ev
hair on end, found *caches* of tricolour cockades. The Duke was in
element, took pistols with him in his carriage, and drafted operat
orders for the defence of Apsley House with armed men at every w
dow and one in poor Kitty's bath-room. But, all things considered
would be just as well to postpone the royal visit to the City. The K
was to have gone in state to the Lord Mayor's Dinner; but there was
dence that Wellington was to be attacked. He was quite equal to atten
upon his life. But a disorderly attack on the procession in the Ki
presence was quite another matter; and the Duke, by what Lord We
ley termed a little bitterly "the boldest act of cowardice he had
known," decided to postpone it. The postponement was a grave hur
tion; stocks fell; and an Opposition bard chanted derisively,

> "Charles the Tenth is at Holie-Rode,
> Louis Philippe will sone be going;
> Ferdinand wyse and Miguel good
> Mourne o'er the dedes their people are doing;
> And ye Kynge of Great Britain, whom Godde defende,
> Dare not go out to dine with a frende."

Outnumbered in the House of Commons, the Government had
confessed its inability to preserve the normal life of London. Hats
still raised to Wellington as he rode down to Whitehall, though a
boys hooted him. But his Government was a doomed fortress; its
were silent now; and the garrison waited behind battered walls fo

st assault. Reform was looming in the Commons; but before they ached it, ministers were defeated on the Civil List. The Duke was ankly startled. He had a dinner at Apsley House that evening (it as November 15); an excited gentleman came in with the news; and e Prime Minister, who was no feminist, said, "Do not tell the women." He took a night to think it over and resigned. If they stayed in, ougham's motion on Reform would be carried against them; but a nely resignation served to postpone it—"indeed it was with that view at I thought it best to lose no time in sending it." Forced to abandon s position, he could still fire a shot against Reform from his retreating arguard. But the Duke was out.

"What is the best test of a great general?"
"To know when to retreat, and to dare to do it."—WELLINGTON.

I

THE Duke, a private gentleman once more, surveyed the unpleasing scene, while Grey assembled the incongruous elements of the first Whig administration since the distant days of Fox. As he sat musing by the fire at Mrs. Arbuthnot's, they overheard him thinking aloud. "They want me to place myself at the head of a faction; but I say them, I have now served my country for forty years—for twenty I have commanded her armies, and for ten I have sat in the Cabinet— and I will not now place myself at the head of a faction."

For he was disinclined to lead the Opposition; the old gamekeeper could not turn poacher. A life of public service is an indifferent training for the Opposition, since he had served the King too long to acquire the habit of obstructing the King's ministers; and Rogers, who was listening, would take his message to Lord Grey. A private gentleman once more, he was still the leading gentleman in England; and gentlemen in 1830 had work to do. County magistrates and Yeomanry must maintain order in the countryside, where something unusual was brewing. Wellington was Lord-Lieutenant of Hampshire; he had already got all the Hampshire gentlemen out of town; and the deep voice still rumbled on.

"When I lay down my office to-morrow, I will go down into my county and do what I can to restore order and peace. And in my place in Parliament, when I can, I will approve; when I cannot, I will dissent; but I will never agree to be the leader of a faction."

A rare mood of despair was on him. "Bad business," was his verdict in Peel's drawing-room, "devilish bad business"; and he looked so grave as he walked out of Downing Street and stepped into his cabriolet that Greville (though he got his customary nod) did not like to speak to him. The times were out of joint. For he was quite convinced that the French meant to go to war, and there was every sign of an impending revolution. The French, of course, were at the bottom of it—"I entertain no doubt that there exists a formidable conspiracy. . . . I am in-

407

clined to think that the operations of the conspirators in his country
are conducted by Englishmen. But that the original focus is at Paris.'
French gold enabled agitators to flit about in gigs; and the Duke waited
grimly for the explosion. He was inclined to blame himself for allowing
"a licentious press to repeat *usque ad nauseam* the misrepresentations of
all parties." But what hope was there that a misguided public could be
preserved by Grey and his Whig colleagues? "The gentlemen now in
power are committed to Revolution by the applause with which, as
private persons, they greeted those in Paris and Brussels." Besides, their
policies were a delirious and conflicting blend of Opposition pledges
And there was little salvation to be hoped for from the Crown. He had
once said that where kings can ride on horseback and inflict punishment, revolution is impossible. Russia, perhaps, enjoyed that happy state
but it was evident that such feats of equitation were far beyond William IV.

What was to be done? The Duke performed his county duties and
returned to town. His first reluctance to lead his friends in Opposition
was passing now; and he gave fifty of his late colleagues a dinner at
Apsley House. They dined in the great gallery among his Spanish pictures; and when the Duke of Richmond proposed his health with the
sentiment that he hoped their host would soon give them the word of
command "As you were," Wellington replied almost cheerfully, "Not
not as you were, but much better." This was a trifle more encouraging
though he still counselled his retreating followers "to remain quiet till
they see real cause to take an active part." For in rearguard actions unnecessary conflicts were to be discouraged. So they fell slowly back
as 1830 went out.

2

The world in 1831 was not more cheerful; and Mr. Croker found
the Duke "in very low spirits about politics," though he still could
not see his way to open fire as leader of an organised Opposition. But
when the Reform Bill was produced, he knew his mind clearly enough
opining that the measure would, "by due course of law, destroy

ountry," while the disfranchisement of existing boroughs would give
a shake . . . to the property of every individual in the country." For
e was more interested in the sanctity of vested interests than in the
orms of Parliamentary representation. But party discipline presented
ritating problems. It had already been revealed to him that a Prime
linister's authority over his followers is considerably less than that of
commander in the field; and he now discovered that an Opposition
ader's is more slender still, complaining bitterly that "nobody does
ything but what he likes, excepting myself. We are all commanders,
d there are no troops. Nobody obeys or ever listens to advice but
yself. Then I am abused because things do not go right." Even the
ithful Peel—"that fellow in the House of Commons"—was trying.
)ne can't go on without him; but he is so vacillating and crotchety
at there's no getting on with him. I did pretty well with him when we
re in office, but I can't manage him now at all. . . ." Wellington was
termined to defeat the Bill and had little patience with half-measures.
s views were plainly stated; but his popularity seemed almost un-
paired. For one day in February he was thrown from his horse at
:ford Circus; they took him to a shop, where he announced that he
s not seriously injured and requested that the mud might be removed
m his clothes; a cab was called; and as he entered it, the Duke was
dly cheered. But he still argued stoutly in the House of Lords that
form involved "the downfall of the constitution," contending shrewdly
t Whig declamations on the toiling masses should be discounted be-
se nobody proposed to enfranchise them, and that it was wise "to
sider what a House of Commons ought to be, and not what the
stituents ought to be" (a devastating test by which to judge some
r extensions of the franchise). His strategy was simple—"to reject
Reform Bill, if only to gain time"—and in order to render their
nsive tactics effective he was urging the divided Tories to close
r ranks. In April a Government defeat in the House of Commons
followed by a dissolution. There was an afternoon of wild con-
n in the Lords; peers shook their fists and bawled abuse at one
her; the Lord Chancellor bounded about the Chamber; and guns
ned the tidings that King William had left his palace for the House.

But the Duke was absent. He was at Apsley House by Kitty's bed
side. For poor, faded Kitty was sadly ailing. An Irish friend, who saw
her early in the year, was shocked to find her on a sofa, "paler than
marble . . . a miniature figure of herself in wax-work." A tiny head
on a big pillow, she stirred a little as her visitor arrived; and a familiar
voice said faintly, "O! Miss Edgeworth, you are the truest of the true
—the kindest of the kind." A thin white hand stole out to greet her
and a faint touch of colour returned with the shadow of a smile. She lay
on the ground-floor of his great London house among the trophies,
glass cases full of china given by respectful monarchs, stupendous can
delabra from the Portuguese, and the Homeric shield, gift of a grateful
City. Her visitor stared at them; and a faint voice behind her murmured
"All tributes to merit! there's the value, all pure, no corruption ever
suspected even. Even of the Duke of Marlborough that could not be said
so truly." For her Duke was perfect, though he could never bear it when
she told him so. He alarmed her sometimes. But then great men were
bound to be alarming; and her brother's boys used to run up
back-stairs, when they came to see her, for fear of an encounter with
their terrifying uncle. He was gentle with her now and positively wrote
to Alava about her health. She seemed to rally in the spring; but he still
sat with her. Her thin fingers strayed inside his sleeve and found a
circlet fastened on his arm years before by Kitty Pakenham. The guns
were booming for King William now across the Park. That afternoon
the House of Lords was full of agitated peers; but her Duke was there
beside her, as his poor, faded Kitty died.

Parliament had been dissolved, and London illuminated for Reform.
A cheerful mob paraded Piccadilly on the look-out for recalcitrant house
holders. Dark windows meant a Tory occupant; and the great house at
Hyde Park Corner with its tall portico stood out against the summer
night in sombre outline. Mourning apart, the Duke was the last man
in London who was likely to put candles in his windows for Reform in
order to oblige a mob; and presently the stones began to crash in
the silent rooms (one did some damage to a picture), until a servant
on the roof let off a blunderbuss, and the crowd moved off to draw Park
Lane for Tories.

3

The twin scourges of Reform and cholera strode on through 1831. Reform was grave enough; but the Duke was not afraid of cholera—the only thing I am afraid of is fear. . . . If three or four hundred Notables were to leave London for fear of it, they would be followed by three or four hundred thousand, and then this country would be plunged into greater confusion than had been known for hundreds of years." But Reform was a more formidable menace. His fears of violent revolution had vanished now; but he was frankly alarmed by the prospect of a measure which "totally alters all the existing political interests of the country, creates one-fourth entirely new interests . . . and this at the most critical period in the history of the world." He was inclined to blame himself for the destructive power of the press—"I allowed my contempt for the newspapers—a contempt founded upon the experience of a long life, of their utter inefficiency to do an individual any mischief . . . —to influence my conduct in respect to the press, when I was in office. The press is an engine of a very different description, when it attacks individuals, and when it attacks the institutions of the country. It is powerful in respect to the latter, and no man can blame my own neglect more than I do." Meanwhile, deluded citizens were voting readily for Reform; there would be a majority of Reformers in the new House of Commons; and what was to be done? It might be coming to sit at Walmer talking of old times to Alava and Croker. But what was he to do? Reform was a chimera menacing the "last asylum of peace and happiness," where great towns with no members of Parliament enjoyed "the benefit of being governed by the system of the English constitution without the evil of elections" and an eccentric franchise secured the Parliamentary services of steady persons whose presence "constitutes the great difference between the House of Commons and those assemblies abroad called Chambers of Deputies." His contempt for the new members was profound—"they dare not vote according to the suggestions of their own judgment after discussion; they are sent as delegates for a particular purpose under particular instructions, and not members of Parliament sent to deliver it *de arduis regni*." He was acting on the defensive now; and the first necessity was to unite his forces. This was achieved by midsummer. Peel was still enigmatic; but the Tories were aligned behind the Duke. Even Lord Winchilsea was reconciled, and Wellington went over to inspect his Yeomanry.

Their course in Parliament was plain. The Bill must be defeated, though the Duke retained his old reluctance to declare a general war upon the Whigs—"I could not be a party to any violent or factious opposition against any government named by the King." For he was a public servant; and his services were at Lord Grey's disposal upon matters of foreign policy. He even waited on the Prime Minister in Downing Street, and wrote long memoranda for his guidance. But he was quite unbending on Reform. If the Commons passed the Bill, the Lords must throw it out. For time, he felt convinced, was on their side; rejection meant delay; and under cover of delay sanity might yet prevail. He was in town that autumn; Greville attended a great dinner at Apsley House, where the Duke told him stories about George IV and all the trinkets they had found in his belongings—gloves, *gages d'amour*, and women's hair of every colour with the powder and pomatum still upon it—and what a trial the Duchess of Kent had been with her commanding ways. But with Reform impending it was impossible for him to find a refuge in talk about old times. The Tory peers must be convened, and he wrote argumentative letters in all directions. That autumn his old mother died at eighty-nine, having seen her incomparable pair of Gracchi on every eminence in two continents. The Opposition leaders met at Apsley House, and Eldon came in after dinner, post-prandial in the extreme. If the Bill passed the Commons, the Lords must do their duty. Wellington informed his peers that Reform was synonymous with democracy—"this fierce democracy"—and that democracy involved immediate onslaught upon property:

> "A democracy has never been established in any part of the world, that it has not immediately declared war against property—against the payment of the public debt—and against all the principles of conservation, which are secured by, and are in fact the principal objects of the British Constitution as it now exists. Property and its possessors will become the common enemy. . . ."

The Spanish precedent still haunted him; for he insisted that Reform would paralyse "the strength which is necessary to enable his Majesty to protect and keep in order his foreign dominions, and to ensure the obedience of their inhabitants. We shall lose these colonies and foreign possessions, and with them our authority and influence abroad." Four days later angry Reformers read in black-edged newspapers that the Bill was dead, rejected by the House of Lords. An undergraduate was driving back to Christ Church in the Oxford coach, and confided to his diary Gladstone's impressions of his first debate.

The Bill was dead; but, with the country in an ugly ferment, it might rise again. The Duke's windows suffered once more; and when he went to Walmer, six gentlemen, headed by a fighting Army chaplain, rode as his escort. It was November now, and Wellington drove in his britzka—that open carriage in which everyone caught colds—with an armed servant on the box and a brace of double-barrelled pistols by his side. The Arbuthnots were at the Castle; and his tone was frankly pessimistic. Then Croker and a house-party arrived; Lord Stanhope been asking him questions about the Peninsula, retiring to his room to write down all his answers; and they found the Duke looking grave. He faced the facts about Reform, announcing that "the disfranchisement of any place is a painful thing to swallow. I don't mean that we shan't be obliged to swallow it—but it is a monstrous gulp." The closing sentence of his speech had urged the Lords to leave the door open:

"In recommending to your Lordships to vote against this Bill, I earnestly entreat you to avoid pledging yourselves, whether in public or private, against any other measure that may be brought forward. I recommend to you to keep yourselves free to adopt any measure upon this subject which shall secure to this country the blessings of a government."

This was the strategy of retreat once more: the enemy were pressing hard, and it might be necessary to fall back to the next ridge. But warfare extended now far beyond the walls of Parliament; for crowds were on the move in every quarter of the kingdom, and Wellington's first instinct was to repress them. Crowds almost invariably warped his judgment. He sent his sovereign a warning letter on the subject of the Political Unions; they were reported to be arming now, and he advised their prompt suppression, pointing his advice with the alarming prec-

edents of the National Guard and the Irish Volunteers. The letter con
veyed a hint that Wellington was prepared to take the helm again
rescue the King from his Whig captors, fight a General Election upor
the issue of public order, and restore England to her senses. But hi
bewildered sovereign was unresponsive.

To restore public order was the main problem now. As the Duk
wrote, "that once done, the reform of the Parliament might be consid
ered with honour and safety, if not with advantage. Till these union
are put down, it does not much signify, in reality, what course is taken.
In this mood he was frankly indifferent to the negotiations in progres
between ministers and the more cautious of his Tory followers in th
House of Lords. What did the details of Reform matter, if revolutio
went unchallenged on its way? But the Duke could see that events ha
made Reform quite inevitable—"the King has . . . pronounced himse
for Reform, and it would not be easy to govern in his name witho
Reform. But the more gentle and more gradual the reform, the bett
for the country. . . ." His mind was moving towards a fresh stage
the long retreat; but he must not be hurried.

4

The next attack would come in 1832. For the Bill was passing throu
the Commons for the third time. How was it to be received when
reached the House of Lords? That fortress was not quite impregnat
since it was generally known that Grey proposed to spike its sligh
antiquated guns by a creation of sufficient peers to pass the Bill; a
in January one enthusiast was pressing Wellington to see the Ki
advise him to refuse this exercise of the prerogative, form a T
Government, and go to the country. But the Duke refused. He alw
thought of details; and one detail of Parliamentary routine stood in
way. For this exhilarating programme would leave no time for Pa
ment to renew the Mutiny Act before a dissolution. Besides, he doub
how far the King would play his part. He had every reason to, si
when he had been prepared to act on similar lines in the autumn,
King hung back and the moment for the *sortie* passed. Now there

nothing to be done except to stand on the defensive; and he waited for the Bill behind the ramparts of the House of Lords.

An unwise "endeavour to bully slight colds" had ended in a temperature, and shooting gave him bad headaches before Christmas; but he was soon restored, out in the saddle through six hours of February rain, and riding sixty miles a day to hounds. As for the situation, he was past tactics now. A gloomy certainty possessed him that "we are governed by the mob and its organ—a licentious press . . . the mob and Mr. Place the tailor!" Convinced that "the monarchy . . . approaches its termination," he was averse from ingenious manœuvres designed to avert the creation of Whig peers. Indeed, he rather welcomed this expedient, since its very ruthlessness would expose Grey's *coup d'état* in all its nudity and spare noblemen the degradation of changing their minds. The King might still prevent it—"The King of this country is a tower of strength"—but Wellington would put no pressure on him.

The Bill reached the House of Lords in March, and Wellington fired a warning shot from the battlements. Even Greville, who had been busy in the negotiations for a compromise, found his tone "fair and gentlemanlike . . . a speech creditable to himself, useful and becoming . . . very handsome speech." He opposed the second reading at length, though in a tone of marked restraint. But months of negotiation between Whig ministers and "Waverers" had weakened his defences; and the Bill passed its second reading. The enemy had penetrated his position now; for the Lords' vote admitted that there was to be a Reform Bill of some sort, and the Duke faced the uncomfortable fact—"my own opinion is, that we shall not escape a Reform Bill on the principle of that now in the House of Lords, and that the efforts of all ought to be directed to render that bill as little noxious as possible." The threatened fortress was quite indefensible, and the heroic gesture of a last stand among the ruins made no appeal to Wellington. Always practical, he was prepared to abandon the position and fall back fighting. But he had few illusions as to the final outcome since he was frankly sceptical of the value of any possible amendments of the Bill. What else was there to do, though, unless the King came to his senses? The world was more than usually out of joint; for Wellington could scarcely take a ride in London without hearing angry cries though Croker was con-

soled to notice "with what respectful, I should say *increased* attention
he is received by every well-dressed person, and even by a vast majority
of the lower orders." But his health was glaringly omitted from a long
toast-list at the King's dinner to the East India directors. The skies were
dark indeed; and the Duke ruefully confessed that "I am out of the
whole affair."

Grey's temper changed the situation. The Bill was in committee now;
and when the House of Lords shewed signs of independence in the first
week of May, the Prime Minister posted off to Windsor with a peremp-
tory demand for the creation of fifty peers. This was too much for his
much-enduring sovereign, who refused to give the required assurance.
The Government resigned; King William sent for Lyndhurst; and, in
Endymion's gleeful narrative, "the bold chief baron advised His Majesty
to consult the Duke of Wellington."

5

Was he to be Prime Minister again? He had his chance; and this
was the precise situation for which he had played in November, 1831—
the King at bay, the Whigs dismissed, and loyal subjects to the rescue.
But the *sortie*, which might have saved the fortress six months before,
was now little more than a forlorn hope. For it was 1832. However, it
might still serve a useful purpose; for Wellington was thoroughly alive
to "the advantage of taking the King out of the hands of the Radicals,
that is, in reality—of giving the country the benefit of some government"—and taking the sting out of the Reform Bill.

It was a Thursday when Lord Lyndhurst saw him, and they went
in search of Peel. The three men met at Apsley House; Croker was there
as well, and asked who was to be Prime Minister. Lyndhurst nodded
towards Peel, and said that he must tell them. Peel spoke with his
accustomed emphasis: if the new Government proposed to carry a Reform Bill, he could not and would not have anything to do with it. He
had already made a *volte face* on Catholic Relief, and was quite determined not to repeat the experience. Croker suggested that Lord
Harrowby, who had been prominent among the "Waverers," might play
the part; but the Duke disliked the idea, doubting if Harrowby would

be acceptable to the Tory peers. That night he wrote a note to Lyndhurst:

> "I shall be very much concerned indeed if we cannot at least make an
> effort to enable the King to shake off the trammels of his tyrannical Minis-
> ter. I am perfectly ready to do whatever his Majesty may command me. I
> am as much averse to the Reform as ever I was. No embarrassment of that
> kind, no private consideration, shall prevent me from making every effort
> to serve the King."

So he was prepared to abandon his defensive strategy and lead the forlorn hope; and on Friday Lyndhurst went down to Windsor and informed the King.

Croker saw the Duke again on Saturday, and found him grim, but not
uncommunicative. "Well," he remarked, "we are in a fine scrape, and
really do not see how we are to get out of it." Harrowby, he said, had
declined; so had the Speaker; and if no one else would act, he must form
a Government himself. As the Duke remarked to Croker, he had
passed his whole life in troubles and was now in troubles again, but it
was his duty to stand by the King. That was his leading thought; the
royal summons was a command to Wellington; and he pressed Croker
to let Peel know that he would serve with him or under him or in any
way that Peel might think best for the common cause. But Peel had
little taste for a second recantation followed by a second martyrdom, and
kept carefully aloof. That day the printers were at work on Place's wily
placard, "To stop the Duke, go for Gold"; a general run on the banks
might paralyse the new Tory Government; and windows in Birmingham already displayed the threat, "No taxes paid here until the Reform
Bill is passed." But though the King was hissed as he drove up from
Windsor, a crowd cheered Wellington outside the palace. He told the
King that, "happen what would, he would stand by him and endeavour
to extricate him from the difficulty in which he was placed." But he must
have colleagues; and the King, who took a hand in the Duke's game, had
no success with Peel or the Speaker. That afternoon Wellington interviewed a long procession of reluctant Tories; but none of them would
serve except his military stalwarts, Murray and Hardinge. For the Tory
intellect was not equal to the Duke's conception of a rearguard action in

politics, his incessant series of retreats to the next ridge in rear; and their civilian weakness for consistency was strangely troubled by the prospect of helping to pass Reform after resisting it so long. But they all dined together at the Carlton Club that night. The Duke was in the chair and listened to innumerable speeches, followed by a long session with the reluctant Speaker.

More interviews filled Sunday. His patience was beginning to wear a little thin, since he observed to Croker (who was hanging back) that in such a crisis, if a man put himself on the shelf, it might not be so easy to take him off the shelf when he perhaps might desire it. That night he saw the Speaker once again without success; for that dignitary's eloquence, repressed by his official situation, found release in a disquisition that lasted for three hours, led nowhere, and provoked from Lyndhurst the disrespectful comment that his prospective colleague was "a damned tiresome old bitch." The Speaker asked for time; but on Monday night the House of Commons intervened with a debate, which proved conclusively that the Duke's forces were inadequate. He faced the facts at once, and informed the King on Tuesday morning that he could not form a Government.

The *sortie*, which lasted for five breathless days, had failed; and the long siege was nearly over. For Wellington had failed to break the Whig blockade of the House of Lords. The Whigs were back again in office; and the peers, surrounded by a hostile Government and an angry House of Commons, were bound to capitulate. But it had been a gallant effort, though *Coningsby* conjectures that "the future historian of the country will be perplexed to ascertain what was the distinct object which the Duke of Wellington proposed to himself in the political manœuvre of May 1832," and concludes disapprovingly that "this premature effort of the Anti-Reform leader to thrust himself again into the conduct of public affairs . . . savoured rather of restlessness than of energy." But did it? His objectives were plain enough—to form a Tory Government which would preserve public order and pass a moderate Reform Bill. If he failed, it was because his followers permitted him to fail. Opponents of Reform, they were unable to share his willingness to pass the Bill. For they viewed it as good partisans were bound to view it: Reform was not a Tory measure, and what Tory could square his princples with voting for it? The Duke took another view. Never a good party man, he was prepared to sacrifice Tory orthodoxy in a crisis. Indeed, he did not regard himself as a mere party leader—"I was not acting for any body of men, but for the King." That was the key to all his actions. The King was in difficulties, and must be rescued; the King had summoned Wellington, and Wellington had eaten the King's salt. However desperate the adventure, he could not refuse. He did not spare himself, offering to serve under Peel and enduring endless interviews with his reluctant followers. But persuasion was not his *forte*; and if his followers thought more of Tory principles than of the King's dilemma, the Duke was not to blame.

Reform rolled on implacably; and Wellington, determined to avert the final ignominy of a wholesale creation of Whig peers by an unwilling King, withdrew his opposition to the Bill; his followers "skulked in clubs and country houses," whilst it passed through its remaining stages; and on a summer afternoon Whigs crowded to the House of Lords to hear the royal assent recited to the empty benches opposite.

6

One June morning he rode out of Apsley House to give a sitting to Pistrucci at the Mint. An ugly crowd collected in the City to wait for him on his return, and a magistrate offered his assistance. The Duke's reply was practical.

"You can do nothing. The only thing you can help me in is to tell me exactly the road I am to take to get to Lincoln's Inn; for the great danger would be in my missing my way and having to turn back on the mob."

He started with his groom, and the mob followed them. They tried to drag him from his horse in Fenchurch Street; but two Chelsea pensioners appeared, whom he stationed at each stirrup with orders to face about whenever he was forced to halt. There was some stone-throwing in Holborn; and when he saw a coal-cart in the distance, "Hillo!" said the Duke in a grim aside, "here's the Artillery coming up; we must look out." But an obliging gentleman, who drove a tilbury behind him for some time, gave valuable cover, and earned the Duke's esteem by "never

looking towards me for any notice." Two policemen joined the little
party; and the Duke disposed them at his horse's head as an advance
guard. When they reached Lincoln's Inn, the mob was still at his heels.
He surveyed the situation and enquired if there was another exit. It
seemed there was. "Then be so good," said the Duke, "as to shut the
gate." The enemy detained by this simple strategem, he rode out into
Lincoln's Inn Fields; but the mob was after him again. His horse
was walking, and an excited gentleman named Martin Tupper leapt
on the steps of Surgeons' Hall, exclaiming loudly, "Waterloo, Waterloo!" The mob was slightly awed; the Duke raised two fingers to his
hat; and the strange ride went on, "the cast-metal man" (as Carlyle wrote
to his mother) "riding slowly five long miles all the way like a pillar of
glar!" He had a little escort now, as they went up the Strand and along
Pall Mall; gentlemen in club windows saw him staring straight between
his horse's ears. They rode up Constitution Hill; but the mob headed
him by a dash across the Park; and they were waiting outside Apsley
House to hoot, as he reached home at last. It was June 18. "An odd
day to choose," the Duke said to somebody. "Good morning."

THE new world, where Reform was law and Mr. Creevey boarded his first omnibus, filled Wellington with grave misgivings. He was quite convinced that the revolution had begun, and waited for the end with dignity. The least of troubles was his personal unpopularity. An emblem of opposition to Reform, he was continually hooted; but he had grown accustomed to the mob outside his house, and even to the groans of village Radicals as he rode home from hunting. He faced it in his quiet way, reporting calmly that "I think that I have got the better of the mobs in London by walking about the town very quietly, notwithstanding their insults and outrages. It is certain that the better class are ashamed of them, and take pains upon all occasions to testify every mark of respect for me." But the prospect was dark—"the government of England is destroyed"—and his mind ran on revolutionary precedents. The monarchy might still survive, if only the army remained sound; but the Jacobins were in the saddle, and he might live to see a National Guard. He even detected symptoms of the Great Rebellion—"the times are much more similar to those of Charles I than people are aware of. The same parties, almost under the same denominations, are *en presence*. . . ." But the French precedents unnerved him; for it was 1789 over again. The road had forked once more towards safety or revolution; and when his countrymen made the wrong choice, how could the old duellist of the *ancien régime* feel anything but dark forebodings? "Our wise rulers prefer the course which faction suggested forty years ago to that of wisdom, of experience, and reflection. God knows what will happen to the world."

His course was clear, though. A Tory clergyman, who was inclined to emigrate from his ungrateful country, had asked for the Duke's advice.

"You have, I understand, a cure of souls. Can you abandon your post in a moment of crisis and dangers for worldly objects? Your flock ought to

provide for your decent and comfortable subsistence; and they not only c
not perfom that duty, but they persecute you! Still, ought you to abandc
them? Is it not your duty to remain at your post? Expect better times. Mal
every exertion, every sacrifice to enable you to do justice by everybod
including your family; but I confess, if I was in your situation, I would n
quit my post."

The parable applied as plainly to himself: he could not quit his po
For though the Duke was out of office, he was keenly aware that, po
tics apart, he was a public institution. As the late King's executor, l
had assumed peculiar and delicate duties towards the Crown. Besid
the world conspired to regard him as a universal dispensary of go
advice. "Every man," as he once wrote, "has one resource only; that
to apply to the Duke of Wellington." A mannerism grew upon him
alluding to himself in the third person. Cæsar had done the same; b
in Cæsar's case the habit was a mere convenience for narrative.
Wellington's it served to indicate an odd dualism. For he seemed
recognise two persons in himself—an ageing gentleman of modest tas
who could be happy in congenial society, and a public figure wh
requirements were often more majestic. In this mood of queer deta
ment he wrote to Croker of his own state appearance as Chancellor
Oxford, "I am the Duke of Wellington, and, *bon gré mal gré*, must
as the Duke of Wellington doth." That was his duty for the future.
was far pleasanter, no doubt, to sit gossiping about the past in the l
rooms at Stratfield Saye, or to pace the sunny flagstones of his battleme
at Walmer eluding Stanhope's endless questions. But there was
duty to be done. He could not quit his post; the splendid *rôle* must
played out to the end.

The new Parliament met early in 1833; and Wellington retur
from a stroll into the House of Commons to view the children of
form with the chilly verdict, "I never saw so many shocking bad l
in my life." He feared the worst, informing Greville that his first c
sideration was to keep a roof over his head, the next to support G
as the sole alternative to anarchy; for "I consider Lord Grey's Governm
as the last prop of the Monarchy." Besides, Opposition had never been
forte—"I have been in office, and have served the King throughout
life; and I know all the difficulties in which the Government are plac

ut since the revolution was over and the House of Lords had ceased
count, he saw no reason for regular attendance. Now he was al-
ost irresponsible, and wrote cheerfully that "I have been here generally
ausing myself with the Foxhounds," gaily attired in a scarlet coat,
apped trousers, and a lilac waistcoat. But he was in the Lords some-
nes; and the devoted Haydon watched him speaking with such a manly
or deliberately fetching out his glasses to read a quotation. He was
calmer water now; and someone who rode with him in St. James's
rk noticed how everyone got up and all hats came off at his ap-
oach. He was still convinced that "we are going, but I think it will
gradually. There will be no catastrophe; we are not equal to one.
e shall be destroyed by the due course of law, unless the Virgin of
Pillar or some miracle saves us." But the process was comfortingly
adual; and when the King came to his Waterloo banquet that year, he
I his windows mended for the occasion.

Not that he mitigated his despair, writing to Stanhope that he would
anything to be able to quit this unfortunate and unhappy country."
t how could he? There was nothing for it but to visit country houses,
end the House of Lords, and install a novel system of warming Strat-
d Saye by hot-water pipes. (He was a domestic pioneer, even achieving
amphs in the uncharted field of household sanitation.) This mild
tine carried him through 1833, until the University of Oxford brought
a upon the stage again as Chancellor. The honour pleased him, though
protested that he "knew no more of Greek and Latin than an Eton
in the remove." H. B. poked pleasant fun at *A Great Doctor of
non Law*, and the Duke conjectured gaily that "I shall get to the
olsack at last." In June, 1834, he went to Oxford for his installation.
vas a great occasion, with the Sheldonian packed to receive him and
. Arbuthnot there to share his triumph. The Oxford Tories took him
heir bosoms; Eldon was there as well, and the Duke gave a degree
is old adversary, Winchilsea. He had learnt with some apprehension
a speech in Latin was expected—"Now, any speech is difficult, but
atin one was impossible; so in this dilemma I applied to my physician,
nost likely, from his prescriptions, to know Latin, and he made me a
ch, which answered very well. I believe it was a very good speech,
I did not know much of the matter." His Latin quantities were un-

certain, and a shocked university heard its heroic Chancellor affront th
rules by mispronouncing *Jacobus* as three short syllables. This was er
couraging for the prospects of *Carolus*; but the incalculable Latinist defie
convention once again with a protracted "o." False quantities were a
forgiven, when a tactful prizewinner declaimed the Newdigate an
reached the apostrophe,

> "And the stern soul the world could scarce subdue
> Bowed to thy Genius, Chief of Waterloo."

The packed Sheldonian rose at the Chancellor, roaring its homage; ca
waved, feet stamped, and an impassive figure was seen rigid in its se
through a haze of dust. He noticed them at last, lifted his tasselled ca
and signalled to the poet to proceed; and then the cheerful uproar bro
out again.

The Arbuthnots went off to Woodford. They were to meet aga
as usual in the autumn; but she died with dreadful suddenness in Augu
"Only think," wrote Mr. Creevey in his unpleasant idiom, "of the Bea
flirt, Mrs. Arbuthnot, being dead!" He was at Hatfield, when the ne
arrived. The letter fell from his hand, and he flung himself down or
sofa; then he rose on the verge of sobs and paced the room. That nig
he thought of poor Arbuthnot. They had both loved her; and
Duke felt that he must go to him. Early the next morning he pos
off to console the widower. But the loss was Wellington's. For he had l
the only home that he had ever had. An exile until middle life, he l
returned at fifty to his two big houses where poor, fluttered Kitty m
dled accounts and failed to recognise his guests. That had been noth
like a home. But he was always at his ease in his chair at Mrs. Arbu
not's. They had met first in Paris, when it was no novelty for Welling
to meet handsome women. Harriett Arbuthnot was quite as handsc
as the rest, and far more sensible. She listened well, entered into p
tics, and could be trusted not to talk. She did not gush over him
public; and her slight tendency to order him about was an agree
change for an authoritative man. Besides, her husband was an invalu
subordinate with vast official knowledge; and Wellington could alv
find sanctuary at her house in Parliament Street. All this was er
now; there would be no more talks beside her fire, no more little j

bout the implacable *Tiranna* and her Slave. There was still Arbuthnot; nd the two lonely men drew silently together. He had once shared rbuthnot's home with him, and now the Duke gave Arbuthnot a shel-r. They would be widowers together. But when the world watched im speaking calmly in the House of Lords that week, it thought him ard. For the world knew nothing of his stricken letters to Frances helley, who had once shared their jokes—all ended now.

2

An ageing, lonely man, he had his work, his friends, and his in-rminable correspondence. His friends receded now behind the distances hich separate deaf men from the world; their voices came to him ross the silence, and he answered loudly from the farther shore. But his ntact with the world was principally maintained on paper; and he d little reason to complain of any lack of it. For everybody wrote him; and from a constitutional inability to ignore a letter he wrote ck to everyone. Stray correspondents invariably received the Duke's mpliments and a full, if occasionally acid, statement of his point of w. Remedies for ailments from which he did not suffer were civilly urned; and unsolicited precautions for his spiritual welfare received e acknowledgment. For he was never frivolous about religion. A hful Churchman, he was no church-goer in London because "in point act, I never hear more than what I know by heart of the Church serv-and never one word of the sermon"; besides, the precious remnants his hearing would be imperilled by sitting "for two hours every k uncovered in a cold church." He had tried St. James's, Piccadilly, found it too chilly for him. But he invariably attended divine wor-) at Stratfield Saye and Walmer, where "my presence at church operate as an example." He explained, for his correspondent's benefit, he was not "a person without any sense of religion. If I am so, I am ardonable; as I have had opportunities to acquire, and have ac-ed a good deal of knowledge upon the subject. . . . I am not ostenta-s about anything. I am not a 'Bible Society man' upon principle, and ake no ostentatious display either of charity or of other Christian ues."

His correspondent in this instance was a zealous bishop. But he ha
other correspondents upon spiritual themes. Early in 1834 he receiv
an exhortation from a young lady much addicted to good works ar
playing on the harp, who had been encouraged by her success with
convicted murderer to try her hand upon the Duke. Exhorted to spiritu
rebirth by a total stranger, he answered promptly. Two blots, an err
and the circumstance that he misdated his reply convinced her that t
Duke was overwhelmed by his emotions, although the month was Jan
ary when the most hardened sinners frequently mistake the year witho
spiritual commotion, and he had made precisely the same error wh
writing to the King about his Cabinet in January, 1828. Heartened
this conviction, Miss Jenkins called at Apsley House and left a Bib
The Duke resisted the temptation to present his compliments and
quaint Miss Jenkins that there were several in the house already. Inde
he made no reply, although the gift was accompanied by a "suita
note." This was in April; and Miss Jenkins' note remained unanswe
for four months. But Mrs. Arbuthnot died in the first week of Augu
and before the month was out, the Duke's mind had turned to his
ligious correspondent, who received an answer (addressed to "M
Jenkins") acknowledging her gift and asking whether he might h
the pleasure of meeting her. It was most unlike him to wait four mor
before answering a letter or, having waited so long, to answer it
all. But in the interval something had gone out of his life with M
Arbuthnot; was it possible that Mrs. Jenkins might replace her? I
reply enlightened him, revealing that, though willing to receive h
she was *Miss* Jenkins after all. The young evangelist had reached
great decision in consultation with her friend, Mrs. L., "a perfect wor
of the world." The Duke, a little startled, rejoined that he was not
the habit of visiting young unmarried ladies with whom he is not
quainted"; but he proposed to call, when he was next in town.

He called upon her in November. Miss J. was fortified by pr
for the ordeal, "praying to God to be with me every moment of
time, directing even my dress." Divine guidance had indicated her
dark green merino as most suitable for the occasion; and as she w
downstairs to receive her formidable guest, dear Mrs. L. cried after
"Now if the Lord should send His arrow into his soul!" The Duke

standing by the fire; and she was quite surprised to notice that he had such a beautiful silver head, such as I always from my childhood admired." Her mission would, it seemed, be less distasteful than she had feared. "This," she remarked, "is very kind of your Grace." He took her hand without a word; and the odd pair sat in two chairs on each side of the little fire. Miss Jenkins rose, exclaiming, "I will show you *my Treasure*"; the Duke got up politely; and his hostess returned to her seat clasping an enormous Bible. Then she began to read, announcing that her reading was from the third chapter of the Gospel according to St. John:

"There was a man of the Pharisees, named Nicodemus, a ruler of the Jews: The same came to Jesus by night, and said unto him, Rabbi, we know that thou art a teacher come from God: for no man can do these miracles that thou doest, except God be with him. Jesus answered and said unto him, Verily, verily, I say unto thee, Except a man be born again, he cannot see the kingdom of God. Nicodemus saith unto him, How can a man be born when he is old? can he enter the second time into his mother's womb, and be born? Jesus answered, Verily, verily, I say unto thee, Except a man be born of water and of the Spirit, he cannot enter into the kingdom of God. That which is born of the flesh is flesh; and that which is born of the Spirit is spirit. Marvel not that I said unto thee, Ye must be born again. . . ."

As she reached these words, Miss Jenkins emphasised her Scripture lesson by pointing at the Duke. His reply was slightly unexpected, since he promptly clasped her outstretched hand and said with emphasis, "Oh, how I love you! how I love you!" Some arrow, as Mrs. L. had hoped upstairs, had pierced him; but was it quite the arrow for which Mrs. L. had hoped? His hearing was imperfect, and it may be doubted whether he had caught the sacred words. But his sight was unimpaired; and he could see a pretty girl in a green dress.

He left, saying that he should call again, and made Miss Jenkins promise to write to him. She made several attempts, but finally desisted from this arduous composition, "considering such was not the will of God." The weeks went by, and his time was fully occupied. For the Whigs were out; Sir Robert Peel was on his way from Rome; and the Duke held the fort, acting temporarily as Prime Minister and all three

Secretaries of State. These administrative exercises would have kept mo
men busy at sixty-five. But though the Duke was the entire Cabinet i
his own person, he found time in those crowded weeks for a note to Mi
Jenkins asking the reason of her silence and proposing to visit her agai
Her silence was unbroken; but the Duke persisted. He called one Su
day afternoon and seemed a little flurried. It appeared that he was goin
on a visit to the King, on hearing which his pious hostess expressed
wish that it had been to the King of Kings. His conversation was e
citing, since he alluded once more to his feelings for her and exclaime
"This must be for life!" Indeed, he said it twice, and positively asked h
if she felt sufficient for him to be with him a whole life. Miss Jenkin
who was quite prepared to be a Duchess, modestly replied: "If it be t
will of God." He left her hurriedly and was a shade annoyed to fir
on his return that she had locked the door. Her explanation, which
received in silence, was that she had shut herself in to pray. He ask
her why she had not written; and when she pleaded divine guidan
he was silent again. A doubt was growing on him. Locked doors, exc
sive piety, devotions at unseasonable moments, and a tendency to confu
the King of Kings with William IV—these were disturbing sympto
Was Miss Jenkins all that the Duke had hoped?

He kept his distance for a fortnight; and as the days went by
dreadful doubt grew on Miss J. as well. Was she to be a Duchess a
all? A newspaper (for she did not disdain earthly means of intelligen
informed her that he was in town; and she put the matter to the
by a note entreating him to cease his visits. Her love for him was c
didly avowed; she was fully aware that his intentions could not be otl
wise than strictly honourable; but for religious reasons (which were
out at length) it was advisable that their meetings should remain pu
spiritual. The Duke's reply conveyed (in three sentences) his entire c
currence. Miss J. was horrified. His answer had confirmed her w
suspicions, and her racing pen bombarded him with texts. Page a
page informed him of his degradation and excused her own pro
acceptance of his proposal by her firm conviction—how could he l
ever doubted it?—that Miss Jenkins would "confer as high an hor
on a Prince in bestowing my hand on him as he would on me in
ceiving it." He answered almost humbly:

428

"I beg your pardon if I have written a line or used an expression which could annoy you. Believe me; it is the thing of all others that I would wish to avoid! And that there is nobody more strongly impressed than I am with veneration for your Virtues, attainments, and Sentiments!"

But though his tone was highly apologetic, there was nothing here about marriage. Quite undeterred, Miss Jenkins received his letter with the raptures appropriate to a repentant sinner. For a Duke penitent might be a Duke redeemed, a Duke set on the right path and looking for a Duchess. That was her dream; she never wavered in her faith that Providence had "influenced the Duke of Wellington to love me above every other lady upon earth from the first moment he beheld me." Her devoted Mrs. L. was of the same opinion; and how could Mrs. L.—"a perfect woman of the world in her early life"—be wrong?

There was an interval from January to June, 1835; and then the extraordinary couple resumed their comedy—she still convinced of her power to elevate him (as well as his to do the same for her), and he anything but reluctant to continue his association with a pretty girl. For the attentions of twenty-one are flattering to sixty-six. Besides, if she was so uncompromisingly good, she would at least be safe. Letters written to Miss J. would hardly find their way into the newspapers; she was unlikely to divert the town (like Miss Harriette Wilson) by publishing reminiscences; and he could meet her without fear of awkward consequences. So by midsummer their meetings were resumed. She had been writing letters to him without posting them; he asked to see them and was favoured with the loan of much improving literature. He seemed to enjoy her narratives of conversation with irreligious strangers in stage coaches, discussed the merits of a preacher whose ministrations she enjoyed at Ramsgate, and was almost meek in his request that her more voluminous epistles should (in view of excess postage) be confided to several envelopes. He asked to see her; but the whilst Miss Jenkins practised with skill the tactics of the flying nymph. He took pleasure in their correspondence. For it was always to his taste to be treated without undue deference; Mrs. Arbuthnot had continually ordered him about; and Miss Jenkins, with all Scripture at her back, was nothing if not authoritative. Indeed, her habits of command impelled her to rebuke him for ceasing to seal his notes with a coronet and signing

them with a bare initial. This was gross disrespect—she should retur
his letters and receive none from him in future unless they bore his fu
insignia. It was years since anyone had dared to question the Duke
conduct; and he replied with the familiar irony that he had "alwa
understood that the important parts of a Letter were its Contents. I nev
much considered the Signature; provided I knew the handwriting;
the Seal provided it effectually closed the Letter." But he accepted t'
rebuke and undertook that future letters should be "properly signed a
sealed to your Satisfaction," noting with some relief that she propos
to send him back his letters and adding helpfully that he would sa
her the trouble of burning them. Before this olive-branch appeased h
a second furious epistle sped from Miss J. to Apsley House. This w
too much for Wellington, who took refuge in his chilliest third pers
presented compliments, repeated his apology, and gave detailed instr
tions for the return of his letters. Miss Jenkins was distracted. Shou
she abandon her letters and her Duke? The tactics of the flying nym
had yielded excellent results; she had sixty letters from him; a
she spread them out before the Lord, asking His guidance as to their
posal. Her prayer was answered when Mrs. L., always the woman
the world, advised her not to part with them. It was His will; for had
Miss J. "asked the Lord to put it into her heart to advise me agrea
to His will"? So Mrs. L. prevailed; Miss Jenkins kept her letters;
an irritated Duke informed her coldly that "it is a matter of Indiffere
whether Miss J. has burnt the Letters; or kept them; or sent them ba

They corresponded still; for Wellington lived in the grip of a nerv
inability to refrain from answering letters. Composing suitable rep
was, with him, an automatic reaction. But he was chilly now, regrett
bleakly that "Miss J. is not satisfied with the formal style of his No
She was not satisfied when he wrote to her in a form more consis'
with familiarity. . . . The Duke assures Miss J. that he can reply to
letter which she may think proper to address the Duke as fully in
form as the other." When she asked him to return one of her letters
replied coldly that as "they are in general long and they succeed
other rapidly," it was his practice to destroy them. She pelted him
tracts and hymns in manuscript adorned with four distinct grade
underlining; on one sublime occasion she ran to "nineteen side

aper under three covers"; each family bereavement brought him her
onsolations; and she formed an irritating habit of entrusting him with
ulky letters for transmission to royal personages on the subject of
unday observance, the rates of Marlborough House (upon which she
ad some texts unfamiliar to rating lawyers), and more eternal themes.
hey met once in 1836, with Mrs. L. safely ensconced behind the fold-
g doors. But this time there were no scenes; and the female Polonius
ard little more than her fearless friend admonishing the Duke; though
hen Miss Jenkins asked about the trouble in his knee, he seemed quite
atified, drawing his chair a little nearer, "which of course met with
e withdrawal on my part due to Christianity."

They did not meet again for years, although the nymph was now
rsuing. She sent him wipers for his spectacles and for his pens; she
ered him a Bible in large print, which elicited the cautious answer
t "that which I now have answers perfectly, and I will not deprive
1 of another." For he was wary now and less inclined to notify her
his movements. By 1840, faint but pursuing, she was offering to come
1 nurse him; but he assured her of his perfect health, adding de-
sively that "he has no reason to believe that he will have occasion to
ble her upon any subject whatever." For she was quite unbearable,
ting with alarming frequency and getting little in return beyond
e acknowledgments, until "the Duke would recommend [her] to
herself from such anxiety in future by omitting to write to him."
last shot was still more final—"to avoid disappointment he now
her that he will write no more."

/as this the end? Plainly, if Wellington had anything to do with it.
four years of silence were too much for Miss J.; and in 1844 she
ned fire again. His replies at first were passive—he was obliged for
kind enquiries, reluctant to embark upon religious topics, and re-
d to learn that her misunderstanding with Mrs. L. was at an end.
that year he called on her again and, on leaving, found quite a
d round his horses. Indeed, he sent her his sole recorded present—
x impression of his features on half a ducal visiting-card. This treas-
eft her in grave doubt as to its ultimate disposal—whether it should
se for ever in the British Museum or be realised in order that its
eds might be sent upon the thankless task of propagating the Gos-

pel among the Jews. More visits followed; and his notes grew friendlie
again, though they were mainly filled with brave assertions of his rud
health and the intolerable burden of affairs. (Her new *rôle* as the Lad
with the Lamp must be repelled at all costs.) But she soon grew exactin
expecting him to answer every letter. This was bad enough; but whe
she wrote a rambling story about money troubles, his patience final
ran out:

> "I will give her any reasonable assistance she may require from n
> when she will let me know in clear distinct Terms what is the Sum s
> requires.
> "But I announce again; that I will never write upon any other Subjec

Such brutality sent her into apocalyptic transports; she even contemplat
returning the precious seal and a lock of his hair. But Mrs. L., s
worldly, pressed her to keep them both; and the Duke, sternly appri
that he had totally misunderstood, was unexpectedly apologetic—"P.S
wrote Wellington, "I never will offend again in any manner." I
humility was quite astonishing. He had been humouring his fractic
correspondent for twelve years, and her most extravagant *boutades* seen
powerless to exasperate him into a final breach. He made one attempt
1847, in which "Field Marshal the Duke of Wellington presents
Compliments. . . . He declines to [write] anything further to Miss
being convinced that as usual any correspondence will end in his giv
her Offence, however much he may desire and endeavour to please h
But this attempted *Nunc dimittis* elicited no more than a stern intima
that his correspondent "cared no more for his Field Marshalship than
Generalship"; and within three months they were both correspond
hard, the Duke complaining helplessly that "you write at great len
with much celerity, in light coloured Ink." He seemed to find distrac
in the taming of this spiritual shrew. It was such a change to encou
someone who stood up to him; he always liked commanding wor
Besides, he was not far off eighty; and the solicitude of thirty-three
his welfare was distinctly gratifying. But when she favoured him
letters for transmission to Miss Coutts and Sir Robert Peel, he sent t
back with a sharp intimation that "I am not the Post Man! nor the S
tary of Sir Robert Peel nor your Secretary!" His patience was evapor

ice again, and in a *cri de cœur* he wrote that "to read one letter from
ou is as much as I can do."

A gleam of hope appeared in 1850, when she announced her impending
parture to the United States, and the Duke eagerly enquired her new
ddress. But she stayed on relentlessly; and with exaggerated caution for
r health he begged her to avoid fatiguing herself by excessive letter-
riting. His request was vain; for shortly afterwards he received a wild
rrago, in which her pen wandered distractedly among her symptoms,
nseed poultices, the cost of jellies, and the inadequacy of her income,
e whole richly decorated with appropriate texts. He asked how much
e needed and what was her banker's name—"all this *legibly written*!"
ut she answered him with more texts. The Duke was helpless; and
nen Miss Jenkins grew reproachful, he bowed himself out with awful
urtesy in a note concluding, "He thus finally takes his Leave!" But
did nothing of the kind. Involved in her epistolary toils, he was
helpless as Laocoon. When she informed him of her health, the
ce of habit was too strong for him, and he replied. The stern pietist was
n rebuking him for regular attendance at earthly ceremonies; but he
wered (with fervent requests that she should write no more) that
"considers it his Duty to serve the Public to the best of his Ability."
at was in March, 1851. She never heard from him again, though he
rd frequently from her. Indeed, a letter to the Duke was waiting
her table to be posted when the doctor called eighteen months later.
was always so kind about posting her letters. "That," she remarked,
for the Duke." But he informed her gently that there was no Duke
ead it. He had eluded her at last; and she departed for New York,
qualify still further for her heavenly crown by writing up her Jour-
re-reading his three hundred and ninety letters, and reposing in
happy consciousness of a Duke very nearly saved from the burning.

III

I<small>T WAS</small> still 1834, and the Duke stared about him in the uncomfortab
world created by Reform. But there were compensations; for th
Whigs were breaking fast. First, Lord Grey resigned; Melbourne su
ceeded him; but when Lord Spencer died, removing Althorp to th
Lords, there was a sudden buzz.

"It is an immense event," said Tadpole.

"I don't see my way," said Taper.

"When did he die?" said Lord Fitz-Booby.

"I don't believe it," said Mr. Rigby.

"They have got their man ready," said Tadpole.

"It is impossible to say what will happen," said Taper.

"Now is the time for an amendment on the address," said Fitz-Boo

"There are two reasons which convince me that Lord Spencer is
dead," said Mr. Rigby.

But Mr. Rigby was wrong as usual. Spencer was dead beyond a dou
Althorp succeeded to the title; and Lord Melbourne must find some
else to lead the House of Commons. His sovereign made difficulties a
with a sudden access of resolution, dismissed his ministers. For th
were still the Tories; and the King sent for Wellington. The Duke
at Stratfield Saye. He was up early that November morning; for
was going hunting. But the King's letter came at six o'clock. His hun
countermanded, he ordered post-horses, was off by eight, and by din
time had seen the King at Brighton. His sovereign asked him to f
a Government; but he "told his Majesty that the difficulty of the
consisted in the state of the House of Commons, and that all our eff
must be turned to get the better of these difficulties, that I earnestly rec
mended to his Majesty to choose a Minister in the House of Commc
and that Peel should be his choice. This was rare unselfishness, s
their relations had been a little strained by Peel's refusal to join
in the forlorn hope of 1832. But the Duke's mind was quite mad
that Peel must be Prime Minister; Arbuthnot had conveyed as muc

Robert in the summer; and now Wellington informed the King.
t where was Peel? With rare improvidence he was abroad. For Sir
bert had gone off to Italy. He must be sent for. Meanwhile, the Duke
I Lyndhurst could govern England until he returned. Lyndhurst was
be Lord Chancellor, and the Duke calmly assumed all the remaining
ces of state, writing gleefully that "I am in harness again; and I have
t to bring home Sir Robert Peel."

le was indeed in harness; for that week, "after much fumbling for
spectacles," he was sworn in as First Lord of the Treasury, Home
retary, Foreign Secretary, and Secretary of State for War and the
onies. He was the government of England. H. B. portrayed a soli-
figure at the head of the Cabinet table asking two lines of empty
rs, "How is the King's Government to be carried on?—that is the
stion"; whilst a rival caricaturist depicted *The United Administra-*
, all clean-shaven, trim, and aquiline—Wellingtons to a man—in
in blue, in black, in wig and gown, in capes, frock-coats, and robes,
ng with splendid unanimity and encouraged by their sovereign's ex-
ation, "Now, my chosen friends and Ministers, I sincerely hope
e will be none of those dissensions and disputes between you there
e with the last." Their offices and titles filled the margin of this
sing scene:

First Lord of the Treasury .	.	DUKE OF WELLINGTON
Home Secretary .	.	DUKE OF VITTORIA
Foreign Secretary .	.	PRINCE OF WATERLOO
War and Colonies .	.	DUKE OF CIUDAD RODRIGO
Lord Privy Seal .	.	COUNT VIMIERA
First Lord of the Admiralty .	.	BARON DOURO
Chancellor of the Exchequer	.	ARTHUR WELLESLEY
Lord High Chancellor .	.	VISCOUNT WELLINGTON

d for three flurried weeks the charge was very nearly true. Taking
ssion as Home Secretary before his predecessor's papers had been
ed away, he was reported by scared officials to have "fixed his head-
ters at the Home Office, and occasionally roves over the rest." His
y was simple: "all that he knew, which he told in his curt, husky
ier, was, that he had to carry on the King's government." This was
finite relief after the crotchets of the Whigs; and the world shared
Salisbury's consciousness that "it was really a moment worth living

for to see that great man once more where he ought to be, appreciate
as he deserves by his King, and at the head of this great country." F
there could be few finer sights than the industrious old hero in tempora
charge of England.

But Mr. Hudson reached Rome at last; Sir Robert raced across t
Alps, "the great man in a great position, summoned from Rome
govern England"; and the Duke subsided into the Foreign Office, whe
he soon impressed ambassadors that "thirty minutes with him suff
to transact what can never be accomplished in as many hours with c
wavering ministers of France." For Wellington was still as punctual a
decisive as ever. But administrative virtues could not win Gene
Elections, and the future of Peel's Government depended on the po
Electioneering was hardly the Duke's province, though echoes of the
tant warfare sometimes came his way. A young gentleman with sligh
fluctuating principles, who had once asked him (without success)
accept the dedication of an epic poem, wrote imploring his support
High Wycombe. But nothing came of it; his correspondent was at
bottom of the poll once more, exclaiming darkly that he was now a cip
and chivalrously assuring the Duke that he might always count on
support of Benjamin Disraeli.

The elections went against them; and Wellington was soon assur
country neighbours that, "whatever way the Cats jump in this Quart
he would not miss his hunting in the autumn of 1835. They had b
five months in office; they would be out again at any moment;
when Peel was threatened with a final defeat in the House of C
mons, an obliging colleague offered to send news of the division
Apsley House. But the Duke was perfectly prepared to wait until
morning.

"I am quite satisfied to have it when the newspapers come in at
o'clock. If I could do any good by having it earlier, I would; bu
I can't, I'd just as soon wait."

A friend interposed, remarking that he took it coolly and enqui
if anxiety ever kept him awake.

"No," said the Duke, "I don't like lying awake; it does no goo
make a point never to lie awake."

IV

THE brief interlude of Tory government worked wonders with the
Duke's popularity. Oxford in 1834 had marked his readmission
the canon of Tory saints; but the next year restored him to a wider
cle of good graces. Not that the world of 1835 had any wish to be
verned by the Tories. But it was profoundly touched by the spectacle
Wellington in harness once again. His obvious good faith, his chivalry
wards Peel, his willingness to serve under a younger man were in
id contrast with the normal appetites of party politics; and the old
n resumed his place in popular regard as a national institution. He
nt to Cambridge in the summer and was triumphantly received by
vn, gown, and Yeomanry; Vauxhall shouted itself hoarse when he
peared; and roaring crowds greeted him at a Hyde Park review. His
simism had begun to melt.

It is very bad," he observed to somebody at dinner, "but I consider
country on its legs again."

Do you?" said Greville. "I am glad you think so."

Oh yes," the Duke replied, "I think that, however this may end;
ink the country is on its legs again."

ven his Parliamentary authority was recovering. The House of
ds had never lost its habit of attending to his simple arguments; as
ng Disraeli allowed, "there is a gruff, husky sort of a downright
ntaignish naïveté about him, which is quaint, unusual, and tells."
when he silenced Brougham, the Boanerges of the new era, in mid-
t by lifting a warning forefinger and murmuring across the House,
w, take care what you say next," it was a veritable triumph. For he
come into his own again. Young men of promise in 1836 noted
s of his approval with avidity, Disraeli writing gleefully that the
e had told somebody at dinner that his Aylesbury speech was "the
: manly thing done yet" and positively asked, "When will he come
Parliament?" And the less ardent Gladstone, who met him at
Robert Peel's and noted that "he receives remarks made to him very

frequently with no more than 'Ha!' a convenient suspensive expressio
which acknowledges the arrival of the observation and no more," co
mented favourably on his mental powers.

His life was easier again; and he could return to his normal occu
tions. The past absorbed him now; for Gurwood was editing his *L*
patches, and the Duke turned over old papers to elucidate doubtful poir
Then there were endless sittings to be given to portrait-painters. Inde
the reckless Haydon had laid siege to him whilst he was still in off
but Wellington refused to sit. Quite undeterred, the painter called
Apsley House, borrowed his clothes, and asked the Duke to look at
completed picture. This was too much. The indignant hero had '
objection to any gentleman painting any picture of me that he n
think proper; but if I am to have anything to say to the picture, eit
in the way of sitting or sending a dress, I consider myself, and s
be considered by others, as responsible for it. . . . Paint it, if you ple
but I will have nothing to say to it. To paint the Emperor Napoleon
the rock of St. Helena is quite a different thing from painting me
the field of battle of Waterloo. The Emperor Napoleon did not con
to be painted. But I am to be supposed to consent; and moreover, I
the field of battle of Waterloo am not exactly in the situation in w
Napoleon stood on the rock of St. Helena." This was discouraging;
Haydon urged that with six children to support he could scarely ig
a good commission. The Duke, who felt that Haydon had made
with his wardrobe, was obdurate, though he consented rather sulki
the persisent artist "painting and engraving a picture of me in any
you please, and in any costume."

But his defence was not always so successful; and in his later y
artists became a plague. Indeed, the pestilence was almost endemic
he wrote helplessly from Walmer, "I did not . . . ask you to c
here . . . as I expected a descent of artists. I have had one; some
remain, and more are coming—two from Scotland. I literally lead
life of the subaltern officer of a regiment. I parade, dressed for dut
nine in the morning, and again once or twice a day. There is not a
ment of the day or night that I can call my own. These gentlemen a
breakfast, dinner, and supper, and all the evening my existence is at

leasure; I cannot move along the passage, or on the staircase, or the amparts, without meeting them. . . ."

He had his public duties, too—meetings of Tory peers at Apsley House, dinners at Kensington with Princess Victoria and her overpowering mamma, his correspondence with Sir Robert on Opposition tactics, ad regular attendance in the House of Lords where he spoke twenty-e times in 1836 upon every topic from insolvent debtors to railways. is course in politics was slightly complicated by his leader; for he had leader now. Peel was sometimes a little trying, though the Duke was better terms with him and took his hunting-coat to Drayton with gay intimation that he was "prepared to do whatever you please." at Sir Robert's aptitude for chilling followers was impressive; even ellington complained that "our leader does not excite enthusiasm"; and eir relations sometimes resembled an exchange of signals between pass-g icebergs. But it was no time for dashing tactics, as the Tory rear-ard receded slowly before Melbourne's languid advance. It was the wn of a new age, although the dawn crept imperceptibly up the sky, til the apprehensive gaze of Wellington grew almost accustomed to e change of colouring.

A new age was dawning, although Greville wrote comfortably that *thing* will happen, because, in this country, *nothing* ever does." miliar outlines of the night began to vanish. Beaux of the Regency pt silently away; royal uncles receded; and Mrs. Fitzherbert died ong her memories. The Duke appeared in Tilney Street. He was the King's executor, and Mrs. Fitzherbert's papers had presented prob-s of unusual delicacy which he had dealt with while she was still e. Some had been sealed up and sent to Coutts' Bank; but the grate re-ed a generous supply; and as the fire roared up, Wellington said nly to his companion, "I think, my lord, we had better hold our hand a while, or we shall set the old woman's chimney on fire." A new day climbing up the sky; and as Kensington flushed in the summer vn of 1837, two kneeling men informed a sleepy girl that she was en of England.

O good gray head which all men knew.

ODE ON THE DEATH OF THE
DUKE OF WELLINGTON.

THE past receded now—the legendary past, where Nelson walked his quarter-deck and Mr. Pitt, sharp-nosed among the candles of ᵁuildhall, urged England to save Europe, and a trim frock-coated figure ᵁntered along the lines to lift a low cocked hat and point through the ᵁinning smoke towards the French. The past receded into a middle ᵁistance hazy with patriotic folklore, a region of soldiers' tales and steel ᵁgravings. But one figure held the foreground still, where Wellington ᵁngered indomitably on the bright Victorian scene. A hero of the last ᵁign but two, he was the past incarnate. Men saw his profile and heard ᵁe guns of Badajoz; a spare, familiar figure brought back forgotten ᵁhoes; and the deep voice took them into their fathers' memories of ᵁys before Reform, before Waterloo, before Vimeiro, before . . . His ᵁalks abroad became a progress, upon which the London streets turned ᵁspectfully to watch the past go by. Every hat came off; genteel persons ᵁade excuses to stop and stare; across the way young surgeons crowded ᵁ the steps of St. George's Hospital to watch him pass; and as he ᵁrned slowly in at Apsley House, the butcher's boy pulled up his cart ᵁ see. Not that he was a passive spectacle. A cheering crowd once fol-ᵁwed him up Constitution Hill until he reached his gate; he turned ᵁ the saddle, pointed to the iron shutters on the windows that they ᵁd broken once, swept them a bow, and then rode in without a word. ᵁe roads near Walmer knew him well, driving a pair-horse phaeton ᵁm the left-hand seat in order that his companion might have his good ᵁ. His driving was a little wild, but his talk was always on the target ᵁconomy, dockyard employment as a method of reducing the poor-ᵁe, the futility of supposing that England would be the workshop of ᵁ world for ever, foreign markets, means of securing them by lower ᵁts of manufacture (they were just driving into Ramsgate and stopped ᵁ the first draper's shop where he bought a white cotton handkerchief ᵁh red spots, emerging with the sage reflection that it had only cost ᵁhilling and was an article which, one would think, might find a mar-

ket anywhere), and so back to Walmer, dinner at seven o'clock, a littl
talk, and candles at eleven. For the Duke lived on, half national monu
ment, half Delphic oracle.

I

His talk was never better than in those later years. It had lost nothin
of its astringent quality; yet somehow it was mellower. For he coul
be almost genial with the omniscient Croker, stepping in from the battl
ments at Walmer with a sardonic intimation that "I've just been receivir
a lecture from Croker on fortification," and protesting amiably at tl
dinner-table, "My dear Croker, I can yield to your superior information (
most points, and you may perhaps know a great deal more of wh
passed at Waterloo than myself; but, as a sportsman, I will maintain n
point about the percussion caps."

This was the speech of his briefest sayings. Uttered in his distir
voice, these oracles were patiently collected, not infrequently improv
upon, and assembled like Sibylline leaves to form a canon of *stacce*
wisdom. Debt, discretion, habits of industry, and early rising were amo
his austere themes; his views were obstinately normal, and his co
clusions wholly to the taste of the age of Samuel Smiles. If he spo
at any length, it was generally about the past. Respectful interlocut-
headed him firmly in the direction of the Peninsula and pelted him w
questions. Stanhope was quite incorrigible in this vein, making a t
ment of his evenings, when the old man would have so much prefer-
a quiet hour between his candles with a paper. But the implacable
quisitor nightly perched beside him on his reading-table, until a thoug
ful lady piled it high with books. Quite undeterred, the relentless St
hope took them off and installed himself as usual.

"I don't think much of your fortifications," said a deep voice fr
the Duke's armchair.

Not that his topics were exclusively martial. For one day he read th
the report of *Bardell* v. *Pickwick*; and he was occasionally enga
by deeper themes provided by his religious correspondents. Some
found him deep in a forbidding work by Habershon upon the Prophe
and he was known to recommend a learned publication which proved

he aid of Scripture) that the aboriginal population of America had
riginally come from Tyre. He found it quite convincing and regarded
heir successful navigation of the Atlantic without compasses as conclu-
ive evidence of the activities of a higher Power. Then he talked of old
imes in India, told stories about Talleyrand, and went off on the cam-
aign of Vimeiro. For it was more comforting to recall the past than to
ontemplate a present where O'Connell was haranguing crowds. Crowds
lways irritated him; as he thought of them, a little rhyme came back
him—

> *"Pour la canaille*
> *Faut la mitraille"*

nd he murmured it quite lovingly as they went in to dinner. But his
d despairs had very nearly vanished, since his countrymen showed sense
ough to discard the Whigs; and though there were difficulties in sight,
do not conceive them to be insurmountable, and I have good hopes
r the future." For though the world was changing fast, perhaps it would
t change too much.

2

The customary scene was Walmer, though the big house at Hyde
rk Corner and the long rooms at Stratfield Saye still knew their mas-
. But his most frequent setting in those later years was the low, castel-
ed house beside the Kentish sea. Its aspect, like the Lord Warden's,
s strictly military. But time had made them both civilians; its port-
les were bedroom windows now, its platform a verandah, and the moat
rformed the peaceful office of a kitchen-garden. No less civilian, the
ke, white-trousered and blue-coated, emerged at six o'clock, tramped
and down his battlements, enjoyed the morning sun, and reappeared
breakfast. A morning with his papers, a ride to Dover in the afternoon,
other turn upon the flagstones, dinner, a quiet evening (unless Stan-
e was in the house), and a bowed figure with a silver head lit the
candlesticks and wished them all good-night.

His life was easy there, though he had his Cinque Ports business, giving
countersign to the Dover garrison each day and walking through
lmer in procession with the pilots when his Court was held. He

was a friendly neighbour, strolling unasked into Deal lodging-house
in order to invite a wholly unimportant stranger to shoot his woodcock
or sending somebody at Dover his garden key. Stray visitors with children found themselves miraculously asked to dinner; and when someone
in the neighbourhood complained of the devastations of the Castle
rooks, he replied meekly that they should be destroyed. He had his
sterner moments, though, when a female was summarily deported from
the neighbourhood; and a letter asking him to make some charitable
award to a young lady, who pleaded that she was eligible for an annuity
bequeathed to Kentish girls and that her father (whom she supported by
dressmaking) was seventy-eight, provoked the Duke's compliments and
his desire "that she will specify in clear and distinct terms what is the
benefit in the way of annuity which is in the gift of the Duke; which he
has the power of conferring on young ladies *seventy-eight years old* of the
County of Kent."

He had his garden; though he was no gardener, admitting to an applicant for employment who had confessed that he knew nothing of
gardening, "No more do I, but you can learn." His grounds were full
of robins, because the wintry old man had quite a feeling for them.
But a slow walk up and down the ramparts was his invariable resource.
He tramped them with Arbuthnot; and an indulgent housekeeper enjoyed the sight of "our two dear old gentlemen so happy together."
The Duke, however, was the younger, and on occasion youth would assert
itself. For sometimes as they paced the path along the beach at dusk
the younger man halted.

"Now, Arbuthnot," said a deep voice, "you've been out long enough.
The dew is falling and you'll catch cold; you must go in."

So Arbuthnot, slightly protesting, went back to the Castle; and the
Duke tramped on alone.

A cloud of witnesses observed him, but none more eagerly than Haydon. The preliminaries of his visit were much as usual. A Liverpool
committee had commissioned a large picture of the Duke musing on
the field of Waterloo. True, he had never mused there; but the sublime
in art is not easily discouraged, and Haydon leapt at the canvas with
a muttered prayer that he might be no less victorious than his heroic
subject. In the intervals of lecturing all over the country and designing

446

Nelson monument, he painted hard. Would the Duke sit to him? There was a chance. Meanwhile, the busy painter improved the occasion by writing to him on the subject of the Nelson project (eliciting the slightly ominous reply that Wellington was "not the committee, nor the *secretary to the committee*; and, above all, not the *corresponding secretary*"). He painted hard, borrowed a sketch of "Copenhagen," and traced his saddler; and when that deserving tradesman revealed that he had made all the Duke's saddles from Salamanca to Waterloo, this information "so increased my reverence I offered him my arm." Small wonder that he glowed over the discovery of a small niece of Wellington's who called her uncle, "Dukey." "The terror of Napoleon—Dukey to his niece!" But there were still the elusive clothes. The Duke remained inexorable and hopes that he will have some cessation of note-writing about pictures. The Duke knows nothing about the picture Mr. Haydon proposes to paint. At all events, he must decline to lend to anybody his clothes, arms and equipments." Was this the end? In spite of everything his picture grew; D'Orsay called at the studio one day, sublime in scented gloves, white greatcoat, blue cravat, and "hat of the primest curve and purest water," picked up a brush and gave a touch. This would never do—"Frenchman touch Copenhagen!"—and the indignant patriot rubbed out the sacrilegious brushwork. The Duke's clothes still defeated him. But not for long, since the indomitable Haydon had traced his tailor and ordered himself a pair of trousers of the Duke's own pattern, "so that I shall kill two birds with one stone,—wear 'em and paint 'em. So, my Duke, I *do* you in spite of you."

Not quite in spite of him; for one October day the postman brought an invitation to go down to Walmer. The eager guest set off by way of Ramsgate; the Castle bell was sounded when he arrived; and he met the party at dinner. He found them gossiping about a circus lady, coast erosion, and Napoleonic personages. The Duke averred that the French system was "bullying and driving—they robbed each other, and then poured out on Europe to fill their stomachs and pockets by robbing others." So much for the French. As for Don Carlos, he was "a poor creature." Mankind in general, it seemed, was not much better, since that evening Wellington was of the opinion that the natural state of man was plunder; society was founded upon property, and that was going

fast. The talk strayed, as usual, to Spain—how they had burnt house
for fuel and how the British soldier must always have a home to go t
at night.

"Your Grace," Haydon courageously remarked, "the French alway
bivouac."

"Yes," said the Duke, "because French, Spanish and all other natio
lie anywhere. It is their habit. They have no homes."

Arbuthnot nodded in his chair; Haydon was studying the Duke
head, until the hero gave a tremendous yawn and rang for candles. H
lighted two and gave one to his latest guest. "God bless your Grace," sa
Haydon, and retired to struggle with the inspiring consciousness of t
greatest man on earth asleep just through the wall.

They breakfasted at ten. "Which will ye have," asked Wellingto
"black tea or green?" Six children clamoured at the windows. "Let the
in," said Wellington. The invading hordes arrived, charging the Du
with cries of "How d'ye do, Duke? how d'ye do, Duke?" One urch
clamoured thirstily, "I want some tea, Duke."

"You shall have it, if you promise not to slop it over me, as you o
yesterday."

The speaker hugged them, three a side; and then they all romp
wildly up and down the ramparts, with the Duke in full cry afte
small girl. "I'll catch ye," said the Duke, "ha, ha, I've got ye."

He went out hunting in the morning; and after hunting he sat
Haydon, "like an eagle of the gods who had put on human shape, a
had got silvery with age and service." His ride had made him "rosy a
dozy"; and after dinner he read the *Standard* until bedtime. The next
was Sunday; and Haydon very nearly sat in the Duke's pew, profoun
affected by the spectacle of the conqueror in church. That night he r
his paper again. He seemed a little aged when he sat again on Mon
"like an aged eagle beginning to totter from his perch." But a Russ
diplomat appeared at lunch; and the Duke "put on a fine dashing w
coat" for the occasion. More sketching in the afternoon with Lady B
hersh to keep his subject talking. But he was done at last.

"It's very fine," said Lady Burghersh.

"Is it though?" said the Duke. "I'm very glad." He never looked a
But Arbuthnot and Lady Burghersh both begged Haydon not to a

t, as he had caught the likeness. One more evening at the Castle; then candles and a loud good-night, and Haydon ended his last day at Walmer.

But sometimes they had statelier visitors. The Duke always prided himself that he possessed "the most charming marine residence he had ever seen—that the Queen herself had nothing to be compared with it." And one day in 1842 he received an intimation of the royal pleasure to visit him in force. The preparations were extensive; Pitt's room was hastily partitioned off and gaily papered to form a royal dining-room; the village carpenter put up a little shelf to hold a timepiece in view of the royal bed (understood to be required for Albert's full happiness); and their careful host gave detailed directions for the guard of honour to parade "at a distance from the road and the Castle; so as not to frighten the Queen's horses." The Duke himself removed to the Ship Hotel at Dover. Even his laundry, evacuated by the Duke's mangle, became a royal guard-room; and H. B. depicted him surrendering his fortress and treating with Lady Douro and his humble belongings. It was all a great success. The Duke rode over every day; the royal couple read Hallam's *Constitutional History* (varied with doses of St. Simon by way of light refreshment) or went out for excursions. But they found the house a little draughty; the Queen caught a cold; and it was three weeks before the Duke got back his Castle. Someone remarked that they had knocked about his rooms a little.

"Yes," he replied with a little smile, "yes, oh yes, they have rather. Put up Mr. Pitt's room and turned it into a dining-room, but it don't signify, I'll soon knock all that down again."

For it was not so easy to displace the past at Walmer.

3

His thoughts were much in the past. With Arbuthnot dozing in his chair and Alava's endless Spanish chatter, how could he escape the past? Not that his life was a mere retrospect, since it was full of children. They came to stay with him, made havoc of his breakfast, played hide-and-seek with him along the ramparts, and bombarded him with cushions in the drawing-room. The *rôle* was most unlikely; but, as he wrote, "it is my fate to be all things to all men, women, and children." Indeed, a small

boy, interrupted in a raid upon the Walmer fruit-trees, paid him a
unusual compliment—"Never mind, let's go to the Duke; he alway
allows everything and gives you what you like directly."

He had been fond of children in the East; the war deprived him o
the nursery days of his own sons; and when he was restored to then
they were too old for him to do much more than give directions t
their tutors, pay their bills, and send their Latin verses to Richard fo
that connoisseur's approval. But his later years were bright with childre:
Dickens once saw him at Vauxhall "in a bright white overcoat" with tw
little girls and Lady Douro; grave visitors to Stratfield Saye were slight
embarrassed at being received by an old gentleman on all fours amon
the crumbs under the dining-table; and a staid individual who warne
a fellow-traveller on the Deal steam-boat that he should really tell h
little girl not to romance, as she had just told him that she had a pillo
fight with the Duke of Wellington, was pained to learn that it was t
strictest truth. When children stayed with him, he sometimes wrote the
letters to arrive by post; his bulletins to anxious parents were rich
detail—"Bo was indisposed while I was away. He says himself that I
Indisposition was occasioned by his eating too much dinner; which
not unlikely." He shipped them off to France with the precautions app
priate to a well-timed invasion; and when he wrote to them, he w
particularly careful not to write to their parents by the same post, '
I recollected that it was necessary that a letter should be brought
herself by the Postman in order to produce all the Satisfaction that
was capable of producing." His evening pillow-fight (known as t
"battle of Waterloo," conducted in the drawing-room and usually oper
by a judicious cushion hurled through his newspaper) was almost
ritual; and he had a pleasing habit of carrying a store of shillings hu
on red and blue ribbons for distribution to stray children. "Are you
Navy," asked the Duke, "or Army?" Intending sailors got a blue ribl
and soldiers scarlet, though in one disastrous instance a small child,
whom he had promised a commission in the Guards, objected loud
"But I am a dirl, Mr. Dook." It was all, as Dickens wrote, "good, a
aged, and odd."

There was a saving streak of oddity about him. With strongly individ
tastes and personal requirements he ran largely to unusual contraptio

and his mind, as fertile as the White Knight's in strange devices of his own invention, soared far beyond the commonplace in household and personal appointments. The lives of visitors were darkened by a teapot perched in some complicated way on a hot-water jug, which appeared to possess no merit except that of capsizing more easily than usual; he loved to demonstrate his patent finger-bandage; a supply of sword-umbrellas afforded him protection against assassins in wet weather; and he gratified his fancy by appearing on the road in queer, boat-like conveyances of personal design. Strange clothing fascinated him in later years. Always susceptible to colds, he had a weakness for unusual cloaks and mufflers; overalls of strange construction seemed to appeal to him; and he had been known to appear on horseback with a fur collar and an umbrella. His passion for such ingenuities had made him a domestic pioneer. Guests at Stratfield Saye were nearly suffocated by his novel heating system; and, born a century before his time, he was a sanitary enthusiast.

His tastes were simple. A modest standard of barrack-room discomfort satisfied him, though he was conscious of the arts. The windfall of King Joseph's coach at Vitoria gave him the nucleus of a picture gallery, supplemented by judicious purchases in Paris. He was still buying Dutch and Italian pictures; and occasionally he took a fancy to commission a particular scene. Wilkie's *Chelsea Pensioners* originated in one of his ideas, and he had the notion of setting Landseer to paint a dramatic moment in a lion-tamer's exhibition. But he was more at home in music. His guests were firmly led off to the Ancient Concerts, where he was sometimes gratified by hearing his father's compositions; Grisi was brought down to sing at Walmer; and he arranged his programmes with precision—a selected vocalist and instrumentalists to taste ("If they want the horn I'll have Puzzi. I used to like the violincello").

So he lived on amongst his friends. Douro was married to a charming young lady, of whom he saw a great deal; and sometimes there were additions to his circle, when Alava made him receive "Mons. Merimée . . a sort of lion." But strange faces were infrequent among his grown-up visitors; for his taste in acquaintances was formed. He had a home at last, a refuge from the innumerable contacts of his official life. The world complained that he did not surround himself with Peninsular veterans. But why should he? He had lived half his life among them; and it was far pleasanter to gossip to his little court. Gossip, alas! was not so easy across the silence of his deafness; and he turned increasingly to paper, writing innumerable little notes to privileged young ladies about his garden and the weather and the vexations of his public life. Almost indecipherable now, those scribbled pages, where a rose-leaf or a lock of his white hair is often pressed, hold in their trivialities the brave secret of his long struggle against loneliness and silence.

But he could still be formidable. The uneasy figure of John Gurwood moved in the outer circle of his intimates. Brought into early prominence by reckless galantry at Ciudad Rodrigo, his subsequent career failed to live up to his own expectations. A slight display of temperament before Waterloo was scarcely helpful; and he spent the next few years in almost constant disappointments and the gloomy survey of *Gazettes* in which his name did not appear. An obscure love-affair assisted his decline, and so early as 1823 his nerves were gravely shaken by a hold-up in Spain. But the Duke, on taking over at the Horse Guards, promptly promoted him; and Gurwood responded by publishing his master's *General Orders*. This led him to a larger project, and he prepared to edit the entire *corpus* of Wellington's *Dispatches*. Close association with the Duke made him a devotee; and when the work concluded, the Duke reciprocated by obtaining him a pension and the post (after a struggle with Macaulay) of Deputy-Lieutenant of the Tower. Gurwood expanded in the sunshine of success. It was extremely pleasant to frequent the little circle at Stratfield Saye—so pleasant that he consented to be seen there without his wife. For Mrs. Gurwood's antecedents would hardly bear the strict examination to which pedigrees were subjected in the Duke's social neighbourhood. A bright Parisian *brunette*, she was unlikely to associate on easy terms with Lady Douro. First heard of as the widow of an invisible M. Mayer, deceased (it was charitably supposed) in Africa, Fanny Gurwood, *née* Kreilssamner, of Mulhouse, had two sisters of whom one worked at a Paris dressmaker's, while the other enjoyed the less arduous protection of the Director of the *Comédie Française*; and it was Gurwood's practice to accept the Duke's invitations as a bachelor. But in spite of everything his nerves continued to grow worse; and they were not improved by a sharp controversy with Napier, in which he

Peninsular laurels were impugned. As years went by, he had recourse to mediums; animal magnetism fascinated him; and he dabbled in the new wonders of mesmerism. His work grew heavier than ever, as he was now deep in an enlarged edition of the *Dispatches*. Mountains of documents confronted him, all clamouring to be copied out, arranged in order, printed, and indexed. At last he finished them; but the index was too much for him. Sleep left him; he was dreadfully depressed, spending a good deal of his time burning his precious papers; and the Duke gave him leave to go to Brighton, where he sat brooding in his lodgings until one afternoon he cut his throat. The Duke's consolations to his widow included a request for papers; for Wellington, it seemed, had heard from somebody that Gurwood had kept notes of his conversation. But Fanny answered that the unhappy man had destroyed all his documents "from an overstrained sense of delicacy towards Your Grace." The Duke replied with a detailed reiteration of the story:

"A few days after the funeral of the lamented Colonel Gurwood, the Duke was informed by different persons, by some verbally, by others in writing, that the Colonel had been in the habit, when associating with him, of retiring to his room early at night, or as soon as possible, in order to write down a memorandum of what the Duke had said. . . .

"The Duke does not believe that there is an instance in history of a similar act. It is anti-social; it puts an end to all the charms of society, to all familiar and private communication of thought between man and man; and, in fact, it places every individual in familiar society in the situation in which he puts himself in a publick assembly, with a gentleman of the press to report what he says. . . ."

Sublimely unaware that Stanhope had been doing the same thing for years, the Duke continued in a tone of stern reproof. He was at pains to demonstrate the depravity of such a practice in order to establish that the notes had better be destroyed for Gurwood's sake. This was too much for Fanny Gurwood, who answered hotly. Wellington, quite unabashed, restated his position at length, reminding Mrs. Gurwood a trifle unkindly that "he was in the habit of daily intercourse with the Colonel, that he has had the pleasure of receiving him at his house in Hampshire, and at Walmer Castle, to both of which he was constantly invited, and always welcome whenever he chose to come, and that he did come frequently; but the Duke had never had the honour of receiving Mrs. Gurwood, excepting at balls, concerts, or publick breakfasts"; and that, in consequence, she was without sufficient knowledge of her late husband's practice when in contact with the Duke. He was still painfully explicit upon the story which had reached him and the iniquity, if credible, of such proceedings. It was all a trifle heavy-handed although Fanny had given quite as good as she got. But the calm waters of his later years were rarely ruffled; and his letters dealt more frequently with less exciting themes, as the sea-wind rattled his windows and the sun crept along his battlements.

II

THE long procession of public life went slowly by, and the Duke rode with it. Indeed, he rode in the procession now rather than at its head. His juniors tasted the doubtful joys of leadership, whilst he played to perfection the *rôle* of Elder Statesman. It was a rewarding part, invariably greeted by rounds of affectionate applause. For they cheered him now. Cæsar's Commentaries were unfavourably compared with his *Dispatches*, and "Atticus" wrote respectful things about "the aquiline supremacy of the Cæsars" in a prose style that bore a strong resemblance to Disraeli's. Dispraise of him was out of fashion; only perverse persons like Mr. Borrow, who had once used his fists upon a Radical in the Duke's defence, were goaded into finding fault with him for being overrated and with "the loathsome sycophantic nonsense which it has been the fashion to use with respect to Wellington these last twenty years." Even the sharp eye of Jane Carlyle was melted by his "clear kind face"; and her formidable mate, who once heard him for a quarter of an hour in the House of Lords, confessed that "Wellington awking, haing, humming—the worst speaker I had ever heard—etched and scratched me out gradually a recognisable *portrait of the fact*, and was the only noble lord who had *spoken* at all." Indeed, a glimpse of Wellington, seen at a ball of Lady Ashburton's in 1850, moved Carlyle to rhapsodies—"Truly a beautiful old man; I had never seen till now how beautiful, and what an expression of graceful simplicity, veracity, and nobleness there is about the old hero when you see him close at hand. His very size had hitherto deceived me. He is a shortish slightish figure, about five feet eight, of good breadth however, and all muscle or bone. His legs, I think, must be the short part of him, for certainly on horseback I have always taken him to be tall. Eyes beautiful light blue, full of mild valour, with infinitely more faculty and geniality than I had fancied before; the face wholly gentle, wise, valiant, and venerable. The voice too, as I again heard, is "aquiline," clear, perfectly equable—uncracked, that is—and perhaps almost musical, but essentially tenor or almost treble voice—eighty-two, I understand. He glided slowly along, slightly saluting this and that other, clear, clean, fresh as this June evening itself, till the silver buckle of his stock vanished into the door of the next room and I saw him no more."

He was sometimes a spectator now, watching the young Queen at her first Council and telling somebody that if she had been his own daughter he could not have desired to see her perform her part better, watching her Coronation, and watching her reviews a shade derisively— "Much better come in her carriage." What was a young lady doing on horseback "surrounded only by such youths as Lord Hill and me, Lord Albemarle and the Duke of Argyll—and if it rains and she gets wet, or if any other *contretemps* happens, what is to be done? All these things sound very little, but they must be considered in a display of that sort. As to the soldiers, I know *them*; they won't care about it one sixpence. It is a childish fancy, because she has read of Queen Elizabeth at Tilbury Fort; but *then* there was threat of foreign invasion, which was an occasion calling for display; what occasion is there now?" Such was the chilly welcome offered by one legendary figure to its successor.

He watched her hanging on Lord Melbourne's words and drew the sage conclusion that "she does nothing without consulting him, even up to the time of quitting the table after dinner and retiring to bed at night." But he was disinclined to active Opposition, though he assured Arbuthnot that "I have always been and shall always be in front of the Battle. I cannot hold back." He could not, if by holding back he meant retirement into private life. For the Duke of Wellington, that public character which he sustained with an increasing effort, still made demands upon him which were not to be denied. He must continue to speak his mind in public and, in that sense, to stand in the forefront of the battle. The only doubt that Tories sometimes felt was upon which side he was fighting. The Duke had never been a good Tory. Indeed, his hostility to all the arts of party was frankly expressed—"There nobody who dislikes, so much as I do, and who knows so little of Party Management. I hate it. . . ." Such prejudices were a rare handicap for leadership in Opposition. Besides, he often had his doubts; and Oppo-

tion leaders who give way to doubts are lost. There was so much to be
said for a Government supported by all moderate men. Not that he
had the slightest taste for Coalitions; Canning had formed a Coalition
once; and "the truth is that *Coalitions* have a bad name!" But, from his
point of view, there were worse fates than being governed by Lord Melbourne; and it would be extremely awkward to impose the Tories on
the House of Commons, the country, and the Queen. His sense of
public duty always kept him in close relations with the Government,
writing memoranda for their guidance on Canada and Indian defence.
Indeed, he often felt himself obliged to intervene in their support. This
was exasperating to eager Tories, who muttered angrily about his failing
powers; for what could be more distressing to the Greeks than to observe
their great Achilles in a constant posture of defence over the body of a
Whig Patroclus? But the Whigs acclaimed his statesmanship; and
even from a Tory standpoint there was something to be said for his
magnanimity, if England was to be preserved by perpetuating Melbourne and averting a dark future ruled by O'Connell and the Radicals.
The past engaged him too, when Soult came to London for the
coronation and the Duke tactfully postponed publication of the Toulouse
volume of his *Dispatches*. The long pursuit across the Pyrenees was
ended in a drawing-room at Buckingham Palace, when Wellington came
up with Soult at last; and Soult even went to Apsley House. The Duke
was civil; but when somebody proposed that he should give the health
of the French army, "Damn 'em," he said, "I'll have nothing to do with
'em but beat 'em."

2

He was just seventy, when his course was sharply interrupted. The failing Whigs resigned in 1839, and Melbourne advised his sovereign to
send for the Duke. They spoke about his deafness, and Lord M. impressed her to be sure that the old man understood what she said to him.
She talked to Wellington for twenty minutes and found him kind. He
received her news with concern; but when she asked him to form a
Government, the Duke replied that he had no power over the House of

Commons, that they were sure to contradict him, and that she had better
send for Peel. Then she expressed a hope that Wellington would take
a place in the Cabinet. He made objections, saying that he was old
and deaf and unfit for discussion, but that if he could serve her comfort
he should accept. She mentioned something about the Household; but
he advised her not to make stipulations before anything was proposed.
Then she saw Peel; and "the Queen don't like his manner after—oh! how
different, how dreadfully so, to that frank, open, natural and most kind
warm manner of Lord Melbourne." Their interview was highly unpromising, with Sir Robert stiff and shy and the Queen shy and petulant.
When she announced that she should not part with her Ladies, he
started visibly and said that he must consult the Duke. They both
returned on the next afternoon, and Wellington tried his hand with
her alone. She had been pressing Peel to make him drop his notion
of joining the Cabinet as leader in the House of Lords without office and
become Foreign Secretary instead. She asked the old man thoughtfully
whether it would not be too much for him.

"I'm able to do anything," he said in his decided way.

Then they discussed her Ladies; and the Duke repeated all his arguments—how their opinions were of no significance, but the principle
involved had some importance. The Queen was obdurate; the Duke,
not unaccustomed to young ladies, was less persuasive than usual; they
failed to solve the problem; and Conservatism subsided once more in
Opposition, "brained" (in Disraeli's figure) "by a fan," whilst H.
was moved to unusual bitterness and Alava remarked derisively, "Je
croyais que c'était seulement en Espagne que ces sortes de choses
rivaient."

They were all at a Palace ball on the next evening, and their triumphant
sovereign wrote that "Peel and the Duke of Wellington came by looking
very much put out." But were they? Not Wellington, at any rate;
that day he had been writing gleefully to countless applicants for office that
he "found himself under the necessity of declining to undertake the
Commission with which the Queen was pleased to offer to entrust him,
and recommended that it should be entrusted to Sir Robert Peel. Thank
God! He has resigned the same. . . ."

3

The old man resumed his sentry-go over the Queen, her ministers, and his innumerable charges. It was a weary round. "Rest!" he cried bitterly that autumn. "Every other animal—even a donkey, a coster-monger's donkey—is allowed some rest, but the Duke of Wellington never! There is no help for it. As long as I am able to go on, they will put the saddle upon my back and make me go." The load grew heavier —or did it only seem heavier now? "It is like everything else," he wrote. "Nobody else will do it. The Duke of Wellington *must*." That *rôle* absorbed him, when he would gladly have subsided into leisure. "I am the Duke of Wellington," as he confessed, "and an officer of the army. But there is not an affair of any kind in which I am not required to be a party. And each of these cases is attended by consequences. I am now required to be a party to the establishment of a college in Kent to teach agriculture. . . ." This was too much; his ordinary business included giving brides away, the House of Lords, Cinque Ports matters, and writing sympathetic letters to maiden ladies who enquired about the weight of baggage carried by soldiers on the march. But agriculture was really quite outside his province; and with his customary ardour of exposition he took several pages to say so. That was his Achilles' heel: he could not resist answering his letters. Such fatal regularity breeds correspondence; and as his wrist grew more rheumatic, the notion spread that there was no topic in the world upon which a letter to the Duke would be out of place, until he was left protesting angrily that "they forget that the Duke of Wellington has only one pair of eyes, and only a certain number of hours in the day like other people," or (more touchingly) "that which people will not understand is that the whole labour and business and ceremony and everything else of the world cannot be thrown upon one man, and that an old one!!"

He was unequal to it now. At seventy his health began to fail under his incorrigible abstemiousness. Indeed, a breakfast of dry bread was poor preparation for a morning ride on a November day, enlivened by showers of icy rain and conversation on bimetallism. Chilled to the bone, he sat down to his papers, munched half an Abernethy biscuit, and

collapsed. But his collapse was brief. In a few hours the still figure o
the little bed was up and giving orders once again; in a few days h
answered letters as usual, paid the household bills, attended to his char
ties, tramped up and down the drawing-room urging a visitor to "te
them at Dover that you have seen me walking—and well—instead o
lying speechless at your feet," and posted off in his open britzka for a
eight hours' drive to London, where he sat in Council to hear h
sovereign announce that she proposed to marry Prince Albert of Sax
Coburg-Gotha. But the attacks recurred in 1840 and 1841; for he wa
ageing now, and his austerity impaired his powers of resistance. Did no
Mr. Greville notice how loosely the clothes hung on him and think hi
"only a ruin"? His face grew thinner, and he stooped noticeably; he wa
a little apt to drop asleep over the fire; his step was firm enough, b
he swayed in the saddle (*Punch* turned a kindly eye upon "the ne
white-haired old gentleman, whom we have all seen rolling upon h
horse in the Park and Pall Mall—a wonder to all bystanders that he di
not topple over," and one eye-witness recalls him in the saddle at
perilous tilt, the crop in his right hand rising and falling in a co
tinuous salute all down the Row). There was no more hunting now; an
as it tried his eyes to read without his spectacles, he could not hope
shoot. His recreations were all gone. Even music failed to entertain hi
as the silence of his deafness deepened; and, once a connoisseur of Gri
and Tamburini, he seemed listless now and rarely called for his favori
airs. "One by one," as an observant neighbour wrote, "all his pleasur
have dropped from him like leaves from a tree in winter." For it w
winter now, and the bare boughs of Wellington stood in bleak outline.

He still cast a shadow on the House of Lords, speaking assiduously o
topics of all dimensions from foreign policy to penny postage and t
comparative futility of Indian missions. His vast knowledge was for
fied by an extensive correspondence with contemporary observers. M
Raikes had constituted himself the Duke's Paris correspondent (reward
by an unsuccessful effort to get him Consular employment) and elicit
his comments on the shifting phases of Palmerstonian diplomacy. T
Duke was frankly sceptical of the advantages of **international** contr
versy conducted "for the same cause as those who quarrel in Billingsga
that is for language rather than substance." His aims were simpler—"

ɔring the French government back into its real and beneficial position
n the councils of Europe." For splendid isolation was little to his taste
—"I have no confidence in the system of *isolement*. It does not answer
n social life for individuals, nor in politics for nations. Man is a social
ɪnimal. I have still less confidence in *paix armée*. I will do everything
hat a private individual can do to conciliate and procure peace." (Had
ɪe not informed the House of Lords that he was "one of those who con-
ɪder that the greatest political interest of this country is to remain at
ɔeace and amity with all the nations of the world"?) His comments
ɪanged over the distant past, as he recalled "our absurd declaration of
he independence of the colonies of Spain" or thought of Portugal, which
ɪnce "was not only sound, but, with our assistance, formidable: it was the
ɪasis on which the machinery was founded which finally overturned the
ʋorld."

But the past was very distant now; and the Duke almost felt that
ɪe belonged to it. For when news arrived of armed insurrection in the
Velsh mining valleys and shooting in the streets of Newport, he raised
ʋo hands in helpless protest and exclaimed, "Oh! if I were only twenty
ɪars younger!" That would have made him only fifty; at fifty he
ɪd helped Liverpool and Castlereagh to tame democracy; but he was
ʋenty—and times had changed. "In these times," as he noted later,
ɪnd since the Reform Act, a Tory Government is not to be expected."
ɪhedule A and the extended franchise had done their work, and politics
ʋpeared to be reduced to a mere scramble between democracy and
ɪoperty, in which no single individual counted for anything and min-
ɪrs were under the degrading necessity "of taking their course, not
ɪcording to their notions of what may be wise for the country; but of
ɪat they may be able to carry through both Houses of Parliament." In
ɪch a world what place was there for Wellington? He could still do his
ɪilitary duty and assist in the smooth operation of the House of Lords;
ɪt he found the part increasingly distasteful.

ɪt was some consolation, when Peel brought the Conservatives to power
ɪ 1841. Lord M. departed, and Sir Robert took his place. This time
ɪre was no suggestion that the Duke should form a Government, al-
ɪugh he was still bravely willing "to do anything, go anywhere, and
ɪd any office, or no office, as may be thought most desirable or ex-

pedient for the Queen's service." Indeed, the King of Prussia had en
quired during the alarums of Palmerston's Egyptian crisis in 1840 i
Wellington would command the German armies against France; and
the old man replied that, subject to the Queen's consent, he felt a
equal to the task as ever. But when Peel formed his Government, th
Queen recognised that Wellington's health was "too uncertain, and
himself too prone to sleep coming over him—as Peel expressed it—t
admit of his taking an office in which he would have much to do." S
he joined the Cabinet with the less arduous responsibility of leadin
the House of Lords. His health had rallied, and Greville found him i
better trim. But the fresh burden of official business told upon h
temper. His duties were discharged; but their discharge was painf
now, and his tired fancy magnified them, until he thought himself to
busy to see anyone and refused interviews with terrifying rudeness.

He laboured through the years of Peel's administration. Indeed, whe
Hill died in 1842, he resumed the post of Commander-in-Chief, addir
the Horse Guards to his cares at seventy-three. State ceremonies st
engaged him—he received the King of Prussia in his Prussian unifor
and the Czar in his Russian kit; the Queen came to Stratfield Saye; ar
when the Prince of Wales was christened, he bore the Sword of Sta
The return to duty seemed to revive him; for in 1843 he "spoke wi
extraordinary vigour, and surprised everybody. He is certainly a mu
better man in all respects this year than he was two years ago, mind a
body more firm." His private comments were as tart as ever; and
received the news of Ellenborough's Indian enthronement among scen
of Curzonian magnificence with the grim observation that "he ought
sit upon it in a strait waistcoat." The Cabinet was almost tender w
him, each minister rising from his place when he had anything to s
and going to the chair beside the Duke in order that his views mig
be audible to their old colleague. He had strong opinions of his o
on national defence, which were accentuated by the rising temper of
French; and among graver problems the proposal for a Peninsular me
recurred. He had never reconciled himself to the notion of a gene
award of medals. But when his sovereign deftly combined it with a s
gestion that his veterans would value a memento of the Duke, he
outmanoeuvred; and forty years after Vimeiro a medal was issued

ll survivors of the war, bearing on its reverse a figure of Wellington
kneeling to Queen Victoria.

But home affairs absorbed them, when the rains of 1845 destroyed the
Irish crop. Peel's mind moved rapidly towards Free Trade. The Duke
was sceptical. "Rotten potatoes," he remarked without enthusiasm, "have
done it all; they have put Peel in his d——d fright." He was an old
Protectionist; but caring less for Protection than for national stability,
he argued stoutly that "a good government for the country is more important than the Corn Laws or any other consideration." Unlike the
Prime Minister, he was no convert to Free Trade— "My position is not
the Corn Law; but it is to maintain a Government in the country." This
faith made him a loyal Peelite; long afterwards he wrote that "having in
1834 brought Sir Robert Peel from Rome and handed over to him the
government of the country, and having once found that he possessed
the confidence of the sovereign, of Parliament, and of the country, and
thinking that a *government* is of more importance than any measure
or particular law, since the passing of the Reform Act—I have been
most anxious that Sir Robert Peel shall retain power in his hands; and
I did everything in my power on the one hand to induce him to modify
his proposed measures, and to take time for carrying them into execution, in order that they might satisfy those who supported his Government, and on the other to persuade his colleagues in office to go on."
That was his simple reasoning, when he informed the Cabinet in 1846
that "the Corn Law was a subordinate consideration." The major
problem was the government of England; and when Croker bombarded
him with Protectionist orthodoxy, he replied majestically, "I am the
trained servant of the Sovereign of this empire," and refused to be
distracted from the larger issue. Who was to govern England? His
angry correspondent would prefer the Corn Laws to be repealed, if they
must, by Mr. Cobden. That was politician's logic. But the Duke would
have none of it. He had seen the fatal consequences of permitting Whigs
and Radicals to carry Reform in 1832 instead of letting Tories do it
with a slight sacrifice of consistency; and he was not prepared for a
repetition of the same mistake in 1846—"I will not be instrumental in
placing the Government in the hands of the League and the Radicals."
That was his guiding principle. It was his old strategy of retreat—the

deft withdrawal to the next position in rear, which would keep saf
men in office and leave dangerous characters in Opposition. He had em
ployed it with success on Catholic Emancipation; his own supporter
failed him, when he applied it to Reform; and it was his guide alon
the twisting path that led towards Free Trade. He faced with equanimit
the prospect of separation from a large section of the Tory Party—"I hav
. . . put an end to the connection between the Party and me." Part
loyalties were a secondary matter, if the country was to be saved from
the dubious embraces of Mr. Cobden. Better Free Trade, he reasone
with Sir Robert Peel than Free Trade and the mob. Free Trade wa
quite inevitable either way; and, as in 1829, he gave his orders to th
House of Lords—"My lords! Attention! Right about face! March!" The
wheeled obediently and repealed the Corn Laws at the Duke's con
mand. It was the last and most beneficent of his retreats. The Bill w
passed; and as the old man left the House in the summer dawn, a litt
crowd began to cheer. "God bless you, Duke," a workman shouted. "F
Heaven's sake, people," the gruff answer came, "let me get on n
horse."

4

Peel fell within the month, and the Duke was out again. But Oppo
tion was no place for him; he had never shewn the slightest aptitu
for it; and his position was now more anomalous than ever. His vie
were still Conservative; but it was quite impossible for him to "act w
a party in Parliament," since he was Commander-in-Chief to a Wl
Prime Minister. Lord John was tactful; and the watchful Greville no
that "it is curious to see what good terms he is on with the Duke
Wellington, who is much more cordial and communicative with h
than he was with his former colleagues." They corresponded freely
India and army matters; and the Duke's letters almost relaxed the c
tomary stiffness of his official tone. Not that his approval was extended
all John Russell's colleagues. Lord Palmerston was at the Foreign Offi
and the livelier excursions of Palmerstonian diplomacy failed to cc
mend themselves to Wellington, who was profoundly shocked by spiri
interventions on behalf of British tourists:

"Only conceive calling upon an independent Sovereign to punish one of his subjects *severely* for anything! . . . What we require is to be able to flatter up the vanity of the sovereign people! to be cried up by their vile Press as a Government bullying the world in protection of the sole amusement and habits of each thirty-millionth part of the sovereign people wandering about in search of amusement."

he Duke, it is evident, would not have indulged in heroics over Don cifico. His patriotism, though, burned brightly still. For he was quite sessed by national defence; Arbuthnot reported that "it haunted the uke of Wellington, and deprived him of rest, and night and day he as occupied with the unhappy state of our foreign relations, the nger of war, and the defenceless state of our coasts." His views were gorously expressed to the Prime Minister; and a letter to the Inspectoreneral of Fortifications, dwelling in harrowing detail upon the dangers invasion and closing with a prayer "that the Almighty may protect from being the witness of the tragedy, which I cannot persuade my ntemporaries to take measures to avert," occasioned general alarm. is document was confidential; but the recipient showed it to Lady elley, who lent copies to half the House of Lords. It reached a news-er; and the Duke's annoyance was extreme. His indignation smoul-ed for two years, until he met her husband out one evening. Good evening, Duke," said Shelley. "Do you know, it has been said someone, who must have been present, that the cackling of geese e saved Rome. I have been thinking that perhaps the cackling of old goose may yet save England."

he Duke stared at him and laughed. "By God, Shelley," he said, u are right. Give me your honest hand." And an old friendship been saved.

e still had his friends, his walks upon the Walmer battlements, and correspondence. Mr. Haydon still left little notes at Apsley House ng for an authentic hat to paint from. An application to the Duke ted the stern reply that "those to whom he gives his hats and clothes w best what to do with them"; but a sympathetic valet heard the ter's prayer and succumbed to a sovereign (of which poor Haydon few to spare); and the triumphant hero-worshipper "carried off a

genuine hat—the glorious hat which had encircled the laurelled hea
of Wellington! I trusted it to nobody; I took it in the hat-box, called
cab, and gloried in it." The Duke's life was a protracted triumph now
Warned by the dismal fate of Marlborough, he watched his dignity wit
care—"The Duke of Marlborough, because he was an old man, w;
treated like an old woman. I won't be." No problem caused him moi
anxiety than his own statue. In the beginning he had viewed it with
fine indifference, asking "to be considered as *dead* upon all matte
relating to the statue," and writing that "the Duke is the man of ;
men in England who has the least to do with the affair." When it w
erected on the arch opposite his house, Arbuthnot wrote almost shy
to him that "it seems as if it would be a Gala day in London." B
when it was proposed (on purely æsthetic grounds) to move it, he too
legitimate offence. Even the Queen, it seemed, took sides against hii
More sensitive than anybody seemed to realise, he felt as though t
world was all united in execration of him, "as . . . in 1808, when I w
persecuted by all factions, out of doors as well as in Parliament; and t
Lord Mayor and the City of London, wishing to treat a general offi
according to the precedent of Admiral Byng, petitioned the Ki
George III, in my own presence, to bring me by name to trial befor
general court-martial. I faced them all. . . ." The topic became dangero
even the Prime Minister asked Greville nervously if he should menti
it at Apsley House; and it provoked the Duke to a rare degree
self-consciousness. Reminding Croker that "more than forty years ;
Mr. Pitt observed that I talked as little of myself or my acts as
I had been an assistant-surgeon of the army," he launched into a vigor
protest against the fancied slight. The Prime Minister received a fu
version of the same theme, in which indignation moved him to unus
eloquence—"Without conviction or trial for offence, or complaint
ledged, or even whispered or suspected; displeasure is marked with
conduct, as according to the Hypothesis stated in this letter will be
opinion founded on the removal of the Statue from its pedestal"—
he came near threatening to resign the command of the army.
thunderbolts prevailed; the Queen surrendered; and the Duke
tinued to ride sedately on his arch.

5

He was not far off eighty when the warning bells of 1848 began to
ng. Half Europe was in flames; and a dull glare on the sky warned
ndon, where half a million Chartists were on the march. The Duke
s studiously calm and did his best to steady nervous ministers, beckon-
one across the House of Lords to inform him that "we shall be as
iet on Monday as we are at this hour, and it will end to the credit
the Government and the country." It did; but not without his help.
when the Cabinet decided to stop the Chartist march on Westminster,
Duke was sent for. This was a military matter; and military matters
e plainly for the Duke. The old man came promptly; returns were
ed for; maps were unfolded on the Cabinet table; and as he gripped
problem, his swift decisions put courage into them all. Macaulay
profoundly impressed and thought it the most interesting spectacle
he had ever witnessed. (He told somebody that he should remember
o his dying day; but then Macaulay remembered everything.) The
ke made his plan on Sunday. If London was to be defended, he was
master of the defensive. He had the Guards, some guns, and three
ments of foot. But it had never been his way to show the enemy
strength. Besides, the military were a last resource; for the police
ht be sufficient. On Monday there was nothing to be seen about the
ts except police and special constables (a nephew of the Emperor was
beat in Piccadilly). Somewhere behind them the troops were wait-
as they had waited behind the slope at Salamanca and the long ridge
Vaterloo. But they were never needed; for the great demonstration
ed before a few police inspectors, and revolution drove respectfully
Vestminster with its petition in a four-wheeled cab.
it the storms of 1848 brought shipwrecked mariners for consola-
to the Duke. The Prince of Prussia came to stay at Stratfield Saye;
when Wellington got back to London, he called every day on
ernich at the Brunswick Hotel in Hanover Square. The exiles
Vienna came to Apsley House to see the table laid for his Waterloo
uet; and when Radetzky thrashed the Italians, the Duke wrote to
ratulate him. The world was sadly changed, and universal revolu-

tion had made havoc of the settlement of 1815; but it was sor
consolation to visit the Metternichs on Richmond Green (and give t
Prince a little overcoat of his peculiar design). It was a most disturbi
time, when France resumed the tricolour and Lamartine sent paci
messages to Wellington and Lord Palmerston had questionable dealin
with the most revolutionary governments; but though the world w
changed, the Duke lived bravely on.

III

A NEW decade—his ninth—was opening. His ninth? In one sense it was the tenth decade that Wellington had seen. For his eyes ad opened in 1769; and here was 1850. He was past eighty now; and ne had left the old man almost alone upon an emptying stage. They ere all gone; his colleagues waited for him in stiff, marble attitudes on their monuments; the Emperor was at the Invalides, watched by silent circle of tall Caryatids; Lord Liverpool was gone, with Castle-agh and Canning; and now his juniors were going. Melbourne flick-ed out; a sudden accident took Peel; and when the old man spoke few sentences about him in the House of Lords, his voice was broken. e was a lonely figure; and as he stood beside his brother Richard's en grave in Eton Chapel, his mouth quivered. Even the faithful buthnot deserted him at last. The Duke saw the doctor in his little om at Apsley House and drew a chair close to catch his words. "No, no," he said, taking the doctor's hand between his own and bing it, "he's not very ill, not very bad—he'll get better." The old man stared hopefully into the doctor's eyes. "It's only his mach which is out of order," he suggested. "He'll not die." But there was no hope. Arbuthnot died with his hand in Wellington's, uite tranquil" (the Duke wrote), "as a flame extinguishes when the stance which keeps it alive is consumed"; and the last echo of Har-t Arbuthnot died with him.

His life was full of dying echoes now—of lost ladies and forgotten misters and his poor fluttered Kitty in her white muslin without ellery sitting apart and talking to her boys' tutor instead of to the st of honour, pausing at intervals to gaze with embarrassing devotion his own direction. One echo pleased him; for though he had worn urning for his friend at Hatfield, he took pleasure now in writing little es to a new Lady Salisbury. Sometimes she shared his daily tramp ng the Piccadilly side of the Green Park; and she was always glad nave his letters. She told him so, and he was no less glad to write

them. "They amuse me," he wrote, "as they do you, and I lau
while writing them, thinking of the amusement they will afford you."
she heard all about his minor worries and affairs of state and local politi
at Walmer and cures for colds and Palmerston's iniquities and the d
plorable irregularity of brides' mothers who expected him to give aw
their daughters without informing him whether to meet them at t
hotel or at St. George's, Hanover Square, and if at the church, wheth
at the door or in the vestry. His daily gossip with her was a real pleasu
to him. For the deaf talk freely on paper; and as the silence deepen
round him, the little scribbled notes became his only form of conv
sation.

His correspondence was still a burden, though. "It is quite curiou
he noted, "with what a number of Insane persons I am in relation. M
retired Officers, Mad Women. . . ." But he was gradually learning
elude his persecutors, announcing with an air of discovery that "so
write in order to get an answer which they shew." Indeed, he specula
innocently whether Cæsar and Hannibal had been exposed to the sa
form of persecution. He was to blame, he felt, for letting it be thou
that he was "a good-natured Man, with whom Persons may vent
to take liberties, and what the French call serviceable." (Servicea
indeed to the widowed lady at Boulogne who asked him for five pou
to get her back to England and, when he sent it, asked five more beca
his unexpected bounty had moved her to break a looking-glass v
a large piece of statuary.) Small wonder the Mendicity Society was
voked for his protection and made matters worse by advertising
extent to which he had been imposed upon; for a migratory troop
beggars followed him about and encamped before his doors. The W
Knight was still strong in him; and he was fascinated by the new ele
cable at Dover, though slightly troubled by the problem of avoid
injury from passing ships by fastening it securely to the bottom of
sea. A terrifying machine, known as the "Jump Baby" or "Baby Jum
engaged him deeply; and Lady Salisbury received a gift of one
profuse instructions how to screw it to the nursery ceiling and no
than three reminders that Lord Salisbury or the house carpenter she
test it before a small Cecil was entrusted to this "delightful instrume
He had less taste for large-scale inventions, since the railway faile

mmend itself to Wellington, who felt that it was fraught with peculiar
erils for ladies. "I cannot bear," he wrote, "seeing or hearing of ladies
ing alone by the Trains on the Rail Roads. It is true that you have
ith you your children. But still the protection of a Gentleman is neces-
ry." The gentry, he conceived, had allowed themselves "to be cheated
d bustled . . . out of the best system and establishment for travelling
at existed in any part of the World. England did not require Rail
ads." But, however uncalled for, they had come; and though he used
em on occasion, he remained gravely impressed with their mysterious
enace to England's womanhood—"If I could attain the object, no lady
uld ever go by a Train, at all events without protection. It is horrible
ogether." His greatest heights of ingenuity were reserved, as usual,
sartorial invention. Lady Salisbury, whose taste in costume was unusual,
eived consignments of his waistcoats with detailed instructions for
ir adaptation; and when the polite world giggled discreetly over Mrs.
oomer's epoch-making innovation, the Duke was highly interested. "I
vastly amused," he wrote, "by the Bloomer discussions! I understand
m, being somewhat of a Taylor." But the contemplated revolution in
ale apparel was too much for him; and he concluded that "it is
ossible that the Costume should be adopted!"

he roar of public life receded. But when patriotic draymen mobbed
unpleasant Haynau, he commented grimly that "the travellers of
Bull family will suffer for it." He made a strenuous attempt to induce
nce Albert to be his successor at the Horse Guards. Not that he had
least intention of resigning; for he told the Prince that he was,
nk God, very well and strong and ready to do anything. But he was
rly eighty-one; and it was most desirable, he felt, that the Crown
uld control the army in these democratic times—"the democrats
uld blow me up if they could, but they find me too heavy for them."
said the same thing to the Queen, who countered that Albert already
d as her private secretary and worked far harder than she liked, and
these extra duties might be too much for him. There were more
ferences; memoranda were exchanged; but the proposal dropped. A
ier business occupied him, when a prince was born on May 1, 1850.
lyre was struck by Thackeray:

"To Hapsley Ouse next day
    Drives up a Broosh, and for,
A gracious prince sits in that Shay
    (I mention him with Hor!)

"They ring upon the bell,
    The Porter shows his Ed
(He fought at Vaterloo as vell,
    And vears a Veskit red).

"To see that carriage come
    The people round it press:
'And is the galliant Duke at ome?'
    'Your Royal Ighness, yes.'

"He stepps from out the Broosh,
    And in the gate is gone;
And X, although the people push,
    Says wery kind, 'Move hon.'

"The Royal Prince unto
    The galliant Duke did say,
'Dear Duke, my little son and you
    Was born the self-same day.

" 'The Lady of the land,
    My wife and Sovring dear,
It is by her horgust command
    I wait upon you here.

" 'That lady is as well
    As can expected be;
And to your Grace she bids me tell
    This gracious message free.

" 'That offspring of our race
    Whom yesterday you see,
To show our honour for your Grace,
    Prince Arthur he shall be.

    •   •   •   •   •

" 'You fought with Bonypart,
    And likewise Tippoo Saib;
I name you then with all my heart
    The Godsire of this babe.' "

Albert recorded their selection with a less sprightly pen, reporting for the eye of Stockmar that "his first name is in compliment to the good old Duke, on whose eighty-first birthday he first saw the light. Patrick is a remembrance of our recent visit to Ireland; William, of the Prince of Prussia, whom we shall ask to be godfather, and also in remembrance of poor Queen Adelaide, on whose account we have also selected the Duchess Ida of Saxe-Weimar as godmother. My name the Queen insists on retaining by way of *coda*. I hope you will approve the arrangement. The Exhibition is making good progress. . . ."

The Duke had his cares as Ranger of Hyde Park. For his territory had been invaded by a determined female, who was unlawfully established in a hut by the Serpentine and was suspected of intent to sell cakes and oranges. "We must proceed," he wrote, "with caution and Regularity"; and he rode out to reconnoitre her position as thoroughly as though she had been Masséna. He viewed the ground with care; but before his offensive could develop, the enemy decamped, leaving the Duke victorious again. He had one more victory in 1851, when the Great Exhibition glittered in the Park. The watchful Commons had insisted that the trees should be cut down. A dreadful consequence ensued. For when the marvels of art and industry were exposed to view, the lively sparrows began to spoil them. The dilemma was agonising, since it was impossible to shoot the sparrows without breaking half the glass in the great building. What was to be done? His country turned, as usual, to Wellington. The Duke was sent for; and the Queen herself explained the difficulty. "Try sparrow-hawks, Ma'am," he replied. It was Wellington's last victory.

He found the Exhibition a great resource, rode up to see it every day, talked to the stall-keepers, made appointments to meet ladies in the Glass Palace," and bought Miss Coutts a bracelet there. That summer he met Thiers and "had to make him some phrases about the Emperor Napoleon." There was a fancy ball in Queen Anne costume, to which he dutifully went in powder and three-cornered hat, remembering to show the children how to walk a minuet before he went. Politics were a receding murmur now, though early in the year he had been called on to advise the Queen, when John Russell resigned and nobody could form a Government. The Duke was sent for and advised his

sovereign to try Lord John again. Not that he had turned Whig, sin
he called on Derby afterwards to express his satisfaction and sa
"Well, they are in the mud, and now you can look about you." He w
quite right; for the Conservatives came in the next year. He sat besi
the new Prime Minister in the House of Lords; and as he strained
catch the unfamiliar names of the new Cabinet (a Mr. Disraeli w
to be Chancellor of the Exchequer), the old man kept asking Derl
"Who? Who?" So somebody nicknamed the Government of 1852 "t
Who? Who? Ministry."

The slow weeks of 1852 went by; and Wellington still went his roun
That summer he made quite a long speech in the House of Lords
the Militia Bill; and when the stooping figure rose at the Acade
banquet, they heard him speak of the admirable discipline which h
prevailed on board the sinking *Birkenhead*. He spoke a final senter
on the same subject in the House of Lords. Then the House rose
the recess, and England went on holiday. The Duke, as usual, was
Walmer, pacing slowly up and down his battlements or writing lett
in his little room. (His standing-desk stood in the recess that lool
towards the sea and caught the morning sun; and his camp-bed, w
the silk mattress which he had devised for Russia in 1825, was in
corner of the room.) A Grand-Duchess and her husband came to s
and there were moments when their host could "wish my Impe
Royalties were in Russia." But he saw them off from Dover and
turned to his little fortress with relief. That was the worst of being
—"one gets bored in boring others, and one becomes too happy to
home." Deafness apart, he had little fault to find with life at eig
three—"I really believe that there is not a youth in London who co
enjoy the world more than myself . . . but being deaf, the spirit, not
body, tires!" The body, indeed, was strictly mortified by his rem
able régime, which comprised systematic starving and massage v
vinegar and water.

September came; and he rode into Dover and caught the trair
Folkestone for a call on Mr. Croker. They told him at the station
the house was only half a mile away. So the Duke started out to v
there and discovered that it was a three-mile walk ending with a cl
up a steep hill; and at the end of it he found that Croker had gone

Dover. He started home again, ordered a fly to take him to the station, but positively walked part of the way until his conveyance overtook him. A meeting was arranged with more success a few days later; and the two old men sat gossiping about the past. They talked of old Irish Office Bills which he had left in Croker's charge when he went out to take command in the Peninsula, of the forgotten Parliament on College Green, of his horse "Copenhagen," and the endless complexities of Reparations in 1818. The Duke began to tell a story about a Spanish lady at Salamanca who had hidden some papers about herself, and broke off to spare Mrs. Croker's blushes. Then he explained to her that all the business of war, and indeed all the business of life, is to endeavour to find out what you don't know by what you do; that's what I call 'guessing what was at the other side of the hill.' " The talk ran on French generals, and he said reminiscently that the Emperor was the best of them all. His own success in Spain had come, he thought, because he was "a *conquérant sans ambition*. I had for a time a sovereign power there, but no one suspected me of any design to become King of Spain or Portugal, like Joseph or Soult or Junot. I *was* almost King of Spain. . . ." The time slipped by; and when his carriage came, the Duke walked slowly down the steps counting them aloud for Croker's guidance. A slightly intoxicated Irishman with a Peninsular medal besieged him at the station and received the invariable sovereign. Then the Duke went back to Walmer.

He was not lonely, though; for his son Charles was at the Castle with his children. Besides, there was his correspondence—eight pages of Spanish in pale ink from Ciudad Rodrigo about a local grievance, his daily gossip with Lady Salisbury, and all his begging letters. His mind was running on the past; and he wrote off a long account of the mob that followed him through London in 1832, and how pleased the King had been when Oxford made him Chancellor. He had a letter from a madman, who proposed to call with a message from the Lord. But he was expecting more normal visitors; for Lady Burghersh was due to arrive on Tuesday and Lady Salisbury on Wednesday. He seemed quite well on Monday; and when his servant went to him on Tuesday morning (it was September 14), he ordered his carriage for a drive to Dover. But a little later he felt unwell and, methodical as ever, said: "I feel very ill; send for the apothecary." It was his last order; for the Duke never spoke again. He had been born beside the sea, where the long tide crept slowly round the bay from Dalkey to the hill of Howth; and the sea whispered still beyond the window of his silent room, as the tide ebbed slowly and the Duke sat on, a huddled figure in a high back chair.

IV

ALL through the long November night it rained. The rain fell relentlessly, and London waited for the dawn with gleaming pavements. The Park trees stood dripping in the downpour outside a shuttered house at Hyde Park Corner. It drummed on the Great Hall at Chelsea, where two hundred thousand people had trooped by candlelight for five days past a still pageant of black velvet and silver stars, watched by immobile sentries resting stiffly on their arms reversed. Eastwards across the darkness a gilded cross dripped in the winter night on the Cathedral dome that waited for the day with all its windows darkened; and midway the hours chimed slowly from the Horse Guards. Outside on the parade the water stood in pools, and the rain whispered round the tent where men were working all night long on the great car. The night was paling now; and as it turned to grey, a darker mass was etched upon it, where the long lines of troops moved into place. There was a steady tramp of marching feet; cavalry went jingling by; words of command hung on the chilly morning air; and as the pale winter day came up, the rain checked. For the Duke was riding out again; and it was his way to ride out after rain. (Had it not rained that night before he rode to Waterloo?) It was broad daylight now. A gun thudded in the Park. The ranks stiffened; and as the bands wailed out the slow refrain, his last ride began.

Duke of Wellington, Marquis of Wellington, Marquis of Douro, Earl of Wellington in Somerset, Viscount Wellington of Talavera, Baron Douro of Wellesley, Prince of Waterloo in the Netherlands, Duke of Ciudad Rodrigo in Spain, Duke of Brunoy in France, Duke of Vittoria, Marquis of Torres Vedras, Count of Vimiero in Portugal, a Grandee of the First Class in Spain, a Privy Councillor, Commander-in-Chief of the British Army, Colonel of the Grenadier Guards, Colonel of . . .

The minute-guns spoke slowly from the Park; and the car—twenty-

477

seven feet of assorted allegory—"rolled," in its proud creator's words
"majestically forth." It was a triumph in its way—a triumph over Banting
the undertaker, who had submitted drawings made (*proh pudor!*) by
Frenchman; a triumph for the new superintendent of the Department o
Practical Art, whose modest sketch had drawn from Prince Albert th
rapturous exclamation, "This is the thing." Small wonder that this sub
lime vehicle, all black and gold, was generously adorned with lion
heads, with sabres, with laurel wreaths; and in case its delicate symbolism
should be missed, a thoughtful hand had added an immense trophy c
real swords and muskets. One witness might observe a trifle bleakl
that something in its outline recalled a railway truck. But *The Time*
enraptured eye was fastened on "the magnificent dolphins, symbolica
of maritime supremacy, playfully wrought out along the spokes . .
the sumptuous pall, powdered with silver embroiderings—and the no
less superb canopy of silver tissue, after an Indian pattern, manufacture
with unexampled rapidity and skill by Keith & Co., of Wood-street
Nor was the *Illustrated London News* blind to the marvels of the canopy
supports, since they were halberts—no ordinary halberts, though, b
halberts rising from ornamental tripods and "lowered by machinery i
passing through Temple Bar," itself surmounted by vases burnin
incense and transformed into the semblance of a procenium arch f
some sepulchral pantomime. This portent had a stormy birth. Compe
ing Government Departments hung like rival fairies above its cradl
The Lord Chamberlain was gravely exercised; the Board of Works ha
a word to say; the War Department intervened; and for some occult d
partmental reason the Board of Trade conceived the matter to be its ow
sole concern. Six foundries struggled with the castings; the ladies of t
School of Art stitched with demented fingers; and in three weeks th
monument of art and industry rumbled across the Horse Guards.
rumbled, to be more precise, into the Mall; and there, just opposite t
Duke of York's column, it gave a dreadful lurch and stayed. For t
sodden roadway had collapsed under its weight, and the great whee
were buried up to the lions on their axles. Twelve dray-horses, sublin
with funeral feathers, strained vainly at the traces. But five dozen co
stables leaned on a cable; and the stupendous hearse staggered once mo

into motion. The slow march resumed; and from the Park the minute-guns still thudded on the damp morning air—

> . . . *Field-Marshal of Great Britain, a Marshal of Russia, a Marshal of Austria, a Marshal of France, a Marshal of Prussia, a Marshal of Spain, a Marshal of Portugal, a Marshal of the Netherlands, a Knight of the Garter, a Knight of the Holy Ghost, a Knight of the Golden Fleece, a Knight Grand Cross of the Bath, a Knight Grand Cross of Hanover, a Knight of the Black Eagle, a Knight . . .*

The Queen was waiting at the Palace with a melancholy conviction that "we shall soon stand sadly alone; Aberdeen is almost the only personal friend of that kind we have left. Melbourne, Peel, Liverpool—and now the Duke—*all* gone!" The news had reached them in the Highlands on an excursion from Allt-na-Giuthasach, whilst they were sitting by the side of the Dhu Loch, one of the severest, wildest spots imaginable"; and her pen promptly underlined his epitaph—"the pride and the *bon génie,* as it were, of this country. He was the GREATEST man this country ever produced, and the most *devoted* and *loyal* subject, and the staunchest supporter the Crown ever had. He was to us a true kind friend and most valuable adviser. . . . Albert is much grieved. The dear Duke showed him great confidence and kindness." Even his small godson, Arthur of Connaught, kept murmuring, "The Duke of Wellikon, little Arta's God-papa"; for the pair of them had rambled through the big rooms at Apsley House together, when the Queen sent the baby round for the last anniversary of Waterloo. Small wonder that the long procession and the silent crowds made "a deep and *wehmütige* impression," as the old man passed her Palace windows for the last time. Albert rode with mournful thoughts in the *cortège.* He felt the loss as well, "as if in a tissue a particular thread which is worked into every pattern was suddenly withdrawn." Stockmar responded with a thoughtful analysis of human greatness, concluding with a slightly condescending estimate—"His intellect was not many-sided and mobile, but with all its one-sidedness it was always clear and sound, so that although the principles which lay at the foundation of his character were not of the noblest kind, still they contained a good sprinkling of practical truth, justice, and honesty." His object, it would seem, was to incite his princely pupil "to

replace the Duke for the country and the world." The country was less
ardent to accept the substitute; and a notion that the Prince might be
Wellington's successor as Commander-in-Chief occasioned general alarm.
But he retained his sober predilection for "*silent* influence," and drove
sedately in a mourning carriage. Half England rode in the procession,
watched by the silent pavements. There was no sound along the route
except a sudden, scattered cry of "Hats off" above the rolling of the
wheels, the wail of military bands, the thud of muffled drums, the slow
beat of hoofs, and the dull pulse of tramping men.

> . . . *Knight of the Sword of Sweden, a Knight of St. Andrew of
> Russia, a Knight of the Annunciado of Sardinia, a Knight of the Ele-
> phant of Denmark, a Knight of Maria Theresa, a Knight of St. George
> of Russia, a Knight of the Crown of Rue of Saxony, a Knight of
> Fidelity of Baden, a Knight of Maximilian Joseph of Bavaria, a Knight
> of St. Alexander Newsky of Russia, a Knight of St. Hermenegilda of
> Spain, a Knight of the Red Eagle of Brandenburgh, a Knight of St.
> Januarius, a Knight of the Golden Lion of Hesse-Cassel, a Knight of
> the Lion of . . .*

Still they went by. Three thousand foot brought on the slow *cortège;*
eight squadrons followed, and three batteries of guns clanked past. It was
the strangest medley of his long career slowly passing by. East India
Directors; one rigid private of every British regiment with arms reversed;
Chelsea Pensioners marching a little stiffly; then the civilians—the Bench,
the Cabinet, and Mr. Disraeli in a mourning coach wishing that his
memory of Thiers' obituary of a French Marshal had not been quite so
perfect as to obtrude itself almost *verbatim* into his funeral oration.
The new Laureate, whose *Ode* was out that morning, watched from a
window and was "struck with the look of sober manhood in the British
soldier," as he marched to bury the great Duke; and by the strangest
irony of all a son of the Emperor was waiting gravely at St. Paul's
in diplomatic uniform. For when Walewski hesitated, the Prince-Presi-
dent had sent him orders to attend; and Napoleon's son mourned Wellington by order of Napoleon's nephew, his bland Russian colleague encouraging him with "*Mon cher, si nous allions* ressusciter *ce pauvre
duc, je comprends que vous pourriez vous dispenser d'assister à ces*

érémonie; mais puisque nous sommes invités pour l'enterrer. . . ." Mr.
Carlyle, much tried by "all the empty fools of creation" crowding to
Chelsea, mourned "the one true man of official men in England, or that
I know of in Europe," from a second-floor in Bath House. Generous to
the *last* perfectly honest and perfectly brave public man," he was highly
disrespectful to the car—"of all the objects I ever saw the abominably
ugliest, or nearly so. An incoherent huddle of expensive palls, flags,
sheets, and gilt emblems and cross poles, more like one of the street carts
that hawk door-mats than a bier for a hero . . . this vile *ne plus ultra*
of Cockneyism; but poor Wellington lay dead beneath it faring dumb to
his long home." That thought almost stifled Lord Shaftesbury's austere
disapproval of so much secular magnificence—"fine, very fine, but hardly
impressive; signs of mortality but none of resurrection; much of a great
man in his generation, but nothing of a great spirit in another; not a
trace of religion, not a shadow of eternity. . . . Stupendously grand in
troops and music. It was solemn, and even touching; but it was a show,
an eye-tickler to 999 out of every thousand—a mere amusement." Perhaps. Yet the crowds watched bareheaded all through the winter morning
(outside St. Paul's they were so closely packed that the lamplighters never
reached the street-lamps, and the lights burned all day above the silent
throng); and as the long procession passed, band after band caught up
the slow refrain—

*. . . The Lord High Constable of England, the Constable of the
Tower, the Constable of Dover Castle, Warden of the Cinque Ports,
Chancellor of the Cinque Ports, Admiral of the Cinque Ports, Lord-
Lieutenant of Hampshire, Lord-Lieutenant of the Tower Hamlets,
Ranger of St. James's Park, Ranger of Hyde Park, Chancellor of the
University of Oxford . . .*

The long lines went by, wound slowly through the Park and past the
blind windows of his empty house, down the long hill towards the City,
until the trumpets died away.

Index

INDEX